EVOLUTIONARY FORENSIC PSYCHOLOGY

EVOLUTIONARY FORENSIC PSYCHOLOGY

Darwinian Foundations of Crime and Law

Edited by
Joshua D. Duntley and Todd K. Shackelford

OXFORD
UNIVERSITY PRESS

2008

OXFORD
UNIVERSITY PRESS

Oxford University Press, Inc., publishes works that further
Oxford University's objective of excellence in research, scholarship, and education.

Oxford   New York
Auckland   Cape Town   Dar es Salaam   Hong Kong   Karachi
Kuala Lumpur   Madrid   Melbourne   Mexico City   Nairobi
New Delhi   Shanghai   Taipei   Toronto

With offices in
Argentina   Austria   Brazil   Chile   Czech Republic   France   Greece
Guatemala   Hungary   Italy   Japan   Poland   Portugal   Singapore
South Korea   Switzerland   Thailand   Turkey   Ukraine   Vietnam

Published by Oxford University Press, Inc.
198 Madison Avenue, New York, New York 10016

www.oup.com

Oxford is a registered trademark of Oxford University Press

Library of Congress Cataloging-in-Publication Data
Evolutionary forensic psychology : Darwinian foundations of crime and law/
edited by Joshua D. Duntley, Todd K. Shackelford.
   p. ; cm.
Includes bibliographical references and index.
ISBN: 978-0-19-532518-8
1. Forensic psychology.   2. Evolutionary psychology.   I. Duntley, Joshua.   II. Shackelford,
Todd K. (Todd Kennedy), 1971–
[DNLM: 1. Evolution.   2. Forensic Psychiatry.   3. Adaptation, Psychological.
4. Crime—psychology.   5. Crime Victims.   6. Genetics, Behavioral. W 740 E93 2008]
RA1148.E98   2008
614'.15—dc22   2007051354

9 8 7 6 5 4 3 2 1
Printed in the United States of America
on acid-free paper

Dedications

Joshua Duntley dedicates this volume to Helena and Paula. Todd Shackelford dedicates this volume to Viviana, Helayna, Avelina, Rex, Ethan, and Mackenzie.

Preface

Evolutionary Forensic Psychology is not a completely accurate title for this volume. It may suggest to some readers that the topics explored here are representative of a subdiscipline of the field of forensic psychology. This is not the case. Evolution by natural selection is the only known process capable of generating the complex adaptations that compose the human mind. Because all psychological mechanisms owe their existence to evolutionary processes, there is no such thing as a nonevolutionary forensic psychology. All forensic psychology is inherently evolutionary, whether or not it is explicitly acknowledged. Our understanding of forensic psychology can benefit from knowledge of the causal processes that designed our psychological mechanisms.

The book is titled *Evolutionary Forensic Psychology* because the profoundly important insights that evolutionary perspectives provide are relatively new. This volume presents a critical introduction to the application of evolutionary perspectives to prominent issues in forensic psychology, exploring theories and research findings that will help to move the field of forensic psychology rapidly forward.

Forensic psychology encompasses a large and diverse range of issues. In constructing this volume, we sought contributions from experts on topics that are of the greatest relevance to the field. Each chapter demonstrates how evolutionary logic has enriched our understanding of topics and generated new hypotheses and research findings, progress that would not have occurred without the unique contribution of a Darwinian perspective.

Although most of the chapters explore the nature of psychological mechanisms that produce criminal behavior, an evolutionary perspective has the power to inform research across domains of forensic psychology. It can help us to differentiate between crimes resulting from psychopathology and those that are the product of cognitive adaptations functioning as they were designed to function. It can help us to understand the origins and evolved functions of cognitive adaptations that produce crime and the psychological mechanisms that generate the perception that some behaviors are criminal. An evolutionary perspective also can inform our understanding of why some crimes are considered to be worse than others, why some people are thought to deserve longer sentences than others who committed the same crime, and why sex differences are pervasive in the commission and perceptions of crime. Current and future forensic psychological research informed by an evolutionary perspective will have an impact on the prevention of crime, how laws are written and enforced, how clinical forensic psychologists and forensic psychiatrists evaluate criminals, the selection of juries and the methods of presenting information to them, and the kinds and structure of punishments in the penal system. The ultimate goal of this volume is much more ambitious than to provide information about how evolutionary theory can inform forensic psychology—we hope it will provide a spark that will ignite theoretical innovation and new programs of research in this important area.

Acknowledgments

We would like to thank the contributors for their brilliant work in the outstanding chapters they wrote for this volume. Our special thanks go to Professor David M. Buss for his mentorship in evolutionary psychology and its application to the dark side of human nature. We would also like to thank Andy Thomson for his insightful feedback during the conception of the volume and on early drafts of the introductory chapter of the book. We extend our gratitude to our editor, Lori Handelman, assistant editor, Jenna Hocut, and production editor, Angelique Rondeau, at Oxford University Press for their insights and support during the production of the volume. Finally, we would like to thank our families for their enduring patience and support, which made it easier for us to spend hours away from them to complete work on this book.

Contents

Contributors

KEVIN BEAVER
College of Criminology and
Criminal Justice, Florida State
University, Tallahassee, Florida

KINGSLEY BROWNE
Wayne State University Law
School, Wayne State University,
Detroit, Michigan

DAVID BUSS
Department of Psychology,
University of Texas at Austin,
Austin, Texas

JOSHUA D. DUNTLEY
Criminal Justice Program,
Richard Stockton College of
New Jersey, Pomona, New Jersey

LEE ELLIS
Department of Sociology,
Minot State University,
Minot, North Dakota

AARON T. GOETZ
Department of Psychology,
California State University-
Fullerton, Fullerton, California

GRANT T. HARRIS
Penetanguishene Mental
Health Care, Penetang,
Ontario, Canada

SATOSHI KANAZAWA
Interdisciplinary Institute
of Management, London
School of Economics and
Political Science, London,
England

DENNIS KREBS
Department of Psychology,
Simon Fraser University,
Burnaby, British Columbia,
Canada

MARTIN LALUMIÈRE
Department of Psychology,
University of Lethbridge,
Lethbridge, Alberta,
Canada

WILLIAM F. MCKIBBIN
Department of Psychology,
Florida Atlantic University,
Davie, Florida

SANDEEP MISHRA
Department of Psychology,
University of Lethbridge,
Lethbridge, Alberta,
Canada

CATHERINE SALMON
Department of Psychology,
University of Redlands,
Redlands, California

TODD K. SHACKELFORD
Department of Psychology,
Florida Atlantic University,
Davie, Florida

VALERIE G. STARRATT
Department of Psychology,
Florida Atlantic University,
Davie, Florida

J. ANDERSON THOMSON JR.
Center for the Study of Mind
and Human Interaction,
University of Virginia,
Charlottesville, Virginia

ANTHONY WALSH
Department of Criminal Justice
Administration, Boise State
University, Boise, Idaho

PART ONE

INTRODUCTION AND OVERVIEW

1

Evolutionary Forensic Psychology

TODD K. SHACKELFORD AND JOSHUA D. DUNTLEY

Forensic psychology is a burgeoning field in the social and behavioral sciences. It explores the application of the science and the profession of psychology, including questions and issues relating to the law and legal systems. Research and practice in forensic psychology have been approached from a broad range of theoretical perspectives, from psychoanalytic to behavioral-genetic. It also has explored issues ranging from the criminal mind to the origins of rules that govern the structure of societies. Despite these achievements, however, differences in theoretical perspectives in forensic psychology have led to an often splintered and incomplete treatment of the field.

Darwin's (1859) theory of evolution by natural selection is the theoretical framework that unifies the field of biology. It unites research and understanding of the development, control, and organization of behavior. It informs domains of research, including communication, territoriality, parenting, and social behavior. The study of humans, which includes all of the social sciences, is part of the field of biology. Evolutionary forensic psychology is a necessary step toward a unified and complete understanding of psychology and the law.

Why *Evolutionary* Forensic Psychology?

Evolutionary psychology uses an adaptationist approach to explore the cognitive foundations of behavior. Over the deep history of humankind, individuals faced specific recurrent problems, generation after generation, that affected how long they survived, how well they lived, and, of greatest relevance for natural selection, how successful they were at reproducing. Some individuals had characteristics that made them better able to solve these problems than others. The better problem-solvers were more likely to survive and reproduce. When there was a genetic basis for characteristics contributing to better problem solving, the genes that contributed to the development of those characteristics were passed on in greater numbers than the genes coding for less successful characteristics. A beneficial characteristic providing even a 1% advantage in reproduction (fitness advantage) over other, less beneficial characteristics could completely replace the poorer characteristics in a few thousand generations (Nilsson & Pelger, 1994). Over the millions of generations of human evolutionary history, characteristics that helped individuals to solve recurrent problems that affected their fitness were gradually sculpted into functional adaptations by the process of natural selection.

Evolutionary processes undoubtedly shaped physiological characteristics to help solve problems of survival and reproduction. The skin is well adapted to protecting the vital organs beneath from injury and infection. The lungs, with their vast surface area and moist membranes, are marvelous adaptations for extracting oxygen and releasing carbon dioxide. The heart is a powerful pump that functions to circulate oxygen and other nutrients to cells throughout our bodies. Just as selection shaped physiological adaptations with specific problem-solving functions, it also shaped the structure of thoughts, preferences, desires, attitudes, and emotions to guide behaviors toward solving historically recurrent problems that affected reproductive fitness. The adaptationist approach used by evolutionary psychologists uses knowledge of recurrent ancestral problems to generate hypotheses about the functions and forms of cognitive mechanisms in human minds.

Humans do not have specialized horns for fighting rivals or teeth for incapacitating prey. Instead, our minds house a large complement of specialized cognitive adaptations that coordinate patterns of behavior capable of solving such problems. Tooby and DeVore (1987) argue that humans occupy the "cognitive niche" in earth's ecosystems. They propose that our place in this unique niche is largely the result of the importance of social interaction over the course of human evolutionary history. Interacting with others can facilitate finding solutions to adaptive problems. However, sociality can also create unique sources of conflict. There would have been significant selection pressure over human evolutionary history in favor of strategies that coordinate cooperation with others in contexts where working together was more beneficial than going it alone (Trivers, 1971), such as hunting large game, building shelter, and defending against attacks from rival groups. There also would have been significant selection pressure for the evolution of strategies to best others in contexts of conflict over scarce resources (Buss & Shackelford, 1997a), including competition for attractive mates and territories.

One general strategy for winning contests over limited resources is inflicting costs on rivals. Damaging rivals in competition for resources makes the net benefit of controlling the resources lower for them. Inflicting enough damage can make the costs of competition for a scarce resource exceed the benefits of controlling the resource, at which point the most adaptive strategy is to disengage from competition, leaving the resource to the cost-inflicting individual. The potential benefits of cost-inflicting strategies in contexts of competition for resources would have created selection pressure for the purposeful infliction of costs as a strategy to outcompete rivals. A special set of adaptations may have evolved for this purpose in psychopaths (see Chapter 10 of this volume).

Several sources of conflict between individuals have been recurrent over human evolutionary history. Understanding the nature of recurrent conflicts between individuals in our evolutionary past can give us insight into the form and function of manifest conflicts between people today. In what follows, we explore some of the most important sources of conflict for our ancestors and briefly discuss their implications for the field of evolutionary forensic psychology.

Interindividual Conflict

Conflict over Status

One broad context of conflict between individuals is the struggle for status. All available evidence indicates that men who are high in status have sexual access to a greater number of women than do men who are low in status (Betzig, 1993; Buss, 2003a; Hill & Hurtado, 1996; Perusse, 1993). Men who are high in status also are more likely than their low-status rivals to seek out younger and more fertile women (Grammer, 1992) and to marry women who are more attractive (Taylor & Glenn, 1976; Udry & Eckland, 1984). An individual in a group cannot ascend a status hierarchy without displacing someone above, bumping that person to a lower position and inflicting costs associated with status loss. The potential for large fitness gains associated with increases in status would have created selection pressures for specialized cognitive adaptations that lead to hierarchy ascension and other cognitive mechanisms to prevent large status falls. Because a greater number of mating opportunities enhances the reproductive success of men more than that of women, there should be greater status striving among men than among women. Research across the life span has found this to be the case, with men placing greater importance on coming out ahead and women focusing more on maintaining social harmony (Maccoby, 1990; Pratto, 1996; Whiting & Edwards, 1988).

Conflict over Material Resources

A second context of ancestrally recurrent conflict was fighting over material resources, specifically resources that helped to solve recurrent adaptive problems. Such resources included territory, food, weapons, and tools. There also was conflict to gain the favor of individuals who were the suppliers of material resources, examples of which include the conflict between siblings for investment from their parents and elder kin (Parker, Royle, & Hartley, 2002) and conflict between women for access to men with resources (Buss, Larsen, & Westen, 1996; Buss, Larsen, Westen, & Semmelroth, 1992). In general, the scarcer and more valuable the resource in terms of its contribution to an individual's reproductive success, the greater the conflict should be between individuals over access to the resource.

Conflict over Mating Resources

Whereas the minimum obligatory parental investment for women is nine months, the minimum investment for men can be as little as a few moments. Because women's minimum investment in reproduction is greater, the costs of a poor mate choice are greater for women than for men (Trivers, 1972). As a result, there is conflict between the sexes about the timing of sexual activity. Because sex is less costly for men than for women, they desire sexual activity much earlier in a relationship than do women (Werner-Wilson, 1998). Men also desire a greater number of sexual partners than do women (Schmitt, Shackelford, Duntley, Tooke, & Buss, 2001) and are more amenable to short-term, uncommitted sex (Buss, 2003a). These differences in men's and women's sexual desires are a clear source of evolutionarily recurrent conflict between the sexes. One hypothesized result of this conflict is sexual harassment, a topic explored by Kingsley Browne in Chapter 5 of this volume. Another is the existence of female prostitution. In Chapter 7 of this volume, Catherine Salmon provides insight into the origins of this cross-culturally ubiquitous phenomenon.

There also is conflict within each sex for access to members of the opposite sex. Women are biologically limited in the number of offspring they can have in their lifetime. In contrast, men are limited reproductively only by the number of female partners they can successfully impregnate. Given an equal sex ratio, men who impregnate more than one woman or who have more than one long-term partner at any time effectively deprive rivals of a potential mate. Human polygynous mating systems, in which males may have more than one mate at a time, lead to greater reproductive success for some men and zero reproductive success for others. Over evolutionary time, the greater reproductive variance among men selected for more extreme male strategies to acquire mates. Daly and Wilson (1988) argue that "risky strategies" such as the use of violence are one outcome of this unique selection pressure on men. Over evolutionary time, men who failed to take risks would have been at a disadvantage in competition for mates and, therefore, less likely to leave descendants. In Chapter 8 of this volume, Martin Lalumière reviews theoretical and empirical work on risk tolerance and risk avoidance from a life history perspective.

Conflict and Kin Selection

Evolutionary researchers have documented that conflict is usually tempered by genetic relatedness. Genetic relatives are less likely to experience conflict over resources than are nonrelatives. Closer genetic relatives do not experience conflict as often as or to the degree that more distant relatives do (see Buss, 2004, for a review). This is argued to be the evolutionary product of kin selection. According to kin selection theory (Hamilton, 1963; Maynard Smith, 1964), humans and other organisms have evolved to act more favorably toward their genetic relatives than toward nonrelatives. If genes that code for altruism exist in an individual, they also are likely to be present in the individual's genetic relatives. Natural selection would favor behaving altruistically toward genetic kin who can convert that investment into reproduction, which translates into the production of additional copies of shared genes.

Daly and Wilson (1988) applied the logic of kin selection theory to family relationships. They hypothesized that genetic relatedness creates a special kind of family bond. Genetic relatives, they argue, should behave more altruistically toward one another than family members who are not genetically related, such as stepparents and stepchildren. To put it another way, stepfamily members should be in greater conflict with each other than genetic family members. To test their hypothesis, Daly and Wilson secured homicide records from the United States and Canada. They used homicide as an assay of conflict between family members. They discovered that children are between 40 and 100 times more likely to be murdered when they reside in a home in which a stepparent is present than when residing with two genetic parents. Adult children are also more likely to kill a stepparent than a genetic parent. Daly and Wilson propose that the greater conflict between stepfamily members is produced by an activation failure of psychological mechanisms that generate closeness between genetic relatives. In Chapter 4 of this volume, Aaron Goetz and Todd Shackelford explore the conflicts between intimate partners that can lead to violence.

Specific Cost-Inflicting Strategies to Outcompete Rivals

Theft

One strategy of cost infliction that may be used to gain an advantage in competition for resources is theft (see Cohen & Machalek, 1988) or otherwise cheating rivals out of their resources. A valuable weapon can be stolen and used against its owner. Valuable territory can be encroached upon and its vegetation, water, shelter, and wildlife exploited (Chagnon, 1983). Mates can be poached from an existing relationship (Buss, 2000; Buss, 2003a; Schmitt & Buss, 2001). Public knowledge that a person has been cheated or has had valuables stolen also can affect the individual's reputation. The person may be viewed by others as someone who is easy to exploit, perhaps increasing the likelihood that others will attempt to cheat or steal from the person in the future. An easily exploitable person will likely be less attractive to members of the other sex. In short, cheating and the theft of resources can be effective strategies of cost-infliction for the gain of reproductively relevant resources, including material resources and status. The topic of theft is explored by Satoshi Kanazawa in Chapter 9 of this volume.

Vigilance and Violence in Romantic Relationships

Buss and Shackelford (1997b) found that men and women engage in tactics that range from vigilance to violence to defend their relationships. Fueled by jealousy, an emotion absent from contexts of material-resource theft, men's tactics of defending against mate poachers were found to be different from women's. Men are more likely to conceal their partners, display resources, and resort to threats and violence, especially against rivals. Men also are more likely to use tactics of submission and self-abasement, groveling or promising their partner anything to get her to stay. Women are more likely to enhance their appearance and to induce jealousy in their partners, demonstrating their desirability by showing that they have other mating options available to them.

Rape

Rape, a topic explored in Chapter 6, is a strategy aimed directly at obtaining reproductive resources at a cost to the victim. A rapist may benefit from the behavior by siring offspring that he may not have otherwise produced. Not only does rape inflict terrible emotional (Block, 1990; Burgess & Holmstrom, 1974) and physical (Geist, 1988) costs on women, it also inflicts fitness costs by bypassing female mate choice mechanisms (Buss, 2004). Although scholars have concluded that there is not enough evidence to determine whether men have adaptations to rape (Buss, 2003a, 2004; Symons, 1979), ethnographies and historical records suggest that rape occurs cross-culturally and was recurrent over the deep time of our evolutionary history (Buss, 2003a). The occurrence of rape would have created selection pressure for strategies to avoid and resist it.

Violence and Homicide

Unlike some other strategies of inflicting costs, violence and homicide represent more flexible solutions to conflicts between individuals. Violence can be used to damage the status of a competitor or as an instrumental measure to facilitate theft. Homicide can free resources from the control of a rival and permanently eliminate cost-inflicting competitors.

Using violence to injure rivals can be an effective strategy to remove them from competition for a valuable resource. A healthy individual can compete more effectively than the rivals he injures. Competitors may be more likely to avoid or to drop out of competition with an individual who has injured them in the past. An individual who is capable of inflicting greater injuries to his competitors than they can inflict on him may gain a reputation of being difficult to exploit. This reputation may protect an individual against violent confrontations and grant easier access to resources with less resistance from competitors.

Daly and Wilson (1988), among others (Chagnon, 1988; Ghiglieri, 1999), have documented that violence and homicide can be outcomes of intraspecific competition.

Competition for mates (Buss, 2000; Weekes-Shackelford, Shackelford, & Buss, 2003), competition for status (Daly & Wilson, 1996; Shackelford, 2005), and competition for resources (Daly & Wilson, 1988; Kruger & Nesse, 2004) have been documented to be sources of violent conflict with the potential to lead to homicide. Even homicides that result from seemingly trivial altercations between two individuals who did not previously know one another can be understood through the lens of evolutionary psychology (Buss, 2005; Daly & Wilson, 1988; Ghiglieri, 1999). For much of our evolutionary history, social reputation carried long-term repercussions that are largely missing from modern societies. An individual's social sphere was smaller in the past, typically consisting of several dozen individuals. The winner of confrontations would garner a reputation as someone who should not be trifled with, and thus would have fewer battles to fight in the future. The loser would garner a reputation as a person who can be exploited and would either have to fight again or cede his resources in future conflicts. David Buss and Joshua Duntley address homicide in Chapter 3 of this volume, and Aaron Goetz and Todd Shackelford explore violence in families in particular in Chapter 4.

Coevolution

From an evolutionary perspective, all crimes can be thought of as strategies that function to benefit the criminal at the cost of the victim. Evolutionary theories of crime are fundamentally coevolutionary theories of adaptations that produce criminal behavior and counteradaptations to defend against being victimized (Buss & Duntley, 2006; Duntley, 2005). Haldane (1932, 1949a, 1949b) was among the first to recognize the importance of coevolutionary arms races in his discussion of the influence of infectious diseases on human evolutionary history. He pointed out that infectious pathogens possess adaptations that enable them to use human tissues to reproduce and that we have evolved counterstrategies to prevent our being invaded by pathogens.

Antagonistic coevolutionary arms races are part of the evolutionary history of all species. They can occur between species, such as the lynx and the hare, or within species between competing adaptations in contexts of social conflict. Such coevolutionary arms races have likely shaped a large number of complex adaptations. They can create massive selection pressures capable of producing quite rapid evolutionary change (see Altizer, Harvell, & Friedle, 2003; Phillips, Brown, & Shine, 2004).

The Fitness Costs of Being Victimized

It is a truism that victims of crime incur fitness costs. Individuals who are victimized are at a competitive disadvantage to those who are not. A victim of homicide provides an extreme example, the fundamental logic of which applies to all forms of victimization. A murder victim's death has a much larger impact on his or her inclusive fitness than just the loss of the genes in the person's body. Death by homicide often has cascading deleterious effects on a victim's inclusive fitness, including (a) the loss of future reproduction; (b) damage to existing children from lack of protection, investment, or the addition of stepparents; and (c) damage to the victim's extended kin group from diminished investment and a reputation for being exploitable.

A murder victim's fitness losses can potentially be translated into a rival's fitness gains. The residual reproductive and parenting value of the mate of a homicide victim may go to a rival, often at the expense of the victim's children with that mate, who may become stepchildren, a condition associated with an increased risk of abuse and homicide (Daly & Wilson, 1988). The murder of a man or woman creates an opening in a social group's hierarchy into which a rival can ascend. The children of rivals who had two surviving genetic parents would thrive relative to the victim's children, who would be deprived of the investment, protection, and influence of two genetic parents.

Victim Defenses

The great costs resulting from being the victim of crime would have selected for adaptations to (a) avoid being victimized; (b) punish conspecifics who damage individuals' inclusive fitness by inflicting costs on others, their genetic relatives, mates, or coalitional allies; and (c) eliminate or otherwise render impotent individuals who presented a persistent threat of inflicting costs in the future on the larger social group of which an individual, his kin, and his coalition are a part (e.g., psychopaths, hostile members of other groups). Inflicting costs on cost-inflicting rivals, including murdering them, is hypothesized to be part of an evolved strategy to avoid or stanch the inclusive fitness costs of being victimized by another individual or group (Buss & Duntley, 2006, in press; Duntley, 2005; Duntley & Buss, 2005).

To avoid being victimized, intended victims must be sensitive to cues indicative of situations in which someone else might benefit from inflicting costs on them. Insight into the likelihood that one will be the victim of crime before the crime occurs requires that the majority of crimes be committed in predictable sets of circumstances. If particular crimes recurrently occurred in response to predictable sets of circumstances over our evolutionary history, selection would be for defense mechanisms capable of recognizing those circumstances and trying to change or avoid them. These and other aspects of victim adaptations are explored in Chapter 11. The evolution of such defense mechanisms, in turn, would have selected for strategies that could circumvent the evolved defenses. In this way, adaptations to avoid being victimized would have served as selection pressures for the refinement of psychological adaptations for inflicting costs over evolutionary time. These new cost-inflicting adaptations would have selected for further refinements in defense adaptations—cost-infliction and defenses against victimization locked in a perpetual, antagonistic, coevolutionary arms race across generations, as illustrated in Figure 1.1.

Demonstration of the existence of crime-specific defenses against victimization that appear to have been designed to defeat corresponding criminal strategies would

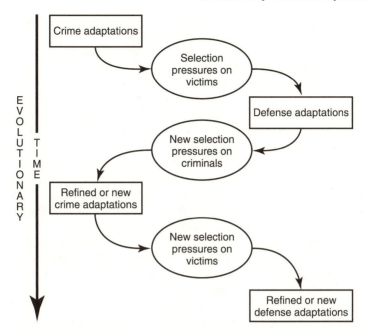

Figure 1.1. Adaptations that produce criminal behavior create selection pressure for the evolution of counter adaptations in victims, which in turn create novel selection pressures for the evolution of counter-counter adaptations in criminals

provide evidence that (a) the crime was likely a recurrent feature of ancestral environments, (b) the criminal strategy occurred in predictable patterns over our evolutionary history and, therefore, (c) there may be adaptations specifically for the crime. The greater the corresponding specificity of design in the psychologies of crime and defenses against crime, the stronger the evidence that the two have had a coevolutionary relationship, and the greater the support for the existence of adaptations for criminal behavior.

There are no perfect solutions to any adaptive problem. Every adaptation is a compromise between the numerous different adaptive problems an organism faces. At the same time as an individual selection pressure operates to shape or refine an adaptation in a certain direction, other selection pressures push and pull on the evolutionary trajectory of its form and precise function, diverting it away from its optimal course for any single adaptive problem. It is unlikely that there would be enough stability in the selection pressures of a coevolutionary arms race, in combination with the other adaptive problems of survival and reproduction, for perfect adaptive solutions to evolve. Therefore, it is unlikely that adaptations that produce criminal behavior and adaptations to defend against being victimized will lead on every occasion to the outcomes for which they were designed. For selection to favor them, they need only lead to greater reproductive success than competing designs *on average* across the individuals in a population over evolutionary time.

Coevolutionary arms races may involve the competing interests of more than two individuals. This is particularly apparent in contexts involving mating (Buss, 2003b). Coevolutionary arms races involving more than two individuals can occur, for example, when a woman who is married to one man becomes interested in another man. There is selection pressure on the woman to be faithful to her husband so as not to lose his investment or risk violent retaliation for her affair. There is also selection pressure on the woman to obtain better or different genes from those possessed by her husband or acquire additional investment from another man. Female adaptations to engage in infidelity in some contexts would select for male adaptations to stanch women's infidelities, especially when a man and woman are in a long-term mating relationship. One hypothesized male adaptation for dealing with infidelity is to inflict costs on the woman—domestic violence, stalking, marital rape, or even murder.

Female adaptations that produce infidelity in certain contexts would select for adaptations in men who are not the woman's long-term mate to lure women or aid them in being unfaithful. These male adaptations that promote female infidelity would, in turn, create selection pressure on men's long-term mating psychology for adaptations to prevent other men from poaching away their long-term partners, including the infliction of costs on the mate poacher, the cheating mate, or both. Any adaptation that results from what Buss (2003b) refers to as "triadic coevolution" is shaped by selection pressures created by the adaptations of the two other individuals involved, as illustrated by Figure 1.2. Newly evolved psychological mechanisms that benefit any one individual in the triadic relationship impose new selection pressures on both of the other individuals. Adaptations in long-term males that lead to cost-infliction as a strategy for dealing with a partner's infidelity, for example, would select for defense adaptations in both romantic partners and poachers. One possible evolved defense against being victimized is to anticipate victimization and preemptively inflict costs on the victimizer. This would select for defense adaptations in victimizers. These defense adaptations are hypothesized to factor into the decision calculus responsible for motivating or inhibiting cost-inflicting patterns of behavior in men who discover that their partners have been unfaithful.

The Importance of Time and Opportunity

Time was likely an important and potentially powerful selection pressure on the psychology of criminal behavior and could have been so in at least two ways. First, the time available to solve a problem may increase or decrease the likelihood with which criminal behavior will be chosen as a solution. The amount of time that people have to react to different adaptive problems varies from situation to situation. Solutions to adaptive problems also vary in terms of how much time they require to be enacted effectively. The interaction of time with adaptive problems and solutions would have created selection pressure for psychological mechanisms capable of calculating the

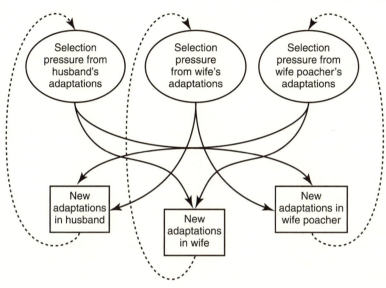

Figure 1.2. When three individuals have conflicting interests in the same adaptive problem domain, an adaptation in one individual can simultaneously create selection pressure on two (or more) other individuals. The counter adaptations that evolve in each of the two other individuals as a result can then create antagonistic selection pressure on the other two. This triadic coevolutionary process can carry on indefinitely through time, as long as there is recurrent conflict between those involved for some fitness-relevant resource.

amount of time available to solve a given problem (Buss & Duntley, in press). Estimates of the amount of time available would have been a source of input for making decisions about which adaptive solution should be employed.

There were likely recurrent contexts of conflict between people who had both a very large potential fitness impact and a narrow time frame in which to enact a solution. Such situations could have selected for some of the risky, cost-inflicting strategies we label as crimes. Examples may include homicides that are committed in self-defense. A woman who is cornered in the kitchen by her abusive husband may reach instinctively for a knife to defend her life with—by ending his. In such situations, homicide may not be the most beneficial possible solution to the problem, but it is the least costly of available alternatives.

The presentation of rare opportunities that put cost-inflicting competitors at a significant disadvantage in highly fitness-relevant situations, if recurrent, could also have acted as selection pressures for the adoption of risky, criminal strategies (Buss & Duntley, in press). For example, a man who walks in on his wife and a rival in the act of having sex is simultaneously assaulted with an extremely significant adaptive problem and presented with a rare opportunity. The rival is naked and distracted, making him vulnerable to attack. The husband may never again have the rival at such a disadvantage. It would be surprising if selection did not fashion adaptations to employ homicide to exploit such rare contexts.

There also may have been recurrent adaptive problems involving social conflict that required a *greater* amount of time to effectively enact a strategy involving criminal behaviors (Buss & Duntley, in press). Cost-inflicting strategies that require the coordination of the efforts of multiple individuals require more time to deploy than strategies perpetrated by one person. Examples include contexts of coalitional aggression or tribal warfare. The raids of rival groups perpetrated by the Yanomamo in order to kidnap women and capture resources (Chagnon, 1988) could not be successful without coordination, which requires a larger window of time than many situations in which individuals commit single murders.

A second way that time could have been an important selection pressure for the evolution of adaptations that produce criminal behavior rests on the importance of responding to costly assaults from others in a timely fashion (Buss & Duntley, in press). Most people are familiar with the proverb, "Revenge is a dish best served cold," which suggests that emotional detachment and planning are best for taking revenge. This may be true for the optimal planning of strategies of revenge. However, there are clear time limits on the effectiveness of strategies for seeking revenge. Waiting too long to avenge being wronged can decrease the effectiveness of vengeance in two ways: first, by allowing more time for a reputation of being exploitable to grow, and second, by creating a larger window for exploitation to occur. Although revenge may be a dish that is best served cold, reputation may be an asset that is best defended by striking while the iron is hot. Inflicting costs on the individual who is the source of reputational damage, including murdering the person, is one effective strategy for the defense of reputation (Buss, 2005; Chagnon, 1988). Murder eliminates the person's ability to inflict costs in the future and clearly signals to other rivals the price they will pay for similar assaults.

As explained by Buss and Duntley (in press), the timing of cost-inflicting, criminal strategies relative to other, complementary strategies is also likely to have been an important source of selection pressure on the function of mechanisms that produce criminal behavior. Adaptations that produce criminal behavior likely comprise a suite of mechanisms designed not only to inflict costs but also to deal with the probable consequences of victimizing someone. Inflicting costs as the solution to a primary adaptive problem is likely to create secondary problems, such as retribution from victims and their genetic relatives. The recurrent costs of secondary problems would have created selection pressure for the evolution of secondary solutions to those problems. Some secondary solutions would be best employed after the secondary problems they created. For example, a criminal could take steps to (a) cover up the crime, (b) subsequently avoid victims and their genetic relatives, (c) threaten to inflict additional costs on them, (d) actually inflict costs on them if they attempt to retaliate, or (e) marshal a formidable coalition to help make the costs of avenging the victim's death too high to be adaptive. Other secondary solutions may be more appropriately adopted before the primary solution involving the infliction of costs

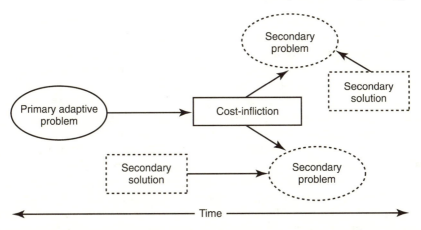

Figure 1.3. The use of cost-infliction to help solve an adaptive problem can create secondary problems, such as retribution from victims and their kin. Selection would have operated on the mind to anticipate likely problems resultant from cost-infliction and shaped a menu of possible solutions. Solutions to secondary problems created by criminal behavior could be enacted before, during, or after the crime

takes place. For example, an individual who may, in the future, adopt a strategy that includes cost-infliction could try to impugn the status and reputation of the person he or she intends to victimize. An intended criminal might also attempt to drive wedges between would-be victims and the kin and coalitional allies who would pose the greatest threat of helping the victims seek revenge, thus eliminating or decreasing the magnitude of secondary problems that will likely result from inflicting costs on victims. These ideas are illustrated in Figure 1.3. Interestingly, adaptations for inflicting costs could use information about the effectiveness of secondary solutions employed in anticipation of the secondary problems that cost-infliction will create as a source of input for the cost-benefit calculus that determines whether to pursue one particular criminal strategy over another, or do something else. In addition, if secondary solutions employed before a cost-inflicting strategy in particular contexts were recurrent over evolutionary time, selection should have operated on victims' defense adaptations to recognize the secondary solutions and motivate people to take action to prevent criminal behavior from occurring.

Implications of Adaptationist Research on the Psychology of Crime

There is great promise in applying the adaptationist approach to all cognitive and behavioral phenomena. Evolutionary theory provides a powerful set of tools for exploring the functions of psychological mechanisms. It suggests specific, novel hypotheses and provides a logical framework that opens and unites data sources not routinely utilized in psychological research (e.g., comparative, ethnographic, bioarcheological).

If it turns out that cognitive mechanisms that produce criminal behavior are biologically engrained in the human psyche, it does not mean that we should be more tolerant of crime because people "can't help themselves." We are not tolerant of a number of behaviors that humans may be biologically disposed to engage in, such as infidelity, spousal violence (Buss, 2000), and violence toward stepchildren (Daly & Wilson, 1988). In fact, there is substantial evidence to suggest that morality itself has evolutionary roots (see Chapter 12 of this volume). The existence of adaptations that produce crime also does not mean that crime is inevitable. Research on homicidal fantasies, for example, demonstrates that the vast majority of murder fantasies are not translated into homicidal reality (Kenrick & Sheets, 1993). Jones (1997) argues that our system of laws is designed to act as a lever to move behavior in desired directions. By gaining a better understanding of how and why our psychology produces criminal behavior, we may be able to create more effective legal interventions to prevent crimes from occurring and more effective psychological treatments for offenders, likely offenders, and victims (see Chapter 14 of this volume). Even if the application of evolutionary logic to help understand criminal behavior turns out to be misguided, the research findings it produces represent a valuable contribution to our understanding of crime.

In conclusion, evolutionary forensic psychology recognizes that crimes such as murder, nonlethal violence, rape, theft, and cheating are manifestations of evolutionarily recurrent conflicts between individuals. The cost-inflicting strategies that we recognize as crimes may have been favored by natural selection when they gave individuals an advantage in competition for resources (see Chapter 2 of this volume). Darwin's theory of evolution by natural selection provides a powerful meta-theoretical framework that has the potential to unify and energize forensic psychology just as it has the biological sciences (see Chapter 13 of this volume). In the future, we predict that evolutionary psychology will revolutionize the field of forensic psychology, including our understanding of the psychology of crime, the cognition and behaviors of victims, jury selection, eye-witness testimony, judges' views of human nature, insanity, competency, and public policy. It is difficult to predict exactly how evolutionary psychology will affect the criminal justice system. The accumulation of research findings grounded in evolutionary theory will refine and change the way we think about legal systems. New discoveries will also open new directions for inquiry and spawn additional research. Evolutionary forensic psychology represents the beginning of a revolution of thought and discovery that will bring us closer to the truth of who we are and what our laws are capable of doing.

References

Altizer, S., Harvell, D., & Friedle, E. (2003). Rapid evolutionary dynamics and disease threats to biodiversity. *Trends in Ecology and Evolution, 18*, 589–596.

Betzig, L. L. (1993). Sex, succession, and stratification in the first six civilizations. In L. Ellis (Ed.), *Social stratification and socioeconomic inequality* (pp. 37–74). Westport, CT: Praeger.

Block, A. P. (1990). Rape trauma syndrome as scientific expert testimony. *Archives of Sexual Behavior, 19,* 309–323.

Burgess, A. W., & Holmstrom, L. L. (1974). Rape trauma syndrome. *American Journal of Psychiatry, 131,* 981–986.

Buss, D. M. (2000). *The dangerous passion.* New York: Free Press.

Buss, D. M. (2003a). *The evolution of desire* (rev. ed.). New York: Free Press.

Buss, D. M. (2003b, June). *Sexual conflict.* Paper presented at the Annual Meeting of the Human Behavior and Evolution Society, University of Nebraska, U.S.

Buss, D. M. (2004). *Evolutionary psychology* (2nd ed.). New York: Allyn & Bacon.

Buss, D. M. (2005). *The murderer next door.* New York: Penguin.

Buss, D. M., & Duntley, J. D. (2006). The evolution of aggression. In M. Schaller, J. A. Simpson, & D. T. Kenrick (Eds.), *Evolution and social psychology* (pp. 263–286). New York: Psychology Press.

Buss, D. M., & Duntley, J. D. (in press). Adaptations for exploitation. *Group Dynamics: Theory, Research, and Practice.*

Buss, D. M., Larsen, R. R., & Westen, D. (1996). Sex differences in jealousy: Not gone, not forgotten, and not explained by alternative hypotheses. *Psychological Science, 7,* 373–375.

Buss, D. M., Larsen, R. R., Westen, D., & Semmelroth, J. (1992). Sex differences in jealousy: Evolution, physiology, and psychology. *Psychological Science, 3,* 251–255.

Buss, D. M., & Shackelford, T. K. (1997a). Human aggression in evolutionary psychological perspective. *Clinical Psychology Review, 17,* 605–619.

Buss, D. M., & Shackelford, T. K. (1997b). From vigilance to violence: Mate retention tactics in married couples. *Journal of Personality and Social Psychology, 72,* 346–361.

Chagnon, N. (1983). *Yanomamo* (3rd ed.). New York: Holt, Rinehart, & Winston.

Chagnon, N. A. (1988). Life histories, blood revenge, and warfare in a tribal population. *Science, 239,* 985–992.

Cohen, L. E., & Machalek, R. (1988). A general theory of expropriative crime: An evolutionary ecological approach. *American Journal of Sociology, 94,* 465–501.

Daly, M., & Wilson, M. (1988). *Homicide.* Hawthorne, NY: Aldine de Gruyter.

Daly, M., & Wilson M. (1996, December 8). Homicidal tendencies. *Demos,* 39–45.

Darwin, C. (1859). *On the origin of species by means of natural selection.* London: John Murray. (Reprinted in 1964 by Princeton University Press.)

Duntley, J. D. (2005). Adaptations to dangers from other humans. In D. Buss (Ed.), *The handbook of evolutionary psychology* (pp. 224–249). New York: Wiley.

Duntley, J. D., & Buss, D. M. (2005). The plausibility of adaptations for homicide. In P. Carruthers, S. Laurence, and S. Stich (Eds.), *The structure of the innate mind* (pp. 291–304). New York: Oxford University Press.

Geist, R. F. (1988). Sexually related trauma. *Emergency Medical Clinics of North America, 6,* 439–466.

Ghiglieri, M. P. (1999). *The dark side of man.* Reading, MA: Perseus Books.

Grammer, K. (1992). Variations on a theme: Age dependent mate selection in humans. *Behavioral and Brain Sciences, 15,* 100–102.

Haldane, J. B. S. (1932). *The causes of evolution.* London: Longmans, Green.

Haldane, J. B. S. (1949a). The rate of mutation of human genes. Proceedings of the Eighth International Congress of Genetics. *Hereditas, 35,* 267–273.

Haldane, J. B. S. (1949b). Disease and evolution. *La Ricerca Scientifica, 19*, 2–11.

Hamilton, W. D. (1963). The evolution of altruistic behavior. *The American Naturalist, 97*, 354–356.

Hill, K., & Hurtado, A. M. (1996). *Ache life history: The ecology and demography of a foraging people.* Hawthorne, NY: Aldine de Gruyter.

Jones, O. D. (1997). Evolutionary analysis in law: An introduction and application to child abuse. *North Carolina Law Review, 75*, 1117–1242.

Kenrick, D. T., & Sheets, V. (1993). Homicidal fantasies. *Ethology and Sociobiology, 14*, 231–246.

Kruger, D. J., & Nesse, R. M. (2004). Sexual selection and the male: Female mortality ratio. *Evolutionary Psychology, 2*, 66–85.

Maccoby, E. (1990). Gender and relationships: A developmental account. *America Psychologist, 45*, 513–520.

Maynard Smith, J. (1964). Group selection and kin selection. *Nature, 201*, 145–147.

Nilsson, D. E., & Pelger, S. (1994). A pessimistic estimate of the time required for an eye to evolve. *Proceedings of the Royal Society of London, 256*, 53–58.

Parker, G. A., Royle, M. J., & Hartley, I. R. (2002). Intrafamilial conflict and parental investment: A synthesis. *Philosophical Transactions of the Royal Society of London B, 357*, 295–307.

Perusse, D. (1993). Cultural and reproductive success in industrial societies: Testing the relationship at proximate and ultimate levels. *Behavioral and Brain Sciences, 16*, 267–322.

Phillips, B., Brown, G. P., & Shine, R. (2004). Assessing the potential for an evolutionary response to rapid environmental change: Invasive toads and an Australian snake. *Evolutionary Ecology Research, 6*, 799–811.

Pratto, F. (1996). Sexual politics: The gender gap in the bedroom, the cupboard, and the cabinet. In D. M. Buss & N. M. Malamuth (Eds.), *Sex, power, conflict* (pp. 179–230). New York: Oxford University Press.

Schmitt, D. P., & Buss, D. M. (2001). Human mate poaching: Tactics and temptations for infiltrating existing mateships. *Journal of Personality and Social Psychology, 80*, 894–917.

Schmitt, D. P., Shackelford, T. K., Duntley, J. D., Tooke, W., & Buss, D. M. (2001). The desire for sexual variety as a tool for understanding basic human mating strategies. *Personal Relationships, 8*, 425–455.

Shackelford, T. K. (2005). An evolutionary psychological perspective on cultures of honor. *Evolutionary Psychology, 3*, 381–391.

Symons, D. (1979). *The evolution of human sexuality.* New York: Oxford University Press.

Taylor, P. A., & Glenn, N. D. (1976). The utility of education and attractiveness for females' status attainment through marriage. *American Sociological Review, 41*, 484–498.

Tooby, J., & DeVore, I. (1987). The reconstruction of hominid behavioral evolution through strategic modeling. In W. G. Kinzey (Ed.), *The evolution of human behavior* (pp. 183–238). Albany: State University of New York Press.

Trivers, R. L. (1971). The evolution of reciprocal altruism. *Quarterly Review of Biology, 46*, 35–57.

Trivers, R. L. (1972). Parental investment and sexual selection. In B. Campbell (Ed.), *Sexual selection and the descent of man: 1871–1971* (pp. 136–179). Chicago: Aldine.

Udry, R. R., & Eckland, B. K. (1984). Benefits of being attractive: Differential payoffs for men and women. *Psychological Reports, 54*, 47–56.

Weekes-Shackelford, V. A., Shackelford, T. K., & Buss, D. M. (2003). Murder in a lover's triangle. In M. D. Smith and P. Blackman (Eds.), *New directions in homicide research* (pp. 219–231). Washington, DC: Federal Bureau of Investigation.

Werner-Wilson, R. J. (1998). Gender differences in adolescent sexual attitudes: The influence of individual and family factors. *Adolescence, 33,* 519–531.

Whiting, B. B., & Edwards, C. P. (1988). *Children of different worlds.* Cambridge, MA: Harvard University Press.

2

The Promise of Evolutionary Psychology for Criminology

The Examples of Gender and Age

ANTHONY WALSH AND KEVIN M. BEAVER

The maladies of sociology are many and grave, so much so that some scholars have deemed the discipline to be terminally ill (Barkow, 2006; Ellis, 1996; Horowitz, 1993; Lopreato & Crippen, 1999; Van den Berghe, 1990; Walsh, 2002) or have wondered if it could, or even should, be saved (Kanazawa, 2006). Sociology is indeed adrift in a foggy maze of theoretical contradictions, ideological self-righteousness, and non-sensical postmodern "display prose," but to declare it beyond hope is premature. The discipline needs a solid anchor to stabilize it while its crew figures out how to steer it out of the swamp. That anchor is biology, the science that sociology divorced itself from by its fundamentalist interpretation of Durkheim's dictum that the cause of social facts should be sought only in other social facts (Udry, 1995). Sociology as a whole took this to mean that there are no other sources of human social behavior, and as a result many sociologists became not simply oblivious to biology but "mili-tantly and proudly ignorant" (Van den Berghe, 1990, p. 177). As a subdiscipline of sociology, criminology is essentially in the same boat, although it seems that more criminologists than scholars in other areas of sociology have heeded biology's call, as evidenced by an avalanche of recent books entirely devoted to or containing signifi-cant coverage of biosocial approaches (Agnew, 2005; Ellis & Walsh, 2000; Fishbein, 2001; Robinson, 2004; Rowe, 2002; Walsh, 2002; Walsh & Ellis, 2003, 2007).

Sociologist Matthew Robinson has said that "the biological sciences have made more progress in advancing our understanding about behavior in the past 10 years than sociology has made in the past 50 years" (2004, p. 4). Robinson is absolutely correct, although we think he is overly generous to sociology. Talk of biology sends shudders down the spines of traditionally trained criminologists, whose understanding of "biology" barely extends beyond the standard textbook fare of phrenology, atavism, and the XYY syndrome. The fears of such people might be allayed if they did just two things: (1) learned a little about that which they fear, and (2) realized that there is no such thing as a strictly biological theory of crime. All existing theories of human behavior that integrate biological insights are *biosocial*. There are three general biosocial approaches: evolutionary, behavior genetic, and neurophysiological. These approaches, while employing different methods, work with different units of analysis and invoke different levels of causation; they are fully complementary (i.e., their principles are conceptually consistent across all three levels of analysis), and they all recognize the tremendous importance of the environment.

Evolutionary psychology is the most environmentally friendly of the three general approaches. It is axiomatic that behavioral patterns of all living things are ultimately the result of evolutionary processes and that human nature is the sum of human adaptations to ancestral environments. There is no *scientifically* viable alternative explanation to evolution by natural and sexual selection for basic behavioral design. There are still those who deny this, believing that because humans have developed culture and possess the cognitive skills to override biological dispositions we have freed ourselves from evolutionary constraints (Ruffie, 1986). John Alcock (2001) has responded to such quasi-existentialist notions by stating the following:

> [T]o say that human behavior and our other attributes cannot be analyzed in evolutionary terms requires the acceptance of a genuinely bizarre position, namely, that we alone among animal species have somehow managed to achieve independence from our evolutionary history, that our genes have for some undefined reason relinquished their influence on the development of human psychological attributes, that our brain's capacity to incorporate learned information has no relation to past selection, that differences in brain functioning in the past had no impact on the genetic success of people, and many other tenets that would be considered outlandish if applied to [other animal life forms]. (p. 223)

In short, the behavior of *Homo sapiens* is subject to the same explanatory framework as the behavior of any other animal. This is decidedly not to say that culture is irrelevant to understanding human behavior. The human behavioral repertoire may be composed of evolved adaptations, but adaptations require evolutionarily relevant triggers from the environment to develop and activate them, and these triggers differ in different cultural contexts. Because of this, Jerome Barkow (1989, p. 635) assures us that we will always need the social sciences to fully understand these triggers, but he also exhorts us not to forget that "psychology underlies culture and society, and biological evolution underlies psychology."

The Evolution of Traits Related to Criminal Behavior

If we accept the notion that evolution shaped human psychology and behavior, we have to accept the companion notion that morally undesirable human traits such as deception and violence owe their existence to their usefulness in the reproductive success of the species' distant ancestors, like the more positive traits such as altruism, nurturance, and love. Needless to say, we do not display evolved patterns of behavior motivated by the desire to maximize genetic fitness: "Evolutionary psychology is not a theory of motivation. . . . Fitness consequences are invoked not as goals in themselves, but rather to explain why certain goals have come to control behavior at all, and why they are calibrated in one particular way rather than another" (Daly & Wilson, 1988a, p. 7). Parents nurture and love their children not because they are motivated by a subconscious genetic voice telling them that if they do they will push more of their genes into the future but rather because ancestral parents who loved and nurtured their children saw more of them grow to reproductive age and pass on those traits down the genetic line. Ancestral parents who neglected and abused their children compromised their viability and thus reduced the probability of their own genes being represented in future generations. This is the ultimate (evolutionary) reason that love and nurturance of offspring are the species norm whereas abuse and neglect are aberrant.

Although evolutionary psychologists consider criminal behavior to be morally regrettable, they also consider it biologically normal behavior for which we all have the potential (Kanazawa, 2003). If behavior we define as criminal today is biologically normal, it must have conferred some evolutionary advantage on our distant ancestors; that is, it must have had positive fitness consequences. But how can morally obnoxious acts such as murder, rape, theft, and assault be evolved adaptations when they are clearly maladaptive in modern environments due to their tendency to result in the perpetrators' being imprisoned, where the opportunities for reproductive success are bleak to say the least? The answer to that is twofold. First, we must understand that specific criminal behaviors are not themselves adaptations: "Genes do not code themselves for jimmying a lock or stealing a car . . . the genome does not waste precious DNA encoding the specifics" (Rowe, 1996, p. 285).

Second, because a behavior is currently maladaptive does not mean that mechanisms underlying it were not designed by natural selection to solve some environmental problem in the distant past. An adaptation is a current feature with a past, and a feature that is currently adaptive may or may not have a future. Modern human environments are different in so many ways from the environments that the species evolved in that traits selected for their adaptive value then may not be adaptive at all today, and traits and behaviors that appear to be adaptive today may not have a history of natural selection (Daly, 1996; Mealey, 1995).

Criminal behavior is a way of acquiring valued resources by force or fraud—that is, by exploiting and deceiving others. Evolutionary psychologists refer to exploitive and deceptive behavior as *cheating*, whether or not it has been culturally defined as criminal. Although we all have the potential to exploit and deceive others, few of us ever do so to a criminal extent. We do not because we are a highly social and cooperative species with minds forged by evolution to form cooperative relationships built on reciprocal trust. We cooperate with others because we feel good when we do so, and because it identifies us as reliable and trustworthy, attributes that confer valued social status on us. In short, cooperation and reciprocal altruism are in the best interests of every member of a social species. Again, cooperation and altruism are not engaged in so that the actor can feel good or because he or she is consciously motivated by the desire for status. Social organisms do so, and are neurologically rewarded when they do, because their distant ancestors who behaved this way enjoyed greater reproductive success than those who did not, thus passing on the genes for the brain structures and neurotransmitters that presumably underlie the propensity (Barkow, 1997).

If cooperation is so rewarding, why do we find individuals who cheat rather than cooperate? The short answer is that getting something for nothing is also rewarding and that cooperative systems create niches for noncooperators to exploit (Tibbetts, 2003). Cheats are individuals who gain resources from others by signaling cooperative intentions but then defaulting. In the absence of internal (self-control, guilt, shame) or external (threats of punishment or ostracism) deterrents, it is in an individual's interests to obtain resources from others under the assumption of reciprocity and then fail to follow through. Such social parasitism has been observed among numerous animal species (Alcock, 1998), which implies that it has had positive fitness consequences. In the human species, criminal behavior may be viewed as an extreme form of defaulting on the rules of cooperation or reciprocity.

The Basic Assumptions of Evolutionary Theories of Crime

All evolutionary theories of criminal and antisocial behavior focus on reproductive strategies and the behavioral tactics that flow from them (see Walsh, 2006, for a discussion of these theories). The reproductive strategies of any species can be apportioned according to the resources (time and energy) devoted to parenting versus mating effort. At one extreme we have species that devote all of their resources to mating and none at all to parenting (e.g., oysters, who lay many thousands of eggs), and at the other we have species such as *Homo sapiens* who devote a huge proportion of resources to parenting effort. Reproductive strategies are underlain by a suite of evolved traits that facilitate their successful pursuit. Among humans, the suite of traits useful for focusing on mating effort includes deceitfulness, impulsiveness, sensation-seeking, and aggression; traits useful for focusing on parenting effort include empathy, conscientiousness, and altruism.

As is readily deduced, the traits useful for mating effort are also useful in pursuing criminal activity, and the traits useful for parenting effort are associated with prosocial activity. As David Rowe (1996, p. 270) phrased it, "[C]rime can be identified with the behaviors that tend to promote mating effort and noncrime with those that tend to promote parenting effort." The strength of these traits is arrayed on a continuum dispersed around an adaptive mean; they are not characteristics one has or has not. For the great majority of people, resources are expended mostly on mating effort at some points over the life course and on parenting effort at other points as reward contingencies shift. The most deceitful, impulsive, aggressive, and sensation-seeking among us are not constitutionally suited to anything requiring long-term commitment, including commitment to marriage and parenting, nor are they suited for pursuing prosocial activities in general. A reproductive strategy emphasizing mating effort is thus similar to criminal behavior in that direct and immediate methods are used to procure resources illegitimately with little thought being given to the consequences. Parenting effort, on the other hand, is embedded in a prosocial lifestyle in which resource procurement relies on the accumulation of social and occupational skills (the ability to delay gratification) that are attractive to females.

The empirical research is unequivocal in its conclusion that an excessive concentration on mating effort is linked to criminal behavior. Ellis and Walsh (2000) reviewed fifty-one studies examining the relationship between number of sex partners and criminal behavior and found fifty of them to be positive. The same authors also reviewed thirty-one other studies and found that age of onset of sexual behavior was negatively related to criminal behavior (the earlier the age of onset, the greater the criminal activity) in all thirty-one.

More recent data from a British cohort study of over 1,100 twin pairs found that 27% of the children were fathered by the most antisocial 10% of males in the cohort (Jaffee, Moffitt, Caspi, & Taylor, 2003). A U.S. study looking at self-selection in different family structures (broken versus intact) found that genetic differences accounted for 94% of the difference on an antisocial subscale between the most at-risk group (single mothers of half-siblings, a structure indicative of mating effort) and the least at-risk group (two-parent family with full siblings, indicative of parenting effort). While the researchers were more concerned with genetics than evolutionary psychology, they concluded, "Although temperament, personality, or cognitive bias toward sexual variety may be proximate causes of single parenthood or multiple matings, they may also comprise components of an overall reproductive strategy that emphasizes mating over parenting effort" (Cleveland, Wiebe, van den Oord, & Rowe, 2000, pp. 744–745). Finally, anthropologists have found striking differences in behavior between cultures that emphasize different reproductive strategies. In cultures emphasizing mating effort significantly more than parenting effort, members exhibit behaviors such as low-level parental care, hypermasculinity, violent competitiveness, and transient bonding, all of which are considered antisocial in Western societies (Harpending & Draper, 1988; Ember & Ember, 1998).

In this chapter, we examine large categories of individuals from an evolutionary perspective rather than individual traits that lead to differences and criminal behavior. The two best demographic predictors of where reproductive effort is focused are gender and age, which, not coincidently, are also the best demographic predictors of criminal and other antisocial behaviors.

Gender

In every culture and every historical period, males commit far more crime than females, and the more serious the crime, the more males are overrepresented. This so-called gender ratio problem (i.e., why do males and females differ so much in their propensity to commit crimes?) has been identified as one of the key issues in feminist criminology (Daly & Chesney-Lind, 1996). Male and female crime rates are highly correlated (the high 0.80s to low 0.90s) across different nations, states, and cities (Campbell, 1999). These correlations indicate that females respond to the same environmental conditions as males, albeit far less frequently and seriously. Similarly, most female offenders are found in the same social situations as most of their male counterparts—that is, among single-parent families located in poor, socially disorganized neighborhoods. The similarity of environmental conditions coupled with the large differences in criminal activity between the sexes led Daly and Chesney-Lind to ask, "Why do similar processes produce a distinctive, gender-based structure to crime and delinquency?" (1996, p. 349).

Criminologists have attempted to answer this question in a variety of ways, but almost always under the assumption of the psychic identity of the sexes. If males and females are psychically identical, then it makes sense to explain differences between them as products of differential socialization (e.g., men are socialized to be assertive, aggressive, and dominant, and women are socialized to be nurturing, passive, and family oriented).

An example of this thinking is Mears, Ploeger, and Warr's (1998) contention that the gender ratio is the result of the differential exposure of the genders to delinquent peers, the fact that males are more influenced by delinquent peers than females, and the fact that females have greater inhibitory morality than males. This "explanation" says little beyond claiming that boys will be boys and girls will be girls, and it begs the questions of why males are more exposed and more influenced by delinquent peers than females, and why females have a stronger sense of morality (Walsh, 2002). The assumption inherent in the traditional sociological view is that if females were socialized in the same way as males and had similar roles and experiences, their rates of criminal offending would be roughly the same. This is pure nonsense undeserving of additional comment save to quote Dianna Fishbein's (1992, p. 100) summation of the gender ratio issue: "[C]ross cultural studies do not support the prominent role of structural and cultural influences of gender-specific crime rates as the type and extent of male versus female crime remains consistent across cultures."

Males and Mating Effort

So-called radical feminists, on the other hand, reason that because the magnitude of the gender gap varies across time and space and yet still remains constantly wide at all times and in all places, biological factors *must* play a major role. They further note that robust sex differences in dominance and aggression are seen in all human cultures from the earliest days of life, are underscored during the teen years, and are observed in all primate and most mammalian species for which no one would evoke socialization as an explanation (Archer, 1996; Geary, 1998). Neuroscience has long informed us that gender-typical behavior is the result of hormones that organize the brain in male or female directions during sensitive prenatal periods (Amateau & McCarthy, 2004). This neurohormonal process organizes male brains in ways such that males become more vulnerable to the various traits associated with antisocial behavior via the regulation of brain chemistry (Ellis, 2003; Lopreato & Crippen, 1999).

Thus the sexes come into this world with "differently wired brains," and these brain differences "make it almost impossible to evaluate the effects of experience [the socialization process] independent of physiological predisposition" (Kimura, 1992, p. 119). The major biological factor organizing the male brain along male lines and which underlies gender differences in dominance, aggression, violence, and general antisocial behavior is testosterone (Archer, 1996; Kanazawa, 2003). No one claims that testosterone is a major or even minor cause of crime and general mayhem, only that it is the major factor that underlies gender *differences* in crime and general mayhem.[1]

While neurohormonal differences provide a scientifically robust explanation of the genders' different responses to environmental instigation, we also need to know why these differences exist in the first place. Talk of brains and hormones invokes mechanisms operating in real time that explain *how* one thing leads to another. Disciplines such as behavior genetics and neurophysiology are most interested in such proximate-level causal mechanisms. Evolutionary psychology is interested in ultimate-level *why* causes, causes that lead via an extended period of selection to the adaptations we call proximate causes. To answer questions about *why* causes, we are required to consider the different selection pressures that confronted our distant male and female ancestors with respect to reproductive considerations.

As Lopreato and Crippen (1999, p. 114) point out, "The two sexes are endowed with differing reproductive strategies, and from this difference arise various behavioral tendencies." There is much more variability among males than females in terms of reproductive success, with some males leaving no offspring and others fathering large numbers. The nature of female physiology ensures that females have a lower potential reproductive ceiling than males, but few will be reproductive failures relative to males. The major strategy throughout our evolutionary history for increasing a female's reproductive success has been for her to secure and hold on to the assistance of a mate to raise her offspring. Given lower variation but greater reproductive certainty, females have evolved a mating strategy inclining them to be choosier than males about whom they will mate with; indiscriminate mating would have had negative reproductive utility for females (Badcock, 2000; Buss, 1994; Cartwright, 2000). Given the lower reproductive ceiling of females, traits that maximized the probability that existing children would survive (parenting effort) evolved rather than traits designed to maximize mating effort. Simply put, females have more strongly evolved neurohormonal mechanisms that underlie the traits conducive to successful parenting effort than males, and because these traits are essentially prosocial traits, females are less likely to commit crimes.

The only limitation to male reproductive success is access to females; the more females a male can have sex with, the greater his fitness potential. Males have an evolved desire for multiple partners because in fitness terms, there is much to gain and little to lose following this strategy. However, every male is in competition with every other male for access to females, a situation that in evolutionary environments has often resulted in violence. Even in modern times, most nonstate violence in the world is male-on-male violence generated, to a great extent, by sexual competition (Daly, 1996).

In addition to overcoming competition from other males, males also have to respond to the more restrained female reproductive strategy. They can comply with the female preference and commit to a single female and assist her to raise their offspring, or they can trick or force a female to have sex and then move on to the next conquest. These two strategies have been called "Cad vs. Dad" (Cashdan, 1993). To successfully pursue a cad strategy, it would be counterproductive to be distracted by emotional signals, either by guilt, shame, or anxiety from within or the fear and disgust of a potential victim. It would therefore be useful to have mechanisms that mute the neurohormonal regulators of the social emotions so that one is less likely to feel guilt, shame, anxiety, and sympathy (Dugatkin, 1992; Nesse & Lloyd, 1992).

The extreme of the cad strategy is, of course, the psychopath. The greatly reduced ability to experience the social emotions of shame, embarrassment, guilt, empathy, and love has marked psychopaths across time and cultures. One of the most consistent physiological findings about psychopaths is their inability to "tie" the brain's cognitive and emotional networks together (Patrick, 1994; Scarpa & Raine, 2003). David Rowe (2002, pp. 62–63) provides a sketch of the traits useful in supporting the male cad mating strategy, which is incidentally an excellent description of the psychopath:

> A strong sexual drive and attraction to novelty of new sexual partners is clearly one component of mating effort. An ability to appear charming and superficially interested in women while courting them would be useful. The emotional attachment, however, must be an insincere one, to prevent emotional bonding to a girlfriend or spouse. The cad may be aggressive, to coerce sex from partly willing partners and to deter rival men. He feels little remorse about lying or cheating. Impulsivity could be advantageous in a cad because mating decisions must be made quickly and without prolonged deliberation; the unconscious aim is many partners, not a high-quality partner.

Almost all heterosexual males have probably used "cad" tactics (falsely proclaiming love and fidelity or the use of some form of coercion, perhaps even force) to obtain sex at some time or another, although the vast majority will eventually settle down and assist a female in raising their young. A small minority, however, will continue to exploit females across the life course, assisted by the traits that facilitate mating effort, which are, as we have seen, the same traits that facilitate criminal behavior. Males have thus evolved to be more risk-taking, violent, and manipulative in competitive situations than females.

Females and Parenting Effort

We have thus far examined only the male half of the equation—that is, why are males more crime prone? We now turn to the other half: why females are less crime prone. The best evolutionary explanation for all of the sex differences in traits and their neurohormonal bases that make females both more inclined toward parenting effort and less inclined toward criminal behavior is Anne Campbell's (1999) *staying alive/low fear* hypothesis. This hypothesis has to do with the selection pressures faced by ancestral females with regard to parental investment and status striving. The obligatory parental investment of males is limited to a few pelvic thrusts, after which they can be on their way. The obligatory parental investment of females is enormously greater. Only after months of gestation and years of lactation can she contemplate further children, which means that her reproductive success is far more tied to children she already has than is that of a male. The greater dependence of the infant on the mother renders a mother's presence more critical to offspring survival (and hence to the mother's reproductive success) than is the presence of a father. In ancestral environments the care of nursing infants meant that females always kept them in close proximity, and this posed an elevated risk of injury to the child as well as the mother if the mother placed herself in risky situations (Beckerman, 1999). Because female survival is more critical to female reproductive success (in terms of maximizing the probability that offspring will survive) than is male survival, Campbell's hypothesis is that females have evolved a propensity to avoid engaging in behaviors that pose survival risks.

Campbell proposes that the evolved mechanism underlying this propensity is a physiology that responds to many different risky situations and that is subjectively experienced as fear. There are essentially no sex differences in fearfulness across a number of contexts, unless a situation contains a significant risk of physical injury. The greater fear response under such circumstances accounts for the greater tendency of females to avoid potentially violent situations and to employ indirect and low-risk strategies in competition and dispute resolution relative to males. In simple terms, the ancestral females who avoided or removed themselves from situations involving a high risk of physical injury or death were more likely to survive, and their survival increased the probability that their offspring would survive and that their genetic lineage would be perpetuated.

The staying alive/low fear hypothesis also has implications for sex differences in status seeking. Because males have greater variance in reproductive success than females but less parental certainty, they too gain greater fitness benefits by engaging in intrasexual competition for mating opportunities. High-status and dominant males always attract more females than low-status, subservient males (Mazur, 2005). Status and dominance striving is often risky business (and certainly was in evolutionary times), and because attaining status is less reproductively consequential for females than for males, there has been less pressure for the selection of mechanisms useful in that endeavor for females. In environments of evolutionary adaptation, a male's reproductive success often rested on involving himself in risky situations in which high fear levels would have been a definite handicap.

Campbell points out that although females engage in intrasexual competition for mates, it is rarely in the form of violence and aggression, with most of it being low key, low risk, and chronic as opposed to the high key, high risk, and acute nature of male intrasexual competition. Females cannot compete for the female assets most pertinent to attracting a committed mate such as youth and beauty, which a woman either possesses or does not. Male assets that attract females, unlike youth and beauty, can be achieved in competition with other males. Males who are most willing to incur risks to achieve status and dominance gain the resources that come with them and thus potentially gain access to more females.

Women do commit crime, of course; but, as Campbell notes, when they do, their crimes rarely involve risk of physical injury and are almost always committed for instrumental reasons. For instance, Campbell points out that although robbery and larceny/theft involve expropriating resources from others, females constitute about 43% of arrests for larceny/theft and only about 7% of arrests for robbery, a crime carrying a relatively high risk for personal injury. Campbell (1999, p. 210) notes that while women do aggress and do steal, "they rarely do both at the same time because the equation of resources and status reflects a particularly masculine logic." Robbery, and flaunting the material trappings signaling its successful pursuit, is seen ultimately as a campaign for respect and status in the street culture from which most robbers come (Jacobs & Wright, 1999). Studies of female robbers provide no mention that they crave the additional payoffs of dominance that male robbers do, or seek reputations as "hardasses" (Messerschmidt, 1993). Aggressive and dominant females are not particularly desirable as mates, and certainly a woman with a reputation as a "hardass" would be most unattractive.

It is not sex per se that exerts pressure for the selection of the mechanisms that underlie these traits and behaviors; it is *parental investment*. In some bird and fish species, males contribute greater parental investment than females (e.g., incubating the eggs and feeding the young), and in these species the sexes have evolved many behavioral characteristics that are the opposite of the characteristics of males and females in mammalian species in which females assume all or most of the burden of parenting. In these "sex-role reversal" species, females are bigger and more aggressive, they have more testosterone, and they are more promiscuous risk-takers in intrasexual competition for mates than males (Betzig, 1999). Species exhibiting sex-role reversal provide support for Campbell's thesis that parental investment, not simple biological sex, accounts for traits supporting different reproductive strategies and underline the usefulness of cross-species comparisons for understanding human behavior.

Age and Crime

Age is almost as strong a predictor of criminal offending as gender. Across time and space we consistently observe a rapid increase in delinquency at puberty and then a slow decline after reaching its peak between 16 and 18 years of age (Ellis & Walsh, 2000). Why this is so has long been a mystery to criminologists. Some take a stab at explaining it by pointing to the increase in peer involvement in adolescence and the decline in antisocial behavior thereafter resulting from the decreasing influence of peers and the increasing influence of girlfriends, wives, children, and employers (Warr, 2002). It escapes their attention that this simply describes situations that co-occur with the usual beginning and the end of delinquent behavior; it does not explain *why* the period between these events is so filled with such behavior or *why* associations with peers lead to negative behavior more often than to positive behavior. Long ago, Shavit and Rattner (1988, p. 1457) pointed out that the age peak in delinquency is "unexplained by any known set of sociological variables." This view is shared by Gottfredson and Hirschi (1990), who basically conclude that because the age effect is constant across time and place, criminologists should accept it as a fact and go on from there, perhaps reasoning that *age* in this context is simply an index of a certain developmental stage (puberty) we all go through. But this is a message of defeat; there must be something special going on during this period of life that temporarily increases the probability of antisocial behavior, and which demands explanation.

The 2003 New York Academy of Sciences conference on adolescent brain development provided some key points relevant to the age effect (White, 2004, p. 4):

1. Much of the behavior characterizing adolescence is rooted in biology intermingling with environmental influences to cause teens to conflict with their parents, take more risks, and experience wide swings in emotion.
2. The lack of synchrony between a physically mature body and a still maturing nervous system may explain these behaviors.
3. Adolescents' sensitivities to rewards appear to be different from those of adults, prompting them to seek higher levels of novelty and stimulation to achieve the same feeling of pleasure.

Adolescence starts with puberty, a stage in human development that marks the onset of the transition from childhood to adulthood, during which our bodies prepare for procreation. This transition is not without its problems, as we observe that "many happy and loveable children suddenly morph into malcontents acting like they should be in pampers rather than pants" (Walsh & Ellis, 2007, p. 230). Puberty is a series of biological events, and adolescence is a *process* that begins at puberty and ends with adulthood. Adulthood typically means taking on socially responsible roles such as acquiring a full-time job and settling down and taking on family life, roles that define us as independent members of society. In many respects, adolescence is a period in limbo because, although we no longer need parental care, we are not yet ready to take on the roles and responsibilities of adulthood (Moffitt, 1993). Adolescence is a normal and necessary period in the human life span in which one can experiment with a variety of social skills before having to put them into practice as an adult (Bogin, 1993).

Testosterone begins playing its role by organizing the male brain during the second trimester of pregnancy so that it will respond in male-typical ways when the brain is activated in that direction at puberty (Ellis, 2003). After sex-specific brain organization takes place, there is little difference in levels of male and female testosterone until puberty, at which time males have approximately ten times the female level (Felson & Haynie, 2002). Testosterone is most responsible for the development of male characteristics, including behavioral characteristics such as aggression and dominance-seeking (Quadango, 2003).

At the same time as they are experiencing hormonal surges, adolescents' brains are undergoing changes in the ratio of excitatory to inhibitory neurotransmitters. Dopamine and another excitatory transmitter called glutamate peak during adolescence, while the inhibitory transmitters gamma-aminobutyric acid and serotonin are reduced (Collins, 2004; Spear, 2000; Walker, 2002). Additionally, the adolescent brain goes through an intense period of physical restructuring as hormonal surges prompt the increase of gene expression initiating the process of slowly refining neural circuitry to its adult form (Walker, 2002). A series of magnetic resonance imaging studies have revealed that the prefrontal cortex (PFC) undergoes a wave of synaptic overproduction just prior to puberty, followed by a period of pruning during adolescence and early adulthood (Giedd et al., 1999; Sowell, Thompson, Holmes, Jernigan, & Toga, 1999).

In addition to all the synaptic modifications occurring in the PFC, the adolescent PFC is also less completely myelinated (myelin is the fatty substance that coats and insulates axons) than the adult PFC (Sowell et al., 1999). A less myelinated brain means less efficient message transmission and a larger time lapse between the onset of an emotional event in the limbic system and the PFC's rational judgment of it. All this amounts to the conclusion that there are *physical* reasons for the greater ratio of emotional to rational responses often observed in teenagers. Adolescents are essentially operating with a brain on "go slow" superimposed on a hormone-driven physiology on "fast forward." This explains why many teenagers find it difficult to accurately gauge the meanings and intentions of others and why they experience more stimuli as aversive during adolescence than they did as children and will when they are adults (Walsh, 2002, p. 143). Richard Restak (2001, p. 76) perhaps put it best when he wrote, "The immaturity of the adolescent's behavior is perfectly mirrored by the immaturity of the adolescent's brain."[2]

The implications for antisocial behavior in all this are obvious in that the neurohormonal modifications and adjustments going on facilitate a tendency to assign faulty attributions to situations and to the intentions of others. As Agnew (2005) points out, a greater sensitivity to stressors leads to an increase in irritability and a decrease in self-control, which in turn lead to a greater probability of antisocial behaviors. This would be particularly true in so-called honor subcultures, which are defined as "communities in which young men are hypersensitive to insult, rushing to defend their reputation in dominance contests" (Mazur & Booth, 1998, p. 362). Such subcultures develop when there is high risk of one's resources being expropriated by thieves and in which the governing body is too weak (or not trusted) to prevent and punish such theft (Anderson, 1999; Shackelford, 2005). According to Quinsey (2002, p. 3), the intense and often deadly "in your face" rivalry among poor inner-city youths supports the evolutionary contention that "crime is functionally related to inter male competition that has its ultimate roots in reproductive rivalry." Males in honor subcultures are behaving as natural selection designed them and, incidentally, in historically normative ways (honor subcultures in which dueling was an accepted way to settle disputes have existed throughout history [Mazur & Booth, 1998]). This biological and historical normativeness does not, of course, make such behavior morally acceptable.

Adolescence and the behaviors manifested during the period must therefore be viewed as adaptations (Spear, 2000; White, 2004). Evolutionary biologists stress that natural selection favors the most adventurous and dominant males because such characteristics typically result in more mating opportunities and thus greater reproductive success. As among all primate species, mid-adolescence and early adulthood are periods of intense competition among males, particularly where social controls are lacking, for dominance and status aimed ultimately at securing more mating opportunities than the next male (White, 2004, p. 7). As Martin Daly (1996, p. 193) put it, "There are many reasons to think that we've been designed [by natural selection] to be maximally competitive and conflictual in young adulthood."

Mercifully, adolescence is short-lived. Around the age of 20, the ratio of excitatory transmitters to inhibitory transmitters becomes more balanced as the former start to decrease and the latter start to increase (Collins, 2004). With more bio-balanced brain signals, more adult-like personality traits emerge. Findings from five different countries show age-related decreases in personality traits positively related to antisocial behavior (e.g., neuroticism, extraversion) and increases in personality traits positively related to prosocial behavior (e.g., agreeableness, conscientiousness) (McCrae et al., 2000). The fine-tuning of neurological and endocrine systems lays the foundations for the acquisition of responsible social roles that help us stay on the straight and narrow and correlate with the steep declines in antisocial behavior noted everywhere crime statistics are gathered.

Conclusion

It should be clear from the preceding that evolutionary psychology shares with mainstream sociology the belief that Homo sapiens are social beings who desire to follow social rules. However, evolutionary psychology is Hobbesian rather than Rousseauesque in that it tells us this desire comes from the yearning for self-preservation and not from a romanticized notion that we are inherently good beings who will commit antisocial acts only when forced to do so by "society." Evolutionary psychology agrees with Durkheim (cited in Walsh, 2002, p. 99) that society is the moral good guy because "it alone has the power necessary to stipulate law and to set the point beyond which the passions must not go."

We have evolved to be reciprocal altruists who know that we can realize our self-interests more often by following rules than by not following them. The apparent paradox of social beings committing antisocial acts is resolved when we realize that our desire to cooperate with our fellows provides opportunities for noncooperators to victimize us. The individuals most likely to do so are those who are disadvantaged in the competition for wealth, power, and status, which is what most mainstream criminological theories express. There is agreement between mainstream theories and evolutionary psychology on many aspects of crime and criminality. Adding evolutionary explanatory concepts to these theories would not only enrich and broaden their repertoire of concepts; it would also ground them in the one existing theory that has the potential to add unity and coherence across all disciplines that study the behavior of living things. Evolutionary psychology highlights the kinds of environments in which those behaviors that trouble us most are likely to emerge, and it is the only extant metatheory capable of uniting, integrating, and making sense of the disparate data on human behavior coming to us from many theories and many disciplines. Criminology will ignore this perspective at its peril.

Notes

1. Ellis (2005) notes that the average correlation between testosterone and criminality is a modest 0.20 to 0.25, although Mazur (2005) indicates that this correlation is higher for behavioral measures than for self-report measures.

2. Several studies show generally that the earlier the onset of puberty, the greater the level of problem behavior for both girls and boys (Beaver & Wright, 2005; Caspi et al., 1994; Felson & Haynie, 2002). Juveniles who enter puberty significantly earlier than their peers must confront their "raging hormones" with a brain that is no more mature than those of their peers. In one study, testosterone level predicted future problem behavior, but only for boys who entered puberty early (Drigotas & Udry, 1993). Felson and Haynie (2002) found that boys who experienced early onset of puberty were more likely to commit a number of delinquent and other antisocial acts than other boys, but that they were also more autonomous and better psychologically adjusted and had more friends.

References

Agnew, R. (2005). *Why do criminals offend? A general theory of crime and delinquency.* Los Angeles: Roxbury.

Alcock, J. (1998). *Animal behavior: An evolutionary approach* (6th ed.). Sunderland, MA: Sinauer Associates.

Alcock, J. (2001). *The triumph of sociobiology.* New York: Oxford University Press.

Amateau, S., & McCarthy, M. (2004). Induction of PGE2 by estradiol mediates developmental masculinization of sex behavior. *Nature Neuroscience, 7*, 643–650.

Anderson, E. (1999). *Code of the street: Decency, violence, and the moral life of the inner city*. New York: W. W. Norton.

Archer, J. (1996). Sex differences in social behavior: Are the social role and evolutionary explanations compatible? *American Psychologist, 5*, 909–917.

Badcock, C. (2000). *Evolutionary psychology: A critical introduction*. Cambridge, UK: Polity Press.

Barkow, J. (1989). *Darwin, sex and status: Biological approaches to mind and culture*. Toronto: University of Toronto Press.

Barkow, J. (1997). Happiness in evolutionary perspective. In N. Segal, G. Weisfeld, & C. Weisfeld (Eds.), *Uniting psychology and biology* (pp. 397–418). Washington, DC: American Psychological Association.

Barkow, J. (2006). *Missing the revolution: Darwinism for social scientists*. New York: Oxford University Press.

Beaver, K. M., & Wright, J. P. (2005). Biosocial development and delinquent involvement. *Youth Violence and Juvenile Justice, 3*, 168–192.

Beckerman, S. (1999). Violence, sex, and the good mother. *Behavioral and Brain Sciences, 22*, 215–216.

Betzig, L. (1999). When women win. *Behavioral and Brain Sciences, 22*, 217.

Bogin, B. (1993). Why must I be a teenager at all? *New Scientist, 137*, 34–38.

Buss, D. (1994). *The evolution of desire: Strategies of human mating*. New York: Basic Books.

Campbell, A. (1999). Staying alive: Evolution, culture, and women's intrasexual aggression. *Behavioral and Brain Sciences, 22*, 203–214.

Cartwright, J. (2000). *Evolution and human behavior*. Cambridge, MA: MIT Press.

Cashdan, E. (1993). Attracting mates: Effects of paternal investment on mate attraction strategies. *Ethology and Sociobiology, 14*, 1–23.

Caspi, A., Moffitt, T., Silva, P., Stouthamer-Loeber, M., Krueger, R., & Schmutte, P. (1994). Are some people crime-prone? Replications of the personality-crime relationship across countries, genders, races, and methods. *Criminology, 32*, 163–194.

Cleveland, H., Wiebe, R., van den Oord, E., & Rowe, D. (2000). Behavior problems among children from different family structures: The influence of genetic self-selection. *Child Development, 71*, 733–751.

Collins, R. (2004). Onset and desistence in criminal careers: Neurobiology and the age-crime relationship. *Journal of Offender Rehabilitation, 39*, 1–19.

Daly, K., & Chesney-Lind, M. (1996). Feminism and criminology. In P. Cordella & L. Siegel (Eds.), *Reading in contemporary criminological theory* (pp. 340-364). Boston: Northeastern University Press.

Daly, M. (1996). Evolutionary adaptationism: Another biological approach to criminal and antisocial behavior. In G. Bock & J. Goode (Eds.), *Genetics of criminal and antisocial behaviour* (pp. 183–195). Chichester, UK: Wiley.

Daly, M., & Wilson, M. (1988a). *Homicide*. New York: Aldine De Gruyter.

Daly, M., & Wilson, M. (1988b). Evolutionary social psychology and family homicide. *Science, 242*, 519–524.

Draper, P., & Harpending, H. (1982). Father absence and reproductive strategies: An evolutionary perspective. *Journal of Anthropological Research, 38*, 255–273.

Drigotas, S., & Udry, J. (1993). Biosocial models of adolescent problem behavior: Extensions to panel design. *Social Biology, 40*, 1–7.

Dugatkin, L. (1992). The evolution of the con artist. *Ethology and Sociobiology, 13,* 3–18.

Ellis, L. (1996). A discipline in peril: Sociology's future hinges on curing its biophobia. *American Sociologist, 27,* 21–41.

Ellis, L. (2003). Genes, criminality, and the evolutionary neuroandrogenic theory. In A. Walsh & L. Ellis (Eds.), *Biosocial criminology: Challenging environmentalism's supremacy* (pp. 13–34). Hauppauge, NY: Nova Science.

Ellis, L. (2005). A theory explaining biological correlates of criminality. *European Journal of Criminology, 2,* 287–315.

Ellis, L., & Walsh, A. (2000). *Criminology: A global perspective.* Boston: Allyn & Bacon.

Ember, M., & Ember, C. (1998, October). Facts of violence. *Anthropology Newsletter, 14*–15.

Felson, R., & Haynie, D. (2002). Pubertal development, social factors, and delinquency among adolescent boys. *Criminology, 40,* 967–988.

Fishbein, D. (1992). The psychobiology of female aggression. *Criminal Justice and Behavior, 19,* 9–126.

Fishbein, D. (2001). *Biobehavioral perspectives in criminology.* Belmont, CA: Wadsworth.

Geary, D. (1998). Functional organization of the human mind: Implications for behavioral genetic research. *Human Biology, 70,* 185–198.

Geary, D. (2000). Evolution and proximate expression of human paternal investment. *Psychological Bulletin, 126,* 55–77.

Giedd, J., Blumenthal, J., Jeffries, N., Castellanos, F., Liu, H., Zijenbos, A., et al. (1999). Brain development during childhood and adolescence: A longitudinal MRI study. *Nature Neuroscience, 2,* 861–863.

Gottfredson, M., & Hirschi, T. (1990). *A general theory of crime.* Stanford, CA: Stanford University Press.

Harpending, H., & Draper, P. (1988). Antisocial behavior and the other side of cultural evolution. In T. Moffitt & S. Mednick (Eds.), *Biological contributions to crime causation* (pp. 293–307). Dordrecht: Martinus Nyhoff.

Horowitz, I. (1993). *The decomposition of sociology.* New York: Oxford University Press.

Jacobs, B., & Wright, R. (1999). Stick-up, street culture, and offender motivation. *Criminology, 37,* 149–173.

Jafee, S., Moffitt, T., Caspi, A., & Taylor, A. (2003). Life with (or without) father: The benefits of living with two biological parents depend on the father's antisocial behavior. *Child Development, 74,* 109–126.

Kanazawa, S. (2003). A general evolutionary psychological theory of criminality and related male-typical behavior. In A. Walsh & L. Ellis (Eds.), *Biosocial criminology: Challenging environmentalism's supremacy* (pp. 37–60). Hauppauge, NY: Nova Science.

Kanazawa, S. (2006). Can the social sciences be saved? Should they? *Evolutionary Psychology, 4,* 102–106.

Kimura, D. (1992). Sex differences in the brain. *Scientific American, 267,* 119–125.

Lopreato, J., & Crippen, T. (1999). *Crisis in sociology: The need for Darwin.* New Brunswick, NJ: Transaction.

Mazur, A. (2005). *Biosociology of dominance and deference.* Lanham, MD: Rowman & Littlefield.

Mazur, A., & Booth, A. (1998). Testosterone and dominance in men. *Behavioral and Brain Sciences, 21,* 353–397.

McCrae, R., Costa, P., Ostendorf, F., Angleitner, A., Hrebickova, M., Avia, M., et al. (2000). Nature over nurture: Temperament, personality, and life span development. *Journal of Personality and Social Psychology, 78,* 173–186.

Mealey, L. (1995). The sociobiology of sociopathy: An integrated evolutionary model. *Behavioral and Brain Sciences, 18,* 523–559.

Mears, D., Ploeger, M., & Warr, M. (1998). Explaining the gender gap in delinquency: Peer influence and moral evaluations of behavior. *Journal of Research in Crime and Delinquency, 35,* 251–266.

Messerschmidt, J. (1993). *Masculinities and crime.* Lanham, MD: Rowman & Littlefield.

Moffitt, T. (1993). Adolescent-limited and life-course persistent antisocial behavior: A developmental taxonomy. *Psychological Review, 100,* 674–701.

Nesse, R., & Lloyd, A. (1992). The evolution of psychodynamic mechanisms. In J. Barkow, L. Cosmides, & J. Tooby (Eds.), *The adapted mind: Evolutionary psychology and the generation of culture* (pp. 601–620). New York: Oxford University Press.

Patrick, C. (1994). Emotions and psychopathy: Startling new insights. *Psychophysiology, 31,* 319–330.

Quadango, D. (2003). Genes, brains, hormones, and violence: Interactions with complex environments. In A. Walsh & L. Ellis (Eds.), *Biosocial criminology: Challenging environmentalism's supremacy* (pp. 167–184). Hauppauge, NY: Nova Science.

Quinsey, V. (2002). Evolutionary theory and criminal behavior. *Legal and Criminological Psychology, 7,* 1–14.

Restak, R. (2001). *The secret life of the brain.* New York: Dana Press and Joseph Henry Press.

Robinson, M. (2004). *Why crime? An integrated systems theory of antisocial behavior.* Upper Saddle River, NJ: Prentice Hall.

Rowe, D. (1996). An adaptive strategy theory of crime and delinquency. In J. Hawkins (Ed.), *Delinquency and crime: Current theories* (pp. 268–314). Cambridge: Cambridge University Press.

Rowe, D. (2002). *Biology and crime.* Los Angeles: Roxbury.

Ruffie, J. (1986). *The population alternative: A new look at competition and the species.* New York: Random House.

Scarpa, A., & Raine, A. (2003). The psychophysiology of antisocial behavior: Interactions with environmental experiences. In A. Walsh & L. Ellis (Eds.), *Biosocial criminology: Challenging environmentalism's supremacy* (pp. 209–226). Hauppauge, NY: Nova Science.

Shackelford, T. (2005). An evolutionary psychological perspective on cultures of honor. *Evolutionary Psychology, 3,* 381–391.

Shavit, Y., & Rattner, A. (1988). Age, crime, and the early lifecourse. *American Journal of Sociology, 93,* 1457–1470.

Spear, L. (2000). Neurobehavioral changes in adolescence. *Current Directions in Psychological Science, 9,* 111–114.

Sowell, E., Thompson, P., Holmes, C., Jernigan, T., & Toga A. (1999). In vivo evidence for post-adolescent brain maturation in frontal and striatal regions. *Nature Neuroscience, 2,* 859–861.

Tibbetts, S. (2003). Selfishness, social control, and emotions: An integrated perspective on criminality. In A. Walsh & L. Ellis (Eds.), *Biosocial criminology: Challenging environmentalism's supremacy* (pp. 83–101). Hauppauge, NY: Nova Science.

Udry, J. (1995). Sociology and biology: What biology do sociologists need to know? *Social Forces, 73,* 1267–1278.

Van den Berghe, P. (1990). Why most sociologists don't (and won't) think evolutionarily. *Sociological Forum, 5,* 173–185.

Walker, E. (2002). Adolescent neurodevelopment and psychopathology. *Current Directions in Psychological Science, 11*, 24–28.

Walsh, A. (2002). *Biosocial criminology: Introduction and integration.* Cincinnati, OH: Anderson.

Walsh, A. (2006). Evolutionary psychology and criminal behavior. In J. Barkow (Ed.), *Missing the revolution: Darwinism for social scientists* (pp. 225–268). Oxford: Oxford University Press.

Walsh, A., & Ellis, L. (Eds.). (2003). *Biosocial criminology: Challenging environmentalism's supremacy.* Hauppauge, NY: Nova Science.

Walsh, A., & Ellis, L. (2007). *Criminology: An interdisciplinary approach.* Thousand Oaks, CA: Sage/Pine Forge Press.

Warr, M. (2002). *Companions in crime: The social aspects of criminal conduct.* New York: Cambridge University Press.

White, A. (2004). *Substance use and the adolescent brain: An overview with the focus on alcohol.* Durham, NC: Duke University Medical Center.

PART TWO

ADAPTATION AND VIOLENT CRIMES

3

The Origins of Homicide

JOSHUA D. DUNTLEY AND DAVID M. BUSS

Why people kill their fellow human beings is a question whose answer has thus far eluded a comprehensive scientific explanation. This chapter describes homicide adaptation theory, a recent theoretical contender that offers an evolutionary psychological explanation of the most common forms of homicide. We begin by reviewing some key statistics about homicide. We discuss examples of the unique selection pressures created by human cognitive adaptations for social exchange that are hypothesized to have selected for homicide. We explore the coevolutionary arms race between adaptations for homicide and defenses against being killed. We compare homicide adaptation theory to nonadaptationist explanations for conspecific killings in humans. Finally, we explore how an evolutionary perspective sheds light on why the law does not treat all forms and contexts of homicide the same.

In the United States, you are ten times more likely to be murdered on the day you are born than at any other time during your life (Centers for Disease Control, 2006). If you survive your first day, you still have a greater risk of being murdered during your first year of life than in any other year of childhood (Overpeck, Brenner, Trumble, Trifiletti, & Berendes, 2002).

Homicide in modern societies is less rare than is often believed. Crime rates are typically reported as the number of incidents per 100,000 people per year. In the United States, for example, there were 17,034 homicides in 2006, which translates to a homicide rate of 5.7 per 100,000 people that year (U.S. Department of Justice, 2007). At first glance, this may make homicide seem like a fairly rare event. However, if you compute this risk over the average life span of a U.S. citizen (77.8 years), it translates to roughly a 1 in 225 lifetime risk of being a victim of homicide.

In 2004, homicide ranked fifteenth among the leading causes of death for men and women of all ages (Centers for Disease Control, 2006). Women and men, however, did not have the same likelihood of being killed by someone else. For men, homicide was the thirteenth leading cause of death. For women, homicide didn't crack the top twenty.

41

The likelihood of being killed also differed as a function of age and ethnicity. For all men between the ages of 15 and 24 years, homicide was the second leading cause of death, but for black men in the same age group it was the number one cause of death.

We propose that homicide rates are not accurate indicators of the number of times that people adopt strategies of lethal aggression against others. The homicide rates in many nations would undoubtedly be much higher were it not for emergency medical interventions that were not available to our ancestors for most of our evolutionary history. Researchers in the United States found that faster ambulances and better emergency room care, much of which was developed during the first Gulf War between the United States and Iraq from 1990 to 1991, are largely responsible for much of the decrease in homicide rates over the last three decades in the United States. It has been estimated that there would be 30,000 to 50,000 *additional* killings in the United States each year—at least tripling or quadrupling the current homicide rate—without the advances in emergency care technology that have occurred during the last thirty years (Harris, Thomas, Fisher, & Hirsch, 2002). Thirty thousand more homicides each year would translate into a 1-in-81 lifetime risk of being murdered. Fifty thousand additional homicides per year would create a 1-in-57 lifetime murder risk in the United States. If we eliminated medical advances that occurred before the 1990s, such as the advent of antibiotics and other important innovations, the lifetime homicide risk would reach much higher levels.

Homicide rates vary predictably from culture to culture. Some cultural variation has been traced to factors such as resource discrepancy (Wilson & Daly, 1997) and the relative costs and benefits of killing a conspecific versus other strategies for solving problems (Buss & Duntley, 2006), suggesting that humans may possess decision rules that guide the implementation of homicidal behaviors (Duntley & Buss, 2005). This should lead to predictably different rates of conspecific killing wherever there are differences in the costs and benefits of eliminating conspecifics. Regional differences in homicide rates have been well documented. In the United States, the rates of killing are much higher than in many industrialized nations, exceeding those in the United Kingdom and Japan by a factor of ten; exceeding those in France, Austria, Sweden, and Germany by a factor of nine; and exceeding the rates in Canada, Italy, Portugal, Korea, and Belgium by a factor of five. But the homicide rates in many other countries are equivalent to or exceed those in the United States (United Nations, 1998). The lifetime probability of being a homicide victim in Venezuela and Moldova is 1 in 90, twice that of the United States. In Estonia and Puerto Rico, the likelihood is 1 in 60, three times that of the United States. And in Colombia and South Africa, the likelihood is greater than 1 in 20 that a person will die at the hands of a killer, more than ten times the lifetime homicide risk in the United States. Even among those nations that currently exhibit low homicide rates, much higher frequencies of conspecific killing were a consistent part of their histories. Historical evidence suggests that the relatively low homicide rates in many modern societies is a recent phenomenon (e.g., Dower & George, 1995; Ruff, 2001). Additionally, the rates of homicide recorded by nations typically do not include casualties of warfare or genocide.

The homicide rates in industrialized nations pale in comparison to the risk of being killed by a competitor in many preindustrial cultures. Including deaths resulting from lethal raids and tribal warfare, homicides account for roughly one in ten deaths of adult men among the Huli; one in four deaths among the Mae Enga; and one in three deaths among the Dugum Dani and Yanomamo (Chagnon, 1988). Even among the so-called gentle people or peaceful !Kung San of Botswana, there were twenty-two homicides over a twenty-five-year period in a population of 1,500, more than four times the rate of killing in a typical year in the United States (Lee, 1984).

For our understanding of homicide to be complete, we must explain observed patterns of conspecific killing, including (a) why men are vastly overrepresented among killers across cultures (87%); (b) why men are also overrepresented among homicide victims across cultures (75%); (c) why women across cultures commit some kinds of homicide more than men (e.g., infanticide of their genetic children soon after birth); (d) why people in every culture kill in qualitatively distinct conditions, leading to predictable infanticides, stepchild killings, men killing women, women killing men, intrasexual rivalry homicides, and warfare killings; and (e) why people experience homicidal fantasies in circumstances that correspond closely to the contexts in which people actually commit murder (Buss & Duntley, under review).

Homicide Adaptation Theory

Buss and Duntley (1998, 1999, 2003, 2004, under review) have proposed a theory that humans possess adaptations designed specifically for killing conspecifics. Psychological adaptations for homicide are argued to be the outcome of the process of natural selection. Like all adaptations, they were favored when they contributed better solutions to recurrent ancestral problems, on average, than competing adaptive mechanisms. Information processing adaptations evolved to scrutinize and sometimes produce homicidal behavior in adaptive problem contexts recurrently solvable by homicide in the past. Although some have suggested the possibility of adaptations for homicide (Ghiglieri, 1999; Pinker, 1997) and others have argued that humans may have an instinct to kill (e.g., Chagnon, 1988), no other theorists have gone into depth in exploring the design of adaptations for homicide (see a notable exception dealing with warfare: Tooby & Cosmides, 1988).

Buss and Duntley (under review) hypothesize that homicide was functional in solving a variety of adaptive problems. Specifically, the killing of a conspecific could have contributed to (a) preventing the exploitation, injury, rape, or killing of self, kin, mates, and coalitional allies by conspecifics in the present and future; (b) reputation management against being perceived as easily exploited, injured, raped, or killed by conspecifics; (c) protecting resources, territory, shelter, and food from competitors; (d) eliminating resource-absorbing or costly individuals who were not genetically related (e.g., stepchildren); and (e) eliminating genetic relatives who interfered with investment in other vehicles better able to translate resource investment into genetic fitness (e.g., deformed infants, the chronically ill or infirm).

Homicide is a unique and potentially powerful strategy with dramatic fitness consequences for both perpetrator and victim. It is reasonable to hypothesize that conspecific killing has been subjected to evolution by natural and sexual selection. Homicide is different from other strategies for inflicting costs because it leads to the absolute end of direct conflict or competition between individuals. People who are killed can no longer compete with or inflict costs on their killers. Dead competitors can no longer directly influence the environment or social context that they shared with their killers. These distinct outcomes of homicide would have created unique selection pressures to shape psychological mechanisms to produce homicidal behavior in contexts in which the elimination of a conspecific yielded better fitness outcomes than other available strategies (Buss & Duntley, under review; Duntley, 2005).

Adaptations for homicide would be more likely to evolve when they reliably contributed to the solution of an adaptive problem with a high impact on individual fitness, such as preventing a rival from killing one's child. Adaptations for homicide also would be more likely to evolve when a large number of different adaptive problems could be solved, or at least partially solved, by eliminating a conspecific. Consider, for example, the intrasexual rival of a man who was preventing his ascension in a status hierarchy, attempting to poach away the man's mate, monopolizing a scarce and valuable shelter as winter approaches, and who took every opportunity to publicly humiliate the man's brother. A large number of fitness costs are being inflicted by a single individual, and a significant amount of benefits could be gained through his elimination. The greater the fitness costs that a rival imposes on an individual, and the greater the benefits that would become available if the rival died, the heavier the weight of selection pressure would be for the evolution of homicidal strategies.

Different ancestral problems required different specific solutions. Homicide adaptation theory proposes that there are multiple, different psychological adaptations for homicide, each of which is devoted to the solution of different kinds of adaptive problems. By this logic, psychological design for infanticide is distinct from psychological design for warfare; psychological design for mate homicide in men is distinct from psychological design for mate killing in women. Some information processing mechanisms are undoubtedly shared between the different adaptations for homicide and with adaptations for the solution of other domains of adaptive problems. Selection would favor the sharing of subroutines performing the same function over reinventing them anew for each psychological adaptation. To be capable of addressing the unique combinations of characteristics inherent in different adaptive problems, however, each homicide adaptation must have at least one design feature that is distinct from other adaptations. In short, homicide adaptation theory proposes that selection has fashioned a number of specialized psychological adaptations in humans to solve distinct and historically recurrent adaptive problems.

Homicide adaptation theory is a coevolutionary theory. Just as killers obtained large ancestral benefits from the use of homicide in some contexts, victims and their genetic kin suffered extraordinary costs. The costs are hypothesized to have created selection pressure for the evolution of defenses against becoming a victim of homicide and to adaptations in victims' genetic kin to prevent relatives' untimely deaths or to minimize the costs in the aftermath. The evolution of defenses against lethal aggression would have made killing less beneficial, creating new selection pressure for design features capable of bypassing victims' defenses. This coevolutionary arms race between homicide adaptations and victim defenses is hypothesized to have contributed to rapid evolutionary change and elaborate design in both.

Homicide adaptation theory does *not* propose that homicide evolved to be the *preferred* strategy for any adaptive problem in all situations. In most circumstances, the high costs of committing homicide would have outweighed its benefits. However, homicide adaptation theory does propose that homicidal behavior was the best solution for rare combinations of adaptive problems and circumstances. It is these relatively rare adaptive problem contexts that provided selection pressure for the evolution of homicide adaptations. As a result, it is not possible to point to just one feature of a situation that will activate a psychology of homicide in every instance, in every person. There are other, mitigating environmental factors (Gartner, 1990), heritable personality features (Rhee & Waldman, 2002), and hormonal (Niehoff, 1999) and developmental influences (Dodge, Bates, & Pettit, 1990) that contribute to the adoption of homicidal behavior. These influences were likely part of the selection pressures that shaped homicide adaptations. The presence of these influences, as well as their magnitudes, can help us to predict when conspecific killing will be more or less likely to occur. Without complete knowledge of how the various influences interact with human psychology to produce homicidal behavior, however, it is not possible to make perfect predictions about whether homicide will occur in any individual case. This problem is not idiosyncratic to the prediction of homicide. The same is true in making predictions about any behavior. We hypothesize that psychological mechanisms for homicide steer an individual in the direction of adaptive behaviors that reliably result in the death of another individual. This is accomplished through a variety of affective, motivational, and computational systems that narrow in on homicide as the solution to adaptive problems.

The adaptive problems to which we are referring are fluid, unfolding and changing over time. As time passes and other individuals pursue adaptive strategies, the nature of adaptive problems changes, and the solution to one set of adaptive problems may reliably create others. It is the reliable unfolding of adaptive problems that shaped psychological adaptations in humans over evolutionary time, including those that end others' lives.

In sum, homicide adaptation theory proposes a new explanation of homicide: Over the long expanse of human history, there were recurrent sources of conflict between individuals, such as conflict over reputation and social status, conflict over resources, and conflict over romantic partners. Killing is hypothesized to be one among an arsenal of context-contingent strategies shaped by natural selection to win conflicts with others. Homicide differs qualitatively from nonlethal solutions to conflict.

Once dead, a person can no longer damage the killer's reputation, steal his resources, prevent the killer from attracting a romantic partner, or have sex with the killer's spouse. According to homicide adaptation theory, our evolutionary heritage has endowed all of us with a psychology to kill others. These psychological processes lead us to entertain fantasies of killing and, in rare instances, act on them when we encounter sources of conflict that were successfully won by homicide in the evolutionary past.

Pathways for the Evolution of Homicide Adaptations

Homicide adaptation theory proposes that there were more numerous selection pressures for the evolution of psychological mechanisms that produce conspecific killings in humans than there were in other animals, including other social primates. One source of selection pressure is humans' unique psychological mechanisms for social exchange (Cosmides & Tooby, 2005). Human psychology is exquisitely sensitive to the details of reciprocal exchange relationships. People have long memories for their histories of social exchange with different individuals. We intuitively represent the quantity and quality of social goods that change hands, the debts we owe to others, and the debts that others owe us. We are capable of representing a range of reproductively relevant resources, including tangible items (e.g., food, tools), social favors (e.g., assistance in preparing food, shelter), and sexual access. The values of some evolutionarily recurrent and reproductively relevant resources are hypothesized to have been built into human cognitive systems by selection (e.g., sexual access, items of food, protection from hostile conspecifics). Our calculus for social exchange intuitively represents equivalent values across different types of resources, allowing us to perceive, for example, the number of arrowheads that would be equivalent in value to a serving of meat or an introduction to a desirable potential mate. We also can represent future social debts and balances across resource types, designing near-optimal plans for future patterns of resource allocation and debt.

We hypothesize that people have evolved to be equally adept at representing the magnitude of costs inflicted on them by conspecifics. As with social debts and balances, the values of reproductively relevant, ancestrally recurrent costs are hypothesized to have been built into our evolved psychology by selection. In addition, humans are hypothesized to have developed the ability to forecast the values of costs that they may incur at the hands of conspecifics in the future.

Not all social exchange relationships are the same. Every category of social relationship, be it a friendship or a mateship, has, at its foundation, an implicit social contract—a mutually agreed-upon code of conduct that delineates the majority of what constitutes acceptable and unacceptable behavior in the context of the relationship. The rules of implicit social contracts are hypothesized to have been shaped by selection and represent co-evolved compromises between the individual interests of those involved in relationships. For example, having sex with a romantic partner is viewed as acceptable conduct in the explicit social contract of long-term relationships (Shackelford & Buss, 1996). It can be mutually beneficial to the reproductive success of both participants. Having sex with someone other than one's long-term romantic partner, however, is a rule violation. It inflicts costs on the partner who was cheated on. Different social relationships have different implicit rules of conduct. For example, although having sex outside of a long-term romantic relationship usually constitutes a rule violation for long-term mating relationships, it does not constitute a violation of the rules that comprise the implicit social contracts between close genetic relatives.

These three classes of evolved mechanisms—those that track social debts, those that represent the values of reproductively relevant resources, and those that form the foundation of the implicit rules that guide social exchange for each type of ancestrally recurrent relationship—are hypothesized to have opened a new adaptive design space in which natural selection could experiment with a range of behavioral strategies to best rivals and achieve a fitness advantage. We propose that one of the strategies was homicide.

Individuals can adopt a range of strategies to obtain benefits, including harvesting resources directly from the environment, cooperating with conspecifics to be effective in this task, or inflicting costs on conspecifics to steal or to gain control of resources. Because a co-evolved victim strategy against attack is to violently resist attackers, selection should have favored the use of cost-inflicting strategies to gain only resources of exceptional fitness value, valuable enough to outweigh the costs of violent victim resistance and subsequent retaliation (Buss & Duntley, 2005; Duntley, 2005; Duntley & Buss, 2004; also see Chapter 11 of this volume). For resources with the greatest fitness values, victims' violent defenses and retaliation would have evolved to be particularly fierce to protect their resources, defend hard-won reputations of being difficult to exploit, and reappropriate that which was forcibly taken. The recurrent use of violence to defend the most valuable reproductively relevant resources is hypothesized to have provided selection pressure for the only strategy capable of completely and permanently eliminating the costs of victim resistance and retaliation—homicide. Ironically, effective victim defenses against cost-inflicting strategies may have selected for the ultimate cost-inflicting behavior.

Individuals also can adopt a range of behaviors to address costs inflicted by others when they violate the rules of social contracts. Like strategies to obtain benefits, a range of strategies is proposed to have evolved to deal with violations of social contracts. Social contract violations that inflicted the greatest ancestral fitness costs would have selected for evolved strategies powerful enough to stanch the costs of the violations and prevent their recurrence. We hypothesize that the costs resulting from some social contract violations were large enough to have favored the evolution of homicidal strategies to address them. For example, sexual infidelity represents a social contract violation for both men and women in the context of a long-term mating relationship. For men, the fitness costs of a partner's sexual infidelity can be particularly large. Cuckolded men may unknowingly invest in a rival's offspring at a cost to their own genetic fitness. Being made a cuckold by an unfaithful wife causes reputational damage to the husband in all cultures for which there are relevant data (Daly & Wilson, 1988). Because experiencing deep emotional bonding with another man is a reason women have affairs (Greiling & Buss, 2000), unfaithful wives also may share information about their husband's vulnerabilities, secrets, and social weaknesses with their affair partners. The costs of being cuckolded would be particularly damaging for high-status men, who have the most to lose from their partner's affair. Higher-status men also are more protected from being punished for inflicting costs on others and could more easily replace a mate than lower-status men. The homicide of an unfaithful wife or the rival with whom she was unfaithful would have deprived male competitors of her residual reproductive value, helped to ameliorate reputational damage, contained leaked information about the husband's vulnerabilities, and possibly eliminated the prenatal child of a competitor. For these reasons, we hypothesize that killing by high-status men in response to their partner's infidelity was favored by selection.

In sum, we propose that cognitive adaptations that evolved to facilitate social exchange in human relationships created a design space for the evolution of novel behavioral strategies to best competitors that was unique among the social primates and other species. Homicide is one strategy hypothesized to be selected for because of its distinct evolutionary outcome—the permanent elimination of a strategically interfering or cost-inflicting conspecific.

Intentionality

As shorthand, the description of how psychological adaptations function to produce behavior is sometimes phrased as if the content of the cognitive processes is available to conscious awareness and under the intentional control of the individual. There are many possible functions of making the content of information processing available to conscious awareness. First, it may have no function, a by-product of memory systems or of metacognitive mechanisms (Wegner, 2002). Second, conscious awareness may be a true reflection of the most relevant or important information processing that is occurring at a given time and may function to allow an individual to exert his or her will. Third, conscious awareness may function only to motivate behavior and not to afford humans "free will" over their actions. By this account, our conscious experience of the world may or may not be a veridical representation of events. Consistent with the logic of error management theory (Haselton & Buss, 2000), conscious experience may contain biases that lead to inaccuracies in the representation of information and function only to motivate individuals to pursue adaptive strategies. We propose that humans are aware of only a subset of their cognitive machinery dedicated to homicide. Evidence from studies of homicidal ideation suggests that some of the content of homicide mechanisms is available to conscious awareness. But conscious awareness of the cognitive processes that motivate homicidal behavior and a conscious intention to kill are not requisite features of adaptations to kill others. All that is required in order to kill is a cognitive program capable of producing behavior that reliably leads to the death of conspecifics. For some contexts, lack of conscious knowledge of the functioning of one's homicide mechanisms could be beneficial in a number of ways, including (a) preventing other mechanisms from derailing or decreasing the likelihood of success of a homicidal strategy, or (b) allowing killers to more convincingly argue to others that the death they caused was unintentional, possibly decreasing or eliminating sanctions for the act.

Uncertainty

An important factor hypothesized to increase the complexity of killing others as part of a strategy to solve adaptive problems is uncertainty. Varying degrees of uncertainty pervade every aspect of adaptive problems solvable by homicide. There is uncertainty about the reliability of the environmental cues that activate adaptations for homicide. For example, is a rival having clandestine sexual encounters with a person's mate, or are the two of them just friends who enjoy each other's company? Uncertainty also surrounds the estimates of variables entered into calculations of every aspect of a homicide scenario—from how much physical force a particular weapon will require to end someone's life, to how vigorously the victim will fight back, to how easily the killing could be covered up, to how likely genetic relatives of the victim will be to seek revenge. Seeking out additional information is one strategy to decrease uncertainty. A person can test the strength of social alliances, check the lethality of a weapon, or learn the daily routine of an intended victim to discover when he or she is most vulnerable. Meticulous planning of every detail of a homicide informed by additional information may also make killers' minds more certain of the outcome of their plans. Some degree of uncertainty, however, always remains.

As a homicidal strategy unfolds over time, some aspects of a situation may occur in ways that were not anticipated. This can happen for at least three reasons. First, incorrect knowledge may be entered into the calculations that form the plans for homicide. For example, assumptions may be made about the formidability of a victim based only on the person's size and weight and observations made of the person in limited contexts. Uncertainty would remain about the range of possible effective homicidal methods in the absence of observing the victim's fighting ability. Second, unanticipated events may confound a plan to kill. For example, a victim may unexpectedly bump into a friend while jogging in the evening, an activity he or she usually does alone. The presence of the friend may be enough to derail a killer's plans for the victim's death. Finally, killers may fail to enter a relevant piece of information into their homicidal plans. A homicide may be planned for night, for example, after a victim is asleep in his or her house. Killers may fail to consider the extent to which the darkness will cripple their ability to navigate through their victim's home.

It is important to understand how uncertainty can limit the power of homicide-scenario building for at least two reasons. First, it suggests that cognitive adaptations for killing others must have evolved ways of dealing with the different kinds of uncertainty. Second, it illustrates how errors in plans to kill that stem from problems of uncertainty can derail an attempt at homicide and effectively save a victim's life. In many contexts, we propose that the psychology of would-be killers is not absolutely committed to ending the life of another person rather than doing something else, even if they have a complete plan for the homicide that they have begun to implement. Other intervening factors can redirect a killer's homicidal strategy to nonlethal alternatives at any point in time until the moment when the victim is dead.

Homicide Adaptation Theory and Other Theories of Conspecific Killing

There are many different explanations for homicide. Each has a unique perspective on killing and seeks to explain different aspects of the psychological and behavioral phenomena surrounding it. The purpose of homicide adaptation theory is to explain the origins and functions of the psychological processes that produce reliable patterns of homicidal behavior. By itself, it does not provide a complete explanation for why every individual who commits homicide does so. A number of other factors may lead to individual differences that influence the likelihood that a person will kill, including heritable individual differences in personality, exposure to violence during development, frontal lobe damage, personality disorders, and psychopathology. An evolutionary perspective on homicide is not at odds with any of these individual difference explanations. Homicide adaptation theory proposes the existence of organized, species-typical psychological processes responsible for producing homicidal behavior. Individual difference theories identify sources of variation between individuals that may affect an individual's probability of committing violent acts, including killing others.

Different theories of homicide need not be in competition. They are often complementary, capable of accounting for unique variance in why people kill others in any individual case. When there is competition between different explanations of homicide, it is most often between different theories at the same level of explanation. Buss and Duntley (2006; under review) and Daly and Wilson (1988), for example, have proposed competing theories at the ultimate level of explanation, which focus on the evolutionary origins, design, and functions of psychological mechanisms involved in producing homicide. We conclude this section with a discussion of the differences between these two evolutionary explanations of homicide. Now, we consider a range of other psychological explanations for why people kill and explore their compatibility with homicide adaptation theory.

Cultural Theories

Many explanations for homicide have focused on the role of cultural norms (Gelles & Strauss, 1979; Rummel, 1991). According to these theories, homicide is the result of exposure to cultural influences that may promote violence and which are inculcated into the human psyche. According to cultural theories, those individuals exposed to cultural influences that promote homicide should be more likely to kill others than those who are not exposed to such influences. Two similar examples of cultural theories invoked to explain homicide are the subcultures of violence (Wolfgang & Ferracuti, 1967) and culture of honor (Nisbett, 1993) theories. Designed to explain why homicide rates vary from culture to culture, these theories propose that, at least within the United States, some subcultures exist that encourage the use of violence in settling interpersonal disputes.

These theories may help to explain some of the cultural variability in homicide rates. For example, there is some evidence that conspecific killing is more common in the cultures of honor in the southern United States than in cultures in the northern United States that valorize violence less (Cohen, 1998). However, a limited number of hypotheses have been derived from these theories, and only a minority have been confirmed (Avakame, 1997; Hagan, Simpson, & Gillis, 1987; Simpson, 1991). In addition, Daly and Wilson (1989) have pointed out that many cultural theories are not complete because they merely describe the cultural differences they are supposed to explain. Similar arguments criticizing the circular reasoning of these theories have been made by others (e.g., Hagan, Gillis, & Simpson, 1985).

Social Theories

One of the earliest social theories of crime was proposed by Sutherland (Sutherland & Cressey, 1974). According to differential association theory, criminal behavior, including homicide, is just another kind of behavior that is learned from people with whom an individual interacts. Sutherland also argued that everyone has an equal potential to learn to be a criminal.

Social learning theory was first proposed as a general explanation of human behavior (Bandura, 1973) and only subsequently revised to explain some aspects of homicide (Berkowitz, 1993). Patterson (1982), in another version of social learning theory, argues that parents, teachers, and peers sometimes unintentionally reinforce what starts out to be occasional and rather trivial antisocial behavior in children that later escalates into serious offending behavior during adolescence. Patterson's version focuses primarily on experiences in the early years of development and little on experiences during adolescence as causes of criminality. Social role theory (Eagly, 1995) and socialization theory (Berkowitz, 1993) share many assumptions with social learning theory. Each of these theories proposes that behaviors originate in the process of observing and imitating others. Some behaviors are rewarded and others are punished, gradually shaping an individual's range of behaviors. These social theories have been used to explain sex differences in homicide rates and the imitation of violent behavior (Daly & Wilson, 1989).

A core assumption of social theories that leads them to predict that men should be more likely to commit homicide than women is that observing violence in the world causes violent behavior. Because humans observe more instances of men perpetrating violent acts in life and in the media, the theories propose, men are more likely than women to engage in similar behaviors. The causal arrow linking violence in the world to the violent behavior of individuals, however, need not run in this direction. For example, evidence shows that boys preferentially seek out violent toys and media images (Hoyenga & Hoyenga, 1993). When parents encourage their boys to be tough and their girls to be gentle, they may be responding to existing predispositions in each sex. Popular media may target boys with more violent programming than girls to exploit the preferences and desires that each sex naturally possesses.

The imitation of violence in the media is also limited in its explanatory power as a causative influence of homicide because it cannot explain evidence of killing in the distant past. One of the earliest pieces of evidence for outright homicide comes from a site in Shanidar, in Iraqi Kurdistan (Tattersall, 1999). This site, located in the Zagros Mountains near the Turkish border, was excavated in the 1950s by archeologist Ralph Solecki, and dates to about 60 to 100 thousand years ago. The human remains at this site include nine different Neanderthal individuals. Their skeletons show varying degrees of trauma, but one stands out. Shanidar 3 is a fragmentary skeleton and includes a partially healed injury on the top of the left ninth rib. The injury consists of a parallel-sided groove. Pathologists who have seen it agree that it was caused by a penetrating wound, about what one would expect if a right-handed individual stabbed Shanidar 3 while the two were standing face-to-face (Trinkhaus & Shipman, 1993).

In sum, cultural and social theories of homicide propose that the process of learning from the social environment is responsible for differences in homicide rates between cultures and differences in men's and women's propensity to kill. Cultures of honor valorize violence as a solution to interpersonal disputes, and violence is socially encouraged in male children but discouraged in female children. Learning is undoubtedly important for the adaptive calibration and activation of adaptations for homicide and the pursuit of homicidal strategies, accounting for some of the variance in why people kill. However, cultural and learning theories in their present form are too general to generate specific hypotheses of how experience affects psychological processes involved in producing homicide differently from psychological processes involved in addressing other domains of human experience, such as mating relationships and food preferences. The addition of an evolutionary perspective to the study of how social and cultural processes affect individuals' psychology of homicide has great potential to suggest fruitful directions for future research and may help to account for many observed patterns of homicide (e.g., infanticide perpetrated primarily by young mothers) (Gove, 1985). This would allow novel, specific predictions to be generated about trends in homicide that may be the function of different social environments and help to explain why people sometimes commit homicide instead of doing something else.

*Homicide Adaptation Theory and Cultural
and Social Theories of Homicide*

Because ancestral environments were likely recurrently variable in a limited number of reproductively relevant ways (Tooby & Cosmides, 1990), learning adaptations probably evolved to be sensitive to relevant patterns of variability in the environment that provided information about the adaptiveness of employing homicide as the solution to specific problems. Growing up in a country ravaged by war, for example, may have the effect of leading an individual to be more likely to kill in response to social conflicts with others than a person whose childhood development occurred in a more peaceful environment, such as the wealthy suburbs of a city in the United States. Homicide adaptation theory proposes that mechanisms that function to end the lives of others should be sensitive to the costs and benefits of killing in the local environment and should use that information to calibrate the likelihood of adopting a homicidal strategy. A decreased threshold for killing, in this example, is the designed, adaptive product of adaptations for homicide. Implicit in this account of homicide mechanisms is the existence of learning algorithms sensitive to specific environmental inputs that calibrate the action of homicide adaptations. It is beyond the scope of this chapter to discuss the nature of evolved learning mechanisms. From an adaptationist perspective, such mechanisms should have evolved to be as domain-specific as the other design features of adaptations for homicide proposed in this book and elsewhere (see Buss & Duntley, under review; Duntley, 2005; Duntley & Buss, 2005).

Individual Differences as Sources of Error Leading to Homicide

Individual difference factors may interact with evolved psychological mechanisms for homicide to produce a decreased threshold for conspecific killing by leading to the inappropriate activation of adaptations for homicide (see Cosmides & Tooby, 1999, for a general discussion of this topic). The mistaken activation of adaptations that lead to lethal aggression may have several sources, including (a) the presence of evolutionarily novel stimuli in modern environments that "trick" homicide adaptations into recognizing a problem as potentially solvable by killing when it is not; (b) errors in the mechanisms that weigh the costs and benefits of homicide, leading to the underestimation of costs, the overestimation of benefits, or both; and (c) a failure of some mechanisms that are necessary for the normal functioning of homicide adaptations to activate, leading to incomplete processing and the erroneous motivation of homicidal behaviors. In each of these cases, the majority of evolved mechanisms for homicide would need to function properly in order for a person to produce the organized behavior capable of killing someone else. Thus, despite systematic errors at some levels of cognitive processing, a complete explanation of killing others that is partially the result of inappropriate activation of psychological adaptations or other psychological dysfunction must still include an analysis of the evolved mechanisms involved. One prominent source of psychological dysfunction is mental illness. A number of different forms of psychopathology have been implicated in contributing to an increased likelihood of killing.

Psychopathology Theories

Psychopathology is a factor in many homicides. Molecular genetic studies have begun to identify the specific genes that may have some involvement in conspecific killing. In one study of schizophrenics, a genetic polymorphism that led to low catechol o-methyltransferase activity occurred more frequently among violent than nonviolent schizophrenic patients and also occurred more frequently among homicidal than nonviolent patients (Kotler et al., 1999).

A prospective study of major mental disorders and criminality conducted using a birth cohort in Northern Finland found that violent offenses were most prevalent among males with alcohol-induced psychoses or schizophrenic alcohol users. Those suffering from depression were least likely to kill (Tiihonen, Isohanni, Rasanen, Koiranen, & Moring, 1997). Research conducted in Australia (Mouzos, 1999) found a similar trend in the disorders that are most common among killers, which also include bipolar disorder, psychopathy, dissociative identity disorder, and unipolar mania. In both studies, people with mental illness were found to be more likely than people not suffering from a disorder to kill members of their families. Proximity theory (Hindelang, 1976; Hindelang, Gottfredson, & Garofalo, 1978), long dismissed by homicide researchers as an explanation for homicide (Daly & Wilson, 1988), may be somewhat compatible with the trends in homicide apparent among the mentally ill.

The percentage of all homicides that can be attributed to psychopathology in a particular region appears to be linked to the homicide rate. Where homicide is rare, a higher proportion of killings are committed by people suffering from disorders like schizophrenia or other psychoses. Where homicide is more frequent, a smaller percentage of killers are identified as suffering from major psychopathology. For example, studies of the perpetrators of homicide in Britain found that 39% of killers suffered from a mental disorder (Gibson, 1975). In Sweden, 53% of killers were found to be mentally ill (Lindqvist, 1986), as were 35% of Canadian killers (Cote & Hodgins, 1992). Britain, Sweden, and Canada have some of the lowest homicide rates in the world (Ghiglieri, 1999). In contrast, only 19% of killers in New York City (Grumberg, Klinger, & Grumet, 1977), 4.4% of killers in Detroit (Boudouris, 1974), and 4.4% of homicidal offenders in Australia (Wallace et al., 1998) were found to suffer from mental illness.

These differences may provide insight into the evolved functioning of adaptations for lethal aggression. In both the United States and Australia, there may be environmental cues that are more likely to activate psychological adaptations for homicide as the solution to adaptive problems faced by individuals. The global criminological literature is not in a state for precise comparisons of the circumstances that may lead to cultural differences in the cost-benefit calculus of whether an individual should kill (Ellis & Walsh, 2000). However, some factors are possible candidates. The magnitude of discrepancy in resources between the rich and the poor may be important (Wilson & Daly, 1997). A greater resource discrepancy may lead to greater average payoffs for adopting risky strategies. Cross-cultural differences in the reputational damage suffered as a result of committing homicide versus the reputational benefit from being known as a killer may also be important. The reputations of gang members in Los Angeles and New York have been shown to improve after killing a member of a rival gang (Alvarez & Bachman, 2002; Vigil, 2003). Higher-status gang members have more mating partners (Ghiglieri, 1999). The reputational effects of committing homicide are similar among the Yanomamo of Venezuela (Chagnon, 1988).

In sum, there is evidence that psychopathology is a contributing factor in some (albeit a minority of) homicides, and that these killers are more likely to manifest symptoms of mental disease by engaging in nonadaptive forms of homicide, such as eliminating genetic relatives. This does not mean, however, that psychopathology is the sole cause of such homicides. Psychopathology and likely most personality differences do not add additional information-processing capabilities to the adaptations that produce homicide. These sources of individual differences more likely distort cognitive adaptations, sometimes affecting the likelihood that a person will kill. An individual with schizophrenia who has delusions that his mother is an extraterrestrial who has plans to eliminate all of humanity, for example, obviously has errors in the interpretation of information from the environment. Despite these errors in interpreting input, the activation of psychological mechanisms to produce homicide may be appropriate and adaptive if indeed his mother were an extraterrestrial. It is difficult to kill someone. The production of a sequence of behaviors capable of successfully ending another person's life requires a large number of calculations that cognitive system errors, by themselves, would be incapable of producing. One reasonable hypothesis is that psychopathology leads to the inappropriate activation of patterned mechanisms capable of producing successful homicidal behavior. A challenge for future research is the identification of how, specifically, different forms of psychopathology interact with the psychological processes that produce homicide to lead to the inappropriate motivation of lethal aggression.

Homicide as a By-product of Other Adaptations

Adaptations for homicide need not be involved in the production of all homicidal behavior. Another evolutionary explanation of killing was proposed first by Daly and Wilson in their book *Homicide* (1988). According to Daly and Wilson, homicide may be considered an overreactive mistake, the by-product of psychological adaptations designed for nonlethal outcomes. They argue that homicide should only be used "as a sort of 'assay' of the evolved psychology of interpersonal conflict" and that it "does not presuppose that killing per se is or ever was adaptive" (Wilson, Daly, & Daniele, 1995, p. 12). For example, the behavior of a teenage mother who abandons her newborn in a dumpster to die may be explained by the failure of her psychological mechanisms for parenting to engage. Similarly, in the case of a husband who kills his wife for being sexually unfaithful, Daly and Wilson have argued that male mechanisms for sexual jealousy and the coercion and control of their mates may mistakenly overreact, leading the man to kill his wife. Despite their contention that homicide is a maladaptive by-product of psychological adaptations, Daly and Wilson (1989) emphasize that an evolutionary account of homicidal behavior is extremely important: "[W]hat is needed is a Darwinian psychology that uses evolutionary ideas as a metatheory for the postulation of cognitive/emotional/motivational mechanisms and strategies" (pp. 108–109).

There are reasons to question whether Daly & Wilson's (1988) theory is an adequate explanation of *all* homicides. First, if lethal aggression has never been adaptive, as Daly and Wilson propose it may not have been, then selection could not have fashioned adaptations for homicide. The only remaining possibilities are that homicide was neutral in terms of selection or that it had negative selective consequences. In contexts in which homicide yielded recurrently negative fitness consequences, there would have been active selection pressure against killing others. Yet currently, homicide continues to take place. In some cultures, the lifetime risk of being killed is as high as 1 in 3 for men (Ghiglieri, 1999). Daly and Wilson do not explain how a behavior with negative selective consequences could be maintained over our evolutionary history, but there are at least two possible explanations. First, the overall benefits of psychological adaptations that sometimes produce homicide as a by-product may have outweighed the occasional costs associated with killing a conspecific over our evolutionary history. One other, related possibility is that selection *has* operated to eliminate by-product homicides in contexts where such killing was too costly, modifying or fashioning new psychological mechanisms for this purpose. This explanation, however, is no longer a strict by-product hypothesis of the origins of homicide. It suggests that selection has acted to inhibit homicide in some contexts while allowing it to persist in others. Instead of an argument against adaptations for homicide, this seems a plausible explanation for the origins of homicide adaptations—through the gradual selection of mechanisms to produce homicide in the rare subset of situations in which killing leads to greater benefits than costs.

Second, the by-product explanation of homicide fails to identify the specific overreactive cognitive mistakes that lead people to kill. In fact, the by-product theory does not explore how information is processed in any of the adaptations shaped for their nonlethal consequences that sometimes lead people to kill. Without understanding their normal function, it is impossible to determine how these mechanisms may malfunction to produce homicide. Third, the by-product theory of homicide has difficulty explaining the double standard it applies to conspecific killing in other species and homicide in humans. Humans are not the only species that kill their own kind.

Numerous species kill conspecifics in predictable contexts. Among insects (including mantids, black widow spiders, jumping spiders, and scorpions), females commonly end the lives of their male mates when subsequent consumption of the male leads to a greater number or increased viability of offspring. The males of these species do not sacrifice themselves willingly. In the sexually cannibalistic black widow spider *Latrodectus mactans*, for example, males that escape their cannibalistic mates can often fertilize multiple other partners (Breene & Sweet, 1985). Males across sexually cannibalistic species use a diverse array of strategies to decrease their chances of being eaten by their mates: male scorpions sometimes sting their mates after depositing their spermatophore (Polis & Farley, 1979); male crab spiders (Bristowe, 1958) and black widows (Gould, 1984) sometimes wrap up females in silk before mating with them.

Among mammals, there are many well-documented patterns of conspecific killing. Male lions, wolves, hyenas, cougars, and cheetahs have been observed to kill the offspring of rival males (Ghiglieri, 1999). Killer lions often benefit because the mothers of the infants that are killed go into estrus sooner, allowing the infanticidal males to impregnate them earlier. Among primate species, infanticides have been documented in similar contexts, including langur monkeys (Hrdy, 1977), red howler monkeys (Crockett & Sekulic, 1984), mountain gorillas (Fossey, 1984), chimpanzees (Bygott, 1972), and others (Hausfater & Hrdy, 1984). The killing of rival adult males has also been well documented among mountain gorillas (Fossey, 1984) and the chimpanzees of Gombe (Wrangham & Peterson, 1996), two of our closest genetic relatives. In all of these species, the researchers concluded that the conspecific killings were evolved strategies shaped by selection to produce lethal consequences. Without marshalling any empirical evidence in support of its contention, the by-product theory of homicide argues that humans are different from all other animal species.

Finally, the by-product theory of homicide has difficulty accounting for premeditated killings—those perpetrated by people who have planned out their deadly act for weeks, months, or even years. Premeditated homicides are likely only the tip of the iceberg of cognitive effort devoted to killing. The majority of male and female undergraduates report having at least one homicidal fantasy in their lifetime (Kenrick & Sheets, 1993). The by-product theory of homicide has no explanation for the existence of homicidal ideation and no explanation for why people devote a significant amount of time and cognitive energy to building scenarios about ending the life of another individual. The by-product theory also does not specify whether homicidal ideations are also by-products of mechanisms selected for their nonlethal consequences or if they may be adaptive. Advocates of the by-product theory have not addressed the topic of homicidal ideations at all.

From the adaptationist perspective of homicide adaptation theory, the contexts that produce homicide as a by-product are unlikely to be contexts for which homicide evolved to be a possible solution. True by-product homicides should not be associated with circumstances that could be adaptively addressed with lethal aggression. For example, a single woman at a wedding who dies as a result of being pushed against a wall by other women seeking to obtain the bouquet tossed by the bride has not died as a result of adaptations for killing. Her death was more likely the result of adaptations for social or mate competition selected for their nonlethal outcomes. If the death of an individual could have led to a net benefit, on average, over our evolutionary history, it is plausible that the killing could be the functional output of adaptations for homicide. Homicide adaptation theory proposes that the majority of killings are the functional outputs of adaptations to produce lethal aggression (Buss & Duntley, under review; 2006).

By this logic, there are no random homicides. Even those killings that are influenced by severe psychological disorders may have random or inappropriate targets, but random cognitive processes are unlikely to be able to produce the highly patterned sequences of behaviors that might lead to a person's death. Even homicides that may be true by-products of adaptations designed for their nonlethal outcomes are likely not to be patterned randomly but instead to be highly correlated with specific categories of interpersonal conflict over reproductively relevant resources.

In sum, nonadaptationist explanations of homicide may be able to predict some variance in who is likely to become a killer and to identify some broad features of contexts that may trigger homicidal behavior. When considered individually, they all share similar weaknesses, which include (a) a failure to provide a comprehensive explanation of the patterns of homicide; (b) not making predictions about when homicide, instead of some other criminal behavior, is likely to occur; (c) not offering explanations for a large number of the observed patterns of homicide; (d) not specifying whether homicide is a kind of criminal behavior that could have ever been adaptive during our evolutionary history; (e) failure to provide an explanation for why people who are not pursuing a general strategy of criminality would ever commit homicide; (f) an inability to explain why the majority of normal people report experiencing homicidal fantasies; and (g) failure to explain the patterns of people's homicidal fantasies.

Homicide Adaptations and the Law

Homicide adaptation theory proposes that humans have evolved adaptations to kill to solve a variety of adaptive problems, from self-defense homicide to warfare killings. From a legal perspective, however, some homicides are viewed as warranting more severe punishment than others. Some contexts of homicide are viewed as murder, others manslaughter, and some not as crimes at all (e.g., self-defense homicide; defense of kin). A "crime of passion" in which a man kills his wife or a mate poacher when he finds them in bed together often gets treated with special leniency in the courtroom compared to a man who has a long, detailed, premeditated plan to kill his wife or the poacher. From our adaptationist perspective, both killings are the products of evolved psychological circuitry, and both have the same outcome. Legally, however, they are treated differently. Why?

Like Krebs (Chapter 12, this volume), we hypothesize that the answer can be found in our human evolutionary history. Like people today, ancestral humans were extraordinarily social. For most of our uniquely human evolutionary history, our ancestors lived in groups of between roughly 50 and 150 individuals. They depended on a web of relationships with others to survive and reproduce. Conflicts between individuals that led to homicide would have directly affected the killer and the victim, but also would have impacted everyone else in the social group.

Some homicides would have delivered an average benefit to members of the social group, while others would have delivered a cost. For example, a killing might free up resources that benefit a large number of individuals in the group or eliminate a cost-inflicting, exploitative bully. Alternatively, homicide could be used as a tactic of exploitation to monopolize resources or assert greater social dominance. We hypothesize that homicides that recurrently delivered benefits to individual group members would have selected for cognitive biases leading people to consider killing in such contexts to be justified. Homicides that recurrently led to the incursion of costs among individual group members, however, would not be viewed as justified. This perspective helps to clarify why many warfare homicides, killing members of rival groups, are not typically viewed as crimes. When groups compete with one another over reproductively relevant resources such as territory or women, killing those in the rival groups typically weakens the victimized groups, allowing resources to flow more freely to the group that successfully kills.

This is, clearly, a simplified account. Who receives benefits and who incurs costs largely would have been a function of individuals' relationships to the killer and the victim. Allies of the exploitative bully might suffer from decreased access to resources and a loss of protection. Allies of a person who kills to maintain dominance and monopolize resources would stand to benefit from their association. Thus, people's biases about whether homicide is justified are hypothesized to be highly context-sensitive. Essentially, however, the same logic applies. Individuals should view homicides as more justified when the resources that flow to them as a result are greater.

Our ancestors benefited from stable, cooperative relationships with others in their social group. Many reproductively relevant resources can be obtained more easily and efficiently with the assistance of others. The killing of one individual by another had the potential to polarize ancestral communities and destabilize cooperative alliances. Family members and close allies of both the killer and the victim likely would have appealed to others in the group for support. Individuals would have benefited from predicting how particular contexts of homicide would be viewed by others in their group. This would have allowed them to strategically distance themselves from killers more likely to be ostracized or otherwise punished by the group.

Cosmides and Tooby (1999) have proposed that humans have evolved adaptations for social exchange, including psychological mechanisms to detect cheaters. Cheaters fail to reciprocate. They are individuals who accept a benefit from someone else without fulfilling the agreed-upon requirement for it. The magnitude of cheating is a product of the discrepancy between the values of the resources exchanged. A person who is paid $100 an hour and sleeps on the job is a bigger cheater than a person who is paid $5 an hour and sleeps on the job.

We hypothesize that humans apply rules of cheater detection to evaluate the degree of justification or evilness of different contexts of homicide. Contexts of homicide in which a killing occurs in response to or to prevent heavy cost-infliction by the victim will be viewed as more justified than contexts of killing in which the costs from the victim are lower. For example, a husband who kills his wife after she has sex with another man would be viewed as more justified and less evil than a husband who kills his wife after she kisses another man. A husband whose wife has sex

with another man incurs greater evolutionary costs because he may end up investing in another man's child. A woman who kills a badly deformed newborn would be
viewed as more justified than a woman who kills a healthy baby of the same age. A
deformed newborn is unlikely to reproduce and represents a fitness cost to its mother.
A healthy newborn could reproduce and deliver fitness benefits to its mother. In sum,
our sense of whether a homicide is justified or evil is hypothesized to be a function of
the magnitude of discrepancy between the costs to the victim of being killed and the
past or likely future costs inflicted on the killer by the victim. Greater discrepancies
will be viewed as less justified and more evil.

Many aspects of human legal systems have been argued to represent the codi-
fication of our evolved sense of morality and justice (see Chapter 11). When it
comes to homicide, we propose that patterns in the severity of homicide charges
and punishments result from evolved patterns in our representations of the costs
incurred by victims and killers. When people kill in response to or to prevent high
fitness costs, their penalties tend to be lower (Costanzo, 2003). Penalties also tend to
be lower when victims suffer lower fitness costs by losing their lives.

Conclusion

In this chapter, we outlined homicide adaptation theory and explored its fundamental logic. We discussed examples of the unique selection pressures created by human
cognitive adaptations for social exchange that are hypothesized to have selected for
homicide. We compared homicide adaptation theory to nonadaptationist explanations for conspecific killings in humans. Finally, we explored why the law has a range
of treatments for different contexts of homicide. There is much work to be done before we have a complete understanding of the causes of homicide. Given the available evidence, we are confident that homicide adaptation theory is significant step
in the right direction. It provides a framework for viewing homicide not as a unitary
phenomenon but as a collection of diverse phenomena. It leads to a host of novel
hypotheses about the psychological mechanisms tributary to killing. And it parsi-
moniously accounts for existing patterns of homicide that are inexplicable on more
domain-general and adaptation-agnostic theories of homicide.

References

Alvarez, A., & Bachman, R. (2002). *Murder American style*. Belmont, CA: Wadsworth.
Altizer, S., Harvell, D., & Friedle, E. (2003). Rapid evolutionary dynamics and disease threats
    to biodiversity. *Trends in Ecology and Evolution, 18*, 589–596.
Avakame, E. F. (1997). Modeling the patriarchal factor in juvenile delinquency: Is there room
    for peers, church, and television? *Criminal Justice and Behavior, 24*, 477–494.
Bandura, A. (1973). *Aggression: A social learning analysis*. Englewood Cliffs, NJ: Prentice-
    Hall.

Berkowitz, L. (1993). *Aggression: Its causes, consequences, and control.* Philadelphia: Temple University Press.

Boudouris, J. (1974). A classification of homicides. *Criminology, 11,* 667–676.

Breene, R. G., & Sweet, M. H. (1985). Evidence of insemination of multiple females by the male black widow spider, *Latrt, dectus maclans* [I'Araneae, Theridiidae] *Journal of Arachnology, 13,* 331–336.

Bristowe, W. S. (1958). *The world of spiders.* London: Collins.

Buss, D. M., & Duntley, J. D. (1998, July). *Evolved homicide modules.* Paper presented to the Annual Meeting of the Human Behavior and Evolution Society, Davis, CA.

Buss, D. M., & Duntley, J. D. (1999, June). *Killer psychology: The evolution of intrasexual homicide.* Paper presented to the Annual Meeting of the Human Behavior and Evolution Society, Salt Lake City, UT.

Buss, D. M., & Duntley, J. D. (2003). Homicide: An evolutionary perspective and implications for public policy. In N. Dess (Ed.), *Violence and public policy.* Westport, CT: Greenwood.

Buss, D. M., & Duntley, J. D. (2004). The evolution of gender differences in aggression. In S. Fein (Ed.), *Gender and aggression.* New York: Guilford.

Buss, D. M., & Duntley, J. D. (2006).The evolution of aggression. In M. Schaller, J. A. Simpson, & D. T. Kenrick (Eds.), *Evolution and social psychology* (pp. 263–286). New York: Psychology Press.

Buss, D. M., & Duntley, J. D. (under review). Homicide adaptation theory.

Bygott, J. D. (1972). Cannibalism among wild chimpanzees. *Nature, 238,* 410–411.

Centers for Disease Control and Prevention, National Center for Injury Prevention and Control. (2006). *WISQARS Leading Causes of Death Reports, 1999 – 2005.* Retrieved October 26, 2007, from http://webapp.cdc.gov/sasweb/ncipc/leadcaus10.html.

Chagnon, N. (1988). Life histories, blood revenge, and warfare in a tribal population. *Science, 239,* 985–992.

Cohen, D. (1998). Culture, social organization, and patterns of violence. *Journal of Personality and Social Psychology, 75,* 408–419.

Cosmides, L., & Tooby, J. (1992). Cognitive adaptations for social exchange. In J. Barkow, L. Cosmides, & J. Tooby (Eds.), *The adapted mind.* New York: Oxford University Press.

Cosmides, L., & Tooby, J. (1999). Toward an evolutionary taxonomy of treatable conditions. *Journal of Abnormal Psychology, 108,* 453–464.

Cosmides, L., & Tooby, J. (2005). Neurocognitive adaptations designed for social exchange. In D. M. Buss (Ed.), *Evolutionary psychology handbook.* New York: Wiley.

Costanzo, M. (2003). *Psychology applied to law.* New York: Wadsworth.

Cote, G., & Hodgins, S. (1992). The prevalence of major mental disorders among homicide offenders. *International Journal of Law and Psychiatry, 15,* 89–99.

Crockett, C. M., & Sekulic, R. (1984). Infanticide in red howler monkeys In G. Hausfater & S. B. Hrdy (Eds.), *Infanticide: Comparative and evolutionary perspectives* (pp. 173–192). New York: Aldine.

Daly, M., & Wilson, M. (1988). *Homicide.* Hawthorne, NY: Aldine.

Daly, M., & Wilson, M. (1989). Homicide and cultural evolution. *Ethology and Sociobiology, 10,* 99–110.

Dodge, K. A., Bates, J. E., & Pettit, G. S. (1990). Mechanisms in the cycle of violence. *Science, 250,* 1678–1683.

Dower, J. W., & George, T. S. (1995). *Japanese history and culture from ancient to modern times.* Princeton, NJ: Markus Wiener.

Duntley, J. D. (2005). Adaptations to dangers from other humans. In D. Buss (Ed.), *The hand-book of evolutionary psychology* (pp. 224–249). New York: Wiley.

Duntley, J. D., & Buss, D. M. (2005). The plausibility of adaptations for homicide. In P. Carruthers, S. Laurence, & S. Stich (Eds.), *The structure of the innate mind* (pp. 291–304). New York: Oxford University Press.

Eagly, A. H. (1995). The science and politics of comparing women and men. *American Psychologist, 50,* 145–158.

Ellis, L., & Walsh, A. (2000). *Criminology: A global perspective.* Needham Heights, MA: Allyn & Bacon.

Fazel, S. F., & Grann, M. (2004). Psychiatric morbidity among homicide offenders: A Swedish population study. *American Journal of Psychiatry, 161,* 2129–2131.

Fossey, D. (1984). *Gorillas in the mist.* Boston: Houghton Mifflin.

Gartner, R. (1990). The victims of homicide: A temporal and cross-national review. *American Sociological Review, 55,* 92–106.

Gelles, R. J., & Strauss, M. A. (1979). Family experience and public support for the death penalty. In R. F. Gelles (Ed.), *Family violence.* Beverly Hills, CA: Sage.

Ghiglieri, M. P. (1999). *The dark side of man: Tracing the origins of violence.* Reading, MA: Perseus Books.

Gibson, E. (1975). *Homicide in England and Wales 1967–1971.* Home Office Research Study, No. 31, London.

Gould, S. J. (1984). Only his wings remained. *Natural History, 93,* 10–18.

Gove, W. R. (1985). The effect of age and gender on deviant behavior: A biopsychological perspective. In A. S. Rossi (Ed.), *Gender and the life course* (pp. 115–144). Hawthorne, NY: Aldine.

Greiling, H., & Buss, D. M. (2000). Women's sexual strategies: The hidden dimension of extra pair mating. *Personality and Individual Differences, 28,* 929–963.

Grumberg, F., Klinger, B., & Grumet, B. (1977). Homicide and deinstitutionalization of the mentally ill. *American Journal of Psychiatry, 134,* 685–687.

Hagan, J., Gillis, A. R., & Simpson, J. (1985). The class structure of gender and delinquency: Toward a power-control theory of common delinquent behavior. *American Journal of Sociology, 90,* 1151–1178.

Hagan, J., Simpson, J., & Gillis, A. R. (1987). Class in the household: A power-control theory of gender and delinquency. *American Journal of Sociology, 92,* 788–816.

Harris, A. R., Thomas, S. H., Fisher, G. A., & Hirsch, D. J. (2002). Murder and medicine. *Homicide Studies, 6,* 128–166.

Haselton, M. G., & Buss, D. M. (2000). Error management theory: A new perspective on biases in cross-sex mind reading. *Journal of Personality and Social Psychology, 78,* 81–91.

Hoyenga, K. B., & Hoyenga, K. T. (1993). *Gender-related differences: Origins and outcomes.* Boston: Allyn & Bacon.

Hausfater, G., & Hrdy, S. B. (Eds.). (1984). *Infanticide: Comparative and evolutionary perspectives.* New York: Aldine.

Hindelang, M. (1976). *Criminal victimization in eight American cities.* Cambridge, MA: Ballinger.

Hindelang, M., Gottfredson, M., & Garofalo, J. (1978). *Victims of personal crime: An empirical foundation for a theory of personal victimization.* Cambridge, MA: Ballinger.

Hrdy, S. B. (1977). Infanticide as a primitive reproductive strategy. *American Scientist, 65,* 40–49.

Kenrick, D. T., & Sheets, V. (1993). Homicidal fantasies. *Ethology and Sociobiology, 14,* 231–246.

Kotler, M., Barak, P., Cohen, H., Averbuch, I. I., Grinshpoon, A., Gritsenko, I., et al. (1999). Homicidal behavior in schizophrenia associated with a genetic polymorphism determining low catecho o-methyltransferase (COMT) activity. *American Journal of Medical Genetics (Neuropsychiatric Genetics), 88*, 628–633.

Lee, R. B. (1984). *The Dobe !Kung*. New York: Holt, Rinehart and Winston.

Lindqvist, P. (1986). Criminal homicide in Northern Sweden 1970–1981: Alcohol intoxication, alcohol abuse, and mental disease. *International Journal of Law and Psychiatry, 8*, 19–37.

Mouzos, J. (1999). Mental disorder and homicide in Australia. *Trends and Issues in Crime and Criminal Justice, 133*, 1–6.

Niehoff, D. (1999). *The biology of violence*. New York: Free Press.

Nisbett, R. E. (1993). Violence and U.S. regional culture. *American Psychologist, 48*, 441–449.

Overpeck, M. D., Brenner, R. A., Trumble, A. C., Trifiletti, L. B., & Berendes, H. W. (2002). Risk factors for infant homicide in the United States. *New England Journal of Medicine, 339*, 1211–1216.

Patterson, G. R. (1982). *A social learning approach: Vol. 3. Coercive family process*. Eugene, OR: Costalia.

Pinker, S. (1997). Why they kill their newborns. *New York Times*, November 2.

Polis, G. A., & Farley, R. D. (1979). Behavior and ecology of mating in the cannibalistic scorpion *Paruroctonus mesaensis* Stahnke (Scorpionida: Vaejovidae). *Journal of Arachnology, 7*, 33–46.

Rhee, S. H., & Waldman, I. D. (2002). Genetic and environmental influences on antisocial behavior: A meta-analysis of twin and adoption studies. *Psychological Bulletin, 128*, 490–529.

Ruff, J. R. (2001). *Violence in early modern Europe 1500–1800*. Boston: Cambridge University Press.

Rummel, R. J. (1991). *The conflict helix: Principles and practices of interpersonal, social, and international conflict and cooperation*. Rutgers, NJ: Transaction.

Shackelford, T. K., & Buss, D. M. (1996). Betrayal in mateships, friendships and coalitions. *Personality and Social Psychology Bulletin, 22*, 1151–1164.

Simpson, S. S. (1991). Caste, class, and violent crime: Explaining differences in female offending. *Criminology, 29*, 115–135.

Sutherland, E. H., & Cressey, D. (1974). *Principles of criminology* (7th ed.). Philadelphia: Lippincott.

Tattersall, I. (1999). *The last neanderthal*. Boulder, CO: Westview Press.

Tiihonen, J., Isohanni, M., Rasanen, P., Koiranen, M., & Moring, J. (1997). Specific major mental disorders and criminality: A 26-year prospective study of the 1966 Northern Finland birth cohort. *American Journal of Psychiatry, 154*, 840–845.

Tooby, J., & Cosmides, L. (1988). *The evolution of war and its cognitive foundations*. Institute for Evolutionary Studies, Technical Report #88-1.

Tooby, J., & Cosmides, L. (1990). The past explains the present: Emotional adaptations and the structure of ancestral environments. *Ethology and Sociobiology, 11*, 375–424.

Trinkaus, E., & Shipman, P. (1993). *The Neanderthals: Changing the Image of Mankind*. New York: Alfred A. Knopf.

United Nations. (1998). *United Nations 1996 Demographic Yearbook*. New York: Author.

U.S. Department of Justice, Federal Bureau of Investigations, Criminal Justice Information Services Division. (2007, September). *Crime in the United States, 2006*. Retrieved April 10, 2008, from http://www.fbi.gov/ucr/cius2006/index.html.

Vigil, J. D. (2003). Urban violence and street gangs. *Annual Review of Anthropology, 32,* 225–242.

Wallace, C., Mullen, P., Burgess, P., Palmer, S., Ruschena, D., & Browne, C. (1998). Serious criminal offending and mental disorder. *British Journal of Psychiatry, 172,* 477–484.

Wegner, D. (2002). *The illusion of conscious will.* Cambridge, MA: MIT Press.

Wilson, M., & Daly, M. (1997) Life expectancy, economic inequality, homicide, and reproductive timing in Chicago neighbourhoods. *British Medical Journal, 314,* 1271–1274.

Wilson, M. I., Daly, M., & Daniele, A. (1995). Familicide: The killing of spouse and children. *Aggressive Behavior, 21,* 275–291.

Wolfgang, M. E., & Ferracuti, F. (1967). *The subculture of violence.* London: Tavistock.

Wrangham, R., & Peterson, D. (1996). *Demonic males.* Boston: Houghton Mifflin.

4

Intimate Partner Violence

AARON T. GOETZ, TODD K. SHACKELFORD, VALERIE G. STARRATT, AND WILLIAM F. MCKIBBIN

Violence in Families

The theory of evolution by natural selection revolutionized the study of biology. So too is it revolutionizing the study of human psychology and behavior. Charles Darwin himself predicted, "Psychology will be based on a new foundation, that of the necessary acquirement of each mental power and capacity by gradation. Light will be thrown on the origin of man and his history" (1859, p. 488). Modern evolutionary psychological perspectives have been used to predict and understand a diverse array of human behaviors, such as altruism, mating, and violence. In the past few decades, many psychologists have begun to recognize the value of using an evolutionary perspective to guide their research. With a focus on evolved mechanisms and associated information-processing features, evolutionary psychology has risen as a powerful heuristic tool for the study of human psychology and behavior. Evolutionary psychology leads researchers to look at old phenomena in a different light. Such a new perspective potentially offers powerful insights into human psychology and behavior. In this chapter, we use the tools provided by evolutionary theory to explore why violence and abuse occur between intimate partners. Specifically, we focus our discussion on physical and sexual intimate partner violence.

Paternal Uncertainty and the Function of Male Sexual Jealousy

Jealousy is an emotion that is experienced when a valued relationship is threatened by a real or imagined rival, and it generates responses aimed at stifling the threat. Jealousy functions to maintain relationships by motivating behaviors that deter rivals from mate poaching and deter intimate partners from infidelity or outright departure from the relationship (Buss, Larsen, Westen, & Semmelroth, 1992; Daly, Wilson, & Weghorst, 1982; Symons, 1979). Because ancestral men and women recurrently faced the adaptive problems of retaining partners and maintaining relationships over human evolutionary history, men and women today do not differ in the frequency or intensity of experienced jealousy (Shackelford, LeBlanc, & Drass, 2000; White, 1981). A sex difference, however, is evident when considering two basic types of jealousy: emotional and sexual. This sex difference coincides with sex differences in the adaptive problems that ancestral men and women recurrently had to solve over human evolutionary history in the context of their mating relationships (Buss, 2000; Symons, 1979). Ancestral women's adaptive problem of securing the paternal investment needed to raise offspring exerted a selection pressure for women to be more sensitive to and more distressed by cues associated with a partner's *emotional* infidelity. Ancestral men's adaptive problem of paternal uncertainty (i.e., uncertainty regarding biological parenthood), however, exerted a selection pressure for men to be more sensitive to and more distressed by cues associated with a partner's *sexual* infidelity. Because emotional infidelity and sexual infidelity were highly correlated throughout evolutionary history (i.e., if an individual were engaging in one type of infidelity, he or she was often engaging in the other type of infidelity as well), researchers studying sex differences in jealousy have used forced-choice methods in which participants are asked to select which type of partner infidelity upsets them more. Recently, however, some researchers, such as Sagarin, Becker, Guadagno, Nicastle, and Millevoi (2003) and Wiederman and Allgeier (1993), also have found a sex difference in jealousy using continuous measures. At least two dozen studies have provided evidence of this sex difference in jealousy, documenting that men experience greater jealousy in response to the sexual aspects of an intimate partner's infidelity whereas women experience greater jealousy in response to the emotional aspects of an intimate partner's infidelity. These results are corroborated by experimental data (e.g., Schützwohl & Koch, 2004), physiological data (Buss et al., 1992), patterns of divorce (Betzig, 1989), and the behavioral output of jealousy, such as mate retention behaviors (e.g., Buss & Shackelford, 1997).

Men's sensitivity to and distress as a result of a partner's sexual infidelity are not surprising given the severe reproductive costs to men of cuckoldry (the unwitting investment of resources in genetically unrelated offspring). Some of the costs of cuckoldry include the potential misdirection of a man's resources to a rival's genetic offspring, his partner's investment in a rival's genetic offspring, and reputational damage if the cuckoldry becomes known to others (see Buss, 2000; Platek & Shackelford, 2006). Perhaps with the exception of death, cuckoldry is associated with the most severe reproductive costs for an individual man. It is therefore likely that selection will have resulted in the evolution of male strategies and tactics aimed at avoiding cuckoldry and decreasing paternal uncertainty.

Intimate Partner Violence and Sexual Jealousy

Male sexual jealousy is one of the most frequently cited causes of intimate partner violence (e.g., Buss, 2000; Daly & Wilson, 1988; Daly et al., 1982; Dobash & Dobash, 1979; Dutton, 1998; Dutton & Golant, 1995; Frieze, 1983; Gage & Hutchinson, 2006; Russell, 1982; Walker, 1979). Intimate partner violence is a tactic used by men to restrict a partner's sexual behavior (Buss & Malamuth, 1996; Daly & Wilson, 1988; Wilson & Daly, 1996) and may be best understood as a behavioral output of male sexual jealousy. A man may afford his partner many freedoms, but these freedoms rarely include sexual activity with other men (Buss, 1996, 2000). Men are hypothesized to have evolved mechanisms dedicated to generating risk assessments of a partner's sexual infidelity. These mechanisms include, for example, assessments of the time spent apart from his partner (i.e., time during which she might have been sexually unfaithful), the presence of potential mate poachers, his partner's reproductive value (i.e., expected future reproduction) and fertility (i.e., current likelihood of conceiving), and his partner's likelihood of committing infidelity (e.g., Goetz & Shackelford, 2006; Peters, Shackelford, & Buss, 2002; Schmitt & Buss, 2001; Shackelford & Buss, 1997; Shackelford et al., 2002; Trivers, 1972; Wilson & Daly, 1993). Moreover, the male mind may be designed to be hypersensitive to cues of his partner's sexual infidelity, motivating more false positives than false negatives because the benefits of the former outweigh the costs of the latter (Haselton & Nettle, 2006). Together with assessments of the likelihood of a partner's sexual infidelity, contextual factors—such as social and reputational costs, proximity of the partner's adult male kin (who might be motivated to retaliate for a man's violence against his partner), and economic dependency (Figueredo & McClosky, 1993; Wilson & Daly, 1993)—are processed by mechanisms of the male mind to inhibit or motivate men to inflict violence on their partners.

Occasionally, men's use of violence against their partners is lethal. As with nonlethal partner violence, male sexual jealousy is a frequently cited cause of intimate partner homicide across cultures (Daly & Wilson, 1988; Serran & Firestone, 2004). Killing an intimate partner is costly. But under specific circumstances, might the benefits have outweighed the costs enough for selection to produce a psychology that motivates partner killing? According to Daly and Wilson (Daly & Wilson, 1988; Wilson & Daly, 1998; Wilson, Daly, & Daniele, 1995), killing an intimate partner is not the designed product of evolved mechanisms but instead is a by-product of mechanisms selected for their nonlethal outcomes. This by-product or "slip-up" hypothesis states that men who kill their partners have "slipped up" in that their violence—which was intended to control an intimate partner's sexual behavior—inadvertently resulted in their partner's death.

The by-product hypothesis is attractive in that it would seem too costly to kill an intimate partner. Why kill a partner and risk the enormous costs that often flow from such actions when a man could simply end the relationship with the woman he suspects of sexual infidelity? But consider this: If killing an intimate partner is a slip-up or accident, as argued by Daly and Wilson, why are so many partner ho-micides apparently premeditated? Hiring someone to kill a partner, aiming at and shooting a partner with a firearm, and slitting a partner's throat appear to be in-tentional killings, not accidental killings. Although some partner homicides may be accidental, too many seem premeditated and intended. This is one observation that led Buss and Duntley (1998, 2003; see also Buss, 2005) to propose that many intimate partner homicides are motivated by evolved mechanisms designed to moti-vate killing under certain conditions. Discovering a partner's sexual infidelity, Buss and Duntley argue, may be a special circumstance that motivates partner homicide. This "homicide adaptation theory" does not argue that discovering a partner's infi-delity inevitably leads to homicide, but it does suggest that this circumstance would activate mechanisms associated with weighing the costs and benefits of homicide, and that under certain circumstances partner killing might be the designed out-come (for a fuller treatment, see Buss, 2005).

Daly and Wilson's (1988; Wilson & Daly, 1998; Wilson et al., 1995) and Buss and Duntley's (1998, 2003; Buss, 2005) competing hypotheses have not yet been examined concurrently to determine which hypothesis best accounts for the data (but see Shackelford, Buss, & Weekes-Shackelford, 2003). Our intention is not to crit-ically evaluate these competing hypotheses. We intend to argue that intimate part-ner homicide, by design or as a by-product, is often the behavioral output of male sexual jealousy stemming from paternal uncertainty.

Men's "mate retention" or "mate guarding" behavior is another example of the behavioral output of jealousy. Buss (1988) identified specific mate guarding behav-iors, such as vigilance (e.g., dropping by unexpectedly to check up on a partner) and concealment of mate (e.g., taking a partner away from a social gathering where other men are present). These mate guarding behaviors vary in ways that suggest they are produced by mechanisms that evolved as paternity guards. For example, a man guards his partner more intensely when she is of greater reproductive value (as indexed by her youth and attractiveness) and when the perceived probability of her sexual infidelity is greater (Buss & Shackelford, 1997). In addition, men who are partnered to women who have characteristics that make them more likely to com-mit sexual infidelity guard their partners more intensely (Goetz et al., 2005). Men also guard their partners more intensely after spending a greater proportion of time apart from them—a situation that inherently increases the possibility of sexual in-fidelity (Starratt, Shackelford, Goetz, & McKibbin, in press)—and when she is near ovulation, a time when an extra-pair copulation or sexual infidelity would be most costly for the in-pair man (Gangestad, Thornhill, & Garver, 2002).

Recognizing that men's mate retention behaviors are manifestations of jealousy, Shackelford, Goetz, Buss, Euler, and Hoier (2005) investigated the relationships between men's mate retention behaviors and intimate partner violence, specifi-cally whether some mate retention behaviors and seemingly innocuous romantic gestures may be harbingers of violence. Securing self-reports from men, partner-reports from women, and cross-spouse reports from married couples, Shackelford and his colleagues found that men's use of particular mate retention behaviors was related to partner violence in predictable ways. For example, men who dropped by unexpectedly to see what their partner was doing or who told their partner that she would "die" if she ever left him were most likely to use serious violence against their partners, whereas men who attempted to retain their partners by expressing affection and displaying resources were least likely to use violence against their partners. These findings corroborated the results of research conducted by Wilson, Johnson, and Daly (1995), who found that women who affirmed statements such as, "He insists on knowing who you are with and where you are at all times" and "He tries to limit your contact with family or friends" were twice as likely to have experienced serious violence by their partners.

Sexual Violence in Intimate Relationships and Sexual Jealousy

Between 10% and 26% of women experience rape in marriage (Abrahams, Jewkes, Hoffman, & Laubscher, 2004; Dunkle et al., 2004; Finkelhor & Yllo, 1985; Hadi, 2000; Painter & Farrington, 1999; Russell, 1982; Watts, Keough, Ndlovu, & Kwaramba, 1998). Rape also occurs in nonmarital intimate relationships. Goetz and Shackelford (2006) secured prevalence estimates of rape in intimate relationships from a sample of young men and from an independent sample of young women in a committed relationship. They documented that 7.3% of men admitted to raping their current partner at least once, and 9.1% of women admitted that they had experienced at least one rape by their current partner. Rape by physical force is just one form of sexual coercion in intimate relationships (Koss & Oros, 1982; Weis & Borges, 1973). Pressure may take the form of threats of violence, physical force, or intoxication but also may include more subtle tactics such as emotional manipulation (Shackelford & Goetz, 2004). Questions concerning sexual coercion and rape in relationships often do not encompass this wide range of behaviors; they also are emotionally loaded, and may be subject to social desirability concerns. These percentages therefore may be underestimates of the prevalence of rape in intimate relationships among young men and women who are not married.

Many hypotheses have been generated to explain why, across cultures, women are sexually coerced by their partners. Some researchers have hypothesized that sexual coercion in intimate relationships is motivated by men's attempts to dominate and control their partners (e.g., Basile, 2002; Bergen, 1996; Frieze, 1983; Gage & Hutchinson, 2006; Gelles, 1977; Meyer, Vivian, and O'Leary, 1998; Watts et al., 1998) and that this expression of power is the product of men's social roles (e.g., Brownmiller, 1975; Johnson, 1995; Yllo & Straus, 1990). Results relevant to this hypothesis are mixed. Several studies have found that physically abusive men are more likely than nonabusive men to sexually coerce their partners (Apt & Hurlbert, 1993; DeMaris, 1997; Donnelly, 1993; Finkelhor & Yllo, 1985; Koziol-McLain, Coates, & Lowenstein, 2001; Shackelford & Goetz, 2004), a result that is consistent with the domination and control hypothesis. Gage and Hutchinson (2006), however, found that women's risk of sexual coercion by their partners is not related to measures assessing the relative dimensions of power in a relationship, such as who has more control over decision making. That is, women partnered to men who hold the dominant position in the relationship are not more likely to experience sexual coercion by their partners than women partnered to men who do not maintain the dominant position in the relationship, a result that does not support the domination and control hypothesis. Although many researchers agree that *individual men* may sexually coerce their partners to gain or maintain dominance and control in the relationship, proponents of the domination and control hypothesis often argue that men are motivated *as a group* to exercise "patriarchal power" or "patriarchal terrorism" over women (e.g., Brownmiller, 1975; Johnson, 1995; Yllo & Straus, 1990).

An alternative hypothesis has been advanced by researchers studying sexual coercion from an evolutionary perspective: sexual coercion in intimate relationships may be related to paternal uncertainty, with the occurrence of sexual coercion related to a man's suspicions of his partner's sexual infidelity (Camilleri, 2004; Goetz & Shackelford, 2006; Lalumière, Harris, Quinsey, & Rice, 2005; Thornhill & Thornhill, 1992; Wilson & Daly, 1992). Sexual coercion in response to cues of his partner's sexual infidelity might function to introduce a male's sperm into his partner's reproductive tract at a time when there is a high risk of cuckoldry (i.e., when his partner has recently been inseminated by a rival male). This sperm competition hypothesis was proposed following recognition that forced in-pair copulation (i.e., partner rape) in nonhuman species followed female extra-pair copulations (sexual infidelities; e.g., Barash, 1977; Cheng, Burns, & McKinney, 1983; Lalumière et al., 2005; McKinney, Cheng, & Bruggers, 1984) and that sexual coercion and rape in human intimate relationships often followed men's accusations of their partners' sexual infidelity (e.g., Finkelhor & Yllo, 1985; Russell, 1982). Before considering the case of partner rape in humans, we review briefly the animal literature on forced in-pair copulation. Examining the adaptive problems and evolved solutions to these problems in nonhuman animals may provide insight into the adaptive problems and evolved solutions in humans (and vice versa). Shackelford and Goetz (2006), for example, argued that because humans share with some avian species a similar mating system (social monogamy) and similar adaptive problems (e.g., paternal uncertainty, paternal investment in offspring, cuckoldry), humans and some birds may have evolved similar solutions to these adaptive problems. Identifying the contexts and circumstances in which forced in-pair copulation occurs in nonhuman species may help us to understand why forced in-pair copulation occurs in humans.

Forced In-Pair Copulation in Nonhuman Animals

Instances of forced in-pair copulation are relatively rare in the animal kingdom, primarily because males and females of most species (over 95%) do not form long-term pair-bonds (Andersson, 1994). Without the formation of a pair-bond, forced in-pair copulation, by definition, cannot occur. Many avian species form long-term pair-bonds, and researchers have documented forced in-pair copulation in several of these species (Bailey, Seymour, & Stewart, 1978; Barash, 1977; Birkhead, Hunter, & Pellatt, 1989; Cheng et al., 1983; Goodwin, 1955; McKinney et al., 1984; McKinney & Stolen, 1982). Forced in-pair copulation reliably occurs immediately after female extra-pair copulations, intrusions by rival males, and female absence in many species of waterfowl (e.g., Bailey et al., 1978; Barash, 1977; Cheng et al., 1983; McKinney, Derrickson, & Mineau, 1983; McKinney & Stolen, 1982; Seymour & Titman, 1979) and other avian species (e.g., Birkhead et al., 1989; Goodwin, 1955; Valera, Hoi, & Kristin, 2003). Forced in-pair copulation following observed or suspected extra-pair copulation in these avian species is often interpreted as a sperm competition tactic (Barash, 1977; Cheng et al., 1983; Lalumière et al., 2005; McKinney et al., 1984).

Sperm competition is a form of male-male postcopulatory competition. Sperm competition occurs when the sperm of two or more males concurrently occupy the reproductive tract of a female and compete to fertilize her egg(s) (Parker, 1970). Males can compete for mates, but if two or more males have copulated with a female within a sufficiently short period of time, males must compete for fertilizations. Thus, the observation that in many avian species forced in-pair copulation immediately follows female extra-pair copulations has been interpreted as a sperm competition tactic because the in-pair male's forced in-pair copulation functions to place his sperm in competition with sperm from an extra-pair male (Birkhead et al., 1989; Cheng et al., 1983). Reports of forced in-pair copulation in nonhuman species make it difficult to claim that males rape their partners to humiliate, punish, or control them—as is often argued by some social scientists who study rape in humans (e.g., Pagelow, 1988).

Mounting evidence suggests that sperm competition has been a recurrent and important feature of human evolutionary history. Psychological, behavioral, physiological, anatomical, and genetic evidence indicates that ancestral women sometimes mated with multiple men within sufficiently short time periods so that sperm from two or more males concurrently occupied the reproductive tract of a woman (Baker & Bellis, 1993; Gallup et al., 2003; Goetz et al., 2005; Kilgallon & Simmons, 2005; Pound, 2002; Shackelford & Goetz, in press; Shackelford & Pound, 2006; Shackelford, Pound, & Goetz , 2005; Shackelford et al., 2002; Smith, 1984; Wyckoff, Wang, & Wu, 2000). This adaptive problem led to the evolution of adaptive solutions to sperm competition. For example, men display copulatory urgency, perform semen-displacing behaviors, and adjust their ejaculates to include more sperm when the likelihood of female infidelity is higher (Baker & Bellis, 1993; Goetz et al., 2005; Shackelford et al., 2002).

The selective importance of sperm competition in humans, however, is an issue of scholarly debate. Those questioning the application of sperm competition to humans (e.g., Birkhead, 2000; Dixson, 1998; Gomendio, Harcourt, & Roldán, 1998) do not contend that sperm competition in humans is not possible or unlikely but rather that it may not be as intense as in other species with adaptations to sperm competition. When considering all the evidence of adaptations to sperm competition in men and current nonpaternity rates, which range from 1% to 30% (see Anderson, 2006; Bellis, Hughes, Hughes, & Ashton, 2005), it is reasonable to conclude that sperm competition may have been a recurrent and selectively important feature of human evolutionary history. Below, we discuss theory and research related to forced in-pair copulation in humans. In keeping with the established animal literature and a comparative evolutionary perspective, we often refer to partner rape in humans as forced in-pair copulation—the forceful act of sexual intercourse by a man against his partner's will.

Forced In-Pair Copulation in Humans

Noting that instances of forced in-pair copulation follow extra-pair copulations in waterfowl and documentation that forced in-pair copulation in humans often follows accusations of female infidelity (e.g., Finkelhor & Yllo, 1985; Russell, 1982), Wilson and Daly (1992) suggested in a footnote that "sexual insistence" in the context of a relationship might act as a sperm competition tactic in humans as well. Sexual coercion in response to cues of his partner's sexual infidelity might function to introduce a male's sperm into his partner's reproductive tract at a time when there is a high risk of cuckoldry.

Thornhill and Thornhill (1992) also hypothesized that forced in-pair copulation may function as an anti-cuckoldry tactic designed over human evolutionary history by selective pressures associated with sperm competition. Thornhill and Thornhill argued that a woman who resists or avoids copulating with her partner might thereby be signaling to him that she has been sexually unfaithful and that the forced in-pair copulation functions to decrease his paternal uncertainty. Thornhill and Thornhill argued that the fact that the rape of a woman by her partner is more likely to occur during or after a breakup—times in which men express greatest concern about female sexual infidelity—provides preliminary support for the hypothesis. For example, they cited research by Frieze (1983) indicating that women who were physically abused and raped by their husbands rated them to be more sexually jealous than did women who were abused but not raped. Similar arguments were presented by Thornhill and Palmer (2000), and Lalumière et al. (2005) suggested that antisocial men who suspect that their female partner has been sexually unfaithful may be motivated to engage in forced in-pair copulation.

Both indirect and direct empirical evidence supporting this hypothesis has been documented. Frieze (1983) and Gage and Hutchinson (2006), for example, found that husbands who raped their wives were more sexually jealous than husbands who did not rape their wives. Shields and Hanneke (1983) documented that victims of forced in-pair copulation were more likely to have reported engaging in extramarital sex than women who were not raped by their in-pair partner. Studying men's partner-directed insults, Starratt, Goetz, Shackelford, McKibbin, and Stewart-Williams (under review) found in two studies that a reliable predictor of a man's sexual coercion is his accusations of his partner's sexual infidelity. Specifically, men who accuse their partners of being unfaithful (endorsing items such as "I accused my partner of having sex with many other men" and "I called my partner a 'whore' or a 'slut'") were more likely to sexually coerce them.

Direct empirical evidence supporting this hypothesis is accumulating. Camilleri (2004), for example, found that the risk of a partner's infidelity predicted sexual coercion among male participants but not female participants. It is biologically impossible for women to be cuckolded, so one would not expect women to have a sperm competition psychology that would generate sexually coercive behavior in response to their male partner's sexual infidelity. Goetz and Shackelford (2006) documented in two studies that a man's sexual coercion in the context of an intimate relationship is related positively to his partner's infidelities. According to men's self-reports and women's partner-reports, men who used more sexual coercion in their relationship were partnered to women who had been or were likely to be unfaithful, and these men also were likely to use more mate retention behaviors.

Because cuckoldry is associated with substantial reproductive costs for males of paternally investing species, men are expected to have evolved adaptations to address the adaptive problem of paternal uncertainty. One such adaptation may be a sperm competition tactic whereby sexual coercion and forced in-pair copulation function to increase the likelihood that the in-pair male, and not a rival male, sires the offspring that his partner might produce. It may be that a proportion of sexually coercive behaviors (in the context of an intimate relationship) are performed by antisocial men who aim to punish, humiliate, or control their partners *independent of their perception of cuckoldry risk*. We are not arguing that all sexual coercion and forced in-pair copulations are the output of evolved mechanisms designed to reduce the risk of being cuckolded. Instead, we are suggesting that sexual coercion might sometimes be the result of male evolved psychology associated with male sexual jealousy.

Conclusion

It is possible to study intimate partner violence with little or no knowledge of evolution. Most do. Those who study intimate partner violence from an evolutionary perspective often ask questions that are different from those asked by most clinical and forensic psychologists. Evolutionary psychologists are interested in ultimate (or distal) explanations, referring to the evolved function of a trait, behavior, or mechanism. This is in contrast to proximate explanations, which refer to the immediate causes of a trait, behavior, or mechanism. Although the explanations are different, they are compatible and equally important (Sherman & Alcock, 1994). A fuller understanding of intimate partner violence will be reached when both ultimate and proximate explanations are empirically supported.

References

Abrahams, N., Jewkes, R., Hoffman, M., & Laubscher, R. (2004). Sexual violence against intimate partners in Cape Town: Prevalence and risk factors reported by men. *Bulletin of the World Health Organization, 82,* 330–337.

Anderson, K. G. (2006). How well does paternity confidence match actual paternity? Results from worldwide nonpaternity rates. *Current Anthropology, 48,* 511–518.

Andersson, M. (1994). *Sexual selection.* Princeton, NJ: Princeton University Press.

Apt, C., & Hurlbert, D. F. (1993). The sexuality of women in physically abusive marriages: Comparative study. *Journal of Family Violence, 8,* 57–69.

Baker, R. R., & Bellis, M. A. (1993). Human sperm competition: Ejaculate adjustment by males and the function of masturbation. *Animal Behaviour, 46,* 861–885.

Bailey, R. O., Seymour, N. R., & Stewart, G. R. (1978). Rape behavior in blue-winged teal. *Auk, 95,* 188–190.

Barash, D. P. (1977). Sociobiology of rape in mallards (*Anas platyrhynchos*): Response of the mated male. *Science, 197,* 788–789.

Basile, K. C. (2002). Prevalence of wife rape and other intimate partner sexual coercion in a nationally representative sample of women. *Violence and Victims, 17,* 511–524.

Bellis, M. A., Hughes, K., Hughes, S., & Ashton, J. R. (2005). Measuring paternal discrepancy and its public health consequences. *Journal of Epidemiology and Community Health, 59,* 749–754.

Bergen, R. K. (1996). *Wife rape: Understanding the response of survivors and service providers.* Thousand Oaks, CA: Sage.

Betzig, L. (1989). Causes of conjugal dissolution: A cross-cultural study. *Current Anthropology, 30,* 654–676.

Birkhead, T. (2000). *Promiscuity.* London: Faber and Faber.

Birkhead, T. R., Hunter, F. M., & Pellatt, J. E. (1989). Sperm competition in the zebra finch, *Taeniopygia guttata. Animal Behaviour, 38,* 935–950.

Brownmiller, S. (1975). *Against our will: Men, women, and rape.* New York: Simon & Schuster.

Buss, D. M. (1988). From vigilance to violence: Tactics of mate retention in American undergraduates. *Ethology and Sociobiology, 9,* 291–317.

Buss, D. M. (1996). Sexual conflict: Evolutionary insights into feminism and the "battle of the sexes." In D. M. Buss & N. M. Malamuth (Eds.), *Sex, power, conflict* (pp. 296–318). New York: Oxford University Press.

Buss, D. M. (2000). *The dangerous passion.* New York: Free Press.

Buss, D. M. (2005). *The murderer next door.* New York: Penguin Press.

Buss, D. M., & Duntley, J. D. (1998). *Evolved homicide modules.* Paper presented at the Annual Meeting of the Human Behavior and Evolution Society, Davis, CA, July 10.

Buss, D. M., & Duntley, J. D. (2003). Homicide: An evolutionary perspective and implications for public policy. In N. Dress (Ed.), *Violence and public policy* (pp. 115–128). Westport, CT: Greenwood.

Buss, D. M., Larsen, R. J., Westen, D., & Semmelroth, J. (1992). Sex differences in jealousy: Evolution, physiology and psychology. *Psychological Science, 3,* 251–255.

Buss, D. M., & Malamuth, N. M. (1996). *Sex, power, conflict.* New York: Oxford University Press.

Buss, D. M., & Shackelford, T. K. (1997). From vigilance to violence: Mate retention tactics in married couples. *Journal of Personality and Social Psychology, 72,* 346–361.

Camilleri, J. A. (2004). *Investigating sexual coercion in romantic relationships: A test of the cuck-oldry risk hypothesis.* Unpublished master's thesis, University of Saskatchewan, Saskatoon, Saskatchewan, Canada.

Cheng, K. M., Burns, J. T., & McKinney, F. (1983). Forced copulation in captive mallards III. Sperm competition. *Auk, 100,* 302–310.

Daly, M., & Wilson, M. (1988). *Homicide.* Hawthorne, NY: Aldine de Gruyter.

Daly, M., Wilson, M., & Weghorst, J. (1982). Male sexual jealousy. *Ethology and Sociobiology, 3,* 11–27.

Darwin, C. (1859). *On the origin of species by means of natural selection.* London: John Murray.

DeMaris, A. (1997). Elevated sexual activity in violent marriages: Hypersexuality or sexual extortion? *Journal of Sex Research, 34,* 361–373.

Dixson, A. F. (1998). *Primate sexuality.* Oxford: Oxford University Press.

Dobash, R. E., & Dobash, R. P. (1979). *Violence against wives.* New York: Free Press.

Donnelly, D. A. (1993). Sexually inactive marriages. *Journal of Sex Research, 30,* 171–179.

Dunkle, K. L., Jewkes, R. K., Brown, H. C., Gray, G. E., McIntyre, J. A., & Harlow, S. D. (2004). Gender-based violence, relationship power and risk of prevalent HIV infection among women attending antenatal clinics in Soweto, South Africa. *Lancet, 363,* 1415–1421.

Dutton, D. G. (1998). *The abusive personality.* New York: Guilford Press.

Dutton, D. G., & Golant, S. K. (1995). *The batterer.* New York: Basic Books.

Figueredo, A. J., & McClosky, L. A. (1993). Sex, money, and paternity: The evolution of domestic violence. *Ethology and Sociobiology, 14,* 353–379.

Finkelhor, D., & Yllo, K. (1985). *License to rape: Sexual abuse of wives.* New York: Holt, Rinehart, & Winston.

Frieze, I. H. (1983). Investigating the causes and consequences of marital rape. *Signs: Journal of Women in Culture and Society, 8,* 532–553.

Gage, A. J., & Hutchinson, P. L. (2006). Power, control, and intimate partner sexual violence in Haiti. *Archives of Sexual Behavior, 35,* 11–24.

Gallup, G. G., Burch, R. L., Zappieri, M. L., Parvez, R. A., Stockwell, M. L., & Davis, J. A. (2003). The human penis as a semen displacement device. *Evolution and Human Behavior, 24,* 277–289.

Gangestad, S. W., Thornhill, R., & Garver, C. E. (2002). Changes in women's sexual interests and their partner's mate-retention tactics across the menstrual cycle: Evidence for shifting conflicts of interest. *Proceedings of the Royal Society of London, 269,* 975–982.

Gelles, R. (1977). Power, sex and violence: The case of marital rape. *Family Coordinator, 26,* 339–347.

Goetz, A. T., & Shackelford, T. K. (2006). Sexual coercion and forced in-pair copulation as sperm competition tactics in humans. *Human Nature, 17,* 265–282.

Goetz, A. T., Shackelford, T. K., Weekes-Shackelford, V. A., Euler, H. A., Hoier, S., Schmitt, D. P., et al. (2005). Mate retention, semen displacement, and human sperm competition: A preliminary investigation of tactics to prevent and correct female infidelity. *Personality and Individual Differences, 38,* 749–763.

Gomendio, M., Harcourt, A. H., & Roldán, E. R. S. (1998). Sperm competition in mammals. In T. R. Birkhead and A. P. Møller (Eds.), *Sperm competition and sexual selection* (pp. 667–756). New York: Academic Press.

Goodwin, D. (1955). Some observations on the reproductive behavior of rooks. *British Birds, 48,* 97–107.

Hadi, A. (2000). Prevalence and correlates of the risk of marital sexual violence in Bangladesh. *Journal of Interpersonal Violence, 15*, 787–805.

Haselton, M. G., & Nettle, D. (2006). The paranoid optimist: An integrative evolutionary model of cognitive biases. *Personality and Social Psychology Review, 10*, 47–66.

Johnson, M. P. (1995). Patriarchal terrorism and common couple violence: Two forms of violence against women. *Journal of Marriage and the Family, 57*, 283–294.

Kilgallon, S. J., & Simmons, L. W. (2005). Image content influences men's semen quality. *Biology Letters, 1*, 253–255.

Koss, M. P., & Oros, C. J. (1982). Sexual experiences survey: A research instrument investigating sexual aggression and victimization. *Journal of Consulting and Clinical Psychology, 50*, 455–457.

Koziol-McLain, J., Coates, C. J., & Lowenstein, S. R. (2001). Predictive validity of a screen for partner violence against women. *American Journal of Preventative Medicine, 21*, 93–100.

Lalumière, M. L., Harris, G. T., Quinsey, V. L., & Rice, M. E. (2005). *The causes of rape: Understanding individual differences in male propensity for sexual aggression.* Washington, DC: APA Press.

McKinney, F., Cheng, K. M., & Bruggers, D. J. (1984). Sperm competition in apparently monogamous birds. In R. L. Smith (Ed.), *Sperm competition and evolution of animal mating systems* (pp. 523–545). New York: Academic Press.

McKinney, F., Derrickson, S. R., & Mineau, P. (1983). Forced copulation in waterfowl. *Behavior, 86*, 250–294.

McKinney, F., & Stolen, P. (1982). Extra-pair-bond courtship and forced copulation among captive green-winged teal (*Anas crecca carolinensis*). *Animal Behaviour, 30*, 461–474.

Meyer, S., Vivian, D., & O'Leary, K. D. (1998). Men's sexual aggression in marriage: Couple's reports. *Violence Against Women, 4*, 415–435.

Pagelow, M. (1988). Marital rape. In V. B. V. Hasselt, R. Morrison, A. Bellack, & M. Hersen (Eds.), *Handbook of family violence* (pp. 207–232). New York: Plenum.

Painter, K., & Farrington, D. P. (1999). Wife rape in Great Britain. In R. Muraskin (Ed.), *Women and justice: Development of international policy* (pp.135–164). New York: Gordon and Breach.

Parker, G. A. (1970). Sperm competition and its evolutionary consequences in the insects. *Biological Reviews, 45*, 525–567.

Peters, J., Shackelford, T. K., & Buss, D. M. (2002). Understanding domestic violence against women: Using evolutionary psychology to extend the feminist functional analysis. *Violence and Victims, 17*, 255–264.

Platek, S. M., & Shackelford, T. K. (Eds.). (2006). *Female infidelity and paternal uncertainty.* New York: Cambridge University Press.

Pound, N. (2002). Male interest in visual cues of sperm competition risk. *Evolution and Human Behavior, 23*, 443–466.

Russell, D. E. H. (1982). *Rape in marriage.* New York: Macmillan.

Sagarin, B. J., Becker, D. V., Guadagno, R. E., Nicastle, L. D., & Millevoi, A. (2003). Sex differences (and similarities) in jealousy: The moderating influence of infidelity experience and sexual orientation of the infidelity. *Evolution and Human Behavior, 24*, 17–23.

Schmitt, D. P., & Buss, D. M. (2001). Human mate poaching: Tactics and temptations for infiltrating existing mateships. *Journal of Personality and Social Psychology, 80*, 894–917.

Schützwohl, A., & Koch, S. (2004). Sex differences in jealousy: The recall of cues to sexual and emotional infidelity in personally more and less threatening context conditions. *Evolution and Human Behavior, 25*, 249–257.

Serran, G., & Firestone, P. (2004). Intimate partner homicide: A review of the male proprietariness and the self-defense theories. *Aggression and Violent Behavior, 9*, 1–15.

Seymour, N. R., & Titman, R. D. (1979). Behaviour of unpaired male black ducks (*Anas rupribes*) during the breeding season in a Nova Scotia tidal marsh. *Canadian Journal of Zoology, 57*, 2412–2428.

Shackelford, T. K., & Buss, D. M. (1997). Cues to infidelity. *Personality and Social Psychology Bulletin, 23*, 1034–1045.

Shackelford, T. K., Buss, D. M., & Weekes-Shackelford, V. A. (2003). Wife killings committed in the context of a "lovers triangle." *Basic and Applied Social Psychology, 25*, 137–143.

Shackelford, T. K., & Goetz, A. T. (2004). Men's sexual coercion in intimate relationships: Development and initial validation of the Sexual Coercion in Intimate Relationships Scale. *Violence and Victims, 19*, 21–36.

Shackelford, T. K., & Goetz, A. T. (2006). Comparative psychology of sperm competition. *Journal of Comparative Psychology, 120*, 139–146.

Shackelford, T. K., & Goetz, A. T. (in press). Adaptation to sperm competition in humans. *Current Directions in Psychological Science.*

Shackelford, T. K., Goetz, A. T., Buss, D. M., Euler, H. A., & Hoier, S. (2005). When we hurt the ones we love: Predicting violence against women from men's mate retention tactics. *Personal Relationships, 12*, 447–463.

Shackelford, T. K., LeBlanc, G. J., & Drass, E. (2000). Emotional reactions to infidelity. *Cognition and Emotion, 14*, 643–659.

Shackelford, T. K., LeBlanc, G. J., Weekes-Shackelford, V. A., Bleske-Rechek, A. L., Euler, H. A., & Hoier, S. (2002). Psychological adaptation to human sperm competition. *Evolution and Human Behavior, 23*, 123–138.

Shackelford, T. K., & Pound, N. (Eds.). (2006). *Sperm competition in humans.* New York: Springer.

Shackelford, T. K., Pound, N., & Goetz, A. T. (2005). Psychological and physiological adaptations to sperm competition in humans. *Review of General Psychology, 9*, 228–248.

Sherman, P. W., & Alcock, J. (1994). The utility of the proximate-ultimate dichotomy in ethology. *Ethology, 96*, 58–62.

Shields, N. M., & Hanneke, C. R. (1983). Battered wives' reactions to marital rape. In R. Gelles, G. Hotaling, M. Straus, & D. Finkelhor (Eds.), *The dark side of families* (pp. 131–148). Beverly Hills, CA: Sage.

Smith, R. L. (1984). Human sperm competition. In R. L. Smith (Ed.), *Sperm competition and the evolution of animal mating systems* (pp. 601–660). New York: Academic Press.

Starratt, V. G., Goetz, A. T., Shackelford, T. K., McKibbin, W. F., & Stewart-Williams, S. (under review). Men's partner-directed insults and sexual coercion in intimate relationships. *European Journal of Social Psychology.*

Starratt, V. G., Shackelford, T. K., Goetz, A. T., & McKibbin, W. F. (in press). Male mate retention behaviors vary with risk of partner infidelity and sperm competition. *Acta Psychologica Sinica.*

Symons, D. (1979). *The evolution of human sexuality.* New York: Oxford University Press.

Thornhill, R., & Palmer, C. T. (2000). *A natural history of rape.* Cambridge, MA: MIT Press.

Thornhill, R., & Thornhill, N. W. (1992). The evolutionary psychology of men's coercive sexuality. *Behavioral and Brain Sciences, 15*, 363–421.

Trivers, R. L. (1972). Parental investment and sexual selection. In B. Campbell (Ed.), *Sexual selection and the descent of man 1871–1971* (pp. 136–179). Chicago: Aldine.

Valera, F., Hoi, H., & Kristin, A. (2003). Male shrikes punish unfaithful females. *Behavioral Ecology, 14*, 403–408.

Walker, L. E. (1979). *The battered woman.* New York: Harper & Row.

Watts, C., Keogh, E., Ndlovu, M., & Kwaramba, R. (1998). Withholding of sex and forced sex: Dimensions of violence against Zimbabwean women. *Reproductive Health Matters, 6*, 57–65.

Weis, K., & Borges, S. S. (1973). Victimology and rape: The case of the legitimate victim. *Issues in Criminology, 8*, 71–115.

White, G. L. (1981). Some correlates of romantic jealousy. *Journal of Personality, 49*, 129–147.

Wiederman, M. W., & Allgeier, E. R. (1993). Gender differences in sexual jealousy: Adaptionist or social learning explanation? *Ethology and Sociobiology, 14*, 115–140.

Wilson, M., & Daly, M. (1992). The man who mistook his wife for a chattel. In J. H. Barkow, L. Cosmides, & J. Tooby (Eds.), *The adapted mind* (pp. 289–322). New York: Oxford University Press.

Wilson, M., & Daly, M. (1993). An evolutionary psychological perspective on male sexual proprietariness and violence against wives. *Violence and Victims, 8*, 271–294.

Wilson, M., & Daly, M. (1996). Male sexual proprietariness and violence against women. *Current Directions in Psychological Science, 5*, 2–7.

Wilson, M., & Daly, M. (1998). Lethal and nonlethal violence against wives and the evolutionary psychology of male sexual proprietariness. In R. E. Dobash & R. P. Dobash (Eds.), *Rethinking violence against women* (pp. 199–230). Thousand Oaks, CA: Sage.

Wilson, M., Daly, M., & Daniele, A. (1995). Familicide: The killing of spouse and children. *Aggressive Behavior, 21*, 275–291.

Wilson, M., Johnson, H., & Daly M. (1995). Lethal and nonlethal violence against wives. *Canadian Journal of Criminology, 37*, 331–361.

Wyckoff, G. J., Wang, W., & Wu, C. (2000). Rapid evolution of male reproductive genes in the descent of man. *Nature, 403*, 304–308.

Yllo, K., & Straus, M. A. (1990). Patriarchy and violence against wives: The impact of structural and normative factors. In M. A. Straus & R. J. Gelles (Eds.), *Physical violence in American families: Risk factors and adaptations to violence in 8145 families* (pp. 383–399). New Brunswick, NJ: Transaction.

PART THREE

ADAPTATION AND SEX CRIMES

5

The Evolutionary Psychology of Sexual Harassment

KINGSLEY R. BROWNE

One of the most dramatic social changes to have occurred in Western society in the past half-century is the tremendous increase in women's participation in the labor force. Women now work side by side with men and compete for status with men in the same hierarchies (Browne, 2002). The results of workplace integration have not always been as some hoped, however, because men and women turn out not to be simply interchangeable. Despite the assumption that prohibitions of discrimination would lead to economic parity between the sexes, for example, men—in large part for reasons traceable to our evolutionary heritage—tend to engage in behaviors that result in their earning more money than women and occupying the highest organizational positions at disproportionate rates. Although men and women have somewhat different occupational preferences (Browne, 2006), men and women mix in the workplace far more than in the past. One effect of the breakdown of the sexual division of labor is the expansion of opportunities for sexual conflict to occur in the workplace. Much of this conflict is today labeled "sexual harassment" (Browne, 1997).

Sexual harassment has been called "one of the most damaging and ubiquitous barriers to career success and satisfaction for women" (Willness, Steel, & Lee, 2007, pp. 73–74), though estimates of its incidence vary widely (Gutek, Murphy, & Douma, 2004). By some counts, 90% of all women have faced some form of workplace harassment (Terpstra & Baker, 1986), yet surveys also reveal that most women do not think that it is a problem in their own workplaces (Gutek, 1985).

The huge disparities in frequency estimates result, in part, from the diversity of definitions of sexual harassment. Conduct that has been included within the concept ranges from comments that make someone feel uncomfortable to forcible rape. Legal and lay meanings are often different, so that some researchers claim many women

81

have been subjected to illegal sexual harassment even though the women themselves do not count themselves as victims (Magley, Hulin, Fitzgerald, & DeNardo, 1999), while women also may label certain conduct "sexual harassment" even though it is insufficiently egregious to satisfy the legal definition.

Because the conduct labeled sexual harassment is so diverse—having a wide array of motivations and effects—developing a unitary view of its causes and, necessarily, of its cures is impossible. Courts have declared, for example, that all of the following conduct may constitute sexual harassment: forcible rape, extorting sex for job benefits, sexual or romantic overtures, sexual jokes, sexually suggestive pictures or cartoons, sexist comments, vulgar language, harassing actions of a nonsexual form, and even "well-intended compliments" (Browne, 1997). A category of conduct that encompasses such a wide range of behavior is unlikely to have a single explanation. Nonetheless, some researchers continue to seek unitary causes. Berdahl (2007, p. 425), for example, poses the question of whether sexual harassment "is motivated by sexual desire or by sexist antipathy," as if it must all be either one or the other.

Despite the multitude of behaviors that may constitute sexual harassment, some patterns recur. The purpose of this chapter is to examine these patterns through the lens of evolutionary psychology, a perspective that makes better sense of this constellation of behavior than its purely sociocultural competitors. As one forensic psychology manual puts it, "Familiarity with sexual harassment research findings enables a forensic psychologist to place a specific case within the larger context of the phenomenon of sexual harassment" (Foote & Goodman-Delahunty, 2005, p. 13). The better one understands socially undesirable conduct, after all, the better armed one is to deal with it, whether in the context of workplace prevention or in court proceedings seeking a remedy for a putative victim.

What Is Sexual Harassment?

Sexual harassment is defined as a form of sex discrimination under the laws of the United States (Browne, 1997), the United Kingdom (Kelly, 2000), and the European Union (Defeis, 2004). Title VII of the Civil Rights Act of 1964—the principal U.S. law governing sex discrimination in the workplace—does not even mention the term *sexual harassment*. Rather, case law has identified some forms of sexual harassment as covered by the general prohibition against discrimination "because of sex." The concept's origin in discrimination law has had substantial influence on the course of its development and has led to some oddities and uncertainties in the doctrine.

Two relatively distinct categories of sexual harassment have been identified in the case law and the academic literature (Browne, 1997). The first, known as "quid pro quo harassment," is perhaps the archetypal form. It entails a claim that an employee was required to submit to sexual advances as a condition of either obtaining a benefit, such as being promoted, or avoiding a burden, such as being fired. A threat of "Sleep with me or you're fired" is a classic case, although courts may find an implied threat in less explicit language. The rationale for viewing such conduct as sex discrimination, as opposed to mere swinish behavior, is that the sexual demand would not have been made had the employee been of the other sex. Female employees, or at least some of them, may thus be faced with burdensome conditions of employment that male employees are not, or, if the offending male supervisor is homosexual, male employees may be subjected to conditions not faced by women.

The case of the bisexual supervisor was a merely hypothetical objection to this rationale until a federal court of appeals actually faced such a case in 2000. The court ruled that a supervisor who had imposed sexual demands on both a husband and a wife had not engaged in unlawful sexual harassment because the harassment was not "discriminatory" on the basis of sex (*Holman v. Indiana*, 2000). The bisexual-supervisor case challenges the notion that sexual harassment is wrong because it constitutes sex discrimination. Most people probably do not believe that a supervisor who extorts sex from male and female employees alike is on a higher moral plane than a supervisor who is less catholic in his tastes. It is the use of the supervisor's workplace power to extort sex that is the primary wrong, not the fact that his targets happen to be of one sex or the other. Of course, litigants must use the tools at their disposal, and the antidiscrimination laws have some characteristics that made them particularly attractive for the task, including the liability of employers for the acts of their employees and the availability of attorneys' fees to the successful plaintiff.

The second form of harassment is "hostile environment" harassment, which involves a claim that the work environment is permeated with sexuality or "discriminatory intimidation, ridicule, and insult" (*Meritor Savings Bank v. Vinson*, 1986). A complaining employee must show that she (or he) was subjected to "unwelcome" conduct, based upon sex, that was "sufficiently severe or pervasive to alter the conditions of the victim's employment and create an abusive working environment." The "severe or pervasive" requirement is intended to preclude liability for isolated incidents or behavior that is "merely offensive." The complainant must also show not only that she perceived the environment to be abusive but also that a hypothetical "reasonable person" or "reasonable woman" (more about this distinction later) would have found it so as well, in order to avoid holding employers hostage to the hypersensitivity of a particular employee.

Hostile-environment harassment consists of a more varied range of behaviors than quid pro quo harassment. A hostile environment can be created by sexual advances that are not tied to tangible aspects of the job; these might come from supervisors, co-workers, or even subordinates or customers. These cases are perceived as discrimination for the same reason that quid pro quo cases are—namely, that the advances were "because of" the target's sex. Other cases may involve harassment of either a sexual or nonsexual form that is directed at a woman because of either sexual desire or hostility to her sex, so they also fit easily within a discrimination rationale, although not necessarily a definition of sexual harassment that requires the conduct to be "of a sexual nature." Other hostile-environment cases are not so easily fit into the discrimination model, however. Many involve complaints that the work atmosphere is generally "sexualized"—filled with sexually provocative pictures, sexual jokes, sexist comments, and the like. Unlike quid pro quo cases, there may be no intended "target" of this harassment at all, and the sexualized atmosphere may have predated the entry of women into that particular workplace. A plaintiff in such a case is not saying that she was treated differently because of her sex but rather that the environment is discriminatory because sexualized environments are inherently more burdensome to women than to men.

This chapter will examine three sexual harassment issues that have been either erroneously or incompletely analyzed because of failure to consider the findings of evolutionary psychology. The first is whether the hostility of an environment should be judged from the perspective of the "reasonable person" or from that of the "reasonable woman" (as in a large portion of cases a woman is the complainant). A perspective that takes seriously the notion that humans are products of natural selection—with the attendant differences in selective pressures to which the sexes have been exposed—suggests that when it comes to matters of sex, there is no such thing as a "reasonable person." There are only "reasonable men" and "reasonable women." An average of the two—a "reasonable androgyne," in the words of Lionel Tiger (1997)—is simply nonsensical.

The second issue involves the frequently repeated but seldom examined assertion that sexual harassment is "not about sex but about power." Under this view, men in quid pro quo cases use sex instrumentally to obtain and retain power over women. An evolutionary perspective does not deny the linkage between power and sex—indeed, it recognizes the link to be a powerful one—but suggests that the direction of causation is misperceived. Rather than using sex to obtain power, it is much more accurate to say that men use power to obtain sex.

The final issue is the accuracy of the assumption that abuse that takes a sexual form, such as sexual epithets or hazing that has sexual overtones, is necessarily directed at the target "because of sex." Even prior to the entry of women into the workforce, men directed such conduct toward one another. When the goal is either to offend or to test a person, the actor is likely to select a form of conduct to which he believes the target will be especially sensitive. For both women and men, that conduct is likely to have sexual overtones. In many of these cases, it would not be inappropriate to say that this conduct really *is* "about power"—in the sense of being related to men's attempt to achieve status and dominance generally—rather than sex, but these cases are often assumed to be inherently more sexual than they actually are.

The "Reasonable Person" or the "Reasonable Woman"?

One of the major unresolved issues in sexual harassment law concerns the appropriate perspective by which to judge whether a work environment is sufficiently hostile as to be illegal. Specifically, the question is whether the "victim's perspective" should take account of sex—that is, whether the environment should be viewed from the perspective of the "reasonable person" or that of the "reasonable woman."

The argument for a "reasonable person" reflects concern that a "reasonable woman" standard is paternalistic and imposes an obligation on men to conform to a standard of conduct that they cannot understand (Adler & Peirce, 1993). One court, in rejecting the "reasonable woman" standard, explained that it "may reinforce the notion that women are 'different' from men and therefore need special treatment—a notion that has disenfranchised women in the workplace" (*Radtke v. Everett*, 1993). In contrast, courts adopting the reasonable woman standard have relied upon perceptions of just the differences that other courts have been reluctant to reinforce. As one court stated, "conduct that many men consider unobjectionable may offend many women" (*Ellison v. Brady*, 1991). That court acknowledged that women are not uniform in their viewpoints but noted that they "share common concerns which men do not necessarily share" and that "women who are victims of mild forms of sexual harassment may understandably worry whether a harasser's conduct is merely a prelude to violent sexual assault." Which of these two standards should be adopted depends in part on just how different men's and women's perspectives actually are.

*"Error Management Theory" and
Sex Differences in Perceptions*

Men and women, it turns out, have substantially divergent views about sexual matters in general and sexual harassment in particular. Women tend to view more kinds of sex-related behavior as harassment, although the sexes differ little in their views of the most serious forms of harassment, such as coerced sex (Corr & Jackson, 2001; Rotundo, Nguyen, & Sackett, 2001). Women are more likely than men to perceive touching or sexual comments to be sexual harassment. One widely reported finding is that a substantial majority of women would be offended by sexual overtures at work, whereas a substantial majority of men would be flattered (Gutek, 1985). A study of attitudes about workplace e-mails similarly found that men rated e-mails containing sexual propositions to be "somewhat enjoyable" whereas women found them to be very offensive (Khoo & Senn, 2004, p. 210). Thus, it seems, where a man might see "opportunity," a woman sees "danger," as illustrated by Struckman-Johnson and Struckman-Johnson's (1994, p. 401) finding that a substantial number of men "viewed an advance by a good looking woman who threatened harm or held a knife as a positive sexual opportunity."

Men inhabit a more sexualized world than women do, and they devote a greater share of their reproductive effort to short-term mating. Because men see the world "through sexual glasses," they tend to see situations as more sexually oriented than women do. In their interactions with women, men often perceive sexual interest where women perceive only friendliness (Abbey, 1987, 1982). The tendency of men to interpret friendly behavior as a reflection of sexual interest coupled with women's tendency to interpret sexually interested behavior as mere friendliness leaves much room for misunderstanding. A woman who has no interest in a sexual relationship with a man may initially act in a friendly manner, which the man may interpret as a sign of sexual interest, leading him to respond flirtatiously. The woman's friendly response in return may be taken by the man as a positive indicator that his interest is reciprocated, which may prompt him to respond with sexual advances that are in fact unwelcome.

The converse of men's bias toward perceiving sexual interest on the part of a woman appears to be women's bias toward perceiving sexual threat on the part of men in circumstances in which a risk of coercion exists. Discomfort should begin well before an overt attempt at physical coercion is made, however, since by then it may be too late. Thus the same behavior that may be perceived as friendly in an unthreatening atmosphere may be viewed as threatening when the possibilities of escape are diminished (whether or not a threat is intended).

The differences in perception that lead to miscommunication are easily understood from the perspective of "error management theory" (Haselton & Buss, 2000). In making judgments under uncertainty, the human mind is biased toward minimizing the reproductive costs of error. As Buss (1994, p. 145) has observed, a male tendency to infer sexual interest would have been selected for "if over evolutionary history even a tiny fraction of these 'misperceptions' led to sex." A man who waits to make advances until he is certain that a woman is sexually interested would tend to be less reproductively successful than a man who tries as long as there is a chance that the woman will be receptive. Men are thus predisposed toward false positives in this context (inferring interest that does not exist) rather than false negatives (failing to pick up on genuine interest). Similarly, because of the substantial fitness costs to a woman who loses control over her choice of sexual partner and the timing of reproduction, natural selection would favor a woman's cautiousness about sexual coercion (Thornhill & Palmer, 2000, pp. 100–103). It is better to infer a threat of sexual coercion that does not exist than to ignore one that does, so women in this context—especially in the fertile phase of the menstrual cycle (Chavanne & Gallup, 1998)—should be biased toward false positives. As Duntley and Shackelford have noted (see Chapter 11), natural selection would favor defense mechanisms against reproductive threats that would have been common in our ancestral environment, and sexual coercion of women by men has been a threat for a very long time.

Misperceptions, Miscommunication,
and Sexual Harassment

The varying perceptions of men and women create ample opportunity for miscommunication in the workplace, as the Safeway corporation learned after it implemented its "superior customer service" program in 1998. Under this program, clerks were directed to smile at customers, make eye contact, and call them by name (Ream, 2000). A number of female clerks ultimately filed charges of sexual harassment, claiming that the overtly friendly behavior required by the policy prompted some male customers to interpret their behavior as flirtatious, leading to sexual comments, propositions, and even stalking. Exacerbating the problem of miscommunication, the Safeway policy did not permit employees to discontinue the friendly behavior when customers responded inappropriately, which resulted in further encouragement of the unwelcome attention. The harassment charges were dropped when Safeway agreed with some of its unions to modify the policy.

The fact that cues typically employed in courtship are inherently ambiguous virtually guarantees that miscommunication will happen with some frequency (Stockdale, 1993). Features of the workplace—such as the need for continued future association—especially encourage ambiguity. As Yagil and colleagues have noted, "to the degree that the target's message is ambiguous it leaves an opening for the perpetrator to interpret the behavior as welcome" (Yagil, Karnieli-Miller, Eisikovits, & Enosh, 2006). When a woman tells a male co-worker that she cannot go out with him because she is busy that night, she may be thinking, "I hope he takes the hint and leaves me alone," while he may be thinking, "Great, she's busy this time, but she didn't reject me altogether; I'll try again and hope she's not busy next time." Sometimes women would have it both ways. They do not want to be explicit about their rejection, in order to avoid creating conflict, but at the same time they resent men for not taking their attempt to spare feelings ("maybe some other time") as a no. This lack of clarity may result in the "persistent requests for a date after repeated refusals" that is often defined as harassment.

The risk of miscommunication is exacerbated by the perception of many men that women often are just "playing hard to get" and often mean "yes" even if they say "no." Although this notion is often referred to as a "myth" (Semonsky & Rosenfeld, 1994, p. 515), there is substantial evidence that some women do employ this tactic (Muehlenhard & Hollabaugh, 1988). As Mealey (1992) noted, the fact that "females are selected to be coy will mean that sometimes 'no' really does mean 'try a little harder.' " Because many men know that "no" can be a prelude to "yes," they may persist even when "no" actually does mean "no." Because of the inherent ambiguity of many such situations, it is naive to assert that "sexual harassment allegations are either true or false" (O'Donohue & Bowers, 2006, p. 56), in the way that one might make such an assertion about the claim of a party to an automobile accident lawsuit about the color of the traffic light.

When sex differences in perspective lead to miscommunication—that is, when the man reasonably (from the perspective of the reasonable man) makes sexual overtures that a woman reasonably (from the perspective of the reasonable woman) finds disturbing or even threatening—who, if anyone, is to blame? The usual answer is that the man is responsible; after all, he has made a sexual advance that was "unwelcome," and sexual harassment doctrine, at least in the United States, does not make the man's intent particularly relevant (Browne, 1997). However, when a person reasonably receives a message different from the one that the sender reasonably intended to convey, both subjects are engaging in miscommunication.

Yet commentators commonly dismiss with disdain any suggestion that women bear some responsibility for avoiding such situations (Ehrenreich, 1990, p. 1208 n.114; Oshige, 1995, p. 578).

The fact that some—though by no means all—sexually harassing behavior results from miscommunication suggests that sexual harassment training might abandon its usual exclusive focus on male behavior and focus as well on educating women that some of their behavior might be misunderstood and that even if they feel threatened, the men may not actually be threatening them. Instead, sexual harassment training is often aimed more at heightening sensitivities than educating recipients to avoid miscommunication. Indeed, it is commonplace in the literature for the success of sexual harassment training programs to be judged by the increase in employees' labeling of particular conduct as sexual harassment (York, Barclay, & Zajack, 1997).

If a biological perspective can contribute anything to the sexual harassment discussion, it must be the insight that a "reasonable person" standard is meaningless. When it comes to matters of sex and sexuality, there are no "reasonable persons," only "reasonable men" and "reasonable women." The discrete sexual natures of men and women cannot be blended into a one-size-fits-all "human sexual nature" that is instantiated in a sexless—or hermaphroditic—"reasonable person." This is not to suggest, of course, that all men and all women agree among themselves about what is abusive. Women differ among themselves about the offensiveness of sexual materials and behaviors in the workplace. For example, those adhering to a feminist ideology are especially likely to find them offensive (Brooks & Perot, 1991).

Although interesting from an academic perspective, there is mixed empirical evidence on the question of whether judges and juries are affected in their decisions by whether they are applying a reasonable woman or reasonable person standard. Laboratory studies typically show that the choice of standard has a modest effect in some kinds of cases, with subjects using a reasonable woman standard being somewhat more likely to label particular conduct as harassing (Blumenthal, 1998; Gutek et al., 1999; Wiener & Hurt, 2000). A study of all reported federal cases in the United States over a ten-year period, however, found no statistically significant difference in outcomes between cases explicitly relying on a reasonable woman standard and those employing a reasonable person standard (Juliano & Schwab, 2001). The fact that most cases did not identify the standard being employed suggests caution in drawing too much from the null results. Another study examining factors in decided cases found that courts deciding cases in "reasonable woman" jurisdictions were slightly more likely to find for the plaintiff (Perry, Kulik, & Bourhis, 2004).

Power versus Sex

Many who write about sexual harassment are certain that sexual harassment is not "about sex" at all but "about power" (Avner, 1994; Bravo & Cassedy, 1992)—echoing equivalent claims often made about the motivations of rapists (see discussion in Palmer & Thornhill, 2003). In support of this suggestion, they argue (or at least imply) that victims are not selected according to criteria of sexual attractiveness but rather chosen more or less at random to be victims of a male need to oppress women. For example, Gutek (1985, p. 54) asserts that sexual harassment "is likely to happen to almost any female worker," but on the next page she points out that victims tend to be young and either single or divorced. Another device is to set up an extreme straw man and, in rejecting it, leave a misleading impression. Thus, Workman and Johnson (1991, p. 766) note that "some individuals believe only attractive women are sexually harassed" but that "empirical studies do not support this belief, since women in all ranges of attractiveness have reported harassment." Although this statement may leave the casual reader with the impression that unattractive women are as likely to be targets as attractive women, all the writers have actually said is that not all victims are attractive (although, for all we know, they may have been the most attractive victims available to their harassers).

Of course, not all sexual harassment is directed toward obtaining sex, and some may have no real target at all. A work environment saturated with sexual pictures and coarse language might be viewed as sexually harassing to all women who find themselves present, and some harassment may be driven by dominance motivations or hostility rather than sexual desire. Nonetheless, quid pro quo harassment—when a superior extorts sex from a subordinate—has clear sexual motives, even if it is the harasser's power that makes such extortion possible.

Because of the centrality of sexual behavior to reproductive fitness, an evolutionary perspective should lead to acute skepticism about a claim that activities that result in sexual intercourse are not "about sex." This skepticism is especially warranted when the claim is that power and sex are unrelated, as dominance and sexuality share similar roots. As Dabbs (2000, p. 10) has noted, "the major social effect of testosterone is to orient us toward issues of sex and power." Sexual coercion is not a cultural invention of humans born of an ideology of patriarchy but rather a widespread pattern across the animal kingdom (Clutton-Brock & Parker, 1995).

Throughout human history, men have used power as a way of obtaining sex, whether coercively or through making themselves attractive as mates. Men with the most power in history—despots whose subjects lived at their sufferance—routinely surrounded themselves with nubile women whose favors they could command at their pleasure (Betzig, 1986). Genghis Khan had hundreds of wives and concubines (Ratchnevsky, 1991), and the Y-chromosome of Genghis and his male relatives is now found in approximately 8% of males throughout a swath of Asia largely congruent with the boundary of the Mongol empire when Genghis died (Zerjal et al., 2003). Quite clearly, he reaped substantial reproductive rewards from his power. Male "despots" in the workplace sometimes adopt a similar strategy, with far less extravagant success, of course. Many litigated cases involve allegations of explicit threats of adverse action if the target refuses to engage in sexual activity (Browne, 1997, pp. 48–49 n. 227). There is little reason to think that the motivations of these supervisors are any less sexual than those of an Eastern emperor. Thus, even the sexual harassment cases that most conspicuously involve power—explicit quid pro quo cases—are about both power *and* sex: a supervisor is using his workplace power to extort sexual compliance. To say that it is *only* about power makes no more sense than saying that bank robbery is only about guns and not about money.

Premature Rejection of the "Natural/Biological" Model

A study commonly invoked to support the argument that sexual harassment is not about sex was conducted by Tangri, Burt, and Johnson (1982). They proposed and tested three models of sexual harassment: the "natural/biological" model, which views harassment as a consequence of natural physical attraction; the "organizational" model, which views harassment as a consequence of organizational hierarchy, allowing individuals to use their organizational power to oppress their subordinates; and the "sociocultural" model, which views sexual harassment as a result of sex-role socialization and the differential distribution of power in the larger society. They concluded that there was evidence to support the latter two models but little to support the first (the explanations are not mutually exclusive, of course). Following the Tangri study, the idea that there is any significant biological contribution to harassment is usually mentioned just to be dismissed.

The rejection of the natural/biological model resulted from the failure of the data to satisfy the predictions that the researchers derived from the model. They had predicted that if this model were correct, harassers and victims would be of both sexes; victims would be similar to their harassers in age, race, and occupational status; both harasser and victim would be unmarried; and the harasser would direct his attention only toward the victim. They also predicted that the behaviors would resemble courtship behaviors, that they would stop once the victim indicated a lack of interest, and that victims would be "flattered" by the behaviors (although why a woman should be expected to be "flattered" by behavior she viewed as harassment is hard to fathom). Because their data did not satisfy those expectations, they rejected the model.

Tangri and associates oddly concluded that the tendency of individuals with greater degrees of personal vulnerability and dependence on their job to experience more harassment was some of the "strongest evidence available in these data against the natural model" (p. 52). Their apparent view was that young, unattached women are particularly vulnerable and that it is simply coincidental that such women would also be sexually attractive to a potential harasser (although they did not explain why a young, single woman is more vulnerable than, say, a 55-year-old woman who has worked for the same employer for thirty years but has no pension). It is not clear, however, why a finding that victims were vulnerable would undermine the natural/biological model. If the harasser's strategy is to convert his workplace power into satisfaction of his sexual urges—which is the essence of quid pro quo harassment—he must focus on targets susceptible to the exercise of that power. It is not just attractiveness that is important to him; it is attractiveness plus accessibility.

The test of a model is meaningful only if the predictions the researchers derive from the model logically follow from it. This study was not constructed to test whether harassers were motivated by sexual attraction, however, but rather whether they were looking for long-term, exclusive mates. But no one has suggested that sexual harassment is mostly "about marriage." What the researchers should have tested was whether the actor and the target tend to possess traits that would be relevant to either long-term *or* short-term mating.

A subsequent study by Studd and Gattiker (1991)—informed by evolutionary psychology—analyzed patterns of sexual harassment and concluded that the demographic profiles of targets were largely what would be expected if harassers were employing short-term sexual strategies (see Buss & Schmitt, 1993). The strongest prediction is that the harasser is male and the victim is female, since men are usually the sexual initiators in both long-term and short-term mating. Other predictions are that the target will be of reproductive age, physically attractive, and not involved in a serious long-term relationship (and therefore lacking a male protector). These predictions are largely satisfied. Less than 1% of federal cases over a ten-year period involved sexually based behavior aimed at a male employee by a female supervisor (Juliano & Schwab, 2001). The overwhelming proportion of victims are single, divorced, or separated women under the age of 35 (Studd & Gattiker, 1991). Studd and Gattiker concluded that the motivation of most men involved in coercive sex in the workplace was indeed sexual (although not romantic). It is worth noting that in laboratory studies, subjects seem to assume that harassers' motives are sexual, as they are substantially more likely to find that sexual harassment occurred when the plaintiff is attractive (Madera, Podratz, King, & Hebl, 2007).

Conflicting Predictions about Status and Unwelcomeness

There is some confusion in the literature about what predictions one should make concerning the effect of a man's status on a woman's reaction to sexual advances in the workplace. For example, Buss (1999, p. 319; 2004, p. 318) has suggested that "The degree of chagrin that women experience after sexual advances . . . depends in part on the status of the harasser," with women being *less* upset by advances from higher-status men. Bourgeois and Perkins (2003) claim to have "overwhelmingly refuted" Buss's prediction through their finding that women report imagining *greater* upset if someone higher in their organization persisted in asking them out on a date despite their repeated refusals than if the requests came from someone with lower status. Thus, they assert, their findings support the sociocultural explanation and refute the evolutionary explanation. It is critical to note, however, that Bourgeois and Perkins's study, unlike the study Buss was referring to, placed the high-status man above the woman in the organization. Bourgeois and Perkins do acknowledge that *absent* power differentials, "the evolutionary hypothesis seems to apply" (p. 349).

Rather than refuting the evolutionary psychology account, the Bourgeois and Perkins results are actually predicted by it. Two well-documented findings are relevant to these predictions. The first is that women tend to prefer high-status men to low-status men (Buss, 2004, pp. 110–115). Thus, all else being equal, they are likely to find advances by the former more welcome than advances by the latter. The second finding is that women are strongly averse to sexual coercion (Thornhill & Palmer, 2000). Thus, women will suffer more distress when the possibility of sexual coercion is high than when it is low. These findings yield two predictions. First, women are likely to find advances by high-status men in their own organizations to be more welcome than advances by low-status men. Second, if the advances are *not* welcome, women are likely to be more upset by persistent advances by their superiors—who have the organizational power to coerce them—than by their peers or subordinates, who likely lack that power. These predictions were tested by Colarelli and Haaland (2002), whose study varied the man's power and status separately. They found that power and status interacted, with harassment ratings increasing as power increased and status decreased. Thus, advances by a relatively low-status man who held power over the woman were most distressing of all.

Weaknesses of a Theory that Neglects Biology

An approach that focuses solely on power without resort to sex differences in sexual psychology cannot explain a number of features of sexual harassment. For example, why do women almost never coerce sex from their subordinates? Some argue that one seldom sees coercion by female superiors because women usually lack the necessary power (Tangri et al., 1982; Fitzgerald & Weitzman, 1990). However, large numbers of women hold management and supervisory positions in organizations and faculty positions in colleges and universities. Nonetheless, reported instances of sexual coercion by female managers and professors are relatively rare. Although one might argue that because of the readiness of many men to engage in casual sex, women have no need to coerce them, that response itself rests on the different sexual psychologies of men and women. There is little evidence that women supervisors engage in frequent *voluntary* sexual relations with their subordinates, either, and women's preference for higher-status mates would suggest that this would be a relatively uncommon occurrence.

One variant of the sociocultural theory holds that sexual harassment is an attempt by men to exert power because of their fear that women constitute a threat to men's economic or social standing (Gutek, 1992). Such an argument suggests an inverse relationship between male societal power and sexual coercion. Yet the most pervasive coercive sex in the history of the master-servant relationship is not between men and women in the modern workplace—where women are participating in the workplace as equals like never before—but rather between a slave owner and his slaves. Female slaves did not constitute a threat to their owner's economic or social standing; indeed, they were a reflection of it. Nonetheless, sexual relations between slave and owner were extremely common, and that phenomenon was one of the principal objections of many abolitionists to the institution of slavery. The historical record is clear that slave owners did not seek slave women at random for sexual relations. Rather, they preferred those who possessed the attributes that men typically value in sexual partners: reproductive value as demonstrated by youth and beauty. This preference was reflected in price, as a prime fieldhand would sell in New Orleans for $1,800, a top-quality blacksmith would go for $2,500, and a "particularly beautiful girl or young woman might bring $5,000" (Genovese, 1976, p. 416).

One recurrent, yet implausible, theme in the literature is that sexual harassment represents an implicit conspiracy through which men combine to oppress women (Farley, 1978, p. xvi). Some researchers have suggested that the reason that married women are less likely to be harassed is not that men are looking for mates but rather that harassers are honoring the "property rights" of other men (Gutek, 1985, p. 57; Lafontaine & Tredeau, 1986), as if men have a pact among themselves that they will sexually coerce each other's daughters and sisters but not their wives. Under this view, male harassers (the majority of whom are married) are more willing to honor the marital vows of other men than they are their own. This "property rights" argument rests uneasily with Schneider's (1982) finding that "closeted" lesbians, who might have a male partner for all the harasser knows, are subjected to *more* sexual advances than "open" lesbians, whose partners are known to be women—a finding suggesting that predicted receptivity is a factor influencing men's overtures.

Power and the Priming of Sexual Psychology

The relationship between power and sexual harassment is considerably more subtle than is often appreciated. Bargh and Raymond (1995) have suggested that many men in supervisory positions do not realize they are exploiting their power, because of an unconscious link between power and sex. When such a man is in a position of power over a woman, an "automatic power–sex association" becomes activated, which enhances both the likelihood that he will perceive sexual interest on the woman's part and his perceptions of her attractiveness (also Bargh, Raymond, Pryor & Strack, 1995; Zurbriggen, 2000). The man may see a sexual situation in which the attraction seems to be reciprocated whereas the woman is simply being deferential and friendly to a man who has power over her.

The finding that many men have an automatic association of power and sex suggests that modification of sexual harassment training may be appropriate. Much of that training is currently focused on warning men that they should not exploit their power over subordinates to coerce sex or, more generally, that sexual relationships between supervisors and subordinates are inappropriate. Neither of these messages is likely to be terribly effective in modifying the behavior of a man having the power/sex association. Such a man would not tend to view his conduct as exploitive if he is unaware that it is his power that creates the attraction. Moreover, if he perceives the relationship as one of mutual attraction, he is less likely to abide by institutional strictures against supervisor–subordinate relationships. Perhaps a better strategy is to educate men specifically that being in a position of power will sometimes result in erroneous perceptions, especially in light of Bargh and Raymond's estimate that three-quarters of harassers do not realize that they are engaging in harassment.

Power is unquestionably an important component of some kinds of sexual harassment. It is an essential ingredient of quid pro quo harassment, since the harasser must have the apparent power to carry through on his threat if sexual access is denied, and therefore vulnerability to the exercise of that power will be a typical feature of extortionate harassment. But the claim that "the goal of sexual harassment is not sexual pleasure but gaining power over another" (Bravo & Cassedy, 1992) gets the relationship exactly backward. The focus on power to the exclusion of sex appears to be an unfortunate side effect of the fact that most of the scholarship on harassment has been from the woman's, if not the feminist's, point of view. From the perspective of the victim, it may seem like all power and no sex. But if the goal of the law is to regulate the harasser's actions rather than simply to provide a remedy to the victim, it is his perspective that must be understood rather than hers.

"Because of Sex"

Although many commentators underestimate the sexual component of quid pro quo harassment, many also overestimate the sexual component of some hostile-environment harassment. When the hostile environment consists of sexual expression or conduct, courts generally view that fact as conclusive proof that the actions were motivated by hostility on the basis of sex (Browne, 1997). Such motivations may in fact exist, but not all hostility or harassment directed toward a woman flows from sex-based animus even if it is expressed in a sex-based way.

Sex-based Language May Have a Variety of Motivations

Women may be called vulgar sexual names, and men may make crude overtures to women that on their face look like "sexual advances." However, when a man says something like "give me some of that stuff," his "request" is not a "sexual advance" in the sense that he is acting in the hope that the woman will respond favorably; instead it is typically a form of insult. In many cases, the insult may arise out of hostility toward women, hostility that is sometimes activated by entry of women into traditionally all-male workplaces. If it is, then the man's behavior would constitute sex discrimination under any definition. On the other hand, the conduct may actually be more about dominance, which may have nothing to do with the sex of the target, or hostility, which is only sometimes based on sex.

Insulting language is seldom sex-neutral in nature. Few of the myriad vulgar epithets that flow like water in today's culture are characteristically applied indiscriminately to both sexes. Indeed, a study that asked subjects to identify the worst things that one could call a man and the worst things that one could call a woman found no overlap in the most frequently named insults (Preston & Stanley, 1987).

Insults to women often impugn their chastity, whereas those directed toward men often challenge their masculinity. Even when the same word is used toward individuals of different sexes, the meaning may be different (for example, calling a woman a "bitch" or a "whore" means something quite different from directing those same epithets at a man).

Many people (perhaps especially men) are prone to cruel and aggressive behavior toward those they dislike or perceive to be vulnerable. Where they see weakness, they may attack. Their dislike may or may not spring from sex-based animus, but regardless of whether it does, their behavior may have sexual overtones, both because of the sexualized worldview that men tend to possess and the fact that attackers will choose language to which they believe the target is particularly sensitive. It is important to remember that men's quest for dominance has not been primarily about attaining dominance over women but rather achieving dominance over other men (Buss, 1996), a fact that may explain Gutek's (1985, p. 32) finding that in the workplace "women are less often treated disrespectfully than men are."

Is Everything "Because of Sex"?

Law professor Julie Seaman has recently argued that even when heterosexual men direct sexual behavior toward other men, their conduct is necessarily "because of sex" (Seaman, 2005, pp. 394–395). Her argument is not limited to circumstances in which men make homosexual advances toward other men, which are unproblematically "because of sex." Rather, she argues that when men gang up on another man and subject him to unwelcome horseplay of a sexual nature, they are engaging in coalition building and dominance activities that are explained "by virtue of the sex of the object of the behavior" and therefore "closely tied" to the sex of the victim (pp. 397, 401).

The only same-sex harassment case decided by the U.S. Supreme Court—*Oncale v. Sundowner Offshore Services, Inc.* (1998)—was a case of the sort that Seaman envisions. The plaintiff alleged that he was repeatedly subjected to humiliating sex-related actions, assaulted in a sexual manner (his supervisor allegedly pushed a bar of soap into his anus), and threatened with rape (although there was no indication that the harassers were homosexual). The Court rejected the lower court's categorical holding that same-sex harassment can never constitute sex discrimination and sent the case back to the lower court to decide whether the conduct was "because of sex," a matter about which the Supreme Court expressed no view. Seaman would view this conduct as clearly "because of sex" and therefore as sex discrimination. In a sense, of course, it is. It is extremely unlikely that the same cruel conduct would have been directed toward a female employee, and the harassers were certainly engaged in coalitionary behavior that is a product of their evolved male psychologies. Moreover, they were directing their aggression against another man—the primary target of men's coalitionary aggression.

The problem with Seaman's argument is that there is no logical basis for limiting it to conduct of a sexual nature. Ultimately, her argument implies that all conflict, whether intersexual or intrasexual, is "because of sex." Federal harassment law does not distinguish between sexual and nonsexual conduct. Thus, nonsexual conduct aimed by men toward women because of their sex is as much sex discrimination (that is, "because of sex") as sexual behavior that flows from the same motivation. Under Seaman's view, ordinary dominance behaviors directed by men against other men are also "because of sex" and therefore in violation of Title VII, but, inexplicably, only if they take a sexual form. By similar reasoning, conflict between women is also in many cases "because of sex," as women's conflicts with other women differ from their conflicts with men. It has often been noted, for example, that across a variety of professions, "women are the first to attack a woman who gets promoted" (Benenson & Schinazi, 2004, p. 329), a phenomenon sometimes labeled the "Queen Bee Syndrome" (Cooper, 1997). Thus conflict arising because one woman was promoted over another—which might be ascribed to simple jealousy—can also be seen, under Seaman's analysis, as "because of sex." Once sexual harassment is defined as workplace conflict of a sexual or nonsexual nature directed at either same-sex or opposite-sex co-workers, the definition expands to include virtually all workplace conflict. That may or may not be a good policy choice, but such an interpretation would "transform Title VII into a general civility code for the American workplace," a course that the Supreme Court has been unwilling to chart *(Oncale v. Sundowner Offshore Services, Inc.*, 1998, pp. 80–81).

Conclusion

The utopian workplace imagined by some—in which men and women are equally represented in all occupations and at all hierarchical levels and behave in the same desexualized, yet fundamentally feminine, manner—is not one likely to be created by our evolved minds. The tabula rasa perspective of human nature—the view that sex is just a "social construct"—has encouraged many to believe that people (especially men) can simply be educated to leave their sexual psychologies behind them and enter a workplace in which they adopt "work roles" wholly disconnected from their psyches. This same perspective has led to the adoption of a sexless "reasonable person" standard in sexual harassment law—an "ideal" androgynous blend of male and female psychologies. Failure to understand male psychology has led many women to assert that they just want to be treated like men when, in fact, for very fundamental reasons, men often do not treat each other very well.

Although many have urged a "desexualization" of the workplace, it is not clear that this is either a practical or desirable goal. A realistic view of human nature suggests that as long as men and women inhabit the same workplaces, they will interact as human beings. Part of the interaction among human beings is sexual and romantic. Although sexual harassment surveys ask whether women have ever received unwanted sexual advances in the workplace, the surveys seldom ask whether women have ever received *welcome* ones. Given the large number of workers who find their romantic partners at work (Hoffman, Clinebell, & Kilpatrick, 1997), the answer for many would probably be in the affirmative.

An understanding of evolved sex differences in sexual psychologies is essential to an understanding of the behaviors produced by those psychologies and can also assist in their management. Sexual harassment training might more productively focus on educating men and women about sex differences in perspectives to avoid miscommunication rather than simply heightening female employees' inclination to be offended. Similarly, because of the association that many men have between power and sex, educating male supervisors about the risk of oversexualized perceptions of interactions when they are in dominant positions over women may forestall much unwelcome sexual attention. Expert witnesses in sexual harassment cases— who to date have virtually all come from the "social construction of gender" school (see O'Connor, 2006)—might be of more assistance to the jury if they incorporated a more robust theoretical perspective.

Recognition of the fact that sexual harassment is a manifestation of our evolved psychologies does not mean that sexual harassment is either good or inevitable. Many behaviors having origins in our evolved psychologies are recognized to be social pathologies even if they do not reflect psychological pathologies (see Buss, 2005). Behaviors are susceptible to modification, even if our underlying psychologies are not. Finally, it should be remembered that our evolved psychologies are the source not only of sexual harassment but also of our desire to combat it.

References

Abbey, A. (1982). Sex differences in attributions for friendly behavior: Do males misperceive females' friendliness? *Journal of Personality and Social Psychology, 42,* 830–838.

Abbey, A. (1987). Misperceptions of friendly behavior as sexual interest: A survey of naturally occurring incidents. *Psychology of Women Quarterly, 11,* 173–194.

Adler, R. S., & Peirce, E. R. (1993). The legal, ethical, and social implications of the "reasonable woman" standard in sexual harassment cases. *Fordham Law Review, 61,* 773–827.

Avner, J. I. (1994). Sexual harassment: Building a consensus for change. *Kansas Journal of Law and Public Policy, 3,* 57–76.

Bargh, J. A., & Raymond, P. (1995). The naive misuse of power: Nonconscious sources of sexual harassment. *Journal of Social Issues, 51,* 85–96.

Bargh, J. A., Raymond, P., Pryor, J. B., & Strack, F. (1995). Attractiveness of the underling: An automatic power → sex association and its consequences for sexual harassment and aggression. *Journal of Personality and Social Psychology, 68,* 768–781.

Benenson, J. F., & Schinazi, J. (2004). Sex differences in reactions to outperforming same-sex friends. *British Journal of Developmental Psychology, 22,* 317–333.

Berdahl, J. L. (2007). The sexual harassment of uppity women. *Journal of Applied Psychology, 92,* 425–437.

Betzig, L. (1986). *Despotism and differential reproduction: A Darwinian view of history*. New York: Aldine.

Blumenthal, J. A. (1998). The reasonable woman standard: A meta-analytic review of gender differences in perceptions of sexual harassment. *Law and Human Behavior, 22*, 33–57.

Bourgeois, M. J., & Perkins, J. (2003). A test of evolutionary and sociocultural explanations of reactions to sexual harassment. *Sex Roles, 49*, 343–351.

Bravo, E., & Cassedy, E. (1992). *The 9 to 5 guide to combating sexual harassment*. New York: Wiley.

Brooks, L., & Perot, A. R. (1991). Reporting sexual harassment: Exploring a predictive model. *Psychology of Women Quarterly, 15*, 31–47.

Browne, K. R. (1997). An evolutionary perspective on sexual harassment: Seeking roots in biology rather than ideology. *Journal of Contemporary Legal Issues, 8*, 5–77.

Browne, K. R. (2002). *Biology at work: Rethinking sexual equality*. New Brunswick, NJ: Rutgers University Press.

Browne, K. R. (2006). Evolved sex differences and occupational segregation. *Journal of Organizational Behavior, 27*, 143–162.

Buss, D. M. (1994). *The evolution of desire: Strategies of human mating*. New York: Basic.

Buss, D. M. (1996). Sexual conflict: Evolutionary insights into feminism and the "battle of the sexes." In D. M. Buss & N. M. Malamuth (Eds.), *Sex, power, conflict: Evolutionary and feminist perspectives* (pp. 296–318). New York: Oxford University Press.

Buss, D. M. (1999). *Evolutionary psychology: The new science of the mind*. Needham Heights, MA: Allyn & Bacon.

Buss, D. M. (2004). *Evolutionary psychology: The new science of the mind* (2nd ed.). Boston: Allyn & Bacon.

Buss, D. M. (2005). *The murderer next door: Why the mind is designed to kill*. New York: Penguin.

Buss, D. M., & Schmitt, D. P. (1993). Sexual strategies theory: An evolutionary perspective on human mating. *Psychological Review, 100*, 204–232.

Chavanne, T. J., & Gallup, G. G. Jr. (1998). Variation in risk taking behavior among female college students as a function of the menstrual cycle. *Evolution and Human Behavior, 19*, 27–32.

Clutton-Brock, T. H., & Parker, G. A. (1995). Sexual coercion in animal societies. *Animal Behaviour, 49*, 1345–1365.

Colarelli, S. M., & Haaland, S. (2002). Perceptions of sexual harassment: An evolutionary psychological perspective. *Psychology, Evolution & Gender, 4*, 243–264.

Cooper, V. (1997). Homophily or the Queen Bee Syndrome: Female evaluation of female leadership. *Small Group Research, 28*, 483–499.

Corr, P. J., & Jackson, C. J. (2001). Dimensions of perceived sexual harassment: Effects of gender and status/liking of protagonist. *Personality and Individual Differences, 30*, 525–539.

Dabbs, J. M. (2000). *Heroes, rogues, and lovers*. New York: McGraw-Hill.

Defeis, E. F. (2004). Equality and the European Union. *Georgia Journal of International and Comparative Law, 32*, 73–98.

Ehrenreich, N. S. (1990). Pluralist myths and powerless men: The ideology of reasonableness in sexual harassment law. *Yale Law Journal, 99*, 1177–1234.

Ellison v. Brady, 924 F.2d 872 (9th Cir. 1991).

Farley, L. (1978). *Sexual shakedown*. New York: McGraw-Hill.

Fitzgerald, L. F., & Weitzman, L. M. (1990). Men who harass: Speculation and data. In M. A. Paludi (Ed.), *Ivory Power: Sexual Harassment on Campus* (pp. 125–140). Albany, NY: SUNY Press.

Foote, W. E., & Goodman-Delahunty, J. (2005). *Evaluating sexual harassment: Psychological, social and legal considerations in forensic examinations.* Washington, DC: American Psychological Association.

Genovese, E. D. (1976). *Roll, Jordan, roll: The world the slaves made.* New York: Vintage.

Gutek, B. A. (1985). *Sex and the workplace: The impact of sexual behavior and harassment on women, men, and organizations.* San Francisco: Jossey-Bass.

Gutek, B. A. (1992). Understanding sexual harassment at work. *Notre Dame Journal of Law, Ethics, and Public Policy, 6,* 335–358.

Gutek, B. A., Murphy, R. O., & Douma, B. (2004). A review and critique of the Sexual Experiences Questionnaire (SEQ). *Law and Human Behavior, 28,* 457–482.

Gutek, B. A., O'Connor, M. A., Melançon, R., Stockdale, M. S., Geer, T. M., & Done, R. S. (1999). The utility of the reasonable woman legal standard in hostile environment sexual harassment cases: A multimethod, multistudy examination. *Psychology, Public Policy, and Law, 5,* 596–629.

Haselton, M. G., & Buss, D. M. (2000). Error management theory: A new perspective on biases in cross-sex mind reading. *Journal of Personality and Social Psychology, 78,* 81–91.

Hoffman, L., Clinebell, S., & Kilpatrick, J. (1997). Office romances: The new battleground over employees' rights to privacy and the employers' right to intervene. *Employee Responsibilities and Rights Journal, 10,* 263–275.

Holman v. Indiana, 211 F.3d 399 (7th Circuit), *cert. denied,* 531 U.S. 880 (2000).

Juliano, A., & Schwab, S. J. (2001). The sweep of sexual harassment cases. *Cornell Law Review, 86,* 548–593.

Khoo, P. N., & Senn, C. Y. (2004). Not wanted in the inbox!: Evaluations of unsolicited and harassing e-mail. *Psychology of Women Quarterly, 28,* 204–214.

Kelly, J. M. (2000). Sexual harassment of employees by customers and other third parties: American and British views. *Texas Tech Law Review, 31,* 807–867.

Lafontaine, E., & Tredeau, L. (1986). The frequency, sources, and correlates of sexual harassment among women in traditional male occupations. *Sex Roles, 15,* 433–442.

Madera, J. M., Podratz, K. E., King, E. G., & Hebl, M. R. (2007). Schematic responses to sexual harassment complainants: The influence of gender and physical attractiveness. *Sex Roles, 56,* 223–230.

Magley, V. J., Hulin, C. L., Fitzgerald, L. F., & DeNardo, M. (1999). Outcomes of self-labeling sexual harassment. *Journal of Applied Psychology, 84,* 390–402.

Mealey, L. (1992). Alternative adaptive models of rape. *Behavioral and Brain Sciences, 15,* 397–398.

Meritor Savings Bank, FSB v. Vinson, 477 U.S. 57 (1986).

Muehlenhard, C. L., & Hollabaugh, L. C. (1988). Do women sometimes say no when they mean yes? The prevalence and correlates of women's token resistance to sex. *Journal of Personality and Social Psychology, 54,* 872–879.

O'Connor, M. (2006). Expert testimony in sexual harassment cases: Its scope, limits, and effectiveness. In M. Costanzo, D. Krauss, & K. Pezdek (Eds.), *Expert psychological testimony for the courts* (pp. 119–148). Mahwah, NJ: Lawrence Erlbaum.

O'Donohue, W., & Bowers, A. H. (2006). Pathways to false allegations of sexual harassment. *Journal of Investigative Psychology and Offender Profiling, 3,* 47–74.

Oncale v. Sundowner Offshore Services, Inc., 523 U.S. 75 (1998).

Oshige, M. (1995). What's sex got to do with it? *Stanford Law Review, 47,* 565–594.

Palmer, C. T., & Thornhill, R. (2003). Straw men and fairy tales: Evaluating reactions to *A Natural History of Rape. Journal of Sex Research, 40,* 249–255.

Perry, E. L., Kulik, C. T., & Bourhis, A. C. (2004). The reasonable woman standard: Effects on sexual harassment court decisions. *Law and Human Behavior, 28*, 9–27.

Preston, K., & Stanley, K. (1987). "What's the worst thing . . . ?" Gender directed insults. *Sex Roles, 17*, 209–219.

Radtke v. Everett, 501 N.W.2d 155 (Mich. 1993).

Ratchnevsky, P. (1991). *Genghis Khan: His life and legacy*. New York: Blackwell.

Ream, S. L. (2000). When service with a smile invites more than satisfied customers: Third-party sexual harassment and the implications of charges against Safeway. *Hastings Women's Law Journal, 11*, 107–122.

Rotundo, M., Nguyen, D.-H., & Sackett, P. R. (2001). A meta-analytic review of gender differences in perceptions of sexual harassment. *Journal of Applied Psychology, 86*, 914–922.

Schneider, B. E. (1982). Consciousness about sexual harassment among heterosexual and lesbian women workers. *Journal of Social Issues, 38*, 75–97.

Seaman, Julie A. (2005). Form and (dys)function in sexual harassment law: Biology, culture, and the spandrels of Title VII. *Arizona State Law Journal, 37*, 321–433.

Semonsky, M. R., & Rosenfeld, L. V. (1994). Perceptions of sexual violations: Denying a kiss, stealing a kiss. *Sex Roles, 30*, 503–520.

Stockdale, M. S. (1993). The role of sexual misperceptions of women's friendliness in an emerging theory of sexual harassment. *Journal of Vocational Behavior, 42*, 84–101.

Struckman-Johnson, C., & Struckman-Johnson, D. (1994). Men's reactions to hypothetical female sexual advances: A beauty bias in response to sexual coercion. *Sex Roles, 31*, 387–405.

Studd, M. V., & Gattiker, U. E. (1991). The evolutionary psychology of sexual harassment in organizations. *Ethology and Sociobiology, 12*, 249–290.

Tangri, S. S., Burt, M., & Johnson, L. (1982). Sexual harassment at work: Three explanatory models. *Journal of Social Issues, 38*, 33–54.

Terpstra, D. E., & Baker, D. D. (1986). A framework for the study of sexual harassment. *Basic and Applied Social Psychology, 7*, 17–34.

Thornhill, R., & Palmer, C. T. (2000). *A natural history of rape: Biological bases of sexual coercion*. Cambridge, MA: MIT Press.

Tiger, L. (1997). Comment on article by Kingsley Browne. *Journal of Contemporary Legal Issues, 8*, 79–86.

Wiener, R. L., & Hurt, L. E. (2000). How do people evaluate social sexual conduct at work? A psycholegal model. *Journal of Applied Psychology, 85*, 75–85.

Willness, C. R., Steel, P., & Lee, K. (2007). A meta-analysis of the antecedents and consequences of workplace sexual harassment. *Personnel Psychology, 60*, 127–162.

Workman, J. E., & Johnson, K. P. (1991). The role of cosmetics in attributions about sexual harassment. *Sex Roles, 24*, 759–769.

Yagil, D., Karnieli-Miller, O., Eisikovits, Z., & Enosh, G. (2006). Is that a "no"? The interpretation of responses to unwanted sexual attention. *Sex Roles, 54*, 251–260.

York, K. M., Barclay, L. A., & Zajack, A. B. (1997). Preventing sexual harassment: The effect of multiple training methods. *Employee Responsibilities and Rights Journal, 10*, 277–289.

Zerjal, T., Xue, Y., Bertorelle, G., Wells, R. S., Bao, W., Zhu, S., et al. (2003). The genetic legacy of the Mongols. *American Journal of Human Genetics, 72*, 717–721.

Zurbriggen, E. L. (2000). Social motives and cognitive power-sex associations: Predictors of aggressive sexual behavior. *Journal of Personality and Social Psychology, 78*, 559–581.

6

Evolutionary Psychological Perspectives on Rape

WILLIAM F. MCKIBBIN, TODD K. SHACKELFORD, AARON T. GOETZ, AND VALERIE G. STARRATT

Rape is a fact of life across cultures (Broude & Greene, 1978; Rozée, 1993; Sanday, 1981). In U.S. samples, estimates of the prevalence of rape are as high as 13% for women (Kilpatrick, Edmunds, & Seymour, 1992; Resnick, Kilpatrick, Dansky, Saunders, & Best, 1993). Rape is likely more common, however, because rapes often go unreported (Kilpatrick et al., 1992). Although other forms of rape occur (e.g., male–male rape), this chapter focuses on the rape of women by men. Definitions of rape vary. It is typically defined, and will be defined in this chapter, as the use or threat of force to achieve sexual penile-vaginal penetration of a woman without her consent (Kilpatrick et al., 1992; Thornhill & Palmer, 2000).

Rape became a public and academic focus following the publication of Brownmiller's (1975) book, *Against Our Will: Men, Women, and Rape*. Brownmiller argued that rape is "a conscious process of intimidation by which *all men* keep *all women* in a state of fear" (p. 15, emphasis in original). Since then, feminist theories of rape have dominated the rape research literature. A prominent version of feminist theory contends that rape is the result of social traditions in which men have dominated political, economic, and other sources of power (Ellis, 1989). Feminist theorists inspired by Brownmiller often interpret rape as a method by which men maintain this power and dominance over women. Moreover, feminist theorists have argued explicitly that rape is not about sexual gratification and often seem more focused on making ideological rather than scientific statements about human psychology and behavior (Thornhill & Palmer, 2000).

This chapter reviews the topic of rape from a modern evolutionary psychological perspective (see, e.g., Barkow, Cosmides, & Tooby, 1992; Buss, 2004). Evolutionary psychology is a powerful heuristic tool that can be used to generate new, testable

101

hypotheses across all domains of psychology. Evolutionary psychology rests on several key premises (Buss, 2004). The first premise states that natural selection is the only known process capable of producing complex functional systems such as the human brain. The complexity of human behavior can only be understood completely by taking into account human evolutionary history and natural selection. Second, behavior depends on *evolved psychological mechanisms*. These are information-processing mechanisms housed in the brain that register and process specific information and generate as output specific behaviors, physiological activity, or input relayed to other psychological mechanisms. Third, evolved psychological mechanisms are functionally specialized to perform a specific task or to solve a specific problem that recurrently affected reproductive success over evolutionary history. This premise is often referred to as *domain specificity*. Finally, the *numerousness* premise states that human brains consist of many specific evolved psychological mechanisms that work together to produce behavior. Together with a number of other theoretical tools and heuristics provided by modern evolutionary theory, these premises are used to generate evolutionary theories of psychology and behavior.

One such heuristic tool that informs evolutionary psychology is parental investment theory (Trivers, 1972). Parental investment theory consists of two important premises. First, in sexually reproducing species, the sex that invests more in offspring (typically the female) will be more discriminating about mating. Second, the sex that invests less in offspring (typically the male) will be more intrasexually competitive for sexual access to the higher-investing sex. These premises have been supported in research with numerous species, including humans. Human females, like the females of most biparental species, invest more in offspring whereas males invest more in mating effort. These sex differences are greatest in short-term mating contexts (Buss, 1994a, 1994b, 2004).

Misconceptions about Evolutionary Psychology

Some scholars believe that evolutionary psychological research is conducted to justify racism, sexism, or other undesirable "-isms." For example, Tang-Martinez (1997, p. 116) describes a common feminist view that evolutionary psychology is "inherently misogynistic and provides a justification for the oppression of women." However, the feminists to whom Tang-Martinez refers are committing what is known as the *naturalistic fallacy*: the error of deriving what *ought* to be from what *is*. This error can be demonstrated clearly with an example: No sensible person would argue that a scientist researching the causes of cancer is thereby justifying or promoting cancer. Yet some people continue to argue that investigating rape from an evolutionary perspective justifies or legitimizes rape (e.g., Baron, 1985; Marshall & Barrett, 1990, cited in Thornhill & Palmer, 2000).

Related to the naturalistic fallacy is the false belief of *genetic determinism*—the idea that behavior is unalterable, programmed, or otherwise unchangeable. This argument has been debunked numerous times. Biologist John Maynard Smith noted that genetic determinism is "an incorrect idea that is largely irrelevant, because it is not held by anyone, or at least not by any competent evolutionary biologist" (1997, p. 524). No evolutionary psychologist would argue that because rape is produced by evolved mechanisms, it cannot be prevented or we should simply accept its occurrence. The goal of evolutionary psychology, like the goal of any science, is to further our understanding of the phenomenon of interest, which in this case is rape. Researching rape from an evolutionary psychological perspective does not justify or promote this heinous act. Whether evolutionary psychological hypotheses about rape are correct, new perspectives often allow researchers to gain new insights into the targeted phenomenon. Gaining a greater understanding about why rape occurs is fundamental to decreasing its occurrence.

Finally, researchers using an evolutionary psychological perspective often frame hypotheses in terms of the costs and benefits to an organism of performing a particular behavior. These costs and benefits refer to the effects on reproductive success over evolutionary time—that is, costs decreased the probability of successful reproduction whereas benefits increased the probability of successful reproduction. These terms are sometimes misconstrued as referring to a more general idea of perceived costs and benefits to the individual or to society. However, these terms carry no moral or ethical meaning and are used only in the context of naturally selected biological functioning.

Comparative Psychology of Sexual Coercion and Rape

Sexual coercion and rape occur in many species. In fact, evolutionary metatheory has been used to generate the hypotheses that sexual coercion and rape occur in species in which males are more aggressive, more eager to mate, more sexually assertive, and less discriminating in choosing a mate (Thornhill & Palmer, 2000). Sexual coercion and rape occur in insects (Dunn, Crean, & Gilburn, 2002; Linder & Rice, 2005; Thornhill, 1980, 1981, 1987; Vahed, 2002), amphibians, reptiles (Olsson, 1995; Reyer, Frei, & Som, 1999, Shine, Langkilde, & Mason, 2003; Sztatecsny, Jehle, Burke, & Hödl, 2006), fish (Magurran, 2001; Plath, Parzefall, & Schlupp, 2003), birds (Gowaty & Buschhaus, 1998; McKinney, Derrickson, & Mineau, 1983; Pizzari & Birkhead, 2000), and primates (Robbins, 1999; Smuts & Smuts, 1993; Wrangham & Peterson, 1996), among other species.

Two species in particular provide clear examples of adaptations in males to sexually coerce and rape females. A large body of evidence demonstrates that male scorpionflies (*Panorpa vulgaris*) have an anatomical feature that is designed to facilitate sexual access to a female in a coercive fashion—that is, rape. They possess a notal organ that is used specifically and exclusively for rape (Thornhill, 1980, 1981, 1987; Thornhill & Sauer, 1991). Scorpionfly males do not always secure copulations through rape. Instead, males display conditional mating strategies. Males that are able to produce a nuptial gift of food for the female are allowed to mate without coercion. Males that are not able to do so resort to the conditional rape strategy and use of the notal organ (Thornhill, 1980, 1981, 1987; Thornhill & Palmer, 2000). Thus, male scorpionflies exhibit evidence of specific anatomical traits that evolved to facilitate rape. They also exhibit evidence of a conditional strategy of sexual coercion.

Male orangutans (*Pongo pygmaeus*) also deploy conditional strategies of sexual coercion and rape. Orangutans are unique among apes in that they live solitary lives rather than in groups. Females therefore do not have mates or kin that may deter or prevent rape (Wrangham & Peterson, 1996). This fact alone makes rape a more viable strategy for male orangutans. Forced copulations account for up to half of all copulations (Mitani, 1985; Wrangham & Peterson, 1996). These forced copulations seem to be performed primarily by a subset of males. Wrangham and Peterson (1996) reviewed evidence indicating that male orangutans exist as one of two distinct morphs or behavioral types. The large morphs weigh significantly more, move much slower, and are typically able to find females willing to mate. The small morphs are typically unable to find females willing to mate with them. These small morphs are more likely to chase down and rape females. This represents a conditional strategy. If the smaller males are unable to gain sexual access to females through intrasexual competition and by being attractive to females, they may use the conditional strategy of chasing down and raping a female.

Comparative evidence indicates that males of many species have evolved strategies to sexually coerce and rape females. Rape in humans must also reflect adaptations constructed over evolutionary time. Although numerous explanations have been offered to explain rape in humans (e.g., learning or enculturation, mental illness, personality differences, drug and alcohol use, and other factors; Bergen & Bukovec, 2006; Brecklin & Ullman, 2001; Dean & Malamuth, 1997; Lalumiére & Quinsey, 1996), these factors alone cannot explain the existence of such seemingly complex behavior. At best, these factors may increase the likelihood of rape, but they cannot explain the complex organized behavior seen in rape. Only two explanations are likely to be true: that rape is the product of specialized psychological adaptation, or that it is a by-product of other adaptations in the male mind (Palmer & Thornhill, 2003a, 2003b; Thornhill & Palmer, 2000). What evidence supports the hypothesis that rape is the result of an adaptation?

Evidence of Human Adaptations for Sexual Coercion and Rape

For rape to be produced by evolved psychological mechanisms, it must have recurrently generated reproductive benefits for ancestral rapists. These benefits must have outweighed the significant costs that men may incur if they attempt or successfully complete a rape. Despite the costs, there is evidence that rape may have increased the number of women with whom ancestral men copulated and, therefore, the reproductive success of rapist males (Gottschall & Gottschall, 2003; Holmes, Resnick,

Kilpatrick, & Best, 1996; Krueger, 1988; Shields & Shields, 1983; Thornhill, 1999; Thornhill & Palmer, 2000).

Men do not exhibit morphological features analogous to the notal clamp of male scorpionflies. Any rape adaptations that men possess are likely to occur in the form of psychological mechanisms. Researchers, particularly Thornhill and Thornhill (1992; see also Thornhill, 1999; Thornhill & Palmer, 2000) have identified several possible rape adaptations. These adaptations are proposed to be universal features of male psychology that are activated under specific circumstances. Empirical support for evolutionary psychological theories of rape has been mixed. For example, the "loser" or mate deprivation model of sexual coercion, in which men with limited or no sexual access to females rape for lack of other options, typically has not been supported (Malamuth, Huppin, & Paul, 2005; but see also later in this chapter).

A hypothesized design feature of rape adaptations involves mechanisms that cause men to evaluate the sexual attractiveness of rape victims differently than that of consensual partners. Specifically, a rapist might be more successful reproductively by maximizing the chance that a one-time forced copulation will result in pregnancy. According to this hypothesis, a would-be rapist may be more likely to target a highly fertile woman than a woman who is less fertile (Thornhill & Palmer, 2000). Human female fertility (current likelihood of conception per copulation) peaks in the early to mid-20s. Therefore, if women in this age range are overrepresented in reports of rape, it is possible that this reflects a male adaptation that leads to raping fertile women more often than nonfertile women. Numerous studies have documented that young women are most often targeted by rapists, and that women of peak fertility are overrepresented in reported and unreported rapes (Ghiglieri, 2000; Greenfield, 1997; Kilpatrick et al., 1992; Shields & Shields, 1983; Thornhill & Palmer, 2000; Thornhill & Thornhill, 1983). This evidence does not support exclusively rape-specific adaptation, however, because men exhibit a preference for sexually attractive partners in general, not just in contexts of rape (see, e.g., Buss, 1994a, 1994b, 2004).

We, like others (e.g., Thornhill & Palmer, 2000), propose that rape is a conditional strategy that may potentially be deployed by any man. Shields and Shields (1983) argued that men use a conditional mating strategy consisting of many mating tactics, including rape. At least one-third of men admit they would rape under specific conditions, and many men report coercive sexual fantasies (see Malamuth et al., 2005, for a review). Such evidence suggests that rape adaptations might be universal features of male psychology. Empirical support for evolutionary psychological hypotheses of rape has been mixed. For example, the mate deprivation model of sexual coercion, in which men with limited or no sexual access to females rape for lack of other options, typically has not been supported (Malamuth et al., 2005; but see also later in this chapter). This mixed support may reflect a lack of appreciation that there may be several distinct types of rapists. For example, Mealey (1995) proposed that men with psychopathy represent a genetically distinct morph different from "normal" men without psychopathy. Lalumière, Harris, Quinsey, and Rice (2005) presented in a related argument that a small proportion of antisocial men who are more likely to rape form a qualitatively distinct portion of the population. Similarly, as a heuristic strategy, we have defined several rapist types. Specifying these types may generate new insights and testable hypotheses. Other researchers have suggested that defining subtypes of rapists can be potentially valuable (Malamuth et al., 2005).

Our view of rape may be a more nuanced view of rape than has previously been explored. We hypothesize that rape may represent a conditional mating strategy, present in all men, that may result from several qualitatively different ancestral contexts combined with individual difference factors among men. Specifically, we propose five types of rapists (or contexts of rape): (1) disadvantaged men who resort to rape, (2) "specialized" rapists who are sexually aroused by violent sex, (3) men who rape opportunistically, (4) high-mating-effort men who are dominant and often psychopathic, and (5) partner-rapists motivated by assessments of increased risk of sperm competition. We next discuss evidence for each of these types of rapists.

The Disadvantaged Male

The first hypothesized rapist type is characterized by men who are motivated to rape if they have no other means of securing copulations. This may be referred to as the *disadvantaged male* hypothesis. This hypothesis has previously been referred to as the *mate deprivation hypothesis* (Lalumiére, Chalmers, Quinsey, & Seto, 1996). It is supported by data indicating that rapes are committed disproportionately by men with low socioeconomic status (Kalichman, Williams, Cherry, Belcher, & Nachimson, 1998; Thornhill & Thornhill, 1983). Furthermore, Krill, Lake, and Platek (2006) presented evidence that men convicted of rape display lower facial symmetry, an indicator of poor genetic quality. Facial symmetry is linked positively with physical and psychological health (Shackelford & Larsen, 1997), and men with lower facial symmetry are perceived as less attractive and as less desirable mates (Gangestad, Thornhill, & Yeo, 1994; Gangestad & Thornhill, 1999; Sugiyama, 2005). Deprived of mates by normal means, some men may resort to rape. Identification of such a rapist type, however, would not necessarily imply a conditional strategy for rape. One can imagine that when reproductive opportunities are dismal, some men might be motivated to take more risks in all domains, with one domain being sexual assertiveness, which might lead to rape.

The Specialized Rapist

Another type of rapist may be the *specialized rapist*. Men in this group are distinguished by being sexually aroused by violent sexual stimuli. These men may possess a psychology that produces differences in sexual arousal in response to depictions of rapes versus depictions of consensual sex. Because rape carries high potential costs for the rapist, particularly if caught in the act, rapists with a psychology that motivated quicker arousal and ejaculation during rape might have been more successful than men who did not possess such a psychology (Thornhill & Palmer, 2000).

Support for the existence of this hypothesized group has been generated by investigating whether men are aroused by depictions of rape versus depictions of casual sex. Meta-analyses indicate that convicted rapists demonstrate greater sexual arousal to scenes of sexual coercion involving force than do nonrapists (Hall, Shondrick, & Hirschman, 1993; Lalumiére & Quinsey, 1994; Lohr, Adams, & Davis, 1997; Thornhill & Thornhill, 1992).

Specialized rapists also might possess mechanisms that cause them to evaluate the sexual attractiveness of rape victims differently than the sexual attractiveness of consensual partners. According to this hypothesis, a rapist will be more likely to rape a highly fertile woman than a woman who is less fertile (Thornhill & Palmer, 2000). Research has demonstrated support for this hypothesis (see earlier sections for details). However, it is unclear whether this reflects a specialized rape adaptation or a more generalized male mating strategy. Future research might test the hypothesis that men evaluate the sexual attractiveness of rape victims differently from the sexual attractiveness of consensual partners by examining whether men target for rape reproductive-aged women who are in the most fertile phases of their menstrual cycles. Such a finding would provide stronger support for this rapist type.

If a rape is a one-time event, it might make adaptive sense for the rapist to inseminate the woman with an ejaculate that contains a high sperm count or that otherwise increases the chance of successful fertilization. Indeed, Thornhill and Palmer (2000) have hypothesized that some rapists may be capable of producing a high-sperm-count ejaculate that would increase the chance of fertilization. Men seem to be capable of unconsciously adjusting sperm number in ejaculates, such as in response to a greater risk of sperm competition (Baker & Bellis, 1989, 1993), but it is unknown whether rapists adjust sperm numbers during rape. Evidence for this would lend support to the specialized rapist type.

Researchers have argued that premature ejaculation might have been adaptive ancestrally, perhaps by minimizing the chances of predation or detection by jealous mates (Hong, 1984; see also Gallup & Burch, 2004). It also might make adaptive sense for a rapist to ejaculate as soon as possible after achieving copulation. This would reduce the chances of being injured or retaliated against. Therefore, it is possible that selection may have acted to minimize the time it takes for a man to ejaculate during a rape. Research is needed to test this hypothesis. For example, one might compare the average pre-ejaculatory copulation length during rape versus during consensual copulation.

There is indirect evidence corroborating the hypothesis that rapists' ejaculates are more competitive than those of nonrapists. Gottschall and Gottschall (2003) estimated that pregnancy rates resulting from rape were two times that of consensual per-incident rates. That is, approximately 6% of rapes result in pregnancy compared to approximately 3% of consensual copulations. Even after controlling statistically for the age of the woman, the researchers identified a higher conception rate for rapes than for consensual sex. This evidence suggests that there may be something different about rapists' psychology or the competitiveness of their ejaculates. Further research is needed, however. One promising area of research is the study of semen chemistry. Burch and Gallup (2006) hypothesized that men may have an adaptation that functions to adjust semen chemistry to cause ovulation immediately following a rape. Future research could profitably test this hypothesis, perhaps by comparing chemical constituents of ejaculates produced by men exposed experimentally to a coercive sexual scenario with ejaculates produced by men exposed experimentally to a noncoercive sexual scenario.

Opportunistic Rapists

The third hypothesized rapist type is that of the *opportunistic rapist*. These men generally seek out receptive women, but they might shift to sexual coercion and rape if women are not receptive or if the associated benefits of coercive sex outweigh the costs—for example, if the chances of injury or retaliation by the victim, the victim's family, or society are particularly low. All rapists are predicted to be attuned to a potential victim's vulnerability, but an opportunistic rapist is especially so. The universality of laws and societal norms prohibiting rape (wife rape being a special exception; see further on) indicates an appreciation that men are more likely to rape when the costs are low (Palmer, 1989; Thornhill & Palmer, 2000). The fact that rapes regularly occur during wartime has been presented as evidence of the assessment of victim vulnerability and decreased likelihood of detection (e.g., Gottschall, 2004). Men in war are likely to assume lowered costs of committing rape because punishment or retaliation is less likely.

The evidence for the existence of this type of rapist, however, is minimal. Theft also is common during war, and for the same reason: punishment or retaliation is unlikely. Support for this hypothesized type may be seen in research demonstrating that women with family members, particularly adult male family members, living nearby are much less likely to be physically assaulted by their partner (Figueredo et al., 2001; Kanin, 1957). This suggests that potential rapists are attending to the probability of retaliation by a victim's adult male family members.

High Mating-effort Rapists

A fourth hypothesized type is the *high mating-effort* rapist. High mating-effort rapists, in contrast to other types, such as disadvantaged rapists, appear to be more sexually experienced (Lalumière & Quinsey, 1996). Rapists of this type may be characterized as aggressive, dominant, and having high self-esteem. These men often are the perpetrators of date or acquaintance rape. Research evidence appears to support this rapist type. Such rapists often may be characterized as psychopathic (Lalumière et al., 2005). Lalumière et al. argue that high mating effort is an important facet of psychopathy. They claim that although most men appear to deploy mating strategies according to environmental contexts, psychopathic men deploy a high mating-effort strategy in most contexts, pursuing many partners with little investment and using coercion and rape when noncoercive tactics fail. There is evidence that psychopathic men display lower fluctuating asymmetry, an index of overall fitness (Lalumière, Harris, & Rice, 2001), further distinguishing this rapist type from others, such as the disadvantaged rapist.

Research evidence corroborates the plausibility of this rapist type. Dean and Malamuth (1997), for example, found that men who scored high on a Sexual Experience measure "were more likely to report sexual coercion if they were also self-centered as opposed to nurturant" (p. 74). Premarital sexual coercion is associated with sexual promiscuity, earlier onset of sexual activity, and greater sexual experience (Christopher, Owens, & Stecker, 1993; Lalumière et al., 2005). Lalumière and Quinsey (1996) found that a strong indicator of past sexual coercion is positive self-perceived mating success and an extensive history of uncommitted sexual relationships. Finally, the risk of date rape is greater when the man initiated the date, spent money on the woman, and provided transportation (Muehlenhard & Linton, 1987). Perceived relative deprivation, in which an individual's (high) expectations about having sex are not satisfied (Malamuth et al., 2005), also may play a role in the sexually coercive behavior of high mating-effort men. For example, men who report a greater likelihood of committing rape tend to endorse statements expressing an increased perception of mate deprivation but do not report an overall fewer number of sexual opportunities (Glick & Fiske, 1996; Lonsway & Fitzgerald, 1995). More research must be conducted to test this hypothesized rapist type. For example, researchers might test whether men convicted of date rape or sexual assault score higher on measures of psychopathy.

Partner Rapists

A final hypothesized rapist type includes men motivated to rape their partners under conditions of increased sperm competition risk. Sperm competition is the competition that can occur between males for each to have his sperm fertilize a female (Parker, 1970). The outcome of sperm competition is favored toward males who produce greater numbers of sperm (Parker, 1970, 1982; Pound, Shackelford, & Goetz, 2006). Rape in response to risk of sperm competition is most likely to occur when a man learns or suspects that his long-term partner recently has been sexually unfaithful (Thornhill & Thornhill, 1992).

Partner rapes account for a substantial proportion of reported rapes (Bergen, 1996; Kilpatrick et al., 1992; Russell, 1990). Between 10% and 26% of women report experiencing rape in marriage (Finkelhor & Yllo, 1985; Hadi, 2000; Painter & Farrington, 1999; Russell, 1990; Watts, Keough, Ndlovu, & Kwaramba, 1998). Women are particularly likely to be raped by their partner during a breakup instigated by men's concerns about their partner's infidelity (Thornhill & Palmer, 2000). Until very recently in Western society, it was not considered a crime if a man forced his wife to have sex with him. The right of men to sexual access to their partner was considered absolute, and only relatively recently in the United States have men been prosecuted for raping their wives (Bergen, 1996; Russell, 1990).

Studying men's psychological reactions to risk of sperm competition is another possible method for testing the hypothesis that men are motivated to rape their partners under conditions of sperm competition. If men exhibit psychological reactions to risk of sperm competition in noncoercive contexts, it is also possible that they do so in coercive or rape contexts. Research evidence indicates that men do display such psychological reactions. For example, men are more aroused by and prefer sexually explicit images that suggest the occurrence of sperm competition than by sexually explicit images that do not suggest the occurrence of sperm competition (Kilgallon & Simmons, 2005; Pound, 2002). Furthermore, men who spend a greater proportion of time apart from their partners since the couple's last copulation (and therefore face a higher risk of sperm competition) report that they find their partner more attractive, are more interested in copulating with their partner, and believe that their partner is more interested in copulating with them (Shackelford, Goetz, McKibbin, & Starratt, 2007; Shackelford et al., 2002). These results are independent of relationship satisfaction, total time since last copulation, and total time spent apart. The psychological mechanisms that lead men to experience greater interest in copulation and to believe their partner is interested in copulation with them also may be part of the suite of mechanisms that lead men to sexually coerce or rape their partners.

Finally, in a direct test of the hypothesis that men may rape their partners under conditions of sperm competition, Goetz and Shackelford (2006) documented in two studies that men's sexually coercive behavior is positively related to their partner's infidelities, that is, to the risk of sperm competition. Men with partners who committed infidelities or who suspected that their partner had committed infidelities (indicating increased risk of sperm competition) were more likely to perform sexually coercive behaviors, including rape. These findings lend support to the hypothesized psychological mechanisms that motivate men to commit partner rape in response to risk of sperm competition.

In summary, it may be useful to characterize rapists as falling into one of several categories or types, specifically (1) disadvantaged men, (2) specialized rapists, (3) opportunistic rapists, (4) high mating-effort men, and (5) partner rapists. Although future research is needed to test the hypothesized types of rapists, prior studies offer some preliminary support for this model. We have identified potential unique ancestral contexts and individual differences that may have selected for conditional rape strategies. But these contexts and individual differences can be overlapping. This is to be expected, however, as we argue that all men may possess adaptations to rape. For example, a high mating-effort context and an opportunity context are not mutually exclusive: a man who devotes much of his time and energy to gaining short-term matings may be even more likely to commit rape when circumstances (such as wartime) allow him to do so at decreased cost (e.g., when there is a low chance of retaliation).

Again, it is important to note that the existence of adaptations to rape does not mean that rape is inevitable or justified. Like any psychological mechanism, rape mechanisms require functioning genetic and environmental components. Rape is predicted to occur only under specific environmental circumstances that activate men's evolved psychology. Furthermore, because rape behaviors may have a genetic component does not mean that men cannot control their behavior. Just as men thwart their evolved psychology every time they choose less calorically dense food over more calorically dense food (as when one is on a diet), so too can men thwart evolved mechanisms that may lead them to sexually coerce or rape. Only through thorough research and a broad understanding of sexual coercion, including its evolved basis, can we hope to reduce or prevent rape.

Women's Defenses against Rape

Rape is a traumatic event that is likely to have been a recurrent problem for women over evolutionary history. Rape often leads to many negative consequences for women; therefore, women may have evolved psychological mechanisms designed to motivate rape avoidance behaviors. There are several reasons that rape is traumatic for women. These include disrupting a woman's parental care, causing a woman's partner to abandon her, and causing a woman serious physical injury (Thornhill & Palmer, 2000) or death. Women are sometimes killed after being raped (Shackelford, 2002a, 2002b). Aside from death, perhaps the greatest cost to women who are raped is the circumvention of their mate choice (Wilson, Daly, & Scheib, 1997). This is because anything that circumvents women's choice in mating can severely jeopardize their reproductive success (Symons, 1979).

Researchers have speculated that a variety of female traits evolved to reduce the risks of being raped. Smuts (1992) argued that women form alliances with groups of men and other women for protection against would-be rapists. Similarly, Wilson and Mesnick (1997) proposed and found support for the *bodyguard hypothesis*: women's mate preferences for physically and socially dominant men may reflect anti-rape adaptation. Of course, women may form alliances or prefer dominant mates for reasons other than to avoid rape. Alliances offer protection from such dangers as assault or predation, and dominant mates may possess higher-quality genes, for example. Finally, Davis and Gallup (2006) proposed the intriguing possibility that preeclampsia and spontaneous abortion may be adaptations that function to terminate pregnancies not in the woman's best reproductive interests, such as those resulting from rape. Relatively little empirical work has been conducted to identify specific psychological mechanisms that evolved to solve the recurrent problem of rape avoidance.

Thornhill and Thornhill (1990a, 1990b, 1990c, 1991) have demonstrated that the psychological pain that women experience after being raped may be produced by evolved mechanisms designed to focus women's attention on the circumstances of the rape, particularly the social cirumstances that resulted in the rape. Thornhill and Thornhill (1990a, 1990b, 1990c, 1991) argue that, like physical pain, psychological pain motivates individuals to attend to the circumstances that led to the pain and to avoid those circumstances in the future. Victims of rape who have more to lose in terms of future reproductive success will also experience more psychological pain relative to women with less to lose in terms of future reproductive success (Thornhill & Thornhill, 1983, 1990a; Thornhill & Palmer, 2000). For example, women of reproductive age are hypothesized to experience more psychological pain due to the greater risk of conception. Thornhill and Thornhill (1990a) demonstrated support for this hypothesis, documenting that reproductive-aged women are more traumatized by rape than are post-reproductive-aged women or pre-reproductive-aged girls.

The research conducted by Thornhill and Thornhill focuses on the aftereffects of being raped and on the psychological pain that may motivate women to avoid the circumstances leading to the rape. Very little research, however, has been conducted to identify the specific behaviors women may deploy to avoid being raped. Scheppele and Bart (1983) conducted interviews of women who had been raped or who had been attacked and successfully avoided being raped. Some of these women described "rules of rape avoidance" (p. 64) and how they followed them—for example, "I would never be alone on the street" and "I would watch what I wear" (p. 65). These qualitative data provide preliminary evidence for rape avoidance adaptations in women.

Petralia and Gallup (2002) examined whether a woman's capacity to resist rape varies across the menstrual cycle. Women in the fertile phase of their menstrual cycle showed an increase in handgrip strength, but only when presented with a sexual coercion scenario. Women not in their fertile phase did not show an increase in handgrip strength. Furthermore, women in all other conditions, including women in the fertile phase who were presented with the neutral control scenario, showed a *decrease* in hand strength post-test. This provides evidence for specialized mechanisms designed to motivate women to behave in ways that cause them to be less likely to be raped. Women who experience increased strength during their fertile phase would be better equipped to defend themselves from would-be rapists. The research by Petralia and Gallup (2002) provides evidence consistent with the hypothesis that women have evolved mechanisms that motivate rape avoidance behaviors.

Chavanne and Gallup (1998) investigated the performance of risky behaviors by women in the fertile phase of their menstrual cycles. A sample of women were asked where they were in their menstrual cycles and to indicate whether they had performed a range of behaviors in the past twenty-four hours. Behaviors were ranked by women in a previous study according to how likely they thought performing the behaviors might be to result in a woman being sexually assaulted, with riskier behaviors given higher risk scores. Individuals' risky behavior was estimated by taking the summed composite score of all performed activities. Women in the fertile phase of their menstrual cycle reported performing fewer behaviors representing a greater risk of being raped. There was no difference in the likelihood of performing low-risk behaviors between women in their fertile phase and women outside their fertile phase. This research has some methodological problems that prevent firm conclusions, however. First, the researchers used only one method (i.e., the forward-cycle method) to assess women's menstrual status. Also, Chavanne and Gallup do not specify how the inventory of risky behaviors was developed, noting only that a preliminary sample of women rated the riskiness of the behaviors. In addition, the dependent variable may be confounded by diversity of activity. For example, a woman who performed ten non-risky behaviors (each scored as a 1 on the riskiness scale) could receive the same score as a woman who performed two high-risk behaviors (each scored as a 5 on the riskiness scale; see Bröder and Hohmann, 2003, for discussion). Despite these methodological issues, this research documented a significant decrease in performance of risky behaviors by women in the fertile phase of their menstrual cycle. This evidence is consistent with the hypothesized function of rape avoidance mechanisms, particularly when women are fertile.

Chavanne and Gallup's (1998) study was replicated by Bröder and Hohmann (2003) using a within-subjects design. Twenty-six women who did not use oral contraceptives were tested weekly for four successive weeks. The results indicated that women in the fertile phase of their cycle selectively inhibit behaviors that would expose them to a higher risk of being raped while performing *more* non-risky behaviors. These results provide a conceptual replication of the results reported by Chavanne and Gallup. Women perform fewer risky behaviors when they are fertile, while still demonstrating a higher overall activity level (Morris & Udry, 1970) and even while engaging in more consensual sex (Morris & Udry, 1982). This selective behavior indicates that women may have evolved specialized psychological mechanisms designed to motivate behaviors that decrease the risk of being raped. Although this study addressed many of the issues in the Chavanne and Gallup research, there is still no indication of how risky behaviors were identified. This study also used the somewhat problematic forward- and reverse-cycle counting methods for identifying the fertile phase of the menstrual cycle, both of which depend on the potentially unreliable self-reports of participants (Bröder & Hohmann, 2003).

A recent study by Garver-Apgar, Gangestad, and Simpson (2007) tested the hypothesis that women are more attuned to signs of a man's potential sexual coerciveness during the fertile phase and are able to more accurately detect sexually coercive men during the fertile phase. A sample of 169 normally ovulating women watched short segments of videotaped interviews of men. The women were then asked to rate the men on several items that were summed to create an overall coerciveness rating. Average coerciveness ratings for each man were computed. Finally, women's menstrual status was estimated using the reverse-cycle counting method. The results indicated that women in the fertile phase of their menstrual cycle rated the men as more sexually coercive. This suggests that women at greater risk of conception may be more attuned to signs of male sexual coerciveness than women at lesser risk of conception. This may represent an evolved cognitive error management bias (see Haselton, Nettle, & Andrews, 2005, for an overview) toward identifying men as sexually coercive, which might serve to protect women from being raped. This research provides more evidence that women may have evolved psychological mechanisms that motivate behaviors to guard against men's sexual coercion and rape. We note, however, that the participants viewed videos of strangers. Studies demonstrate that women have a greater fear of stranger rape than of being raped by someone they know (Thornhill & Thornhill, 1990b), which suggests that stranger rape was the greater adaptive problem. This is despite modern patterns of rape, which indicate that women are more likely to be raped by someone they know (Kilpatrick et al., 1992; Resnick et al., 1993). These results may reflect the greater potential costs associated with stranger rape, such as a decreased likelihood of investment by the genetic father of resulting offspring. Would similar results be found by testing women's coerciveness ratings of acquaintances or other familiar men? Future research is needed to explore these effects in greater detail. For example, researchers might ask women to rate the coerciveness of familiar faces of classmates or celebrities.

In summary, limited previous work suggests that women may have evolved psychological mechanisms that motivate them to avoid being raped. These studies have not assessed specific behaviors performed to avoid rape. Rather, the results of these studies suggest that women may have evolved mechanisms that motivate them to assess the risk of sexual coercion, such as the riskiness of walking in a dark parking lot alone and the coerciveness of a particular man.

Conclusion

Evolutionary psychology is a powerful heuristic tool that allows researchers to consider rape in a new light. Researchers have argued that men possess evolved psychological mechanisms that motivate them to rape in specific contexts. Although some accumulating evidence is consistent with this hypothesis, more research must be conducted before we can conclude that men possess specific adaptations for rape. Furthermore, we propose that a more nuanced view of rapists is needed, in which rapists may be characterized as belonging to one of several types distinguished by the contexts in which they are predicted to commit a rape. Researchers also have hypothesized that women have evolved mechanisms that motivate behaviors to avoid being raped. Some evidence supports this hypothesis. Researchers also must continue to investigate women's evolved rape avoidance mechanisms before generating conclusions. Future research should continue to investigate the psychological mechanisms that may motivate men's rape behavior and women's rape avoidance behavior. Only through continued scientific study of the etiology of rape can we hope to prevent it.

ACKNOWLEDGMENTS

This chapter was adapted from McKibbin, W. F., Shackelford, T. K., Goetz, A. T., & Starratt, V. G. (2008). Why do men rape? An evolutionary psychological perspective. *Review of General Psychology*, 12, 86–97. The authors thank Joshua Duntley for insightful comments.

References

Baker, R. R., & Bellis, M. A. (1989). Number of sperm in human ejaculates varies in accordance with sperm competition theory. *Animal Behaviour, 37,* 867–869.

Baker, R. R., & Bellis, M. A. (1993). Human sperm competition: Ejaculate adjustment by males and the function of masturbation. *Animal Behaviour, 46,* 861–885.

Barkow, J. H., Cosmides, L., & Tooby, J. (Eds.). (1992). *The adapted mind: Evolutionary psychology and the generation of culture.* New York: Oxford University Press.

Baron, L. (1985). Does rape contribute to reproductive success? Evaluations of sociobiological views of rape. *International Journal of Women's Studies, 8,* 266–277.

Bergen, R. K. (1996). Wife rape: Understanding the response of survivors and service providers. In C. Renzetti & J. Edleson (Series Eds.), *Sage series on violence against women.* California: Sage.

Bergen, R. K., & Bukovec, P. (2006). Men and intimate partner rape: Characteristics of men who sexually abuse their partner. *Journal of Interpersonal Violence, 21,* 1375–1384.

Brecklin, L. R., & Ullman, S. E. (2001). The role of offender alcohol use in rape attacks. *Journal of Interpersonal Violence, 16,* 3–21.

Bröder, A., & Hohmann, N. (2003). Variations in risk-taking behavior over the menstrual cycle: An improved replication. *Evolution and Human Behavior, 24,* 391–398.

Broude, G. J., & Greene, S. J. (1978). Cross-cultural codes on 20 sexual attitudes and practices. *Ethnology, 15,* 409–340.

Brownmiller, S. (1975). *Against our will: Men, women, and rape.* New York: Simon & Schuster.

Burch, R. L., & Gallup, G. G. (2006). The psychobiology of human semen. In S. M. Platek & T. K. Shackelford (Eds.), *Female infidelity and paternal uncertainty* (pp. 141–172). New York: Cambridge University Press.

Buss, D. M. (1994a). The strategies of human mating. *American Scientist, 82,* 238–249.

Buss, D. M. (1994b). *The evolution of desire: Strategies of human mating.* New York: Basic Books.

Buss, D. M. (2004). *Evolutionary psychology: The new science of the mind* (2nd ed.). Boston: Allyn & Bacon.

Chavanne, T. J., & Gallup, G. G. (1998). Variation in risk taking behavior among female college students as a function of the menstrual cycle. *Evolution and Human Behavior, 19,* 27–32.

Christopher, F. S., Owens, L. A., & Stecker, H. L. (1993). Exploring the dark side of courtship: A test of a model of male premarital sexual aggressiveness. *Journal of Marriage and the Family, 55,* 469–479.

Davis, J. A., & Gallup, G. G. Jr. (2006). Preeclampsia and other pregnancy complications as an adaptive response to unfamiliar semen. In S. M. Platek & T. K. Shackelford (Eds.), *Female infidelity and paternal uncertainty* (pp. 191–204). New York: Cambridge University Press.

Dean, K. E., & Malamuth, N. M. (1997). Characteristics of men who aggress sexually and men who imagine aggressing: Risk and moderating variables. *Journal of Personality and Social Psychology, 72,* 449–455.

Dunn, D. W, Crean, C. S., & Gilburn, A. S. (2002). The effects of exposure to seaweed on willingness to mate, oviposition, and longevity in seaweed flies. *Ecological Entomology, 27,* 554–564.

Ellis, L. (1989). *Theories of rape: Inquiries into the causes of sexual aggression.* New York: Hemisphere.

Figueredo, J., Corral-Verdugo, V., Frias-Armenta, M., Bachar, K. J., White, J., McNeill, P. L., et al. (2001). Blood, solidarity, status, and honor: The sexual balance of power and spousal abuse in Sonora, Mexico. *Evolution and Human Behavior, 22,* 293–328.

Finkelhor, D., & Yllo, K. (1985). *License to rape: Sexual abuse of wives.* New York: Holt, Rinehart, & Winston.

Gallup, G. G. Jr., & Burch, R. L. (2004). Semen displacement as a sperm competition strategy in humans. *Evolutionary Psychology, 2,* 12–23.

Gangestad, S. W., & Thornhill, R. (1999). Individual differences in developmental precision and fluctuating asymmetry: A model and its implications. *Journal of Evolutionary Biology, 12,* 402–416.

Gangestad, S. W., Thornhill, R., & Yeo, R. A. (1994). Facial attractiveness, developmental stability, and fluctuating asymmetry. *Ethology and Sociobiology, 15,* 73–85.

Garver-Apgar, C. E., Gangestad, S. W., & Simpson, J. A. (2007). Women's perceptions of men's sexual coerciveness change across the menstrual cycle. *Acta Psychologica Sinica, 39,* 536–540.

Ghiglieri, M. P. (2000). *The dark side of man.* New York: Perseus Books.

Glick, P., & Fiske, S. T. (1996). The Ambivalent Sexism Inventory: Differentiating hostile and benevolent sexism. *Journal of Personality and Social Psychology, 70,* 491–512.

Goetz, A. T., & Shackelford, T. K. (2006). Sexual coercion and forced in-pair copulation in humans as sperm competition tactics in humans. *Human Nature, 17,* 265–282.

Gottschall, J. (2004). Explaining wartime rape. *Journal of Sex Research, 41,* 129–136.

Gottschall, J. A. & Gottschall, T. A. (2003). Are per-incident rape-pregnancy rates higher than per-incident consensual pregnancy rates? *Human Nature, 14,* 1–20.

Gowaty, P. A., & Buschhaus, N. (1998). Ultimate causation of aggressive and forced copulation in birds: Female resistance, the CODE hypothesis, and social monogamy. *Integrative and Comparative Biology, 38,* 207–225.

Greenfield, L. (1997). *Sex offenses and offenders.* Washington, DC: Bureau of Justice Statistics, U.S. Department of Justice.

Hadi, A. (2000). Prevalence and correlates of the risk of marital sexual violence in Bangladesh. *Journal of Interpersonal Violence, 15,* 787–805.

Hall, G. C. N., Shondrick, D. D., & Hirschman, R. (1993). The role of sexual arousal in sexually aggressive behavior: A meta-analysis. *Journal of Consulting and Clinical Psychology, 61,* 1091–1095.

Haselton, M. G., Nettle, D., & Andrews, P. W. (2005). The evolution of cognitive bias. In D. M. Buss (Ed.), *The handbook of evolutionary psychology* (pp. 724–746). Hoboken, NJ: John Wiley.

Holmes, M. M., Resnick, H. S., Kilpatrick, D. G., & Best, C. L. (1996). Rape-related pregnancy: Estimates and descriptive characteristics from a national sample of women. *American Journal of Obstetrics and Gynecology, 175,* 320–324.

Hong, L. K. (1984). Survival of the fastest: On the origin of premature ejaculation. *Journal of Sex Research, 20,* 109–122.

Kalichman, S. C, Williams, E. A., Cherry, C., Belcher, L., & Nachimson, D. (1998). Sexual coercion, domestic violence, and negotiating condom use among low-income African American women. *Journal of Women's Health, 7,* 371–378.

Kanin, E. J. (1957). Male aggression in dating-courtship relations. *American Journal of Sociology, 63,* 197–204.

Kilgallon, S. J., & Simmons, L. W. (2005). Image content influences men's semen quality. *Biology Letters, 1,* 253–255.

Kilpatrick, D., Edmunds, C., & Seymour, A. (1992). *Rape in America*. Arlington, VA: National Victim Center.

Krill, A. L., Lake, T. M., & Platek, S. M. (2006, June). Do *"good genes" predict forced copulation? A test of whether facial symmetry is related to sexual battery*. Poster presented at the annual meeting of the Human Behavior and Evolution Society, Philadelphia, PA.

Krueger, M. M. (1988). Pregnancy as a result of rape. *Journal of Sex Education and Therapy, 14*, 23–27.

Lalumiére, M. L., Chalmers, L. J., Quinsey, V. L, & Seto, M. C. (1996). A test of the mate depriva-tion hypothesis of sexual coercion. *Ethology and Sociobiology, 17*, 299–318.

Lalumiére, M. L., Harris, G. T., Quinsey, V. L., & Rice, M. E. (2005). *The causes of rape*. Washing-ton, DC: American Psychological Association Press.

Lalumiére, M. L., Harris, G. T., & Rice, M. E. (2001). Psychopathy and developmental instabil-ity. *Evolution and Human Behavior, 22*, 75–92.

Lalumiére, M. L. & Quinsey, V. L. (1994). The discriminability of rapists from non-sex offenders using phallometric measures: A meta-analysis. *Criminal Justice and Behavior, 21*, 150–175.

Lalumiére, M. L., & Quinsey, V. L. (1996). Sexual deviance, antisociality, mating effort, and the use of sexually coercive behaviors. *Personality and Individual Differences, 21*, 33–48.

Linder, J. E., & Rice, W. R. (2005). Natural selection and genetic variation for female resistance to harm from males. *Journal of Evolutionary Biology, 18*, 568–575.

Lohr, B., Adams, H., & Davis, J. (1997). Sexual arousal to erotic and aggressive stimuli in sexu-ally coercive and noncoercive men. *Journal of Abnormal Psychology, 106*, 230–242.

Lonsway, K. A., & Fitzgerald, L. F. (1995). Attitudinal antecedents of rape myth acceptance: A theo-retical and empirical reexamination. *Journal of Personality and Social Psychology, 68*, 704–711.

Magurran, A. E. (2001). Sexual conflict and evolution in Trinidadian guppies. *Genetica, 112–113*, 463–474.

Malamuth, N. M., Huppin, M., & Paul, B. (2005). Sexual coercion. In D. M. Buss (Ed.), *The handbook of evolutionary psychology* (pp. 394–418). Hoboken, NJ: John Wiley.

Maynard Smith, J. (1997). Commentary. In P. Gowaty (Ed.), *Feminism and evolutionary biology* (p. 522). New York: Chapman & Hall.

McKinney, F., Derrickson, S. R., & Mineau, P. (1983). Forced copulation in waterfowl. *Behavior, 86*, 250–294.

Mealey, L. (1995). The sociobiology of sociopathy: An integrated evolutionary model. *Behav-ioral and Brain Sciences, 18*, 523–541

Mitani, J. C. (1985). Mating behavior of male orangutans in the Kutai Reserve. *Animal Behav-iour, 33*, 392–402.

Morris, N. M., & Udry, J. R. (1970). Variations in pedometer activity during the menstrual cycle. *Sensory Processing, 2*, 90–98.

Morris, N. M., & Udry, J. R. (1982). Epidemiological patterns of sexual behavior in the men-strual cycle. In R. C. Friedman (Ed.), *Behavior and the menstrual cycle* (pp. 129-153). New York: Marcel Dekker.

Muehlenhard, C. L., & Linton, M. A. (1987). Date rape and sexual aggression in dating situa-tions: Incidence and risk factors. *Journal of Counseling Psychology, 34*, 186–196.

Olsson, M. (1995). Forced copulation and costly female resistance behavior in the Lake Eyre dragon, *Ctenophorus maculosus. Herpetologica, 51*, 19–24.

Painter, K., & Farrington, D. P. (1999). Wife rape in Great Britain. In R. Muraskin (Ed.), *Women and Justice: Development of international policy* (pp.135–164). New York: Gordon and Breach.

Palmer, C. T. (1989). Is rape a cultural universal? A re-examination of the ethnographic evidence. *Ethnology, 28*, 1–16.

Palmer, C. T., & Thornhill, R. (2003a). Straw men and fairy tales: Evaluating reactions to *A natural history of rape. Journal of Sex Research, 40*, 249–255.

Palmer, C. T., & Thornhill, R. (2003b). A posse of good citizens bring outlaw evolutionists to justice. A response to *Evolution, gender, and rape* (Edited by Cheryl Brown Travis. [2003]. Cambridge, MA: MIT Press). *Evolutionary Psychology, 1*, 10–27.

Parker, G. A. (1970). Sperm competition and its evolutionary consequences in the insects. *Biological Reviews, 45*, 525–567.

Parker, G. A. (1982). Why are there so many tiny sperm? Sperm competition and the maintenance of two sexes. *Journal of Theoretical Biology, 96*, 281–294.

Petralia, S. M. & Gallup, G. G. (2002). Effects of a sexual assault scenario on handgrip strength across the menstrual cycle. *Evolution and Human Behavior, 23*, 3–10.

Pizzari, T., & Birkhead, T. R. (2000). Female feral fowl eject sperm of subdominant males. *Nature, 405*, 787–789.

Plath, M., Parzefall, J., & Schlupp, I. (2003). The role of sexual harassment in cave and surface dwelling populations of the Atlantic molly, *Poecilia mexicana* (Poeciliidae, Teleostei). *Behavioral Ecology and Sociobiology, 54*, 303–309.

Pound, N. (2002). Male interest in visual cues of sperm competition risk. *Evolution and Human Behavior, 23*, 443–466.

Pound, N., Shackelford, T. K., & Goetz, A. T. (2006). Sperm competition in humans. In T. K. Shackelford & N. Pound (Eds.), *Sperm competition in humans* (pp. 3–31). New York: Springer.

Resnick, H. S., Kilpatrick, D. G., Dansky, B. S., Saunders, B. E., & Best, C. L. (1993). Prevalence of civilian trauma and post-traumatic stress disorder in a representative national sample of women. *Journal of Consulting and Clinical Psychology, 61*, 984–991.

Reyer, H.-U., Frei, G., & Som, C. (1999). Cryptic female choice: frogs reduce clutch size when amplexed by undesired males. Proceedings of the Royal Society B. *Biological Sciences, 266*, 2101.

Robbins, M. M. (1999). Male mating patterns in wild multimale mountain gorilla groups. *Animal Behaviour, 57*, 1013–1020.

Rozée, P. D. (1993). Forbidden or forgiven? Rape in cross-cultural perspective. *Psychology of Women Quarterly, 17*, 499–514.

Russell, D. E. H. (1990). *Rape in marriage* (rev. ed.). Indianapolis: Indiana University Press.

Sanday, P. R. (1981). The socio-cultural context of rape: A cross-cultural study. *Journal of Social Issues, 37*, 5–27.

Scheppele, K. L, & Bart, P. B. (1983). Through women's eyes: Defining danger in the wake of sexual assault. *Journal of Social Issues, 39*, 63–81.

Shackelford, T. K. (2002a). Are young women the special targets of rape-murder? *Aggressive Behavior, 28*, 224–232.

Shackelford, T. K. (2002b). Risk of multiple-offender rape-murder varies with female age. *Journal of Criminal Justice, 30*, 135–141.

Shackelford, T. K., Goetz, A. T., McKibbin, W. F., & Starratt, V. G. (2007). Absence makes the adaptations grow fonder: Proportion of time apart from partner, male sexual psychology, and sperm competition in humans (*Homo sapiens*). *Journal of Comparative Psychology, 121*, 214–220.

Shackelford, T. K., & Larsen, R. J. (1997). Facial asymmetry as indicator of psychological, emotional and physiological distress. *Journal of Personality and Social Psychology, 72*, 456–466.

Shackelford, T. K., LeBlanc, G. J., Weekes-Shackelford, V. A., Bleske-Rechek, A. L., Euler, H. A., & Hoier, S. (2002). Psychological adaptation to sperm competition. *Evolution and Human Behavior, 23,* 123–138.

Shields, W. M., & Shields, L. M. (1983). Forcible rape: An evolutionary perspective. *Ethology and Sociobiology, 4,* 115–136.

Shine, R., Langkilde, T., & Mason, R. T. (2003). Cryptic forcible insemination: Male snakes exploit female physiology, anatomy, and behavior to obtain coercive matings. *American Naturalist, 162,* 653–667.

Smuts, B. B. (1992). Male aggression against women. *Human Nature, 6,* 1–32.

Smuts, B. B., & Smuts, R. W. (1993). Male aggression and sexual coercion of females in non-human primates and other mammals: Evidence and theoretical implications. *Advances in the Study of Behavior, 22,* 1–63.

Sugiyama, L. S. (2005). Physical attractiveness in adaptationist perspective. In D. M. Buss (Ed.), *The handbook of evolutionary psychology* (pp. 292–343). Hoboken, NJ: John Wiley.

Symons, D. (1979). *The evolution of human sexuality.* New York: Oxford University Press.

Sztatecsny, M. Jehle, R., Burke, T., & Hödl, W. (2006). Female polyandry under male harassment: The case of the common toad (*Bufo bufo*). *Journal of Zoology, 270,* 517.

Tang-Martinez, Z. (1997). The curious courtship of sociobiology and feminism: A case of irreconcilable differences. In P. Gowaty (Ed.), *Feminism and evolutionary biology* (pp. 116–150). New York: Chapman & Hall.

Thornhill, N., & Thornhill, R. (1990a). Evolutionary analysis of psychological pain of rape victims I: The effects of victim's age and marital status. *Ethology and Sociobiology, 11,* 155–176.

Thornhill, N., & Thornhill, R. (1990b). Evolutionary analysis of psychological pain following rape II: The effects of stranger, friend, and family member offenders. *Ethology and Sociobiology, 11,* 177–193.

Thornhill, N., & Thornhill, R. (1990c). Evolutionary analysis of psychological pain following rape victims III: The effects of force and violence. *Aggressive Behavior, 16,* 297–320.

Thornhill, N., & Thornhill, R. (1991). An evolutionary analysis of psychological pain following rape IV: The effect of the nature of the sexual act. *Journal of Comparative Psychology, 105,* 243–252.

Thornhill, R. (1980). Rape in *Panorpa* scorpionflies and a general rape hypothesis. *Animal Behavior, 28,* 52–59.

Thornhill, R. (1981). *Panorpa* (Mecoptera: Panorpidea) scorpionflies: Systems for understanding resource-defense polygyny and alternative male reproductive efforts. *Annual Review of Ecology and Systematics, 12,* 355–386.

Thornhill, R. (1987). The relative importance of intra- and interspecific competition in scorpionfly mating systems. *American Naturalist, 130,* 711–729.

Thornhill, R. (1999). The biology of human rape. *Jurimetrics Journal, 39,* 137–147.

Thornhill, R., & Palmer, C. P. (2000). *A natural history of rape.* Cambridge, MA: MIT Press.

Thornhill, R., & Sauer, K. (1991). The notal organ of the scorpionfly (*Panorpa vulgaris*): An adaptation to coerce mating duration. *Behavioral Ecology, 2,* 156–164.

Thornhill, R., & Thornhill, N. (1983). Human rape: An evolutionary analysis. *Ethology and Sociobiology, 4,* 137–173.

Thornhill, R., & Thornhill, N. (1992). The evolutionary psychology of men's coercive sexuality. *Behavioral and Brain Sciences, 15,* 363–375.

Trivers, R. L. (1972). Parental investment and sexual selection. In B. Campbell (Ed.), *Sexual selection and the descent of man: 1871–1971* (pp. 136–179). Chicago: Aldine.

Vahed, K. (2002). Coercive copulation in the Alpine Bushcricket *Anonconotus alpinus* Yersin (Tettigoniidae: Tettigoniinae: Platycleidini). *Ethology, 108,* 1065–1075.

Watts, C., Keogh, E., Ndlovu, M., & Kwaramba, R. (1998). Withholding of sex and forced sex: Dimensions of violence against Zimbabwean women. *Reproductive Health Matters, 6,* 57–65.

Wilson, M., Daly, M., & Scheib, J. (1997). Femicide: An evolutionary psychological perspective. In P. A. Gowaty (Ed.), *Feminism and evolutionary biology: Boundaries, intersections, and frontiers* (pp. 431–465). New York: Chapman & Hall.

Wilson, M., & Mesnick, S. L. (1997). An empirical test of the bodyguard hypothesis. In P. A. Gowaty (Ed.), *Feminism and evolutionary biology* (pp. 505–511). New York: Chapman & Hall.

Wrangham, R., & Peterson, D. (1996). *Demonic males.* New York: Houghton Mifflin.

7

The World's Oldest Profession

Evolutionary Insights into Prostitution

CATHERINE SALMON

Oh, Harlot, you servant of Men
Kings and Princes shall love you
Young Men release their belts
While the old smile in their beards.
For riches you shall both make and destroy
For you, the fertile wife will be foresaken
While priests shall wed you to the Gods.
—Foster, 2001

Prostitution, sometimes referred to as the world's oldest profession, arouses strong sentiment. It is defined as "the act or practice of engaging in sexual activity for money or its equivalent" (Garner, 1999, p. 1238). From a cross-cultural perspective, this definition can be problematic in that gift giving, of goods or money, often occurs in the context of courtship, extramarital affairs, and marital relationships. It is usually males who give such gifts to their sexual partner, even when females have the same degree of sexual freedom as males (Gebhard, 1971). Nevertheless, in the United States (except in certain counties in Nevada) it is illegal to be paid for a sex act, as it is in many other countries. Yet there is strong debate over the nature of the act and whether it should be considered a crime. In this chapter, I examine the insight an evolutionary psychological perspective can provide on these issues; address the reasons for the existence of prostitution; and explore why it is a service almost exclusively provided to men, typically by women.

The History of the Profession

Accounts of prostitution go back to the sexual services provided by priestesses in the temples of Mesopotamia over 4,000 years ago. Such services were frequently performed as religious or fertility rites, often in conjunction with the grain harvest. Even then, there was a hierarchy of prostitution, with high-status temple prostitutes and lower-status ones who worked from roadside inns or other locales. Temple priestesses had greater freedom than the majority of women of the times. Unlike married women, the priestesses had the right to their own possessions and to buy and sell both property and slaves (Ringdal, 2004). Archeology and written accounts suggest a similar hierarchy in Greek society. Elite, educated prostitutes bought their freedom and were able to advance their social status. In this society, the sale of sex was the only option for women who wanted a free life, away from the control of husband and family.

There are many other accounts of prostitution in ancient civilizations. Researchers have found "more than three hundred different words for prostitute in late Sanskrit, something that signifies both a rich language and a comprehensive sex market" (Ringdal, 2004, p. 71). The Kama Sutra is known for its frank discussions of prostitution and sexual behavior, and erotic temple sculptures and paintings are found in India; temple prostitution remained there until the coming of the British and Muslims. There are also accounts of prostitution in China in the eighth and ninth centuries B.C. During the time of the samurai and shoguns in Japan, prostitution flourished, creating an elegant class of social outcasts with significant freedom, including the ability to reject customers they did not desire.

By the Middle Ages, Western attitudes toward prostitution had shifted significantly. "Medieval law understood prostitution as a commercial enterprise the woman engaged in for money" (Karras, 1996). During these times, the role of prostitutes was considered a necessary evil, an outlet for the intense male sex drive that would otherwise build up and threaten "good" women. Prostitutes were both tolerated and marginalized, as a woman's honor depended on her sexual reputation. Church courts imposed moral order and used public shame as a deterrent. Women could even be evicted from a town for multiple offenses of prostitution.

The solution to this problem was officially sanctioned brothels, resulting in the maintenance of public order and protection of respectable women. The brothels catered primarily to young, unmarried men. Women became prostitutes, for the most part, voluntarily, due to economic necessity and a lack of reasonable alternatives. Prostitution substituted for marriage as a form of financial support, as women in the past had few opportunities for employment outside the family (Bullough, Shelton, & Slaving, 1988).

The American Old West was also a time and place where prostitution flourished out of economic necessity (Rutter, 2005). If a woman was not married, there was little available work, and what there was paid even less than the selling of sexual services. Prostitution in these circumstances was characterized by many inherent risks including pregnancy, disease, physical abuse, legal hassles, and social ostracism. There was also a racial hierarchy, with French prostitutes at the top followed in descending order by Caucasian, Mexican, Indian, black, and Chinese workers. Working conditions varied (as always) from common brothels to high-end and parlor houses that were only for the wealthy customer, with an environment of elegance and pampering that required appointments. Such places were safer and provided more financial reward for their workers. Some prostitutes also traveled with railroads, mining camps, and military posts, working out of tent towns or wagons.

The modern phenomenon of Western prostitution shares much with its earlier forms. Since the 1980s, approximately half of Western prostitutes are call girls while about one-quarter are street workers. Escort services are the main form of prostitution in the United States. Perhaps surprisingly, a majority of call girls are from middle-class backgrounds, are young, and are students or have other jobs in addition to their sex work. Few stay in the business more than five years, during which time it serves predominately as a secondary source of income (Ringdal, 2004). In terms of working conditions, street-based sex work is the most dangerous. These women are the worst paid, tend to come from backgrounds of lower socioeconomic status, and are more likely to be arrested than call girls, being much more visible and often considered a public nuisance. Further up the prostitution hierarchy are the escorts. Escort, or indoor, work is safer than street work. The clients are more predictable in number, in repeat business, and often in terms of the services required. Such work also is more private and pays better, and escorts are less likely to be arrested than street workers. High-end call girls (in the model of well-known madam Heidi Fleiss) are the best paid, with usually the best working conditions. Unsurprisingly, indoor workers tend to be the most satisfied with their work and lives (Prince, 1986).

One difference between modern prostitution and its earliest forms is that while a high-class call girl is paid well for her services, she is not accorded the high social status of the temple priestesses or the high-class courtesans of ancient Greece. Like the priestesses, though, high-class prostitutes have economic freedom and are typically well educated.

The Wars over Sex for Pay

The Laws

Different countries have different laws concerning prostitution. Canada punishes both prostitutes and clients (with jail time, fines, or school for johns), as does the United States. Prostitution is illegal in both countries. Finland criminalizes only the client. Italy allows prostitution in the street and in the home but not in a brothel, while Sweden criminalizes the purchase of sexual services. The Netherlands regulates voluntary prostitution as sex work and prosecutes forced prostitution. Brothels and escort agencies are legal in most of Australia. Brothels and their owners (but not the workers) are subject to licensing, and sex workers employed in legal prostitution businesses have many of the same rights as other Australian workers (Sullivan, 2004).

The Players

In many places, the focus seems to be not on eliminating prostitution, despite laws that make it illegal, but on making it invisible to the public eye. If "laws reflect, legitimate, and reproduce social norms" (Scrambler, 1997), then sex work, like all other sexual activity, should not be public. But it is important to remember that street workers are not representative of the majority of sex workers. Approximately 75% are incall or outcall workers (Sullivan & Simon, 1998). Many prostitutes themselves actively call for the decriminalization of prostitution in the United States. COYOTE (Call Off Your Old Tired Ethics) was founded in San Francisco in 1973 by Margo St. James to improve the image and working conditions of prostitutes. One former prostitute, who became an activist for prostitutes' rights, wrote the following:

> A woman has the right to sell sexual services just as much as she has a right to sell her brains to a law firm when she works as a lawyer, or to sell her creative work to a museum when she works as an artist, or to sell her image to a photographer when she works as a model, or to sell her body when she works as a ballerina. Since most people can have sex without going to jail, there was no reason except old-fashioned prudery to make sex for money illegal. (French & Lee, 1988)

Under the decriminalization proponents favor, prostitution would become just another job, subject to normal labor practices like any other occupation. Many prostitutes also argue that they have a useful function in society, providing emotional support to some male clients and sexual services for men who are socially or physically disabled; they also claim that they may help prevent marital dissolution by providing an alternative to an affair, which might lead to a husband leaving his marriage to form a union with his extra-pair partner (Sanders, 2005).

Although temple priestesses are evidence of early religious support for prostitution, the majority of active religions today hold rather a different view. Prostitution, like all sex between unmarried people, has been largely condemned by most Christian religions. Judeo-Christian faiths hold that sex should take place in the context of marriage, as does the Islamic faith. Hinduism also has prohibitions against sex outside of marriage (Nath & Nayar, 1997). Many, though not all, of those opposed to prostitution in the United States today base their arguments on religious or moral grounds. The argument is usually that prostitution undermines the social and religious institution of marriage and exploits women. Sex should be reserved for marriage, or at least, from a moral perspective, to those who are in love. Both religious and moral opposition to prostitution take a very relationship-focused view of the purpose of sexual activity. Many Americans have moral reservations about prostitution. In a 2000 national poll, four out of five teenagers stated that the problem of prostitution was a serious matter to be dealt with (Marcovitz & Snyder, 2004). Such reservations about prostitution are also one reason for the popularity (particularly among those employed in the sex industry) of the term *sex worker* to describe those who work in the industry of providing sex.

The traditional feminist take on prostitution has been that it is misogynistic, driven by male contempt for women. Andrea Dworkin was perhaps the best-known proponent of this view, arguing that prostitution is rape enforced by poverty in which women exist for the sexual enjoyment of men. As such, it is inherently exploitative. She once said in a public speech that "when men use women in prostitution, they are expressing a pure hatred for the human body . . . men use women's bodies in prostitution and gang rape to communicate with each other" (Dworkin, 1994). Other feminists have suggested that while women have the right to use their bodies in whatever way they choose, men should not be allowed to purchase sexual services from women (Brownmiller, 1975). This is a rather odd argument, as it would seem to imply that women should only use their bodies in the service of women! Some feminists seem to believe that in the absence of prostitution and pornography, men will come to want the exact same relationships and activities and have the same desires as women.

Interestingly, the debate over prostitution, like that over pornography, has made strange bedfellows of many feminists and members of the religious right. While the religious right sees it as a threat to morality and the sanctity of marriage and sex, feminists see prostitution as the product of male domination. Most recently, a schism has appeared in the women's movement over sexuality, particularly commercial sexual representations and activities. Anti-prostitution feminists define prostitution as a violation of women's human rights (one reason they also tend to favor punishing the male clients or johns rather than the prostitutes themselves) while the sex workers' rights movement argues that it is the state's repression of prostitutes that is the human rights violation (Alexander, 1997).

What Light Can an Evolutionary Perspective Shed?

There are several important questions concerning prostitution that have legal and social implications for which an evolutionary perspective is highly enlightening. Why does it exist? Why do some men seek it out? Why do some women engage in it? What are the consequences for those women? And why do other people care so much about it? I will consider each in turn, though first I want to make clear the distinction between different levels of explanation. Those who take an evolutionary perspective on human behavior are usually interested in ultimate, or why, explanations rather than proximate, or how, explanations. Proximate explanations refer to the immediate factors, such as internal physiology, environmental stimuli, or previous experience, that produce a particular response. These can be thought of as conditions that trigger a mechanism that produces a physiological, psychological, or behavioral response. Ultimate explanations refer to the conditions of the biological, social, and physical environment that, on an evolutionary time scale, render certain traits (or mechanisms) adaptive and others nonadaptive (Mayr, 1961). The question being asked here is, why does this trait or behavioral mechanism exist—what is its adaptive significance and what advantage did this trait confer?

Consider the example of sexual jealousy in humans. A young man in a bar sees his girlfriend talking to another man and gets jealous. The proximate explanation for any resulting behavior might invoke the fact that he actually saw his girlfriend taking an interest in another man or that he has a history of being cheated on that makes him sensitive to the situation. The ultimate explanation has a different focus. Where does the mechanism that produced this feeling of jealousy come from? Humans, as opposed to other species of primates, have relatively concealed ovulation. There are no obvious signs when a woman is ovulating and able to conceive. In species where this is obvious, males can monopolize sexual access to females through mate guarding when the females are in their fertile period. In humans, this is not possible, as it would have to take place across the cycle because the timing of ovulation is not unambiguously advertised—though recent work by Haselton and Gangestad (2006) suggests that some men increase their mate retention tactics when their partner is near ovulation. One human solution to this problem is marriage, which results in increased paternity certainty (Alexander & Noonan, 1979; Strassman, 1981). But there is always a risk of infidelity, and if a man were not sensitive to such cues, he would pay a fitness cost in being cuckolded. As a result, men prefer a lack of promiscuity in their choice of long-term mates (Thompson, 1983; Weiss & Slosnerick, 1981). Such a focus on the fidelity of their wives has been demonstrated cross-culturally among men (Betzig, 1989; Daly & Wilson, 1988; Tracy & Crawford, 1999).

Ancestral men who failed to adequately address the problem of paternity uncertainty risked not only direct reproductive losses but also loss of status and reputation, which could have had a serious negative impact on their ability to attract other mates. Sexual jealousy is one psychological mechanism that has evolved in men to combat the potential costs of being cuckolded (Buss, 1988; Buss & Shackelford, 1997; Buss, Shackelford, Choe, Buunk, & Dijkstra, 2000; Daly, Wilson, & Weghorst, 1982; Symons, 1979). Considering both ultimate and proximate levels of explanation may deepen our understanding of the development and significance of a behavior, whether that behavior is sexual jealousy or prostitution.

So why does prostitution exist? There are millions of prostitutes working worldwide, both male and female, and in all times and places the majority have and continue to service men. Some suggest that prostitution is rooted in men's feelings about or attitudes toward women, such as disrespect, hostility, or contempt. But such a broad claim should raise questions. If contempt for women is the primary motivation, why does homosexual male prostitution exist? And why are there no significant differences between homosexual and heterosexual prostitution? Prostitution "is not a window into men's feelings about or attitudes toward women; it is a window into the nature of male sexuality" (Salmon & Symons, 2001, p. 48). What is important to remember is that men who purchase the services of a prostitute are not just paying for sex. They are paying for "just sex"—sex without commitment, obligation, and courtship. Of course, that begs the question of why they would want to pay for "just sex."

The reasons are a reflection of basic differences in male and female sexual psychologies. In the environment of evolutionary adaptedness, what would have been the kind of mating strategies that led to reproductive success, the passing on of one's own genes, traits, and predispositions to offspring? If most successful reproduction across human evolutionary history occurred within marriages (or some form of permanent union) and most marriages were monogamous, why is there a male market demand for prostitution and a female willingness to meet it?

Psychological and biological evidence suggests that different strategies led to reproductive success for men and women. Ancestral men and women differed in some of the adaptive problems they encountered in the mating arena. However similar men's and women's typical parental investments may have been, their minimum possible investments differed significantly. If a man fathered a child in whom he did not invest, this reproduction would have occurred at almost no cost. Even if such opportunities did not come along frequently in ancestral human populations, taking advantage of them when they did was adaptive enough that males evolved a sexual psychology that makes low-cost sex with new women exciting both to imagine (fantasy and pornography) and to engage in (one-night stands and prostitutes), and that motivates men to seek out such sexual opportunities (Clark & Hatfield, 1989; Ellis & Symons, 1990; Salmon & Symons, 2001; Townsend, 1995; Wright & Reise, 1997). Compared to females, human males typically invest less in parental investment, are less discriminating in their choice of sexual partners, engage in more low-cost sexual situations, and have sexual encounters with more numerous partners (Clutton-Brock & Parker, 1992; Low, 1989). As a result of different reproductive payoffs, male and female sexual psychologies can be expected to be as different as male and female bodies (Bailey, Gaulin, Agyei, & Gladue, 1994; Symons, 1979).

The vast majority of prostitutes' clients are heterosexual men, often military or business men—those who travel a great deal and are either separated from their sexual partner or do not have one (O'Connell Davidson, 1998). National Health and Social Life Survey data suggest that 36% of those serving in the military have paid for sex (Sullivan & Simon, 1994). Clients themselves suggest several motivations including the thrill, specific types of services not provided by their partner, loneliness, wanting a variety of women, sexual urges, and convenience. The most frequently requested services of prostitutes are vaginal-penile sex, oral sex, and hand jobs, though the specialized fetish market has become more common. The majority of clients in one study were white collar, and more than half were married (Boyle, 1994). Many prostitutes also have regular clients who are socially or physically disabled and have had difficulty finding a regular partner (Sanders, 2005). One could sum up the major conscious motivations as variety, no other partner, cheaper, and less risky than having an affair. This inclination to seek out the services of prostitutes in the pursuit of variety (of partner type and sexual activity) is consistent with the Coolidge effect; this is a phenomenon in which males of a variety of species, including rats, sheep, rhesus monkeys, and humans, who have copulated to the point of satiation with one female can be aroused again in a short period of time if given access to a novel female (Alcock, 2005; Plaud, Gaither, Amato Henderson, & Devitt, 1997). Evolutionary psychologists often point out that, in contrast to males, ancestral females had little to gain and much to lose from engaging in impersonal sex with random strangers and from seeking sexual variety for its own sake, and that they had a great deal to gain from choosing their mates carefully. As such, it is unsurprising that they rarely seek the services of prostitutes, and when they engage in affairs or short-term mating it is not just for the sake of variety. Men and women possess different facultative mating strategies; their mating repertoires differ in adaptive ways (Buss & Schmitt, 1993; Gangestad & Simpson, 2000). This is typically articulated in terms of the conditions that influence the behavioral output of psychological mating mechanisms or the conditions that activate short-term or long-term mating strategies. So why do prostitutes do it? What conditions produce this type of mating strategy on the part of women?

In early Sumerian times, prostitutes were described as "wise women, able to educate, civilize and tame men" (Alexander, 1997, p. 86). A noble pursuit! But such goals are rarely attributed to modern prostitution. The majority engage in sex work for economic reasons. In some cases, it may be a woman's only option, a better option than others, or an appealing option. "Prostitution is like any other work in that some do it because it is the only job available to them, while others do it because it is a good job or because it provides them with money when they need it, or because they enjoy it" (Perkins & Bennett, 1985, p. 213). Many are supporting children in the total absence of the father or in the absence of sufficient financial support. For some young middle-class women, the financial rewards of being a high-priced call girl are appealing, especially in combination with flexible working hours. Essentially, there is a market for sex, and women who need or want to take advantage of that market do so.

Sex differences in the nature of male and female arousal also facilitate the existence of prostitution and explain some of its patterns. Much attention has been paid to the visual nature of male arousal and how this has allowed the pornography industry to flourish (Salmon & Symons, 2001). Among married couples, sex differences in the motivations for extra-pair sexual relations influence the male-oriented nature of prostitution. Married women engaging in short-term mating typically do so in the pursuit of good genes or because they are emotionally unsatisfied in their marriage (Schmitt, 2005). Neither goal would be well served by the services of a prostitute, though they might be by a well-chosen one-night stand or affair. Married men engaging in such mating are more likely to be simply in the pursuit of variety. They often report being quite satisfied with their marital partner (Schmitt, 2005). Thus, their goal is well served through the services of a prostitute.

Another way to consider prostitution is in light of an evolutionary model of courtship framed by social exchange theory. This theory suggests that cooperation between individuals occurs for mutual benefit. From this perspective, parental investment by males is exchanged for sexual access to females. There is an exchange of reproductive goods and services. "Males may have provided food, protection from predators and other males, some parental care, and sex. Females may have provided sex, parental care for children, and labor to gather foods" (Crawford & Johnston,

1999, p. 188). Mechanisms evolved to mediate such social exchanges and in a modern context may result in the exchange of money for service known as prostitution. Resource acquisition mechanisms may also facilitate the prostitution industry.

Why do some people care so much about the sex other people are having? There are a number of reasons. Some see prostitution, like any sex out of marriage, as something bad, something that leads to moral decay. Others may oppose prostitution on the grounds that it is bad for the prostitutes themselves (citing risks of physical and emotional abuse, sexually transmitted disease, and other dangers) and for women as a group. And it is certainly true that there can be significant hazards to sex work, particularly among those who work outcall, including verbal and physical abuse, drugs, depression, disease, and harassment by the police. One might also assume that if men generally value fidelity in a long-term mate, working as a prostitute might impair a woman's likelihood of finding a quality partner. But there is a great deal of evidence that men and women have historically engaged and currently engage in short-term (Gangestad & Thornhill, 1997; Greiling & Buss, 2000) and long-term (Ellis, 1992) mating strategies and have evolved psychological adaptations for enabling these flexible strategies.

> Just one factor stands out to distinguish those who live well with no loss of self-esteem, from those who may find sex work a difficult or even damaging career choice. Most of the former have sufficient sex information and are sex-positive. . . . Most of the latter have internalized negative attitudes about sex. (Queen, 1997, p. 129)

Interestingly, with regard to disease, the data suggest that there is no evidence that sexually transmitted disease rates are higher among prostitutes than in the general population (Pyett, 1996). Another perspective is stated by a prostitute herself: "I think straight women see us as a threat as we take money for something they do for free" (Boyle, 1994, p. 88). In many ways, laws concerning prostitution are a tool for controlling female behavior (Karras, 1996). One imagines men having various reasons to want to do so: religion, to protect "good" women, to provide a sexual outlet for unmarried men. But the strongest opposition to prostitution recently has often been from women, some with genuine concern for the welfare of prostitutes, others with the desire to protect what they have earned through marriage and what may be put at risk by husbands who may divert resources away from their wife to prostitutes. As Symons (1979, p. 259) notes, "to the extent that heterosexual men purchase the services of prostitutes and pornographic masturbatory aids, the market for the sexual services of non-prostitute women is diminished and their bargaining position vis-a-vis men is weakened."

Legal and Public Policy Implications

There are many ways in which evolutionary psychology can inform public policy, but perhaps the most useful is the way it informs about what is or what can be. Much public policy (if not most) is concerned with the way "we" would like the world to be. It is used to try to shape the world (or a particular society or country) into an "ideal" form. In other words, policy is a purposive course of action followed by an actor or set of actors in dealing with a problem or matter of concern (Anderson, 1975). Once an ideal is decided on, the question is whether it will be easy or very difficult to achieve. This is a question that evolutionary psychology is well equipped to address.

It is important to note that evolutionary perspectives give us insight into what is as opposed to what "ought" to be. Using what is to justify what ought to be (rape is natural and therefore should be accepted) is committing the naturalistic fallacy. The fact that ancestral females and males exchanged sex for resources and protection (Symons, 1979) does not imply that women and men today ought to do the same. But an evolutionary examination of the ancestral problems that made it an adaptive solution gives us insight into how it functions today and under what circumstances it may occur with frequency or not at all. The majority of evolutionarily informed work does not make the mistake of the naturalistic fallacy. It can also help us to avoid the moralistic fallacy, or the notion that what ought to be can be. A more complete understanding of human nature, one derived from an evolutionary perspective, can help us to better realize what can really be achieved and at what costs (Crawford, 2004). The policy process can be thought of in the following simple way: People have assumptions about human nature and how the world works. They act on these assumptions, and the outcomes of their decisions will be successful when their assumptions about human nature are correct. When these assumptions are wrong, there will be costs to these decisions, costs that can sometimes, although not always, be unreasonably high.

People have a strong inclination to punish those behaviors they disapprove of as a way of changing or eliminating them. There may be some validity to this approach in that adaptations evolved in response to the costs and benefits of the behaviors they produced in the ancestral environment. As a result, increasing the costs of current behaviors may influence how likely they are to occur (Thornhill & Palmer, 2000). The majority of legal systems rely on a system centered on punishment, and pretty much all such punishments have a fitness cost associated with them. And yet there are problems with a system of punishment as public policy. It's very expensive (Hutsler, 1995).

It can also be difficult to implement severe punishments, especially in democratic societies. Infanticide has been common throughout human history. Some hunter-gatherer societies regard it as a maternal right (Scrimshaw, 1984), while Western European societies regard it as sinful, immoral, and illegal. Historically, many women in Europe were hanged for this crime. However, even all-male British juries were unwilling to convict young, poor, unmarried women for killing their babies when the punishment was death. Judicial authorities were outraged, and for centuries British lawmakers made changes in the law in an attempt to obtain more convictions for infanticide (Hoffer & Hull, 1981). None was successful, and eventually the law was medicalized. Infanticide remains a difficult legal, social, and medical issue.

   Crawford and Anderson (1989) have suggested that prostitution can be considered a pseudopathology—a behavior that has its origin in adaptations that evolved in response to problems human ancestors encountered but which, for one reason or another, is no longer healthy, morally acceptable, or culturally valued. It may have been common for ancestral females and males to exchange sex for resources and protection (Symons, 1979). If so, then modern prostitution may be an exaggerated form of this exchange that occurs when some women need resources and protection and some men lack sexual access to women through normal courtship. If prostitution has its origin in ancestral trading of sex for resources and protection, extensive legal attempts to eliminate it may have other undesirable consequences, such as increased shoplifting and petty robbery by women, increased use of pornography by men, and so forth (Crawford, 2004).

Conclusion

From an evolutionary psychology perspective, all behaviors are either the direct or indirect effects of evolved adaptations. As a result, programs for changing current behaviors should be based on an understanding of how ancestral environmental conditions involved in the development and functioning of the relevant adaptation relate to present environmental circumstances (Crawford, 2000). So, in a sense, taking an evolutionary perspective toward public policy is very practical. Evolved preferences can suggest values and goals, but they will also enlighten us as to evolved constraints on people's preferences, emotions, and behaviors, all factors that will strongly influence the outcome of policy decisions.

   What are U.S. prostitution laws (with the exception of those of some Nevada counties) attempting to do? What is their goal? Is it the eradication of sex for pay? The ways the laws are enforced seems for the most part to target street workers who do not make up the majority of prostitutes in the United States. Even if street workers were eliminated, that would leave close to 75% of sex workers still in business. Is the point to reduce the incidence of sexually transmitted disease? As there is no difference in the disease rates among sex workers and the rest of the population in the United States (Elias, Bullough, Elias, & Brewer, 1998), this seems misguided. More attention to the sexual practices of those most at risk of catching sexually transmitted diseases might seem more useful, particularly when teenagers seem to be one of those groups. Are the laws to protect women? If so, they fail miserably with respect to the prostitutes themselves, who are marginalized, socially ostracized, and denied the protection of the police that most citizens can count on. The decriminalization of prostitution that is called for by organizations such as COYOTE would leave prostitution legal and unregulated—a novel situation, as it is legal and controlled in many other countries (Sullivan, 2004).

   If, however, the prostitution laws are designed to try to control female sexual behavior, they have an impact in the sense that they make the negatives of some forms of sex for pay very high. But they have not eliminated it and are unlikely to do so as long as there are men who are willing to pay for sex and women who need or want the financial rewards of providing that service. People often point to the relatively low rates of prostitution in the United States in recent times and say that this is evidence that the laws do work to discourage it. But others have pointed out that prostitution flourishes under certain social conditions and languishes under others, and those conditions have much more to do with the willingness of unmarried women in general to have sex with unmarried men. In our currently sexually permissive times, the majority of people have had sex before marriage and the majority of women did not need to be paid to do so; dinner and a date were sufficient. Under such circumstances, fewer men need the services of a prostitute than they did in times when women were less willing to share their sexual favors.

It is also important to remember that prostitution laws are not without significant cost, both in the monetary sense and in terms of other consequences. An inordinate amount of taxpayer money goes to policing such laws and arresting prostitutes and clients. There are also personal costs suffered by prostitutes and clients, both financial and social. And if prostitution serves some need, what will be the costs of denying that need? Might women commit other, more violent crimes to get access to resources? Might men who have few sexual opportunities become more coercive? Maybe both, maybe neither, but such consequences should be considered. If a serious attempt is to be made to eliminate, reduce, regulate, or decriminalize prostitution, it will only be successful through an understanding of the functioning of the evolved specialized psychological mechanisms producing the behavior as well as how environmental interactions can influence the functioning of these mechanisms.

References

Alcock, J. (2005). *Animal behavior*. Sunderland, MA: Sinauer.

Alexander, P. (1997). Feminism, sex workers and human rights. In J. Nagle (Ed.), *Whores and other feminists* (pp. 83–97). New York: Routledge.

Alexander, R. D., & Noonan, K. M. (1979). Concealment of ovulation, parental care, and human social evolution. In N. A. Chagnon & W. Irons (Eds.), *Evolutionary biology and human social behavior* (pp. 402–435). North Scituate, MA: Duxbury Press.

Anderson, J. E. (1975). *Public policy making*. New York: Praeger Publishers.

Bailey, J. M., Gaulin, S., Agyei, Y., & Gladue, B. A. (1994). Effects of gender and sexual orientation on evolutionary relevant aspects of human mating psychology. *Journal of Personality and Social Psychology, 66*, 1081–1093.

Betzig, L. (1989). Causes of conjugal dissolution. *Current Anthropology, 30*, 654–676.

Boyle, S. (1994). *Working girls and their men*. London: Smith Gryphon.

Brownmiller, S. (1975). *Against our will*. New York: Simon & Schuster.

Bullough, V. L., Shelton, B., & Slaving, S. (1988). *The subordinated sex*. Athens, GA: University of Georgia Press.

Buss, D. M. (1988). From vigilance to violence: Tactics of mate retention. *Ethology and Sociobiology, 9*, 291–317.

Buss, D. M., & Schmitt, D. P. (1993). Sexual strategies theory: An evolutionary perspective on human mating. *Psychological Review, 100,* 204–232.

Buss, D. M., & Shackelford, T. K. (1997). From vigilance to violence: Mate retention tactics in married couples. *Journal of Personality and Social Psychology, 72,* 346–361.

Buss, D. M., Shackelford, T. K., Choe, J., Buunk, B. P., & Dijkstra, P. (2000). Distress about mating rivals. *Personal Relationships, 7,* 235–243.

Clark, R. D., & Hatfield, E. (1989). Gender differences in receptivity to sexual offers. *Journal of Psychology and Human Sexuality, 2,* 39–55.

Clutton-Brock, T. H., & Parker, G. A. (1992). Potential reproductive rates and the operation of sexual selection. *Quarterly Review of Biology, 67,* 437–456.

Crawford, C. B. (2004). Public policy and personal decisions: The evolutionary context. In C. B. Crawford & C. Salmon (Eds.), *Evolutionary psychology, public policy, and personal decisions* (pp. 3–22). Mahwah, NJ: Erlbaum.

Crawford, C. B. (2000). The future of evolutionary psychology: Counting babies or studying psychological mechanisms. *Annals of the New York Academy of Sciences, 907,* 21–38.

Crawford, C. B., & Anderson, J. L. (1989). Sociobiology: An environmentalist discipline? *American Psychologist, 44,* 1449–1459.

Crawford, C. B., & Johnston, M. A. (1999). An evolutionary model of courtship and mating as social exchange: Implications for rape law reform. *Jurimetrics, 39,* 181–200.

Daly, M., & Wilson, M. (1988). *Homicide.* Hawthorne, NY: Aldine.

Daly, M., Wilson, M., & Weghorst, S. J. (1982). Male sexual jealousy. *Ethology and Sociobiology, 3,* 11–27.

Dworkin, A. (1994). *Prostitution and male supremacy.* Retrieved March 26, 2007, from http://www.nostatusquo.com/ACLU/dworkin/MichLawJourI.html.

Elias, J. E., Bullough, V. L., Elias, V., & Brewer, G. (1998). *Prostitution: On whores, hustlers, and johns.* Amherst, NY: Prometheus.

Ellis, B. J. (1992). The evolution of sexual attraction: Evaluative mechanisms in women. In J. H. Barkow, L. Cosmides, & J. Tooby (Eds.), *The adaptive mind* (pp. 267–288). New York: Oxford University Press.

Ellis, B. J., & Symons, D. (1990). Sex differences in sexual fantasies: An evolutionary psychological approach. *Journal of Sex Research, 27,* 527–556.

Foster, B. R. (Trans.). (2001). *The epic of Gilgamesh.* New York: W. W. Norton.

French, D., & Lee, L. (1988). *Working: My life as a prostitute.* New York: E. P. Dutton.

Gangestad, S. W., & Simpson, J. A. (2000). The evolution of human mating: Trade-offs and strategic pluralism. *Behavioral and Brain Sciences, 23,* 573–644.

Gangestad, S. W., & Thornhill, R. (1997). The evolutionary psychology of extrapair sex: The role of fluctuating asymmetry. *Evolution and Human Behavior, 18,* 69–88.

Garner, B. A. (1999). *Black's law dictionary* (7th ed.). St. Paul, MN: West.

Gebhard, P. H. (1971).The anthropological study of sexual behavior. In D. S. Marshall and R. C. Suggs (Eds.), *Human sexual behavior* (pp. 250–260). New York: Basic Books.

Greiling, H., & Buss, B. M. (2000). Women's sexual strategies: The hidden dimension of short-term mating. *Personality and Individual Differences, 28,* 929–963.

Haselton, M. G., & Gangestad, S. W. (2006). Conditional expression of women's desires and men's mate guarding across the ovulatory cycle. *Hormones and Behavior, 49,* 509–518.

Hoffer, C., & Hull, N. (1981). *Murdering mothers: Infanticide in England and New England (1558–1803).* New York: New York University Press.

Hutsler, J. (1995). *KIDbits: NAYSI Youth, sport, facts & demographics*. North American Youth Sport Institute Web site. Retrieved April 23, 2007, from http://www.naysi.com/kidbits/KB01.htm.

Karras, R. M. (1996). *Common women: Prostitution and sexuality in Medieval England*. London: Oxford University Press.

Low, B. (1989). Cross-cultural patterns in the training of children: An evolutionary perspective. *Journal of Comparative Psychology, 103*, 313–319.

Marcovitz, H., & Snyder, G. (2004). *Gallup youth survey: Major issues and trends*. Broomall, PA: Mason Crest.

Mayr, E. (1961). Cause and effect in biology. *Science, 134*, 1501–1506.

Nath, J. K., & Nayar, V. R. (1997). India. In R. T. Francoeur (Ed.), *The international encyclopedia of sexuality*. London: Continuum.

O'Connell Davidson, J. (1998). *Prostitution, power and freedom*. Ann Arbor: University of Michigan Press.

Perkins, R., & Bennett, G. (1985). *Being a prostitute*. Sydney: George Allen & Unwin.

Plaud, J., Gaither, G. A., Amato Henderson, S., & Devitt, M. K. (1997). The long-term habituation of sexual arousal in human males: A cross-over design. *Psychological Record, 47*, 385–398.

Prince, D. A. (1986). *A psychological study of prostitutes in California and Nevada*. Doctoral dissertation. San Diego: United States International University.

Pyett, P. (1996). Risk practices for HIV infection and other STDs amongst female prostitutes working in legalized brothels. *AIDS Care, 8*, 85–94.

Queen, C. (1997). Sex radical politics, sex-positive feminist thought and whore stigma. In J. Nagle (Ed.), *Whores and other feminists* (pp. 125–135). New York: Routledge.

Ringdal, N. J. (2004). *Love for sale: A world history of prostitution* (R. Daly, Trans.). New York: Grove Press.

Rutter, M. (2005). *Upstairs girls: Prostitution in the American West*. Helena, MT: Farcountry Press.

Salmon, C., & Symons, D. (2001). *Warrior lovers: Erotic fiction, evolution and female sexuality*. London: Weidenfeld & Nicholson.

Sanders, T. (2005). Female sex workers as health educators with men who buy sex: Utilizing narratives of rationalization. *Social Science and Medicine, 62*, 2434–2444.

Schmitt, D. P. (2005). Fundamentals of human mating strategies. In D. M. Buss (Ed.), *The handbook of evolutionary psychology* (pp. 258–291). Hoboken, NJ: John Wiley.

Scrambler, G. (1997). Conspicuous and inconspicuous sex work: The neglect of the ordinary and mundane. In G. Scrambler & A. Scrambler (Eds.), *Rethinking prostitution: Purchasing sex in the 1990s* (pp. 105–120). New York: Routledge.

Scrimshaw, S. (1984). Infanticide in human populations: Societal and individual concerns. In G. Hausfater & S. Hrdy (Eds.), *Infanticide: Comparative and evolutionary perspectives* (pp. 439–462). New York: Aldine.

Strassman, B. I. (1981). Sexual selection, parental care, and concealed ovulation in humans. *Ethology and Sociobiology, 2*, 31–40.

Sullivan, B. (2004). The women's movement and prostitution politics in Australia. In J. Outshoorn (Ed.), *The politics of prostitution: Women's movements, democratic states and the globalization of sex commerce* (pp. 21–40). Cambridge: Cambridge University Press.

Sullivan, E., & Simon, W. (1998). The client: A social, psychological, and behavioural look at the unseen patron of prostitution. In J. E. Elias, V. L. Bullough, V. Elias, & G. Brewer (Eds.), *Prostitution: On whores, hustlers and johns* (pp. 134–154). Amherst, NY: Prometheus.

Symons, D. (1979). *The evolution of human sexuality*. New York: Oxford University Press.

Thompson, A. P. (1983). Extramarital sex: A review of the research literature. *Journal of Sex Research, 19*, 1–22.

Thornhill, R., & Palmer, C. (2000). *A natural history of rape: Biological bases of sexual coercion*. Cambridge, MA: MIT Press.

Townsend, J. M. (1995). Sex without emotional involvement: An evolutionary interpretation of sex differences. *Archives of Sexual Behavior, 24*, 173–205.

Tracy, K., & Crawford, C. B. (1999). Wife beating in evolutionary perspective. In D. Counts, J. Brown, & J. Campbell (Eds.), *To have and to hit: Cultural perspectives of wife abuse* (pp. 27–42). Urbana: University of Illinois Press.

Weiss, D. L., & Slosnerick, M. (1981). Attitudes toward sexual and nonsexual extramarital involvements among a sample of college students. *Journal of Marriage and the Family, 43*, 349–358.

Wright, T. M. & Reise, S. P. (1997). Personality and unrestricted sexual behavior: Correlations of sociosexuality in Caucasian and Asian college students. *Journal of Research in Personality, 31*, 166–192.

PART FOUR

ADAPTATION AND THE PRODUCTION OF CRIMINAL BEHAVIOR

8

Risk-Taking, Antisocial Behavior, and Life Histories

SANDEEP MISHRA AND MARTIN L. LALUMIÈRE

In this chapter we examine the ultimate causes of risk-taking and antisocial behavior. We discuss risk-taking and antisocial behavior together because they have much in common: both often involve impulsive, reckless, immediately rewarding, and self-serving behavior. We examine them together for ease of exposition but also for empirical reasons: many forms of risk-taking (e.g., speeding while driving, promiscuous sex) are tightly associated with antisocial behavior, at both the individual and aggregate levels (reviewed in Mishra & Lalumière, 2008). This observation has led some to propose such broad-spectrum constructs as "taste for risk" (Daly & Wilson, 2001), "generality of deviance" (Osgood, Johnston, O'Malley, & Bachman, 1988), "problem behavior syndrome" (Jessor, 1991), and "low self-control" (Gottfredson & Hirschi, 1990) to reflect the connection between general risk-taking and antisocial behavior. Just as most criminologists have realized the futility of crime-specific etiological explanations, it is becoming clear that the correct target of explanation is something more biologically relevant than legally defined actions or even socially undesirable behaviors.

Longitudinal studies have uncovered reliable developmental trends in antisocial behavior. This research has been mostly descriptive, and explanatory questions have focused largely on proximal factors. In this chapter, we begin by describing three general developmental pathways to antisocial tendencies. We then introduce life history analysis to provide a framework for ultimate explanatory questions about the development of both general risk-taking and antisocial tendencies. In particular, we explore the notion of risky and antisocial behaviors as adapted responses to particular conditions encountered by individuals during their lifetimes; by "adapted," we mean selected over generations because of positive impact on fitness, regardless of current fitness effects. We describe fundamental crossroads all organisms must face—those having to do with growth, maintenance, and reproduction—and examine how these

139

choices are linked to the three developmental pathways. We end with an application of life history analysis to a contemporary criminological phenomenon, the sudden drop in rates of risk-taking and criminal behavior in the 1990s.

The Development of Antisocial Tendencies: Three Pathways

Quinsey, Skilling, Lalumière, and Craig (2004) proposed that there are three key developmental pathways that describe different patterns of antisocial and risky behavior over the life course. A pattern of delinquent behaviors concentrated in adolescence and early adulthood is termed *adolescence-limited delinquency* (after Moffitt, 1993). Antisocial behavior associated with neuropathology and social adversity beginning early in life and persisting over the life span is termed *life-course-persistent offending* (Moffitt, 1993). A third pattern of antisocial behavior is similar to life-course-persistent offending, in that it is characterized by early onset of antisocial behavior and persistence throughout the life span, but individuals do not show any evidence of early neuropathology or social adversity. This pattern is termed *psychopathy* (Harris, Rice, & Quinsey, 1994; Harris, Skilling, & Rice, 2001). There are surely other, less common or more specific pathways (e.g., White, Bates, & Buyske, 2001), but here we concentrate our discussion on these three general pathways.

Delinquent behavior limited to the periods of adolescence and early adulthood is normative, and data suggest that it is somewhat anomalous to refrain from any antisocial behavior during this time (reviewed in Moffitt, 1993). Late adolescence and early adulthood are also rife with other high-risk behaviors, such as speeding while driving, drug use, and promiscuous sexual activity (Gottfredson & Hirschi, 1990). Developmental scientists typically invoke learning theory to explain the ubiquity of adolescence-limited delinquency. For example, adolescents are said to mimic life-course-persistent peers because risky and antisocial behavior in adolescence often leads to desirable outcomes (money, reputation, sex) that cannot be obtained as easily through prosocial means (Moffitt, 1993). Adolescent-limited delinquents desist from antisocial conduct in early adulthood as the benefits of engaging in such behavior diminish relative to rising costs.

Life-course-persistent offending represents a vastly different developmental pattern of antisocial behavior. Life-course-persistent offenders begin engaging in problem behavior early in childhood (e.g., they are hyperactive, aggressive) and display antisocial behavior throughout adulthood. Life-course-persistent offenders are often raised in disadvantaged environments and exhibit evidence of neurodevelopmental perturbations experienced early in life. A number of factors possibly causing neurodevelopmental perturbations have been linked with antisocial behaviors, such as brain injury, malnutrition, maternal smoking during pregnancy, and obstetrical complications (reviewed in Anderson, 2007; Harris, Rice, & Lalumière, 2001). These factors typically interact with other social factors related to delinquency, such as a single-parent upbringing, low socioeconomic status, or parental abuse (Rutter, 1997). Together, neurodevelopmental problems and poor social environments are suggested to decrease intellectual (especially verbal) abilities, leading to increased impulsivity, decreased sensitivity to punishment, and impaired development of pro-social skills, all of which lead to snowballing adjustment problems.

The third pattern of antisocial behavior is psychopathy. Psychopaths exhibit chronic and extreme antisocial behavior throughout their lifetime and across various contexts. They are similar to life-course-persistent offenders in that they experience early onset of antisocial behavior that perseveres throughout the life span, but they exhibit important differences in severity of offending, affect and physiology, interper-sonal relations, and lack of neurodevelopmental pathology (reviewed in Harris et al., 2001; Lalumière, Harris, Quinsey, & Rice, 2005; Quinsey et al., 2004). Research suggests that psychopaths do not exhibit signs of neurodevelopmental perturba-tions experienced by life-course-persistent offenders, and social factors do not seem to have any influence on the development of their persistent antisociality. Compared to other life-course-persistent offenders, psychopaths tend to have broader and more extensive criminal histories, exhibit increased likelihood of reoffending after incar-ceration, commit more violent crimes, are more likely to engage in instrumental (goal-directed) violence, and are more likely to select strangers as victims. Affectively and physiologically, psychopaths also show differences: they exhibit shorter delay of gratification, show less sensitivity to punishment, and are less physiologically reac-tive when exposed to cues of distress, fear, or other aversive signs.

The risk-taking and antisocial behaviors described above for the three pathways are typically seen as a pathological aberration from normal prosocial behavior. Im-plicit in this view is the assumption that engaging in risky and antisocial behavior is irrational or counter-productive and self-destructive. This assumption stems from the perception that risky or antisocial behavior conflicts with an individual's best interests due to its high cost (e.g., physical injuries, jail time). An alternative view is that risky and antisocial behavior may represent an adapted response to particular environmen-tal or situational conditions, an optimal behavioral option in some circumstances, maximizing the likelihood of certain outcomes that were statistically related to fit-ness in ancestral environments. Although risky behavior may lead to costly outcomes (e.g., foreshortening one's life expectancy), it may also have benefits (e.g., increased mating opportunities). When gains and losses are seen in the currency of reproduc-tive success, a tendency to sacrifice life span in exchange for reproduction under some circumstances does not seem so irrational. In the context of adaptive decision making in humans and in light of evolutionary theorizing, when is it beneficial to engage in risky and antisocial behaviors when other alternatives are available? Why are there three general developmental patterns of risky and antisocial tendencies?

Life History Analysis: A Brief Introduction

The central tenet of evolution by natural selection is differential reproductive suc-cess, or fitness, of individuals possessing certain heritable characteristics. There is enormous variability in the ways that organisms can maximize reproductive success. Life history analysis represents a way of conceptualizing the evolution of allocation of effort or energy toward such fitness-relevant characteristics as age of first reproduction, number of offspring, size of offspring, or length of reproductive life span. Life history analysis seeks to understand the selective pressures that influence both the timing and expenditure of limited energy resources under different conditions.

A key concept in life history analysis is trade-off: organisms must allocate a finite amount of effort or energy to endeavors that constrain each other, such as number and size of offspring (Stearns, 1992). Natural selection favors an allocation of effort or energy that optimally maximizes fitness given the features of a particular environment (Kaplan & Gangestad, 2005). A number of trade-offs have been documented in many animal species, including trade-offs between size and number of offspring, mating and parenting, and growth and early reproduction. These trade-offs are relevant in the evolution of a diversity of life histories both between species and within species. Some important trade-offs are discussed in the context of risk-taking and antisocial behavior, particularly in how they affect potentially adaptive risk acceptance in different environmental and situational contexts. We also discuss the relevance of life history analysis for the three general developmental patterns of antisocial behavior.

Survival, the Present, and the Future

Organisms have limited effort and energetic resources to allocate to different essential reproductive activities. This limitation forces trade-offs, such as that between current and future reproduction. Current reproduction incurs costs such as compromised immune function, reduced chance of survival, and lowered expected future reproduction. Delaying current reproduction incurs the risk of not reproducing at all because of potential mortality before other reproductive opportunity (Kaplan & Gangestad, 2005). Organisms "decide" on a schedule of reproduction based on optimality of allocation of resources in a particular environment. If the mortality rate due to extrinsic factors (e.g., predation, accidents) is high, it makes little sense for an organism to delay reproduction given the potentially severe costs of not reproducing at all in a dangerous environment. Consequently, effort and energy in this particular environment should be allocated toward earlier reproduction, minimizing the chances of death without reproducing.

The time horizon of an organism, determined from environmental cues to life expectancy, has a powerful influence on life history. Under the eye of selection, organisms that most accurately assess their time horizons based on internal and external mortality cues and exhibit an appropriate behavioral response would obtain higher fitness and pass this ability on to future generations. In the context of decision making, a limited time horizon leads organisms to value immediate, short-term rewards more highly than larger distal future rewards, a pattern known as future discounting. Discounting of the future may appear on the surface to be a brash strategy, but choosing such a strategy when faced with certain environmental conditions may represent an optimal decision. Harvey and Zammuto (1985) showed that age of first reproduction in females is related to life expectancy at birth both within and across various species of wild mammals.

Humans appear to exhibit similar sensitivity to time horizons by discounting the future if time horizons appear to be short or if the projected quality of one's future is perceived to be poor. In an interesting study, Phillips, Ruth, and Wagner (1993) examined the death rates of Chinese Americans who believed that certain years of birth are associated with susceptibility for certain diseases (e.g., fire years are associated with the heart and therefore heart diseases). Results showed that Chinese Americans died significantly earlier if they contracted a disease associated with their birth year compared to Chinese Americans who contracted a disease not associated with their birth year. Chinese Americans who were less likely to hold traditional beliefs (e.g., not born in China) showed fewer years of life lost if there was a match between disease and year of birth. White Americans, who were not expected to hold such beliefs, did not show an association between year of birth and death rates for any diseases. The findings for Chinese Americans held for all major causes of death and could not be explained by cohort effects, marital status, or changes in the explicit outward behavior of patients, doctors, or other healers. One interpretation of these findings, in light of sensitivity to time horizons, is that certain beliefs about future outcomes implicitly affect physiology and behavior.

Returning to antisocial and risky behavior, the decision to engage in such behavior may be contingent on an individual's assessment (not necessarily conscious) of his own need and how the available present and future behavioral options might meet that need. For example, individuals experiencing economic hardship, poor health, or low social status may rightly perceive that their expected outcome (e.g., a minimum-wage job) will be poor. Such people often appear to engage in behaviors reflective of future discounting, such as competitive risk-taking or interpersonal violence, perhaps because their perceived need for social, reproductive, or financial advancement exceeds the mean advancement resulting from lower-risk behaviors. Engaging in such behaviors may lead to at least short-term gains in reputation, reproductive opportunities, or material resources. Potentially costly risky or antisocial behavior becomes an appealing option, as the benefits may far outweigh the costs for an individual with poor future prospects and a shortened time horizon.

Following this logic, age-specific risk rates reflect different valuations in short- versus long-term rewards. The relative valuation of safety and survival changes in reference to life stages, particularly in comparison to other potential immediate rewards such as mating access (Daly & Wilson, 2001; Hill & Chow, 2002; Rogers, 1994). Young males aged 18 to 24 are particularly likely to engage in antisocial and risk-accepting behavior because competition for status, mates, and resources in that period of time reaches its peak (Wilson & Daly, 1985). Young males compete not only with each other but also with older males who have had more time to accumulate skills, resources, and status, features important to female mate choice. This period of time allows for the potential of high variance in gains, as the costs of not obtaining resources and a mate are significant in a fitness sense, and risk-taking may be necessary to obtain favorable outcomes (Hill & Chow, 2002).

There are also situations in which the future is less discounted and behavior is focused on maximizing long-term outcomes. Other aspects of life history have been associated with decreases in risky behavior, such as obtaining status, gaining a long-term mate, and parenthood (Hill & Chow, 2002). For individuals who have already obtained a mate through competition and are the progenitors of offspring, effort and energy may shift from competition and mating effort to parental effort, facilitating a decrease in risky behavior.

Interpersonal conflict can be thought of as an outcome of steep future discounting and a risk-accepting response to social competition, and many homicides occur as a direct result of male–male competition over status or mates (e.g., Daly & Wilson, 1998, 1990; Wilson & Daly, 1985, 1992, 1997). Wilson and Daly examined homicide rates and reproductive timing as a function of economic inequality and local life expectancy. In the context of limited life expectancy, it is likely that males would escalate competition, and indeed, Wilson and Daly found that the homicide rate increased as local life expectancy decreased, even after statistically removing the effects of homicide on life expectancy. Similarly, a shift toward immediate reproduction trading off with later reproduction should be observed in situations of short time horizons, because the likelihood of successfully reproducing in the future is diminished in such a situation. Wilson and Daly found support for this hypothesis, demonstrating that disproportionately high birth rates among younger mothers were observed in neighborhoods with the lowest life expectancies.

The predictability of environmental cues should also play an important role in the modulation of risky behavior. Risk acceptance may constitute a more effective strategy when future prospects are unknown. If an individual were to utilize a "safe," risk-averse strategy in the face of uncertainty, he might not survive to reproduce again if conditions became particularly bad. In the face of unpredictability, a risky strategy, although paradoxical, may have been associated with greater reproductive success in an ancestral environment. Following from this prediction, Hill, Ross, and Low (1997) found that reported risk-taking behavior in various domains (e.g., sexual, health, financial) was higher in college students who exhibited higher future-unpredictability beliefs and shorter life span estimates. Further research demonstrated that early cues of unpredictability, such as parental divorce or family unreliability, are associated with a risk-accepting life history strategy (Ross & Hill, 2002). It is also possible that divorced or unreliable parents genetically passed on traits that predispose their offspring toward risky behavior, and previous research has shown that there is some genetic transmission of antisocial tendencies from parents to offspring (e.g., Cadoret, Yates, Troughton, Woodworth, & Stewart, 1995). Behavioral genetic studies have also shown, however, that the environment accounts for a large proportion of variance in phenotypes, suggesting that features of the environment may calibrate or activate evolved mechanisms (e.g., sensitivity to predictability cues) associated with risk-taking.

In sum, similar trade-offs are seen in humans that are seen in other animals, wherein short time horizons and unpredictable environments may lead to discounting of the future, as evidenced by greater risky and antisocial behavior in individuals with shorter or less favorable future prospects.

Mating and Parenting Effort

In most species, males have a higher potential reproductive rate than females and so can produce more offspring in a given period of time (Clutton-Brock & Vincent, 1991). One mechanism through which this sex difference can manifest is an imbalance in minimal parental investment (Trivers, 1972). In many species, females incur greater time and energy costs than males in order to produce offspring. In humans, women must invest at least nine months of time for gestation and must go through parturition. Except under exceptional circumstances, energy costs are also incurred in having to provide nourishment for the neonate. In contrast, men need only contribute a single ejaculate to successfully produce an offspring with a fertile woman.

The sex difference in potential reproductive rates creates a situation in which the "slower" sex, usually female, becomes a valuable resource for which members of the opposite sex, usually males, compete (Clutton-Brock & Vincent, 1991). Because a pregnant or lactating female is effectively removed from a pool of potential mates, the effective (or operational) sex ratio is male-biased, facilitating the evolution of intense male–male competition for the limited number of available females. That certain males can monopolize the available pool of females more than others increases male variance in reproductive success, fueling competition (Clutton-Brock & Vincent, 1991).

Over evolutionary time, there may have been stronger selection pressure on men relative to women to seek sexual opportunities, given that an increase in sexual partners likely increased the reproductive success of men more than women over time. A tendency for men to invest more energy in mating effort than women has been well established (reviewed in Low, 2000; see also Schmitt, 2005). Although men are more likely than women to invest in mating relative to parenting effort, there is variation within the sexes. Some men may be monogamous and invest copious amounts of time and energy in their offspring; others may attempt to have as many sexual encounters as possible, never investing in offspring. Similar but smaller variation in allocation of energy to mating and parental effort is seen in women. In both men and women, a tendency toward early reproduction and high mating effort is generally associated with greater risk-taking and antisocial behavior (reviewed in Lalumière et al., 2005).

In both sexes, risk-taking tendencies are highly associated with being or getting someone pregnant in adolescence (Bingham & Crockett, 1996; Jessor, Costa, Jessor &

Donovan, 1983). Teenage fathers are more likely to have committed serious crimes (Stouthamer-Loeber & Wei, 1998) and to have encountered vulnerability factors associated with antisocial behavior, such as low socioeconomic status or parental antisociality (Fagot, Pears, Capaldi, Cosby, & Leve, 1998). Early pregnancy in females has also been associated with antisocial behavior, with childhood aggression predicting early motherhood (Serbin et al., 1998). Other studies have investigated mating effort more generally in relation to antisocial conduct. Lalumière and Quinsey (1996) found that variables measuring antisocial tendencies were also related, in men, to a history of multiple uncommitted sexual relationships. Additionally, antisocial men are more likely to utilize sexual coercion, aggression, or deception in the pursuit of mating opportunities. In many studies, age at first intercourse is strongly related to indicators of antisocial tendencies (e.g., Quinsey, Book, & Lalumière, 2001).

Why are antisocial individuals more likely to engage in potentially costly mating behaviors, exhibiting high mating effort and low parental effort? Adolescence-limited delinquents exhibit a peak in antisocial behavior, including increased sexually coercive behavior, after puberty, with a systematic decline occurring sometime thereafter. As mentioned before, this peak during adolescence may be due to escalated intrasex competition for mates (Campbell, 1995; Daly & Wilson, 1988; Wilson & Daly, 1985). Because of sex differences in potential reproductive rate, there is greater variability in male than in female reproductive success, and thus there are greater fitness benefits bestowed upon males who succeed and greater costs for males who do not.

It should be noted that behaviors that are considered risky may also reflect hard-to-fake displays of prowess or social status, such as willingness to fight, fearlessness, or independence. Adolescent risky and antisocial behavior may thus serve as an "honest signal" of qualities desirable to females (e.g., health, attractiveness; Lalumière & Quinsey, 2000; Zahavi & Zahavi, 1997). This notion is supported by the findings that gang leaders and dominant males enjoy increased access to sexual partners, and young males are more likely to engage in risky behavior when in the presence of peers (reviewed in Daly & Wilson, 2001).

Desistance from criminal and risky behavior for most individuals occurs after adolescence, likely as a function of a shift in allocation of energy from mating to parenting effort. Marriage, stable work, and aging are all reliable correlates of desistance from risky behavior. A shift from mating to parenting effort (or vice versa) should be observed when the cost–benefit ratio favors one type of effort over the other. Investing in a committed relationship with a high-quality mate, for example, may offer greater fitness benefits in the long term. The relative costs of attempting to gain multiple mating opportunities—such as time and effort allocated to courting, risks associated with sexual aggression, or retaliatory violence from partner's relatives—may be too high compared to the relative benefits of investing in a long-term relationship with a single partner and allocating effort and energy to children born of that partnership. Surprisingly, little research has been done to investigate the actual effect of having children on the shift from mating to parental effort. We expect that adolescent-limited delinquents are likely to exhibit diminished risky and antisocial behavior after having children, whereas life-course-persistent offenders would not necessarily do so. Lowered testosterone following the onset of fatherhood has been suggested as a proximal mechanism for this shift (e.g., Gray, Kahlenberg, Barrett, Lipson, & Ellison, 2002). Only adolescence-limited delinquents exhibit a decrease in antisocial behavior with age and so are likely more sensitive to situational or environmental changes, such as having children. Because life-course-persistent offenders do not desist from antisocial behavior with age, different mechanisms are required to explain the persistence of antisocial behavior in this group and in psychopaths.

In sum, individuals must "decide" to invest energy in mating or parenting. Males and younger individuals have more to gain and less to lose from engaging in risky behavior. With age, greater social status, a long-term relationship, and children, however, the relative valuation of benefits and costs from risky antisocial behavior changes significantly, and a shift from mating to parenting effort is observed.

Growth, Reproduction, and Competitive Disadvantage

Life-course-persistent offenders do not exhibit desistance from antisocial or criminal behavior with age, suggesting that a different mechanism is required to explain their consistently high valuation of antisocial behavior relative to its costs. The construct of embodied capital, used in human behavioral ecology, is particularly illuminating of life-course-persistent offending.

Embodied capital refers to intrinsic attributes, such as health, skills, or attractiveness, that allow for successful competition for resources, mates, and status (Lalumière et al., 2005). Individuals with low embodied capital may experience an early and consistent competitive disadvantage, such that a conditional strategy of persistently risky and antisocial behavior may represent the best chance for obtaining resources, status, or mates. Individuals with low embodied capital would likely project their future prospects to be poor, thus affecting the cost-benefit ratio of adopting risky antisocial behavior. The strategy is conditional, in the sense that it facultatively responds to cues of low embodied capital.

Life-course-persistent offenders indeed appear to be at competitive disadvantage relative to others, suffering early from neurodevelopmental problems, poor academic success, and poor social support. As a consequence, antisocial behaviors such as the acquisition of resources through criminal means, establishment of dominance or higher status through violence, or coercion in attempting to gain mating opportunities may represent the most beneficial behavioral option. Competitive disadvantage has been empirically shown to influence rates of antisocial and criminal behavior. Wilson and Daly (1997) demonstrated that Chicago neighborhoods with higher local income disparities also experienced higher homicide rates. If one is able to legitimately compete for resources, status, or mates, it is not beneficial to engage in costly risky or criminal behavior. Low-embodied-capital individuals, however, have much to gain and often little to lose from discounting the future and engaging in antisocial conduct. The constraints of low embodied capital shift the cost–benefit ratio of risky and antisocial behaviors, making such behaviors a more beneficial option. Because low embodied capital may not be easy to remedy, this option remains optimal throughout the life span.

Cues of present or future embodied capital may influence growth trajectories and the adoption of life-course-persistent antisocial behavior, and these outcomes may represent consequences of a life history trade-off between investment in long-term growth and earlier reproduction. Infants exhibit a predictable growth trajectory when they experience typical prenatal conditions. Low birth weight caused by poor maternal nutrition (Godfrey, Robinson, Barker, Osmond, & Cox, 1996), however, can often lead to rapid compensatory growth during the early years of a child's life, in addition to health problems later in life (Gluckman, Hanson, & Spencer, 2004; Lummaa, 2003). The experience of poor maternal nutrition in utero may serve as a cue to the developing fetus that conditions experienced during development (in this case, limited resource availability) are likely to continue after birth and in the future. Thus, compensatory growth and accelerated development in the early part of a child's life may occur as a preemptive physiological adapted response that is likely to confer benefits in anticipation of specific future conditions.

Individuals who exhibit compensatory growth may reproduce earlier in life, but their lack of investment in long-term growth results in an earlier onset of senescence. Such a mechanism may represent an attempt to mature and reproduce earlier than other potential competitors in a cohort, albeit at the cost of not being able to reproduce later. Empirical evidence supports a short-term versus long-term growth life history trade-off in that individuals experiencing early compensatory growth senesce faster and suffer negative reproductive consequences later in life (Lummaa, 2003; Phillips et al., 2001; Eriksson et al., 2001).

Several factors have been implicated in the development of life-course-persistent offending, including parental abuse, poor nutrition (in utero or during childhood), neurodevelopmental perturbations, and general developmental instability (Harris et al., 2001; Lalumière, Harris, & Rice, 2001). Although these factors are typically seen as disrupting normal developmental processes, another interpretation is possible. Neurodevelopmental perturbations and poor nutrition may serve as cues of developmental disadvantage to a mother and her fetus, thus facilitating the development of psychological mechanisms calibrated to produce risk-accepting strategies. Early parental abuse and the subsequent development of persistent antisocial behavior may also reflect the same mechanism, as parental abuse may suggest (analogous to poor nutrition) low embodied capital and a difficult future. Persistent antisocial behavior has also been associated with lower life expectancy, consistent with a life history strategy oriented toward short-term, immediate gains at the cost of long-term survival (Laub & Vaillant, 2000).

An interesting natural experiment provides information relevant to the suggested trade-off between growth (or embodied capital more generally) and reproduction.

During World War II, food supplies were limited by the German army in some parts of the Netherlands, leading to a severe food shortage. Males whose mothers experienced food scarcity during pregnancy had lower birth weight and experienced lower reproductive success over their lifetime (Lumey & Stein, 1997). These males also exhibited much higher frequencies of antisocial behavior in early adulthood compared to males whose mothers did not experience food scarcity (Neugebauer, Hoek, & Susser, 1999).

In sum, persistent antisocial behavior may develop as a conditional life history strategy based on environmental cues predictive of negative future prospects and competitive disadvantage (or low embodied capital), with short-term benefits of immediate reproduction and long-term costs of decreased life span. The lack of desistence of antisocial behavior in life-course-persistent offenders can be explained by low embodied capital and other consequences of compensatory growth (or similar mechanisms) in response to early predictive environmental cues. In both cases, an individual has little prospect of improving competitive standing relative to others in the population and experiences little ability to legitimately acquire a stable job, a long-term relationship partner, or good social standing—all factors that have been shown to be associated with the desistence of antisocial behavior in adolescent-limited delinquents. This framework leads to new expectations regarding the development of antisocial and risky behavior. For example, fast growth during childhood should be associated with life-course-persistent offending but not adolescence-limited delinquency, unless intense remedial measures are put into place.

Life History Strategies as Personalities

Personality describes an individual's consistent pattern of emotional, cognitive, and behavioral responses in multiple contexts (Funder, 2001). Individual differences manifesting as unique personalities may represent different, consistent patterns of solving life history problems. Psychopathy may represent an extreme example of a personality type, in that it is indicative of a consistent pattern of affect, cognition, and behavior that reflects constant risk acceptance and future discounting. At the other extreme, exceptionally risk-averse individuals may always choose the "safest" avenue, whereby risk is avoided and the future is always considered, not discounted. Some studies have identified other personality traits closely associated with criminality and antisocial behavior, such as negative emotionality and weak constraint (Agnew, Brezina, Wright, & Cullen, 2002; Caspi et al., 1994) as well as sensitivity to rewards (Fonseca & Yule, 1995) and low self-control (Gottfredson & Hirschi, 1990).

Although psychopaths share features with life-course-persistent offenders—early onset and persistence of antisocial tendencies, for example—there are important differences to consider. In particular, psychopaths generally do not seem to have experienced the same cues of competitive disadvantage as life-course-persistent offenders. They do not exhibit the same neurodevelopmental pathologies, and they appear to have higher embodied capital. For example, Lalumière et al. (2001) found that adult psychopaths, compared to other adult offenders, had experienced fewer obstetrical complications, exhibited lower fluctuating asymmetry (based on ten features of the head and body), were less likely to be left-handed (a sign of early neuro-developmental perturbations), and were rated as more physically attractive. Other studies have investigated the underlying structure of persistent violence, suggesting that a factor associated with psychopathy and a factor associated with early developmental problems (consisting of obstetrical complications, low IQ, problems in infancy, and so on) were unrelated to each other (Harris et al., 2001). This and other evidence (reviewed in Barr & Quinsey, 2004; Harris et al., 1993; Skilling, Quinsey, & Craig, 2001) suggests that psychopathy represents a separate subgroup of persistent offenders (see Chapter 10 of this volume).

Although engaging in risky behavior is often contingent on fluid environmental or situational conditions, stable patterns of personality may represent attempts to establish "niches" in variable environments. Individuals of average embodied capital who do not suffer from extreme competitive advantage, for example, may engage in consistently low-risk behavior. Investment in low variance outcomes such as commitment to education throughout early childhood, a stable job, and a long-term relationship in life may reflect a long-term, stable, risk-averse personality.

The introversion–extroversion personality dimension may represent behavioral patterns that arise from this scenario. Investment in high mating effort and taking risks that require certain skills may reflect a personality type that is outgoing, risk-accepting, and extroverted. Nettle (2005) has suggested that the introversion–extroversion personality dimension reflects different benefits and costs. Extroversion, for example, was found to be associated with higher mating effort; male extroverts were more likely to have extrapair partners, and female extroverts were more likely to leave existing relationships. Costs of extroversion were also hypothesized and found, with increases in the likelihood of involvement in an accident or illness. In addition, extroverted women were more likely to expose their children to stepparenting, a known risk factor for child abuse and murder (Daly & Wilson, 1988).

Some support for the development of different personality "types" that partially incorporate risk-acceptance and risk-propensity comes from Sulloway's (1997) investigation of birth order and personality. Sulloway suggested that firstborns tend to identify more with their parents, adopting a risk-averse, more conservative strategy over the course of the life span, while later and middle-borns tend to take more risks. Sulloway's characterization of birth order and personality is consistent with the notion that risky or antisocial behavior is an adaptive response contingent on early cues of future prospects and projected time horizons. Firstborns may develop a conservative, risk-averse personality because of the greater certainty of their future resource or status potential derived from parental inheritance. For later-born individuals, certainty of future resources or status is not guaranteed, and a riskier strategy may be required to gain resources, status, and mates. Some empirical evidence supports different personalities and risk propensity based on birth order, suggesting that middle- and later-born offspring are more likely to engage in adolescent anti-social behavior such as substance use, precocious sexual activity, and criminal be-havior (Argys, Rees, Averett, & Witoonchart, 2006). Other studies have linked birth order to personality differences in various domains (e.g., Buunk, 1997; Saroglou & Fiasse, 2003).

Evidence for animal "personalities" has been accumulating and has been a re-cent topic of great interest for behavioral ecologists. Wolf, Sander van Doorn, Leimar, and Weissing (2007) conducted computer simulations that suggest life-history trade-offs favor the evolution of different personalities (e.g., risk-proneness, aggressiveness, boldness). Wolf and colleagues argued that intraspecies variation in the valuation of current versus future fitness returns may lead to polymorphic populations that vary in their propensity toward short-term- and long-term-oriented life history strategies. Animal "personalities" may reflect an attempt to establish behavioral "niches" in a variable environment. Future research using animal models may shed light on the evolution of personalities in humans.

Life Histories and Heritability

In this chapter, we suggest that people's life histories vary with conditions encoun-tered throughout their lifetimes, especially those encountered early in life. Thus, many life histories, including those involving life-course-persistent offending, are likely developmentally conditional (see Lalumière et al., 2005, for a thorough dis-cussion of conditional and obligate strategies associated with antisocial behavior in humans and other species). It is well accepted, however, that personality in general and antisocial tendencies in particular show significant heritability in behavior ge-netic studies (e.g., Mason & Frick, 1994). There are at least three ways to resolve this apparent inconsistency. First, psychopathy is likely part of a heritable and obligate life history (see Chapter 10), and psychopathy has not been considered in behavioral genetics studies of antisocial behavior. Thus, the number of psychopaths in a given behavioral genetic study of antisocial behavior would directly inflate heritability estimates. Second, some factors associated with resistance to developmental pertur-bations must be heritable. Because neurodevelopmental factors are cues to future competitive disadvantage in our hypothetical model of life-course-persistent offend-ing, behavioral genetic studies of persistent offending will inevitably obtain nonzero heritability. Finally, nonzero heritability does not necessarily provide evidence against the existence of condition-dependent life histories.

For instance, the experience of maltreatment is reliably associated with the de-velopment of antisocial tendencies (there is now good evidence that this is an envi-ronmental effect, not simply a genetic transmission effect). Childhood maltreatment may provide a cue to the quality of current and future environments, and people may "adjust" their development accordingly. Caspi et al. (2002), however, found that a genetic polymorphism on the X chromosome associated with the monoamine oxidase A enzyme (which breaks down some neurotransmitters) moderates this relationship: maltreated individuals with a genotype associated with low expression of the gene are much more likely to engage in antisocial behavior as adults than maltreated individuals with a genotype associated with high expression of the gene. Other gene–environment interactions have been detected using large samples and sensitive measures (e.g., a serotonin transporter gene and stressful life events on risk for adult depression; Caspi et al., 2003). Thus, it is likely that the "decision" to adopt a particular life history is dependent on both the conditions encountered and the genotype of the individual. For some people, difficult social conditions may not provide a cue to impending competitive disadvantage because they have the ability to overcome them.

An Application of Life History Analysis: Understanding the 1990s Crime Drop

We now turn our attention to the application of life history analysis to understand a contemporary criminological issue. In the early 1990s, rates for all types of crimes fell sharply in both Canada and the United States (Blumstein & Wallman, 2005; Lalumière et al., 2005; Levitt, 2004; Mishra & Lalumière, 2008). A number of explanations have been offered for the crime drop, including an aging population, increases in the number of police officers, a stronger economy, and changes in abortion laws in the 1970s (Levitt, 2004). Although each explanation can account for a small portion of the decline in crime, none appears to explain a significant amount of the variation in rates of criminal behavior. In addition, many explanations involve U.S.-specific phenomena, such as increased incarceration, and ignore the parallelism between the Canadian and U.S. crime data (Ouimet, 2002). It is quite possible that criminological hypotheses for the decline in crime may be focusing on too narrow a target of explanation.

Our research suggests that existing explanations of the crime drop have not considered the broader category of behavior to which most crimes belong, specifically antisocial behavior and risk-taking (Mishra & Lalumière, 2008). Archival data from the United States and Canada were used to show that since the early 1990s, antisocial and risky behaviors in the domains of violence, some types of drug use, accidents, and sexual behavior have dropped significantly and in a manner that closely parallels the drop in crime. Our results confirm a strong link between crime, antisocial behavior, and risky behavior and suggest that what requires explanation is not simply the drop in crime but a more general drop in risk-taking and antisocial behavior.

What facilitated a decrease in criminal and risky behavior in general in the 1990s? We propose in this chapter that antisocial and risk-taking tendencies are affected by people's time horizons. Here we apply the life history framework presented in this chapter to suggest potential causes of the crime and risk drop in the hope that these suggestions may represent fruitful avenues of research. We identify what may be indicators of a shift from a focus on short-term gains to a focus on long-term gains in the early 1990s and suggest environmental cues that may have influenced such a shift.

The significant drop in antisocial behavior that was observed for the entire population of the United States and Canada in the early 1990s suggests that time horizons were perceived to be longer, and future prospects were perceived as more positive. Therefore, we expect to find *indicators* of investment in long-term, future outcomes instead of short-term outcomes and an increase in behaviors suggestive of an optimistic view of the future. In addition, if risk and antisocial behavior are affected by time horizons and the quality of one's future, then environmental *cues* predictive or indicative of a benevolent future should be observed to precede or accompany the drop in antisocial behavior in the 1990s.

Preliminary data provide some support for the notion that a shift toward a positive future orientation was observed over the course of the 1990s. For example, according to the Youth Risk Behavior Surveillance Survey, teenagers have lived healthier lives by exercising more and eating more fruits and vegetables since the early 1990s. Visits to the doctor for tests diagnostic of long-term chronic diseases such as cancer and diabetes have also increased during that time span despite a drop in the incidence of many diseases, suggesting that people are investing time in physical maintenance. Depression rates, which may be reflective of pessimism about future prospects, have decreased over 25% in Canada since the early 1990s (Patten, 2002). It is important to interpret such data with caution because many other factors could be responsible for these changes, such as increased antidepressant prescriptions affecting depression rates. Together, however, these indicators suggest that as of the early 1990s, people may have exhibited a greater and more optimistic interest in long-term, future-oriented behaviors rather than behaviors reflective of short-term, immediate rewards focused on the present.

Reproductive and parenting behaviors have also changed since the early 1990s. Investment in high mating effort and attempts at immediate reproduction are associated with a shorter time horizon and more negative future prospects, whereas greater investment in parenting and one's offspring suggests a longer-term and more future-oriented perspective. Therefore, we should expect that indicators of parenting effort should have increased and indicators of high mating effort should have decreased since the early 1990s. Since that time, such a shift does appear to have occurred; mothers have delayed reproduction, with decreases in birth rates observed for all ages, except for women aged 30 to 44, whose reproductive future is short (data from the U.S. National Center for Health Statistics, NCHS). There are significantly fewer teen pregnancies (down more than 20% in both the United States and Canada since 1991) in addition to fewer live births among teens (NCHS). It would also be expected that parents allocate more resources to fewer offspring. Even divorce rates have decreased since the early 1990s, suggesting that people may be investing more in long-term relationships (NCHS). Collection of more data relevant to reproductive outcomes and investment in children will provide further tests as to whether there has been a shift toward long-term strategies involving investing in children, as opposed to strategies more oriented to short-term mating effort since the early 1990s. One potentially productive avenue of research would be to examine changes in intensity of parental supervision over the last twenty years (certainly an indicator of parental effort); parental monitoring is one of the best protective factors for anti-social behavior (Donovan & Jessor, 1985).

The dramatic increase in obesity rates since the early 1990s is particularly interesting in the context of the life history trade-off between investment in long-term growth and short-term reproduction (Mokdad et al., 1999). If the decline in crime and risk-taking since the early 1990s is the result of situational cues signaling favorable future conditions, we hypothesize that people would invest more in maintenance and growth than in immediate reproduction. We are currently analyzing data at the state level investigating the relationship of reproductive outcomes and obesity rates since the 1990s. Preliminary results suggest that there is indeed an inverse relationship between indicators of immediate reproduction, such as teenage pregnancy, and long-term investment in growth, such as body mass index. We do not suggest that obesity is adaptive but rather that investment in growth and long-term health means saving calories rather than spending them. In a modern environment with easy access to calorie-rich foods, this process leads to obesity. Such results must obviously be interpreted with caution at present, and further data must be collected, but these preliminary results suggest that a trade-off between immediate reproduction and long-term growth may have occurred in concert with the drop in antisocial and risky behavior in the 1990s. The question still remains, however: What caused this shift from short-term to long-term strategies?

We described several environmental and situational variables associated with increases in antisocial behavior and short-term life history strategies in this chapter, including perceived length of time horizons, projected quality of future prospects, unpredictability of environments, quality of early environment, intensity of competition, and competitive disadvantage. Changes in each of these variables may have preceded or accompanied the drop in antisocial behavior in the early 1990s and would represent important avenues of investigation.

Life expectancy has been increasing for some time in North America. People perceive the length of their time horizon in more ecologically relevant ways than simply looking at a calculated national average life expectancy, and so cues such as the presence of older relatives (parents, grandparents) as well as the presence of older individuals within smaller local populations (e.g., neighborhoods within a city) would be indicative of a lengthier expected future. In communities where there are many sources of extrinsic mortality, such as homicide or accidents, antisocial behaviors are more often observed (Wilson & Daly, 1997). The recent increase in body mass index may itself provide a cue to the health of others, generating positive estimates of one's (or one's children's) future health. A recent study reported that having an overweight spouse, friends, or siblings increases one's odds of obesity (Christakis & Fowler, 2007). Thus it is possible that at the community level, sources of extrinsic mortality have decreased and cues to future health have increased, leading to more future-oriented and less antisocial behavior.

Other cues relevant to time horizons and future prospects may include decreases in perceived inequality, leading to less interpersonal competition and less potential for individuals to suffer competitive disadvantage. Although inequality between the richest and the poorest has actually been increasing at the national level since the early 1990s, it may be possible that communities at a lower level, such as neighborhoods, may have experienced a more egalitarian distribution of wealth, leading to less inequality and fewer costly antisocial behaviors as a response to lesser competition. Comparison of different communities since the early 1990s would shed light on what time-horizon-relevant cues may influence life history strategies.

Conclusion

The application of life history analysis to the development of risky and antisocial behavior may provide a useful framework for thinking about both ultimate and proximal causes, especially hypothetical causes that may not have been postulated under standard development and learning theories. A consideration of ultimate causes, in particular, forces us to think differently about the meaning of pathology, the function of risk and antisocial behavior, the causes of health problems, and how people respond to difficult early conditions. We hope we have shown that a research program informed by life history analysis is a program that may lead to the discovery of proximal—and thus likely modifiable and preventable—causes.

ACKNOWLEDGMENTS

We wish to thank Josh Duntley, Grant Harris, Danny Krupp, Christine Michell, Michael Seto, Vern Quinsey, Todd Shackelford, and Tracey Skilling for providing helpful feedback on an earlier version of this chapter. Thanks also to the Social Sciences and Humanities Research Council for providing a Doctoral Fellowship to S. M. and a Standard Research Grant to M. L. L.

References

Agnew, R., Brezina, T., Wright, J. P., & Cullen, F. T. (2002). Strain, personality traits, and delinquency: Extending general strain theory. *Criminology, 40*, 43–72.

Anderson, G. S. (2007). *Biological influences on criminal behavior*. London: CRC Press.

Argys, L. M., Rees, D. I., Averett, S. L., & Witoonchart, B. (2006). Birth order and risky adolescent behavior. *Economic Inquiry, 44*, 215–233.

Barr, K. N., & Quinsey, V. L. (2004). Is psychopathy a pathology or a life strategy? Implications for social policy. In C. Crawford & C. Salmon (Eds.), *Evolutionary psychology, public policy, and personal decisions* (pp. 293–317). Hillsdale, NJ: Erlbaum.

Bingham, C. R., & Crockett, L. J. (1996). Longitudinal adjustment patterns of boys and girls experiencing early, middle, and late sexual intercourse. *Developmental Psychology, 32*, 647–658.

Blumstein, A., & Wallman, J. (2005). *The crime drop in America*. New York: Cambridge University Press.

Buunk, B. P. (1997). Personality, birth order and attachment styles as related to various types of jealousy. *Personality and Individual Differences, 23*, 997–1006.

Cadoret, R. J., Yates, W. R., Troughton, E., Woodworth, G., & Stewart, M. A. (1995). Genetic-environmental interaction in the genesis of aggressivity and conduct disorders. *Archives of General Psychiatry, 52*, 916–924.

Campbell, A. (1995). A few good men: Evolutionary psychology and female adolescent aggression. *Ethology and Sociobiology, 16*, 99–123.

Caspi, A., McClay, J., Moffitt, T. E., Mill, J., Martin, J., Craig, I. W., et al. (2002). Role of genotype in the cycle of violence in maltreated children. *Science, 297*, 851–854.

Caspi, A., Moffitt, T. E., Silva, P. A., Stouthamer-Loeber, M., Krueger, R. F., & Schmutte, P. S. (1994). Are some people crime-prone? *Criminology, 32*, 163–196.

Caspi, A., Sugden, K., Moffitt, T. E., Mill, J., Taylor, A., Craig, I. W., et al. (2003). Influence of life stress on depression: Moderation by a polymorphism in the 5-HTT gene. *Science, 301*, 386–389.

Christakis, N. A., & Fowler, J. H. (2007). The spread of obesity in a large social network over 32 years. *New England Journal of Medicine, 357*, 370–379.

Clutton-Brock, T. H., & Vincent, A. C. J. (1991). Sexual selection and the potential reproductive rate of males and females. *Nature, 351*, 58–60.

Daly, M., & Wilson, M. (1988). *Homicide*. Hawthorne, NY: Aldine de Gruyter.

Daly, M., & Wilson, M. (1990). Killing the competition. *Human Nature, 1*, 83–109.

Daly, M., & Wilson, M. (2001). Risk taking, intrasexual competition, and homicide. *Nebraska Symposium on Motivation, 47*, 1–36.

Donovan, J. E., & Jessor, R. (1985). Structure of problem behavior in adolescence and young adulthood. *Journal of Consulting and Clinical Psychology, 53*, 890–904.

Eriksson, J. G., Forsen, T., Tuomilehto, J., Osmond, C., Fraser, R. B., & Barker, D. J. P. (2001). Early growth and coronary heart disease in later life: Longitudinal study. *British Medical Journal, 322*, 949–954.

Fagot, B. I., Pears, K. C., Capaldi, D. M., Crosby, L., & Leve, C. S. (1998). Becoming an adolescent father: Precursors and parenting. *Developmental Psychology, 34*, 1209–1219.

Fonseca, A. C., & Yule, W. (1995). Personality and antisocial behavior in children and adolescents: An enquiry into Eysenck's and Gray's theories. *Journal of Abnormal Child Psychology, 23*, 767–781.

Funder, D. C. (2001). *The personality puzzle*. New York: W. W. Norton.

Gluckman, P. D., Hanson, M. A, & Spencer, H. G. (2004). Living with the past: Evolution, development, and patterns of disease. *Science, 305*, 1733–1736.

Godfrey, K., Robinson, S., Barker, D. J. P., Osmond, C., & Cox, V. (1996). Maternal nutrition in early and late pregnancy in relation to placental and fetal growth. *British Medical Journal, 312*, 410.

Gottfredson, M. R., & Hirschi, T. (1990). *A general theory of crime*. Stanford, CA: Stanford University Press.

Gray, P. B., Kahlenberg, S. M., Barrett, E. S., Lipson, S. F., & Ellison, P. T. (2002). Marriage and fatherhood are associated with lower testosterone in males. *Evolution and Human Behavior, 23*, 193–201.

Harris, G. T., Rice, M. E., & Lalumière, M. L. (2001). Criminal violence: The roles of neurodevelopmental insults, psychopathy, and antisocial parenting. *Criminal Justice and Behavior, 28*, 402–426.

Harris, G. T., Rice, M. E., & Quinsey, V. L. (1994). Psychopathy as a taxon: Evidence that psychopaths are a discrete class. *Journal of Consulting and Clinical Psychology, 62*, 387–397.

Harris, G. T., Skilling, T. A., & Rice, M. E. (2001). The construct of psychopathy. *Crime and Justice: A Review of Research, 28*, 197–264.

Harvey, P. H., & Zammuto, R. M. (1985).Patterns of mortality and age at first reproduction in natural populations of mammals. *Nature, 315*, 319–320.

Hill, M. H., & Chow, K. (2002). Life-history theory and risky driving. *Addiction, 97*, 401–413.

Hill, E. M., Ross, L. T., & Low, B. S. (1997). The role of future unpredictability in human risk taking. *Human Nature, 8*, 287–325.

Jessor, R. (1991). Risk behavior in adolescence: A psychosocial framework for understanding and action. *Journal of Adolescent Health, 12*, 597–605.

Jessor, R., Costa, F., Jessor, L., & Donovan, J. E. (1983). Time of first intercourse: A prospective study. *Journal of Personality and Social Psychology, 44*, 618–626.

Kaplan, H., & Gangestad, S. (2005). Life history theory and evolutionary psychology. In D. M. Buss (Ed.), *The handbook of evolutionary psychology* (pp. 68–95). Hoboken, NJ: John Wiley.

Lalumière, M. L., Harris, G. T., Quinsey, V. L., & Rice, M. E. (2005). *The causes of rape: Understanding individual differences in male propensity of sexual aggression.* Washington, DC: American Psychological Association.

Lalumière, M. L., Harris, G. T., & Rice, M. E. (2001). Psychopathy and developmental instability. *Evolution and Human Behavior, 22*, 75–92.

Lalumière, M. L., & Quinsey, V. L. (1996). Sexual deviance, antisociality, mating effort, and the use of sexually coercive behaviors. *Personality and Individual Differences, 21*, 150–175.

Lalumière, M. L., & Quinsey, V. L. (2000). Good genes, mating effort, and delinquency. *Behavioral and Brain Sciences, 23*, 608.

Laub, J. H., & Vaillant, G. E. (2000). Delinquency and mortality: A 50-year follow-up study of 1,000 delinquent and non-delinquent boys. *American Journal of Psychiatry, 157*, 96–102.

Levitt, S. D. (2004). Understanding why crime fell in the 1990s: Four factors that explain the decline and six that do not. *Journal of Economic Perspectives, 18*, 163–190.

Low, B. S. (2000). *Why sex matters: A Darwinian look at human behavior.* New Haven, CT: Princeton University Press.

Lumey, L. H., & Stein, Z. A. (1997). In utero exposure to famine and subsequent fertility: The Dutch famine cohort study. *American Journal of Public Health, 87*, 1962–1966.

Lummaa, V. (2003). Early developmental conditions and reproductive success in humans: Downstream effects of prenatal famine, birthweight, and timing of birth. *American Journal of Human Biology, 15*, 370–379.

Mason, D. A., & Frick, P. J. (1994). The heritability of antisocial behavior: A meta-analysis of twin and adoption studies. *Journal of Psychopathology and Behavioral Assessment, 16*, 301–323.

Mishra, S., & Lalumiere, M. L. (2008). *Did risky behavior decline in the 1990s? An examination of aggregate data in the United States and Canada.* Manuscript submitted for publication.

Moffitt, T. E. (1993). Adolescence-limited and life-course-persistent antisocial behavior: A developmental taxonomy. *Psychological Bulletin, 100*, 674–701.

Mokdad, A. H., Serdula, M. K., Dietz, W. H., Bowman, B. A., Marks, J. S., & Koplan, J. P. (1999). The spread of the obesity epidemic in the United States, 1991–1998. *Journal of the American Medical Association, 282*, 1519–1522.

Nettle, D. (2005). An evolutionary approach to the extraversion continuum. *Evolution and Human Behavior, 26*, 363–373.

Neugebauer, R., Hoek, H. W., & Susser, E. (1999). Prenatal exposure to wartime famine and development of antisocial personality disorder in early adulthood. *Journal of the American Medical Association, 282,* 455–462.

Osgood, D. W., Johnston, L. D., O'Malley, P. M., & Bachman, J. G. (1988). The generality of deviance in late adolescence and early adulthood. *American Sociological Review, 53,* 81–93.

Ouimet, M. (2002). Explaining the American and Canadian crime "drop" in the 1990's. *Canadian Journal of Criminology, 33,* 33–50.

Patten, S. B. (2002). Progress against major depression in Canada. *Canadian Journal of Psychiatry, 47,* 775–780.

Phillips, D. I. W., Handelsman, D. I., Eriksson, J. G., Forsen, T., Osmond, C., Barker, D. J. P., et al. (2001). Prenatal growth and subsequent marital status: Longitudinal study. *British Medical Journal, 322,* 771.

Phillips, D. P., Ruth, T. E., & Wagner, L. M. (1993). Psychology and survival. *The Lancet, 342,* 1142–1145.

Quinsey, V. L., Book, A., & Lalumière, M. L. (2001). A factor analysis of traits related to individual differences in antisocial behavior. *Criminal Justice and Behavior, 28,* 522–536.

Quinsey, V. L., Skilling, T. A., Lalumière, M. L., & Craig, W. (2004). *Juvenile delinquency: Understanding individual differences.* Washington, DC: American Psychological Association.

Rogers, A. R. (1994). Evolution of time preference by natural selection. *American Economic Review, 84,* 460–481.

Ross, L., & Hill, E. M. (2002). Childhood unpredictability, schemas for future unpredictability, and risk taking. *Social Behavior and Personality, 30,* 453–474.

Rutter, M. (1997). Antisocial behavior: Developmental psychopathology perspectives. In D. Stoff, J. Breiling, & J. Maser (Eds.), *Handbook of antisocial behavior.* New York: Wiley.

Saroglou, V., & Fiasse, L. (2003). Birth order, personality, and religion: A study among adults from a three-sibling family. *Personality and Individual Differences, 35,* 19–29.

Serbin, L. A., Cooperman, J. M., Peters, P. L., Lehoux, P. M., Stack, D. M., & Schwartzman, A. E. (1998). Intergenerational transfer of psychosocial risk in women with childhood histories of aggression, withdrawal, or aggression and withdrawal. *Developmental Psychology, 34,* 1246–1262.

Schmitt, D. P. (2005). Sociosexuality from Argentina to Zimbabwe: A 48-nation study of sex, culture, and strategies of human mating. *Behavioral and Brain Sciences, 28,* 247–311.

Skilling, T. A., Quinsey, V. L., & Craig, W. (2001). Evidence of a taxon underlying serious antisocial behavior in boys. *Criminal Justice and Behavior, 28,* 450–470.

Stearns, S. C. (1992). *The evolution of life histories.* Oxford: Oxford University Press.

Stouthamer-Loeber, M., & Wei, E. H. (1998). The precursors of young fatherhood and its effect on delinquency of teenage males. *Journal of Adolescent Health, 22,* 56–65.

Sulloway, F. J. (1997). *Born to rebel: Birth order, family dynamics, and creative lives.* New York: Pantheon Books.

Trivers, R. L. (1972). Parental investment and sexual selection. In B. Campbell (Ed.), *Sexual selection and the descent of man:1871–1971* (pp. 136–179). Chicago, IL: Aldine.

White, H. R., Bates, M. E., & Buyske, S. (2001). Adolescence-limited versus persistent delinquency: Extending Moffitt's hypothesis into adulthood. *Journal of Abnormal Psychology, 110,* 600–609.

Wilson, M., & Daly, M. (1985). Competitiveness, risk taking, and violence: The young male syndrome. *Ethology and Sociobiology, 6,* 59–73.

Wilson, M., & Daly, M. (1992). Who kills whom in spouse killings? On the exceptional sex ratio of spousal homicides in the United States. *Criminology, 30,* 189–215.

Wilson, M., & Daly, M. (1997). Life expectancy, economic inequality, homicide and reproductive timing in Chicago neighbourhoods. *British Medical Journal, 314,* 1271–1274.

Wolf, M., Sander van Doorn, G., Leimar, O., & Weissing, F. J. (2007). Life history trade-offs favour the evolution of animal personalities. *Nature, 447,* 581–585.

Zahavi, A., & Zahavi, A. (1997). *The handicap principle: A missing piece of Darwin's puzzle.* New York: Oxford University Press.

9

Theft

SATOSHI KANAZAWA

An Evolutionary Psychological Perspective on Theft

Theft refers to illicit appropriation of resources that rightfully belong to someone else. Defined as such, the behavior is a cultural universal.[1] Interpol's *International Criminal Statistics* (Interpol, various years) reports some incidence of theft and robbery in each of its 186 member nations every year, so some people steal from and rob others in every nation. Misappropriation of resources (usually food) from rightful owners is also observed among other primate species, such as chimpanzees (de Waal, 1989), bonobos (de Waal, 1992), and capuchin monkeys (de Waal, Luttrell, & Canfield, 1993). That theft is a cultural universal and observed among other species strongly suggests a biological and evolutionary origin.

An evolutionary psychological perspective on theft begins with a recognition of the importance of material resources for both survival and reproduction. Every person needs resources to survive (food, shelter, clothing) and to achieve reproductive success (parental investment). Since not all individuals are equally capable of procuring such resources on their own through legitimate means, it can be expected that some will resort to illicit means to acquire the desired resources.

Besides providing a pan-specific and thus parsimonious explanation for theft and other property crimes, by explaining similar behavior across many species, an evolutionary psychological perspective can simultaneously address four empirical puzzles about theft that no other single criminological theory can: Why do men commit more theft than women? Why are younger men more likely to commit theft than older men? Why are the poor more likely to commit theft than the rich? Why are less intelligent individuals more likely to commit theft than more intelligent individuals?

Empirical Puzzles

1. Why Men and Not Women?

In every human society, men commit an overwhelming majority of both violent and property crimes (Brown, 1991; Kanazawa & Still, 2000). Worldwide, men commit more than 90% of all theft and robberies. Why is this?

One relatively unusual feature of the human mating system can account for the overwhelming male bias toward criminality. Unlike those of most other species, human males make a large parental investment in their offspring. The unusually high degree of *male parental investment* among humans leads to universal human female mate preference for men with a large amount of resources (Buss, 1989). The more resources a potential mate has, the more parental investment he can make in his and his mate's joint children. Men's resources increase their children's chances of survival and their future reproductive prospects.

Because women prefer men with greater resources as their long-term mates, men fiercely compete with one another to accumulate resources and attain higher status. The more resources they possess and the higher the status they occupy, the greater the reproductive opportunities they have. Wealthier men of high status have more sex partners and copulate more frequently than poorer men of low status (Kanazawa, 2003a; Pérusse, 1993). Wealth and status do not have a similar effect on women's desirability as long-term mates (Buss, 1989).

From an evolutionary psychological perspective, this is why men account for an overwhelming majority of thieves and robbers worldwide. Material resources improve men's reproductive prospects much more than they do women's. We would therefore expect men to be much more motivated to accumulate material resources, either through legitimate or illegitimate means, than women. In fact, not only do men commit an overwhelming majority of theft and robberies worldwide but they also make more money through legitimate means, because they are more motivated to do so (Furchtgott-Roth & Stolba, 1999; Kanazawa, 2005a). Men are much more motivated to accumulate resources, whether through legitimate or illegitimate means, in order to attract mates.

My suggestion that men steal in order to attract women might at first appear counterintuitive, because theft, robbery, and other forms of resource malappropriation are universally condemned in human societies (Brown, 1991). It is quite possible, however, that the psychological mechanism that inclines and predisposes men to commit property crimes developed in our ancestors in evolutionary history before the ape–human split (5 to 8 million years ago), and possibly even before the ape–monkey split (15 to 20 million years ago). In fact, an evolutionary psychological perspective on theft logically requires that the key psychological mechanism emerge before the informal norms against theft do; otherwise, resources accumulated through theft will not lead to higher status and reproductive success for men because men engaging in such theft will be ostracized for violating norms (unless, of course, the act of theft goes entirely undetected). I believe that the norms against theft (and other crimes) might have developed *in reaction to* the psychological mechanism that inclines men to steal. The fact that theft appears to be common among our primate cousins who do not have third-party sanctions against such behavior (de Waal, 1989, 1992; de Waal, Luttrell, & Canfield, 1993) seems to suggest that our tendency to steal might have evolved before norms against theft.[2]

That an overwhelming majority of thieves are men does not mean that women never steal; they do. However, an evolutionary psychological perspective on female criminality (Campbell, 1995, 1999, 2002) suggests that men and women may steal for different reasons.

While men steal not only to satisfy their material needs for food, shelter, and clothing but also to compete with other men and gain status, women mostly steal only to satisfy their material needs. Campbell (1999, p. 210) astutely points out that "theft by women is usually tied to economic needs and occurs as part of their domestic responsibilities for their children" whereas "robbery is the quintessential male crime, in which violence is used both to extract resources and to gain status." This is why, when women do steal, they steal much less, and much less frequently, than men do. Women steal what they need; men steal partly to show off.

A personal anecdote illustrates this point well. I moved to the London School of Economics and Political Science in July 2003. Within a month of my arrival in London, someone broke into my new office and stole two blank checks by carefully lifting two nonconsecutive checks from the middle of my new checkbook. When I learned from the bank that the two checks had been cashed for £700 each, I made the (statistically very unlikely to be true) prediction that the thief must have been a woman. As it turned out, it was two women. I later found out their identities from the bank, when they cashed the checks by making them out to themselves *in their real names*, perhaps illustrating another point—that criminals are less intelligent than noncriminals (see later discussion).[3]

As I had read Campbell's work before this 2003 incident, it was immediately obvious to me that the thieves must have been women because it seemed to me that £700 was rent money, not the kind of money used to show off or to attract women. It is the kind of money one *needs*, not the kind of money one *wants*. I felt that a male thief would have made out the check for £700,000. Of course, I do not have that kind of money (nor, I presume, do any of my LSE colleagues). However, from the thief's perspective, if there is at least a 1 in 1,000 chance (0.001%) that the check will clear for that amount, he can still come out ahead by gambling on £700,000 rather than making the check out for a safe £700. Given men's much higher propensity toward risk-taking, I think a male thief might have taken that chance.

2. Why Younger Men and Not Older Men?

One of the advantages of an evolutionary psychological perspective on theft (and crime in general) is that it can explain the universal age–crime curve. In their highly influential 1983 article "Age and Explanation of Crime," Hirschi and Gottfredson claim that the relationship between age and crime is invariant across all social and cultural conditions at all times. In every society, for all social groups, for all races and both sexes, at all historical times, the tendency to commit crimes and other analogous, risk-taking behavior rapidly increases in early adolescence, peaks in late adolescence and early adulthood, rapidly decreases throughout the 20s and 30s, and levels off during middle age. Although there have been minor variations observed around the "invariant" age–crime curve (Greenberg, 1985; Hirschi & Gottfredson, 1985; Steffensmeier, Allan, Harer, & Streifel, 1989), the essential shape of the curve for serious interpersonal crimes remains uncontested in the criminological literature. For empirical examples of the invariant age–crime curve, see Blumstein (1995, Figures 2 and 3), Campbell (1995, Figure 1), Daly and Wilson (1990, Figure 1), and Hirschi and Gottfredson (1983, Figures 1–8).

While Hirschi and Gottfredson claim that the age–crime curve is invariant and holds in all societies at all times, they provide no explanations for this universal observation. They instead argue that no theoretical or empirical variable then available in criminology (in 1983) could explain it. If the age–crime curve is truly constant across all populations, any factor that varies across such populations cannot explain it. Just as a constant cannot explain a variable, a variable cannot explain a constant. The invariant age–crime curve must be explained by something that is constant across all societies and cultures. An evolutionary psychological perspective suggests just such a constant factor (Kanazawa, 2003b; Kanazawa & Still, 2000; Rowe, 2002, pp. 53–55).

There are reproductive benefits for men of intense competitiveness. Those who are highly competitive act violently toward their male rivals. Their violence serves the dual function of protecting their status and honor and discouraging or altogether eliminating their rivals from competition for mates (Daly & Wilson, 1988, 1990). Their competitiveness also predisposes them to accumulate resources to attract mates by stealing from others (via either theft or robbery). The same psychological mechanism induces men who cannot gain legitimate access to women to do so illegitimately through forcible rape (Thornhill & Palmer, 2000). Figure 9.1(A) presents a hypothetical curve depicting the relationship between men's age and their benefit from competition. There are no reproductive benefits from competition (violence and theft) before puberty because prepubertal males are not able to translate their competitive edge into reproductive success. With puberty, however, the benefits of competition skyrocket. Once the men are reproductively capable, every act of violence and theft can potentially increase their reproductive success. The benefits of competition stay high after puberty for the remainder of their lives since human males are reproductively capable for most of their adult lives.

This is not the whole story, however. There are also costs associated with competition. Acts of violence can easily result in the offender's own death or injury, and acts of resource malappropriation can trigger retaliation from the rightful owners of the resources, as well as from their family and allies. Men's reproductive success is

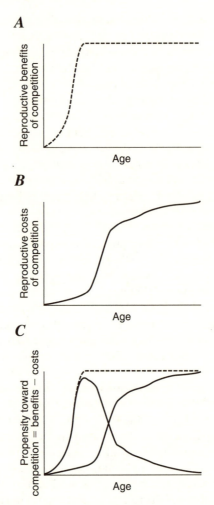

Figure 9.1. The benefits and costs of competition and the age crime curve.
Source: Kanazawa & Still, 2000. Used with permission from the American Sociological Association.

obviously reduced if the competitive acts result in their death or injury. Figure 9.1(*B*) presents a hypothetical curve depicting the costs of competition as a function of age. Before men start reproducing, there are few costs of competition. True, being competitive might result in their death or injury, and they might therefore lose in the reproductive game. However, they also lose by not competing. If they don't compete for mates in a polygynous breeding system (which all human societies are; Daly & Wilson, 1988, pp. 140–142), they'll be left out of the reproductive game altogether and end up losing as a result. In other words, young men *might* lose if they are competitive, but given that polygyny allows some men to monopolize all women, they will *definitely* lose if they aren't competitive. So there's little cost to being competitive even at the risk of death or injury; the alternative—total reproductive failure—is even worse in reproductive terms.

The cost of competition, however, rises dramatically with the birth of the first child and subsequent children. True, men still benefit from competition (as Figure 9.1[A] shows), because such acts of competition might attract additional mates and mating opportunities. However, men's energies and resources are put to better use by protecting and investing in their existing children. In other words, with the birth of children, men should shift their reproductive effort away from *mating effort* and toward *parenting effort*, in the equation: total reproductive effort = mating effort + parenting effort. If men die or get injured in their acts of competition, their existing children will suffer; without sufficient paternal investment and protection, they might starve or fall victim to predation or exploitation by others. The costs of competition therefore rapidly increase after the birth of the first child, which usually happens several years after puberty because men need some time to accumulate sufficient resources to attract their first mate. Nonetheless, in the absence of artificial means of contraception, reproduction probably began at a much earlier age than it does today. There is therefore a gap of several years between the rapid rise in the benefits of competition and the similarly rapid rise in costs.

Figure 9.1(C) depicts a curve that represents the mathematical difference between the benefits and the costs of competition. The curve (in solid bold line) closely resembles the typical age–crime curve. An evolutionary psychological perspective suggests that male criminality varies as it does over the life course because it represents the difference between the benefits and the costs of competition. It is important to note, however, that, unlike actors in decision theories in microeconomics (Grogger, 1998), men, from an evolutionary psychological perspective, do not make these calculations consciously. The calculations have already been performed by natural and sexual selection, so to speak, which then equip men's brains with appropriate psychological mechanisms to incline them to be increasingly competitive in their immediate postpubertal years and to make them less competitive right after the birth of the first child. Men simply don't *feel like* acting violently or stealing, or they just *want to* settle down, after the birth of the child, but they don't necessarily know why.

Fluctuating levels of testosterone may provide the biochemical microfoundation for this psychological mechanism. David Gubernick's unpublished experiment (discussed in Blum, 1997, p. 116) demonstrates that expectant fathers' testosterone levels precipitously fall immediately after the birth of their children. If high levels of testosterone predispose men to be more competitive, then the sudden drop in testosterone after the birth of their children may provide the biochemical reason explaining why men's psychological mechanisms to commit crime "turn off" when they become fathers. Mazur and Michalek's (1998) finding that marriage decreases and divorce increases testosterone levels in men provides a similar microfoundation for the commonly observed negative effect of marriage on criminality (Kanazawa,

2003c; Laub, Nagin, & Sampson, 1998). Further consistent with this perspective, McIntyre et al. (2006) show that married men who actively seek extrapair copulations retain high levels of testosterone characteristic of single men.

Given that human society has always been mildly polygynous, there have been many men who did not succeed at finding a mate and reproducing. These men had everything to gain and nothing to lose by remaining competitive for their entire lives. However, *we are not descended from these men*. As Buss (1994, p. 114) reminds us, all of us are disproportionately descended from men and women who were very successful at reproduction. Contemporary men therefore did not inherit a psychological mechanism that forces them to stay competitive and keep trying to secure mates for their entire lives. An evolutionary psychological perspective can thus explain why criminal behavior, including theft, is largely represented by younger men, not older men.

An evolutionary psychological perspective on property crime in a sense underscores the nondistinctiveness of criminal behavior. Theft and robbery are among a large repertoire of behavior that men engage in to attract mates in order to fulfill their ultimate reproductive goals as biological organisms. In this sense, stealing is no different from anything else men do, such as composing music, painting portraits, writing books, and in fact producing scientific work (Kanazawa, 2003b, 2003c).

3. Why the Poor and Not the Rich?

Criminologists debate whether there is an inverse relationship between social class and criminality. Shaw and McKay (1929) were among the first to show, using official crime statistics, that the poor were more likely to commit crime than the rich. However, later studies claimed that this observation was an artifact of a selection bias, whereby lower-class criminals were more likely to be arrested, prosecuted, and convicted than upper-class criminals and that there were no class differences in self-reported criminality (Short & Nye, 1957). Today some criminologists contend that the negative relationship between social class and criminality is "a myth" (Johnson, 1980; Tittle & Villemez, 1977; Tittle, Villemez, & Smith, 1978), while others claim that there is a genuine relationship (Braithwaite, 1981; Clelland & Carter, 1980; Elliott & Huizinga, 1983). To make matters worse, the debate appears largely driven by ideological conviction rather than empirical data; some scholars conclude that there is no relationship between social class and criminality even when their own data show that the poor are more likely to commit crime than the rich (Dunaway, Cullen, Burton, & Evans, 2000). After nearly a century of debate, consensus on whether there is a negative relationship between social class and criminality appears nowhere near sight, and the best criminologists can offer is that "it remains unclear whether and in what circumstances this negative relationship exists" (Becker & Mehlkop, 2006, p. 194).

Because some criminologists claim that there are no *theoretical* reasons to expect a negative association between social class and criminality (Tittle, 1983), perhaps a new theoretical perspective may help clear the muddy debate. From an evolutionary psychological perspective, it is a straightforward prediction that lower-class men will commit more crimes, particularly property crimes such as theft and robbery, than upper-class men. If women are attracted to higher-status men with greater resources, then lower-class men, who possess and have legitimate access to fewer resources with which to attract mates, should be more motivated to acquire such resources through illicit means than upper-class men. An evolutionary psychological perspective would therefore predict a negative association between social class and criminality. In this connection, it is important to note that some studies of juvenile and adult men show that the social class of their family of origin does not affect their criminality as strongly as their own social class (Stark, 1979; Thornberry & Farnworth, 1982). This is perfectly consistent with an evolutionary psychological perspective on social class and criminality.

An evolutionary psychological perspective on theft can also suggest new hypotheses hitherto unexamined by criminologists. From this perspective, what matters for men's criminality is not social class per se or even resources per se but reproductive opportunities, which highly correlate with their social class and resources (Kanazawa, 2003a; Pérusse, 1993). For example, because women find taller men more attractive as mates than shorter men (Gillis & Avis, 1980; Sheppard & Strathman, 1989), shorter men are more delinquent and criminal than taller men (Farrington, 1992, Table 11.2[g]; 1994, Table 2). Similarly, because women seek out physically attractive men as short-term mates (Gangestad & Simpson, 2000), physically attractive men in general should be less criminal than physically unattractive men. Further, physical attractiveness (or height) and social class should interact in their effects on criminality. Social class should have a weaker negative effect on criminality among physically attractive (taller) men than among physically unattractive (shorter) men. Physically attractive (taller) men of lower class should be less criminal than physically unattractive (shorter) men of lower class. Since social scientists in general and criminologists in particular do not consider physical attractiveness or height to be an important influence on human behavior, these hypotheses are unlikely to be tested by traditional criminologists any time soon.

An evolutionary psychological perspective can also elucidate the mechanism whereby social class influences men's criminality. From this perspective, less intelligent individuals are expected to commit more crime than more intelligent individuals (see later discussion). And social class is significantly negatively correlated with intelligence (Herrnstein & Murray, 2004; Kanazawa, 2005b, pp. 254–255). Thus lower-class men may commit more crime not necessarily or not only because they are poor but because they are less intelligent. I would therefore predict that controlling for men's general intelligence may attenuate or even eliminate the negative effect of social class on their criminality.

4. Why the Less Intelligent and Not the More Intelligent?

Criminologists have long known that criminals on average have lower intelligence than the general population (Herrnstein & Murray, 1994; Hirschi & Hindelang, 1977;

Wilson & Herrnstein, 1985). Juvenile delinquents are less intelligent than nondelinquents (Wolfgang, Figlio, & Sellin, 1972; Yeudall, Fromm-Auch, & Davies, 1982),
and a significant difference in IQ between delinquents and nondelinquents appears
as early as ages 8 and 9 (Gibson & West, 1970). Chronic offenders are less intelligent
than one-time offenders (Wolfgang et al., 1972; Moffitt, 1990), and serious offenders
are less intelligent than less serious offenders (Lynam, Moffitt, & Stouthamer-Loeber,
1993; Moffitt, Gabrielli, Mednick, & Schulsinger, 1981). The negative correlation
between intelligence and criminality is not an artifact of a selection bias whereby
less intelligent criminals are more likely to be caught than more intelligent criminals
because the correlation exists even in self-report studies that do not rely on official
police statistics (Moffitt & Silva, 1988).

Why is this? Why do criminals have lower intelligence than the general population? And why do more chronic and serious criminals have lower intelligence than
their less chronic and serious counterparts? A new hypothesis in evolutionary psychology called the Savanna-IQ Interaction Hypothesis (Kanazawa, 2005b, 2006a,
2006b, 2007a) suggests one possible answer.

Relying on earlier observations made by pioneers of evolutionary psychology
(Crawford, 1993; Symons, 1990; Tooby & Cosmides, 1990), Kanazawa (2004a)
proposes what he calls the Savanna Principle, which states that *the human brain has
difficulty comprehending and dealing with entities and situations that did not exist in the
ancestral environment*. For example, individuals who watch certain types of TV shows
are more satisfied with their friendships, just as they are when they have more friends
or socialize with their friends more frequently (Kanazawa, 2002). This may be because realistic images of other humans, such as those portrayed in television, mov-
ies, videos, and photographs, did not exist in the ancestral environment, where all
realistic images of other humans *were* other humans. As a result, the human brain
may have implicit difficulty distinguishing "TV friends" (characters repeatedly seen
on TV shows) and real friends and may tend to respond similarly to both.

In an entirely separate line of research, Kanazawa (2004b) proposes an evolutionary psychological theory of the evolution of general intelligence. In contrast to
views expressed by Cosmides and Tooby (2000, 2002) and Chiappe and MacDonald
(2005), Kanazawa (2004b) suggests that what is now known as general intelligence
may have originally evolved as a domain-specific adaptation to deal with evolutionarily novel, nonrecurrent problems.[4] The human brain consists of a large number
of domain-specific, evolved psychological mechanisms to solve recurrent adaptive
problems. In this sense, our ancestors did not really have to think in order to solve
such recurrent problems. Evolution has already done all of the thinking, so to speak,
and equipped the human brain with appropriate psychological mechanisms, which
engender preferences, desires, cognitions, and emotions and motivate adaptive behavior in the context of the ancestral environment.

Even in the extreme continuity and constancy of the ancestral environment,
however, there were occasional problems that were evolutionarily novel and nonrecurrent, which required our ancestors to think and reason in order to solve them.

To the extent that these evolutionarily novel, nonrecurrent problems happened frequently enough in the ancestral environment (different problem each time) and had serious enough consequences for survival and reproduction, any genetic mutation that allowed its carriers to think and reason would have been selected for, and what we now call "general intelligence" could have evolved as a domain-specific adaptation for the domain of evolutionarily novel, nonrecurrent problems.

General intelligence may have become universally important in modern life (Gottfredson, 1997; Herrnstein & Murray, 1994; Jensen, 1998) only because our current environment is almost entirely evolutionarily novel. The new theory suggests, and available empirical data confirm, that more intelligent individuals are better than less intelligent individuals at solving problems *only if* the problems are evolutionarily novel but that more intelligent individuals are *not better* than less intelligent individuals at solving evolutionarily familiar problems, such as those in the domains of mating, parenting, interpersonal relationships, and wayfinding (Kanazawa, 2007b).

The logical conjunction of the Savanna Principle and the theory of the evolution of general intelligence suggests a qualification of the Savanna Principle. If general intelligence evolved to deal with evolutionarily novel problems, then the human brain's difficulty in comprehending and dealing with entities and situations that did not exist in the ancestral environment (proposed in the Savanna Principle) should interact with general intelligence, such that the Savanna Principle holds stronger among less intelligent individuals than among more intelligent individuals. More intelligent individuals should be better able to comprehend and deal with evolutionarily novel (but *not* evolutionarily familiar) entities and situations than less intelligent individuals.

There has been accumulating evidence for this Savanna-IQ Interaction Hypothesis. First, individuals' tendency to respond to TV characters as if they were real friends, first discovered by Kanazawa (2002), is limited to those with below-median intelligence (Kanazawa, 2006a); individuals with above-median intelligence do not become more satisfied with their friendships by watching more television.

Second, less intelligent individuals have more children than more intelligent individuals even though they do not want to, possibly because they have greater difficulty effectively employing evolutionarily novel means of modern contraception (Kanazawa, 2005b). Another indication that less intelligent individuals may have greater difficulty employing modern contraception effectively is the fact that the correlation between the lifetime number of sex partners and the number of children is positive among the less intelligent but negative among the more intelligent. The more sex partners less intelligent individuals have, the more children they have; the more sex partners more intelligent individuals have, the fewer children they have.

Third, more intelligent individuals stay healthier and live longer than less intelligent individuals, possibly because they are better able to recognize and deal effectively with evolutionarily novel threats and dangers to health in modern society (Deary, Whiteman, Starr, Whalley, & Fox, 2004; Gottfredson & Deary, 2004; Kanazawa,

2006b). Consistent with the Hypothesis, however, general intelligence does not affect health and longevity in sub-Saharan Africa, where many of the health threats and dangers are more evolutionarily familiar than elsewhere in the world. For example, relative to Western society, comparatively more people die of (evolutionarily familiar) hunger and natural diseases and comparatively fewer from (evolutionarily novel) automobile accidents or gunshot wounds in sub-Saharan Africa. Fourth, more intelligent individuals are more likely to acquire and espouse evolutionarily novel values, such as liberalism, atheism, and, for men, sexual exclusivity than less intelligent individuals (Kanazawa, 2007a). However, consistent with the Hypothesis, intelligence does not affect the acquisition and espousal of evolutionarily familiar values for marriage, children, family, and friends.

Now what does the Savanna-IQ Interaction Hypothesis have to do with crime in general, and theft and robbery in particular? How can it explain the empirical observation that criminals tend to be less intelligent on average than the general population?

From the perspective of the Hypothesis, there are two important points to note. First, much of what we now call interpersonal crime, including theft and robbery, comprised routine means of intrasexual competition and resource acquisition and accumulation in the ancestral environment. This is most obvious from the fact that our primate cousins engage in what we would call theft and robbery if perpetrated by humans (de Waal, 1989, 1992; de Waal et al., 1993). More than likely, ancestral men competed with one another for resources and mating opportunities by stealing from one another if they could get away with it. In other words, most forms of criminal behavior are evolutionarily familiar.

Second, the institutions that deter, control, detect, and punish criminal behavior today—CCTV cameras, police, courts, and prisons—are all evolutionarily novel; there was no third-party enforcement of norms in the ancestral environment, only second-party enforcement (by victims and their kin and allies). In other words, the modern criminal justice system is an evolutionarily novel institution for dealing with evolutionarily familiar criminal behavior.

Thus it makes perfect sense from the perspective of the Savanna-IQ Interaction Hypothesis that men with lower intelligence are more likely to resort to evolutionarily familiar means of competition for resources than to evolutionarily novel means (e.g., theft rather than full-time employment in a capitalist economy). It also makes perfect sense from the perspective of the Hypothesis that men with lower intelligence fail fully to comprehend the consequences of their criminal behavior imposed by evolutionarily novel entities of law enforcement and the criminal justice system. Hence the Hypothesis can explain why less intelligent individuals are more likely to engage in criminal behavior than more intelligent individuals.

The Savanna-IQ Interaction Hypothesis can also suggest a novel hypothesis with regard to IQ and criminality. As mentioned previously, while third-party enforcement (by the police and the criminal justice system) is evolutionarily novel, second-party enforcement (retaliation and vigilance by the victims and their kin and allies) is not. Thus the Hypothesis would predict that the difference in intelligence between criminals and noncriminals disappears in situations where third-party enforcement of norms is weak or absent and where criminal behavior is controlled largely via second-party enforcement, such as situations of prolonged anarchy and statelessness—in fact, any situation that resembles the ancestral environment.

Conclusion

By focusing on the importance of material resources for survival and reproductive success and by underscoring the ultimate reproductive functions of all human behavior, an evolutionary psychological perspective can shed new theoretical light on theft and other property crimes. In particular, it can simultaneously explain why theft and robbery (in fact, all interpersonal crimes) are an overwhelmingly male enterprise; why young men are far more likely to engage in crime than older men (the age–crime curve); why social class and criminality are negatively correlated (the association being far from a "myth"); and why criminals in general tend to be less intelligent than noncriminals. It can also elucidate the causal mechanism behind *why* lower-class men are more likely to engage in crime than upper-class men, and *why* less intelligent men are more likely to engage in crime than more intelligent men.

At the same time, by focusing on individual characteristics that traditional criminologists and social scientists tend to overlook, such as physical attractiveness, height, and general intelligence, an evolutionary psychological perspective on crime can suggest novel hypotheses. For example, lower-class men who are physically more attractive should be less criminal than lower-class men who are physically less attractive, and the difference in intelligence between criminals and noncriminals should weaken to the extent that third-party enforcement (characteristic of modern society but not the ancestral environment) is absent. These and other novel hypotheses from an evolutionary psychological perspective on crime await empirical tests.

ACKNOWLEDGMENTS

I thank Joshua D. Duntley for helpful comments on an earlier draft of this chapter. Direct all correspondence to Satoshi Kanazawa, Interdisciplinary Institute of Management, London School of Economics and Political Science, Houghton Street, London WC2A 2AE, United Kingdom. E-mail: S.Kanazawa@lse.ac.uk.

Notes

1. Strangely, "theft" does not appear on Brown's (1991) list of human universals, even though "males more prone to theft" does. Given that Brown specifically excludes conditional universals ("If theft occurs, then males are more prone to it"), one can safely infer that theft itself is a human universal from the appearance of "males more prone to theft" on the list.

Similarly, one infers that murder is a human universal even though it is not on Brown's list, because "murder proscribed" is. Curiously, both "rape" and "rape proscribed" are on the list.

2. I have elsewhere explored the evolutionary psychological foundations of norms (Kanazawa & Still, 2001).

3. In their defense, however, the thieves were constrained by the (in my opinion) insane UK banking laws, which do not allow individuals to cash checks at all; personal checks must be deposited directly into bank accounts.

4. I concur with Barrett and Kurzban (2006) and believe that the human brain is "massively modular." Like them, I do not believe that any brain function is truly domain-general; I believe even "general" intelligence is domain-specific (Kanazawa, 2004b). Unlike them, however, I do believe in a clear distinction between evolutionarily familiar and evolutionarily novel problems, entities, and situations. For example, I believe that face recognition is a clearly evolutionarily familiar problem (Kanazawa, 2004b, p. 513, Figure 1), despite the fact that faces that we must recognize today never existed in the ancestral environment (Barrett & Kurzban, 2006, p. 635).

References

Barrett, H. C., & Kurzban, R. (2006). Modularity in cognition: Framing the debate. *Psychological Review, 113*, 628–647.

Becker, R., & Mehlkop, G. (2006). Social class and delinquency: An empirical utilization of rational choice theory with cross-sectional data of the 1990 and 2000 German general population surveys (ALLBUS). *Rationality and Society, 18*, 193–235.

Blum, D. (1997). *Sex on the brain: The biological differences between men and women*. New York: Penguin.

Blumstein, A. (1995). Youth violence, guns, and the illicit-drug industry. *Journal of Criminal Law and Criminology, 86*, 10–36.

Braithwaite, J. (1981). The myth of social class and criminality reconsidered. *American Sociological Review, 46*, 36–57.

Brown, D. E. (1991). *Human universals*. New York: McGraw-Hill.

Buss, D. M. (1989). Sex differences in human mate preferences: Evolutionary hypotheses tested in 37 cultures. *Behavioral and Brain Sciences, 12*, 1–49.

Buss, D. M. (1994). *The evolution of desire: Strategies of human mating*. New York: Basic Books.

Campbell, A. (1995). A few good men: Evolutionary psychology and female adolescent aggression. *Ethology and Sociobiology, 16*, 99–123.

Campbell, A. (1999). Staying alive: Evolution, culture, and women's intrasexual aggression. *Behavioral and Brain Sciences, 22*, 203–252.

Campbell, A. (2002). *A mind of her own: The evolutionary psychology of women*. Oxford: Oxford University Press.

Chiappe, D., & MacDonald, K. (2005). The evolution of domain-general mechanisms in intelligence and learning. *Journal of General Psychology, 132*, 5–40.

Clelland, D., & Carter, T. J. (1980). The new myth of class and crime. *Criminology, 18*, 319–336.

Cosmides, L., & Tooby, J. (2000). Consider the source: The evolution of adaptations for decoupling and metarepresentation. In D. Sperber (Ed.), *Metarepresentations: A multidisciplinary perspective* (pp. 53–115). Oxford: Oxford University Press.

Cosmides, L., & Tooby, J. (2002). Unraveling the enigma of human intelligence: Evolutionary psychology and the multimodular mind. In R. J. Sternberg & J. C. Kaufman (Eds.), *The evolution of intelligence* (pp. 145–198). Mahwah: Lawrence Erlbaum.

Crawford, C. B. (1993). The future of sociobiology: Counting babies or proximate mechanisms? *Trends in Ecology and Evolution, 8,* 183–186.

Daly, M., & Wilson, M. (1988). *Homicide.* New York: De Gruyter.

Daly, M., & Wilson, M. (1990). Killing the competition: Female/female and male/male homicide. *Human Nature, 1,* 81–107.

Deary, I. J., Whiteman, M. C., Starr, J. M., Whalley, L. J., & Fox, H. C. (2004). The impact of childhood intelligence on later life: Following up the Scottish Mental Surveys of 1932 and 1947. *Journal of Personality and Social Psychology, 86,* 130–147.

Dunaway, R. G., Cullen, F. T., Burton, V. S. Jr., & Evans, T. D. (2000). The myth of social class and crime revisited: An examination of class and adult criminality. *Criminology, 38,* 589–632.

Elliott, D., & Huizinga, D. (1983). Social class and delinquent behavior in a national youth panel 1976–1980. *Criminology, 21,* 149–177.

Farrington, D. P. (1992). Explaining the beginning, progress, and ending of antisocial behavior from birth to adulthood. In J. McCord (Ed.), *Advances in criminological theory, Volume 3: Facts, frameworks, and forecasts* (pp. 253–286). New Brunswick: Transaction.

Farrington, D. P. (1994). Childhood, adolescent, and adult features of violent males. In L. R. Huesmann (Ed.), *Aggressive behavior: Current perspectives* (pp. 215–240). New York: Plenum.

Furchtgott-Roth, D., & Stolba, C. (1999). *Women's figures: An illustrated guide to the economic progress of women in America.* Washington, DC: AEI Press.

Gangestad, S. W., & Simpson, J. A. (2000). The evolution of human mating: Trade-offs and strategic pluralism. *Behavioral and Brain Sciences, 23,* 573–644.

Gibson, H. B., & West, D. J. (1970). Social and intellectual handicaps as precursors of early delinquency. *British Journal of Criminology, 10,* 21–32.

Gillis, J. S., & Avis, W. E. (1980). The male-taller norm in mate selection. *Personality and Social Psychology Bulletin, 6,* 396–401.

Gottfredson, L. S. (1997). Why *g* matters: The complexity of everyday life. *Intelligence, 24,* 79–132.

Gottfredson, L. S., & Deary, I. J. (2004). Intelligence predicts health and longevity, but why? *Current Directions in Psychological Science, 13,* 1–4.

Greenberg, D. F. (1985). Age, crime, and social explanation. *American Journal of Sociology, 91,* 1–21.

Grogger, J. (1998). Market wages and youth crime. *Journal of Labor Economics, 16,* 756–791.

Herrnstein, R. J., & Murray, C. (1994). *The bell curve: Intelligence and class structure in American life.* New York: Free Press.

Hirschi, T., & Gottfredson, M. (1983). Age and the explanation of crime. *American Journal of Sociology, 89,* 552–584.

Hirschi, T., & Gottfredson, M. (1985). Age and crime, logic and scholarship: Comment on Greenberg. *American Journal of Sociology, 91,* 22–27.

Hirschi, T., & Hindelang, M. J. (1977). Intelligence and delinquency: A revisionist review. *American Sociological Review, 42,* 571–587.

International Criminal Police Organization (Interpol). (Various years). *International criminal statistics.* Lyon: Interpol.

Jensen, A. R. (1998). *The g factor: The science of mental ability*. Westport, CT: Praeger.

Johnson, R. E. (1980). Social class and delinquent behavior: A new test. *Criminology, 18,* 86–93.

Kanazawa, S. (2002). Bowling with our imaginary friends. *Evolution and Human Behavior, 23,* 167–171.

Kanazawa, S. (2003a). Can evolutionary psychology explain reproductive behavior in the contemporary United States? *Sociological Quarterly, 44,* 291–302.

Kanazawa, S. (2003b). A general evolutionary psychological theory of male criminality and related male-typical behavior. In A. Walsh & L. Ellis (Eds.), *Biosocial criminology: Challenging environmentalism's supremacy* (pp. 37–60). New York: Nova Science.

Kanazawa, S. (2003c). Why productivity fades with age: The crime-genius connection. *Journal of Research in Personality, 37,* 257–272.

Kanazawa, S. (2004a). The Savanna Principle. *Managerial and Decision Economics, 25,* 41–54.

Kanazawa, S. (2004b). General intelligence as a domain-specific adaptation. *Psychological Review, 111,* 512–523.

Kanazawa, S. (2005a). Is "discrimination" necessary to explain the sex gap in earnings? *Journal of Economic Psychology, 26,* 269–287.

Kanazawa, S. (2005b). An empirical test of a possible solution to "the central theoretical problem of human sociobiology." *Journal of Cultural and Evolutionary Psychology, 3,* 249–260.

Kanazawa, S. (2006a). Why the less intelligent may enjoy television more than the more intelligent. *Journal of Cultural and Evolutionary Psychology, 4,* 27–36.

Kanazawa, S. (2006b). Mind the gap . . . in intelligence: Reexamining the relationship between inequality and health. *British Journal of Health Psychology, 11,* 623–642.

Kanazawa, S. (2007a). *De gustibus est disputandum II: Why liberals and atheists are more intelligent.* Interdisciplinary Institute of Management. London School of Economics and Political Science.

Kanazawa, S. (2007b). Mating intelligence and general intelligence as independent constructs. In G. Geher & G. F. Miller (Eds.), *Mating intelligence: Sex, relationships, and the mind's reproductive system* (pp. 283–309). Mahwah: Lawrence Erlbaum.

Kanazawa, S., & Still, M. C. (2000). Why men commit crimes (and why they desist). *Sociological Theory, 18,* 434–447.

Kanazawa, S., & Still, M. C. (2001). The emergence of marriage norms: An evolutionary psychological perspective. In M. Hechter & K.-D. Opp (Eds.), *Social norms* (pp. 274–304). New York: Russell Sage Foundation.

Laub, J. H., Nagin, D. S., & Sampson, R. J. (1998). Trajectories of change in criminal offending: Good marriages and the desistance process. *American Sociological Review, 63,* 225–238.

Lynam, D. R., Moffitt, T. E., & Stouthamer-Loeber, M. (1993). Explaining the relation between IQ and delinquency: Class, race, test motivation, school failure, or self control? *Journal of Abnormal Psychology, 102,* 187–196.

Mazur, A., & Michalek, J. (1998). Marriage, divorce, and male testosterone. *Social Forces, 77,* 315–330.

McIntyre, M., Gangestad, S. W., Gray, P. B., Chapman, J. F., Burnham, T., O'Rourke, M. T., et al. (2006). Romantic involvement often reduces men's testosterone levels—but not always: The moderating role of extrapair sexual interest. *Journal of Personality and Social Psychology, 91,* 642–651.

Moffitt, T. E. (1990). The neuropsychology of delinquency: A critical review of theory and research. *Crime and Justice: An Annual Review of Research, 12,* 99–169.

Moffitt, T. E., Gabrielli, W. F., Mednick, S. A., & Schulsinger, F. (1981). Socioeconomic status, IQ, and delinquency. *Journal of Abnormal Psychology, 90,* 152–156.

Moffitt, T. E., & Silva, P. A. (1988). IQ and delinquency: A direct test of the differential detection hypothesis. *Journal of Abnormal Psychology, 97,* 330–333.

Pérusse, D. (1993). Cultural and reproductive success in industrial societies: Testing the relationship at the proximate and ultimate levels. *Behavioral and Brain Sciences, 16,* 267–322.

Rowe, D. C. (2002). *Biology and crime.* Los Angeles: Roxbury.

Shaw, C. R., & McKay, H. D. (1929). *Delinquency areas.* Chicago: University of Chicago Press.

Sheppard, J. A., & Strathman, A. J. (1989). Attractiveness and height: The role of stature in dating preference, frequency of dating, and perceptions of attractiveness. *Personality and Social Psychology Bulletin, 15,* 617–627.

Short, J. F., & Nye, F. I. (1957). Reported behavior as a criterion of deviant behavior. *Social Problems, 5,* 207–213.

Stark, R. (1979). Whose status counts? *American Sociological Review, 44,* 668–669.

Steffensmeier, D. J., Allan, E. A., Harer, M. D., & Streifel, C. (1989). Age and the distribution of crime. *American Journal of Sociology, 94,* 803–831.

Symons, D. (1990). Adaptiveness and adaptation. *Ethology and Sociobiology, 11,* 427–444.

Thornberry, T. P., & Farnworth, M. (1982). Social correlates of criminal involvement: Further evidence on the relationship between social status and criminal behavior. *American Sociological Review, 47,* 505–518.

Thornhill, R., & Palmer, C. T. (2000). *A natural history of rape: Biological bases of sexual coercion.* Cambridge: MIT Press.

Tittle, C. R. (1983). Social class and criminal behavior: A critique of the theoretical foundation. *Social Forces, 62,* 334–358.

Tittle, C. R., & Villemez, W. J. (1977). Social class and criminality. *Social Forces, 56,* 474–502.

Tittle, C. R., Villemez, W. J., & Smith, D. A. (1978). The myth of social class and criminality: An empirical assessment of the empirical evidence. *American Sociological Review, 43,* 643–656.

Tooby, J., & Cosmides, L. (1990). The past explains the present: Emotional adaptations and the structure of ancestral environments. *Ethology and Sociobiology, 11,* 375–424.

de Waal, F. B. M. (1989). Food sharing and reciprocal obligations among chimpanzees. *Journal of Human Evolution, 18,* 433–459.

de Waal, F. B. M. (1992). Appeasement, celebration, and food sharing in the two *Pan* species. In T. Nishida, W. C. McGrew, & P. Marler (Eds.), *Topics in primatology: Human origins* (pp. 37–50). Tokyo: University of Tokyo Press.

de Waal, F. B. M., Luttrell, L. M., & Canfield, M. E. (1993). Preliminary data on voluntary food sharing in brown capuchin monkeys. *American Journal of Primatology, 29,* 73–78.

Wilson, J. Q., & Herrnstein, R. J. (1985). *Crime and human nature: The definitive study of the causes of crime.* New York: Touchstone.

Wolfgang, M. E., Figlio, R. M., & Sellin, T. (1972). *Delinquency in a birth cohort.* Chicago: University of Chicago Press.

Yeudall, L. T., Fromm-Auch, D., & Davies, P. (1982). Neuropsychological impairment of persistent delinquency. *Journal of Nervous and Mental Diseases, 170,* 257–265.

10

In Cold Blood

The Evolution of Psychopathy

MARTIN L. LALUMIÈRE, SANDEEP MISHRA, AND GRANT T. HARRIS

Fool me once, shame on you. Fool me twice, shame on me.
—old (probably Chinese) proverb.

Of all the interesting topics in the field of forensic psychology, psychopathy probably generates the most fascination. In university courses covering psychopathy, students wake from their slumber and knock on professors' doors to ask how they can get involved in research on psychopaths. In crime fiction and historical biographies, psychopathic characters are imbued with iconic qualities. It seems that our minds are attuned to psychopathic characteristics in others, and probably for good reason: if psychopaths have been a constant feature of the ancestral social environment of *Homo sapiens*, they will have exerted significant selection pressure. Researchers have not been immune to this fascination: despite the fact that psychopaths represent a small proportion of criminal offenders, psychological research on psychopathy seems to dominate the forensic literature.

The most important reason for the popularity of psychopathy among forensic researchers is probably the empirical fact that measures of psychopathy are reliable and robust predictors of future criminal behavior in both forensic and nonforensic populations (reviewed in Harris, Skilling, & Rice, 2001; Leistico, Salekin, DeCoster, & Rogers, 2007; Porter & Woodworth, 2006). In fact, one measure of psychopathy, the Psychopathy Checklist-Revised (Hare, 2003), might be the single best psychological predictor of criminal recidivism. In actuarial assessments of dangerousness, scores on measures of psychopathy have very large—often the largest—predictive weights (e.g., Hilton, Harris, Rice, Houghton, & Eke, 2008; Quinsey, Harris, Rice, & Cormier, 2006).

Perhaps even more interesting, scores on measures of psychopathy reveal intriguing interactions in other research with offenders. Psychopathy and measures of sexual deviance (or paraphilia) have been found to exhibit a multiplicative relationship such that sex offenders who are both sexually deviant (e.g., pedophilic) and psychopathic are much more likely to engage in sexually violent recidivism than all other group combinations (Rice & Harris, 1997; Seto, Harris, Rice, & Barbaree, 2004). Psychotherapy effective in reducing the risk of violence among non-psychopaths has been reported to have the opposite effect on psychopaths, increasing their risk of violence (Hare, Clarke, Grann, & Thornton, 2000; Harris, Rice, & Cormier, 1994; Rice, Harris, & Cormier, 1992). Alcohol abuse is a good predictor of criminal recidivism among schizophrenic offenders but not among psychopaths, even though psychopathic offenders are more likely to abuse alcohol than schizophrenic offenders (Rice & Harris, 1995). Even more intriguing are empirical reports that psychopaths rated by therapists as having benefited from treatment are subsequently more dangerous than psychopaths rated as not having benefited (Looman, Abracen, Serin, & Marquis, 2005; Seto & Barbaree, 1999; but see Langton, Barbaree, Harkins, & Peacock, 2007).

Greatly facilitating this burgeoning research activity is a valid and reliable measure of male psychopathy, the Psychopathy Checklist, now revised (PCL-R; Hare, 2003). Researchers have also subsequently developed similar psychopathy measures for nonforensic populations, teenagers, and even children. The PCL-R has provided researchers with a common definition of psychopathy, greatly aiding communication and integration of results in the field. Other terms have sometimes (and mistakenly) been used to mean the same thing as psychopathy, such as *sociopathy*, *antisocial personality disorder*, and *Machiavellianism*. *Psychopathy* now typically refers to "a lifelong persistent condition characterized, in males at least, by aggression beginning in early childhood, impulsivity, resistance to punishment, general lack of emotional attachment or concern for others, dishonesty and selfishness in social interaction, and high levels of promiscuous and uncommitted sexual behavior" (Harris, Skilling, et al., 2001, pp. 197–198). Psychopathy is more restrictive than antisocial personality disorder as defined in the *Diagnostic and Statistical Manual of Mental Disorders* because the customary diagnostic cutoff for psychopathy is more stringent, but in fact the indicators of psychopathy and antisocial personality disorder are highly correlated and can identify essentially the same individuals (e.g., Skilling, Harris, Rice, & Quinsey, 2002)—contrary to the commonly accepted view (e.g., Livesley, 1998). Psychopathy is mostly a male phenomenon, and in this chapter we focus on male psychopathy.

In sum, psychopathy is (perhaps naturally) fascinating, can be measured reliably, and is an important social phenomenon with significant practical implications. It is thus not surprising that it has generated a large amount of theoretical interest. Where does psychopathy come from? Can evolutionary psychology help us generate new hypotheses about the origins and causes of psychopathy? Before we address these questions, let us examine more closely the construct of psychopathy.

The Construct of Psychopathy

Psychopathy as a Clinical Condition

A century and a half ago, the modern concept of psychopathy originated in the observation that a small minority of people seemed to engage in antisocial, irresponsible, extremely selfish (and even apparently self-destructive) behavior without also displaying any obvious signs of mental derangement. Beginning about seventy years ago, Cleckley (1941) applied the term *psychopathy* and added clinical descriptions of other, more affective aspects of this condition: superficial charm and good intelligence, absence of nervousness, dishonesty, lack of remorse, incapacity for love, and shallow emotional responses are examples. For the last four decades, Hare (1970, 1998, 2003) has elaborated on Cleckley's clinical observations and brought the study of psychopathy into the realm of scientific investigation. As mentioned, one of Hare's several contributions has been the development and validation of an effective way to measure the phenomenon. The PCL-R (Hare, 2003) comprises twenty psychopathic characteristics to be assessed primarily based on an individual's life-long pattern of conduct as documented in official records and institutional files, but the scoring of some traits (e.g., grandiose sense of self-worth, lack of remorse, lack of realistic long-term goals, failure to accept responsibility for actions) may also be inferred from a semistructured interview.

Twenty years ago, Hare (Harpur, Hackstian, & Hare, 1988) reported that scores on the PCL-R consisted of two highly related (correlations greater than 0.50) but conceptually and empirically distinct aspects. The first, usually called Factor 1, comprised *interpersonal and affective* characteristics (e.g., conning and manipulation, callousness and lack of empathy), while Factor 2 described a *deviant, antisocial lifestyle* (e.g., proneness to boredom, poor behavioral controls, early behavior problems, impulsivity, juvenile delinquency, parasitic lifestyle). A few characteristics (sexual promiscuity, many short-term marital relationships, and criminal versatility) did not appear to load on either factor. The names given to the factors did not strictly capture their content, of course—boredom is an affective response; poor behavior controls are about irritable, angry, hostile, violent emotional responses; conning and manipulation are about overt antisocial conduct; and criminal versatility is certainly about an antisocial lifestyle. Nevertheless, at the empirical level, this two-aspect nature of psychopathy has generally held up ever since (Benning, Patrick, Hicks, Blonigen, & Kreuger, 2003; Blackburn, 2007; Loney, Taylor, Butler, & Iacono, 2007; Patrick, Edens, Poythress, Lilienfeld, & Benning, 2006; Skeem, Johansson, Andershed, Kerr, & Louden, 2007).

It is evident that those who receive maximal scores on a measure of psychopathy such as the PCL-R would, by definition, exhibit both aspects. Also, the well-established empirical association between the two factors means that those who score highly on one aspect have a high probability of also exhibiting the other (Skilling et al., 2002). Nevertheless, some people who receive high scores on such a measure do so via a maximal score on one aspect and perhaps only a moderate score on the other. Indeed, these two aspects appear to be related in opposite directions to such emotions as anxiety and depression (Hicks & Patrick, 2006). As well, many empirical findings about psychopathic responding in the laboratory or in the natural environment seem particularly characteristic of only one of the two aspects (e.g., Carlson, McLarnon, & Iacono, 2007; Hare et al., 2000; Maccoon & Newman, 2006; Moltó, Poy, Segarra,

Pastor, & Montañés, 2007). Most relevant for forensic application, the second aspect is more predictive of criminal recidivism, violent recidivism, substance abuse, and suicidal behavior (Harris, Skilling, et al., 2001; Leistico et al., 2007; Salekin, Rogers, & Sewell, 1996).

Thus, it appears that some violent offenders have such traits as remorselessness, grandiosity, and insincerity and are presumably deliberately and premeditatedly violent out of emotional detachment and indifference to others' interests. Another group of violent offenders seem to be impulsive and to experience considerable anger, anxiety, and distress, and they are violent due to such negative emotions. This distinction[1] has long been noted in the psychopathy literature and the terms *primary* and *secondary psychopathy*, respectively, are often applied. It is now evident that these two aspects of the phenomenon are, at least partly, due to quite distinct underlying basic processes. It has been assumed that the primary, affectively cold-hearted version is the one that reflects psychopathy's "core personality"and is more constitutional and "biologically" based. On the other hand, the secondary, "behavioral" version has been seen as acquired and contextually caused (Mealey, 1995; Skeem et al., 2007). Current evidence appears, however, to make these etiological assumptions untenable.

Psychopathy in the Context of Development

The first relevant source of data comes from laboratory studies of adults. It is clear that experimenters can arrange test conditions such that psychopaths obtain poorer scores than other groups (e.g., Blair et al., 2006). But it is just as clear that some experimental conditions lead to equivalent or even better performance by psychopathic participants (Book, Holden, Starzyk, Wasilkiw, & Edwards, 2006; Budhani, Richell, & Blair, 2006). Indeed, the core affective psychopathic personality traits appear to be so subtle that it is unclear how they can be characterized (Munro et al., 2007); for example, psychopaths do not seem to exhibit deficits in detecting emotion in others (Glass & Newman, 2006) and might even be better at it than non-psychopaths (Book, Quinsey, & Langford, 2007).

Conversely, the more behavioral, antisocial lifestyle aspects of psychopathy exhibit profound, inescapable (and utterly unsubtle) findings. As mentioned above, these are the psychopathic traits most predictive of forensically relevant outcomes. These so-called externalizing traits have been reported to exhibit a distinct, natural class (Harris, Rice, Hilton, Lalumière, & Quinsey, 2007; Harris, Rice, & Quinsey, 1994; also see Swogger & Kosson, 2007; but also Edens, Marcus, Lilienfeld, & Poythress, 2006), even in juveniles (Skilling, Quinsey, & Craig, 2001; Vasey, Kotov, Frick, & Loney, 2005). Such externalizing traits, together with some callous and unemotional traits, exhibit a distinct developmental trajectory detectable in individuals as young as age 3 (Glenn, Raine, Venables, & Mednick, 2007; Moffitt & Caspi, 2001; Shaw, Bell, & Gilliom, 2000; Shaw, Gilliom, Ingoldsby, & Nagin, 2003; Vizard, Hickey, & McCrory, 2007). There is also clear evidence that this pattern of externalizing traits represents a stable, life-course phenomenon (Loney et al., 2007; Lynam, Caspi, Moffitt, Loeber, & Stouthamer-Loeber, 2007). These externalizing aspects of psychopathy associated with negative emotions are at least as heritable as the affectively coldhearted traits (Burt, McGue, Carter, & Iacono, 2007; Hicks et al., 2007; Larsson et al., 2007; Larsson, Andershed, & Lichtenstein, 2006; Viding, Frick, & Plomin, 2007). Indeed, an externalizing factor among elementary-school-aged children has been reported to exhibit a heritability coefficient of 0.96 (Baker, Jacobson, Raine, Lozano, & Bezdjian, 2007). These externalizing traits seem to be more closely associated with and central to the characteristic cognitive differences associated with psychopathy (Maccoon & Newman, 2006). Finally, externalizing traits, as assessed by the PCL-R, for example, appear to predict violent behavior even among adults who are unlikely to meet any criteria for classification as psychopaths (Harris, Rice, & Camilleri, 2004; Hilton et al., 2008; Rice & Harris, 1992).

The Two Factors Revisited

Recent empirical research on psychopathy has clarified many features of this forensically important and fascinating condition. That same research, however, has also raised new questions. For example, should the condition of psychopathy be conceptualized as a disorder of personality whose core features of callousness and affective shallowness directly (but not inevitably) cause antisocial conduct (e.g., Cooke, Michie, & Hart, 2006; Cooke, Michie, & Skeem, 2007; Widiger, 2006)? Is psychopathy better conceived of as a collection of enduring characteristic behaviors and interpersonal tactics (e.g., Hare & Neumann, 2006; Harris et al., 2007)? Is antisocial and criminal conduct merely the rather obvious and expected consequence of theoretically more interesting core psychopathic personality (e.g., Cooke et al., 2007)? Or are some aggressive and violent behaviors actually so much at the core of psychopathy that such antisocial behaviors are actually most diagnostic (e.g., Harris et al., 2007)? It is likely that not all the phenotypic traits of psychopathy have so far been optimally identified. It also seems possible, even probable, that one aspect of the condition (and its neurophysiological substrates) will ultimately be deemphasized in favor of the other. Though it appears that the externalizing, behavioral horse has a small lead in this race, it is not yet clear which path empirical and theoretical development will take and what the final result will be. In the following section, we describe evolutionary accounts of psychopathy and show that these can generate novel and testable hypotheses about the core features of psychopathy.

Explanations of Psychopathy

Traditional approaches to the study of antisocial behavior assume that the behavior would not occur if appropriate genetic, prenatal, family, socialization, and economic conditions were in place. There is, in fact, some support for these ideas; convincing evidence suggests that antisocial behavior, and especially violent behavior, is some-times associated with some rare genetic mutations, poor prenatal or perinatal con-ditions (e.g., maternal malnutrition, birth complications), family instability, poor parental monitoring during adolescence, and low socioeconomic status (for a re-view see Quinsey, Skilling, Lalumière, & Craig, 2004). Because some of these putative causes involve disruptions of otherwise normally functioning systems, it seems that antisocial behavior can sometimes result from pathological causes.

Elsewhere, we have argued that the presence of pathological causes for a given trait or behavior does not necessarily imply that the trait or behavior in question is a pathological *outcome* (Lalumière, Harris, Quinsey, & Rice, 2005; Quinsey et al., 2004; also see Chapter 8 of this volume). It is quite possible that antisocial behav-ior is part of an adaptive response to specific and difficult conditions. For example, pathological causes having to do with early development (e.g., early malnutrition, the experience of physical abuse) may provide the child with information about the likely features of his future environment. This information may divert the child toward a developmental pathway that facilitates aggression, impulsivity, and high mating effort, tendencies that might better allow him to reach fitness-relevant goals. Alternatively, those early difficult conditions may reduce embodied capital (i.e., intrinsic attributes, such as health, skills, or attractiveness), leading to reduced ability to compete for resources, status, and mates, and forcing the adoption of al-ternative tactics of social competition. These two scenarios imply that antisocial behavior may be an adaptation (i.e., ancestrally selected) specific to "pathological" circumstances (just as an immune response is an adaptation designed to respond to infections). These ideas are discussed in more detail in Chapter 8.

What about psychopathy? Psychopaths are quite different from other offend-ers, even other life-course-persistent violent offenders. They differ, for instance, with regard to some aspects of their criminal behavior (e.g., more violent, more goal-directed), how punishment and rewards affect their behavior in the laboratory, how they process emotional information, their physiological responses to aversive events, and their cerebral lateralization and cerebral activity while processing verbal information (reviewed in Barr & Quinsey, 2004; Harris, Rice, et al., 2001; Lalumière et al., 2005; Lalumière, Harris, & Rice, 2001; Quinsey et al., 2004). Also, signs of early neurodevelopmental problems that are associated with persistent violent crimi-nality are not associated (and perhaps are even negatively associated) with psychop-athy (Harris, Rice, & Lalumière, 2001; Lalumière et al., 2001).

Can conditional (facultative) developmental accounts of the sort mentioned above explain the psychopathic phenotype? Such an account would predict that psychopaths have experienced difficult early conditions statistically predictive of an inhospitable future biotic or social environment or that they have reduced embodied capital and ability to compete. Evidence so far does not support such an account. As mentioned, psychopathy is unrelated to early signs of neurodevelopmental problems (e.g., obstetrical complications, low IQ, learning problems). Also, psychopaths show lower fluctuating asymmetry—a measure of developmental instability and a possible

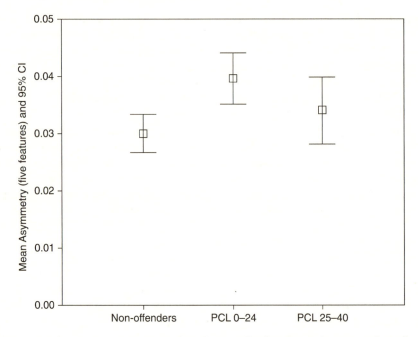

Figure 10.1. Fluctuating asymmetry values for nonoffenders (n = 31), non-psychopathic offenders (n = 25), and psychopathic offenders (n = 15). Adapted from Lalumière, Harris, & Rice, 2001.

indicator of low embodied capital—than other violent offenders (Figure 10.1; Lalumière et al., 2001). In our study of fluctuating asymmetry, the psychopaths with the most extreme PCL-R scores were just as physically symmetrical as the non-offenders (who were members of the hospital staff), and much more symmetrical than violent offenders with low PCL-R scores.

Psychopathy also seems to be unrelated to social factors generally associated with delinquency and conduct problems. For instance, in a study of the link between the quality of parenting and childhood conduct problems, ineffective parenting was associated with a higher number of conduct problems exhibited by children (as expected), but only among the children who did not display lack of empathy, manipulativeness, lack of guilt, or emotional constriction—all features of psychopathy (Wootton, Frick, Shelton, & Silverthorne, 1997; see also Oxford, Cavell, & Hugues, 2003). Children displaying psychopathic features had more conduct problems than other children, regardless of the quality of parenting. In fact, there was a tendency for *fewer* conduct problems among "psychopathic" children who experienced ineffective parenting compared to "psychopathic" children who had experienced more effective parenting. Although more research is needed, so far there is no evidence that the origin of psychopathy involves the types of pathological causes implicated for persistent violent offending more generally. This result should be surprising to developmental psychologists because psychopathic children would be expected to at least *elicit* parental behaviors and social responses that often lead to neural, developmental, and social problems (e.g., excessive physical punishment, withdrawal of parental investment, peer rejection). If psychopathy is not the result of pathological processes of the kind already identified for other life-course persistent offenders, what might explain psychopathy?

Perhaps the most often discussed evolutionary explanation of psychopathy is the frequency-dependent selection account. In the most common version of this account, psychopaths have evolved to take advantage of the fact that most people are cooperators by defecting in social interactions. Thus, psychopathy represents an alternative strategy (in the genetic sense) that is successful only at a particular low relative frequency in the population. If there are too many cheaters (or defectors), nonpsychopaths become very vigilant and cheating opportunities disappear. It is not hard to imagine how the constellation of psychopathic characteristics (e.g., manipulative, charming, lack of empathy, failure to learn from punishment, unresponsive to cues of distress in others) would facilitate such a strategy. By this account, some individuals are born with a propensity for psychopathy, and the phenotype manifests itself early and perhaps without any environmental cues (e.g., Mealey, 1995). This type of obligate strategy has been observed in other species (see Box 10.1), but it is fairly rare compared to conditional (facultative) strategies.

Harpending and Sobus (1987) noted that an evolutionary explanation of psychopathy based on nonreciprocation requires that the psychopath be not only difficult to detect and highly mobile but "especially skilful at persuading females to copulate and at deceiving females about his control of resources and about the likelihood of his provisioning future offspring" (p. 65S). Using contemporary terminology, psychopaths should invest highly in mating effort (energy and resources devoted to increasing mating access) and should advertise parenting effort without actually engaging in it. High mating effort, however, is a hallmark of general criminal offending, not just psychopathy. Interestingly, of the three items that do not load onto one of the PCL-R factors, two involve mating effort (many short-term marital relationships and sexual promiscuity). Could it be that these two items do not capture the type of mating effort that is required by an obligate account of psychopathy?

Harris et al. (2007) hypothesized that although high mating effort is associated with persistent antisocial behavior, early and coercive mating effort should be particularly associated with psychopathy if it is an early-onset, obligate strategy. Harris et al. suggested that the reason these two items are orphans on the PCL-R is because they are diagnostic of antisocial behavior generally (and perhaps even other male life history strategies), not psychopathy in particular. Under the obligate, frequency-dependent selection explanation of the type discussed by Harpending and Sobus (1987), psychopathy should emerge early, and the aspects of sexuality that are diagnostic of psychopathy should not be general features associated with high adult mating effort but functional features that develop and are expressed early.

Box 10.1   Frequency-Dependent Selection
in the Animal World

In the bluegill sunfish, there appear to be three types of males, distinguishable both behaviorally and morphologically (Gross & Charnov, 1980). The largest males, called *parental* types, invest heavily in growth in the first few years of life, delaying reproduction. These males eventually build nests and use their size to defend nesting territories. *Satellite* males mimic females behaviorally and in physical appearance; they attempt to interrupt territorial males that are courting and to intercept females in an attempt to fertilize them. Finally, *sneaker* males tend to stay near the lake bottom and make quick attempts to enter and exit nests, releasing ejaculate quickly. Sneaker males mature in two to three years, investing more in immediate reproductive capabilities than long-term growth. As sneaker males mature, they become satellite female mimics, but never grow to the size of the parental males. The two smaller morphs do not incur the same parental investment costs as the larger parental morphs—building a nest, defending a territory, courting females, and caring for the eggs, a necessary condition for the hatching and survival of young. Instead, the sneaker and satellite morphs parasitize the larger males by attempting to gain fertilizations covertly (Neff, Fu, & Gross, 2003).

Sneaker males have a much larger testis-to-body mass ratio and also have greater sperm counts in their ejaculates. These characteristics lead to increased success in sperm competition. Fu, Neff, and Gross (2001) found that sneaker males fertilize more eggs than parental males during sperm competition, with satellite males falling between the sneaker and parental types in terms of fertilization success. Genetic analyses suggest that the mean paternity estimate for parental males is 76.9% and for cuckolder males (sneakers and satellites) 23.1% (Neff, 2001). Although cuckolder males are more successful in fertilizing females in the context of sperm competition, the higher percentage of paternity in parental males is likely due to increased mating opportunities with females afforded by the defense and maintenance of a stable territory. Previous studies have found that cuckolders form approximately 21% of the bluegill sunfish population, suggesting that the parental and sneaker/satellite strategies have approximately the same mean fitness outcome. Even though both parental and sneaker/satellite strategies appear to offer the same fitness outcomes, the success of alternative cheater strategies is likely contingent on their frequency in the population: modeling of bluegill populations suggests that cuckolders become less successful as their numbers increase (Gross, 1991). Bluegill sunfish are but one of several species that appear to have undergone frequency-dependent selection for stable alternative life history strategies. Alternative reproductive phenotypes have also been observed in isopods, swordtails, and ruffs (Gross, 1996).

Harris et al. tested the predictions that a factor comprising early onset and coercive sexuality items should positively correlate (in a sample of violent offenders) with the traditional PCL-R factors, should show taxonicity (i.e., evidence that scores on the factor identify types of offenders, psychopaths versus non-psychopaths, as opposed to a dimensional trait), and should also show a pattern of correlation with individual characteristics predicted by the account (e.g., negatively associated with signs of early neurodevelopmental perturbations, positively associated with number of victims of reproductive value). All of these predictions were confirmed. These results not only clarified the unique sexuality of psychopaths but also provided support for the idea that evolutionarily informed research can improve the conceptualization and measurement of the phenomenon.

At the moment, there is some evidence that psychopathy might be the product of frequency-dependent selection. At the very least, there is evidence that psychopathy is *not* the result of early pathological conditions, such as those associated with general adult criminality. The particular structure of the definite evolutionary model of psychopathy probably remains to be elucidated, but it is clear that studies designed to test such models will continue to lead to further advances in our understanding of psychopathy. In the remainder of the chapter we discuss the relevance of, and some results from, three active lines of research for the study of the evolution of psychopathy.

Computer Simulations and Experimental Games

Models of the evolution of cooperation can help to shed light on the evolution of psychopathy. These models are also germane to the idea of different "types" of individuals (or strategies) interacting in a social environment. The Prisoner's Dilemma, a non-zero-sum game, has been used to model the evolution of cooperative behavior in the face of defection (Axelrod & Hamilton, 1981; Axelrod, 1984).

In the Prisoner's Dilemma, two players are in a hypothetical situation in which both are imprisoned and accused of having colluded to commit a crime. If both players cooperate and do not implicate the other (mutual cooperation), they each receive a minimum sentence. There is, however, a greater incentive for each player to implicate the other (defection), thus earning his own complete freedom at the expense of the other's maximum sentence. If both defect and implicate the other (mutual defection), both remain imprisoned with a long sentence. In this game, there is a small reward for mutual cooperation, a larger reward for the individual who defects (as long as the other cooperates), and costs for mutual defection. If the Prisoner's Dilemma is played only once, the optimum strategy for each player is to defect. When the same two players play repeatedly (the iterated Prisoner's Dilemma, or IPD), mutual cooperation becomes optimal.

Axelrod and Hamilton (1981) invited game theorists to submit a computer program designed to optimize success in a round-robin IPD tournament. The conditions were as follows: two players (i.e., computer programs) interacted, simultaneous choices were made consisting of either cooperation or defection, the magnitude of payoffs was fixed beforehand, and the history of choices made by the other players was known to each player in the tournament. One simple strategy triumphed over all others, known as *tit-for-tat*. In this strategy, cooperation is the first move of the game, and the other player's move is copied on all subsequent moves. An ecological simulation comparing various strategies of cooperation also showed that tit-for-tat quickly became the most common or evolutionarily stable strategy in a population.

An evolutionarily stable strategy (ESS) is one that, if adopted, cannot be invaded by alternative strategies. In the context of an IPD, Axelrod and Dion (1988) demonstrated that if the chance of future interaction is high, no player in a population can do better than to cooperate. Axelrod and Dion also suggested that even in an already established population of defectors, a small cluster of players using cooperation quickly takes over, and an established population of cooperators cannot be easily invaded (replaced) by those using defection. More recent research, however, suggests that there is no true ESS for the IPD (e.g., Marinoff, 1990). The strategy Axelrod and colleagues (1981, 1984, 1988) described as an ESS is also subject to numerous restrictions, many of which are not ecologically tenable.

Of particular relevance to the study of psychopathy is the requirement of future interaction. The tit-for-tat model of stable cooperation put forth by Axelrod and colleagues specifically requires that players have multiple interactions and that all interactions be remembered. Harpending and Sobus (1987) modeled a population similarly to Axelrod and colleagues and found comparable results: If all players in a simulation have perfect memories, cooperators (engaging in tit-for-tat) always do better than individuals who always defect (cheaters). In a population where players are fallible, however, with a 10% probability of any player forgetting all encounters, it was observed that the relative frequencies of cooperators and defectors varied over time. Harpending and Sobus argued that these findings suggest that a small population of defectors could succeed if they were difficult to detect, mobile, and skilled at manipulating others, with males successfully persuading females to mate. Thus psychopathy is analogous to the strategy of repeated defection in social interactions (perhaps after showing signs of cooperation) and so might persist at a low frequency in a population if an absolute ESS for an "always cooperate" strategy cannot be strictly maintained.

More recent research by Kurzban and Houser (2005) is consistent with the idea that there is not a single ESS for social exchanges but rather that there has been selection for frequency-dependent cooperative "types" in humans, exhibiting a more complex equilibrium, where the success of multiple strategies has been equal over time. Three strategies or types were identified: reciprocity contingent on cooperation by others (analogous to tit-for-tat), cooperation regardless of the actions of others, and "free-riding"—consistent defection regardless of the actions of others. Although groups comprising mostly cooperating or reciprocating types did better than groups that included a free-rider, at the individual level all three types experienced equivalent average earnings. These findings are consistent with the notion of a polymorphic equilibrium where payoffs for different types or strategies are equal.

Simulations and experimental games exploring how evolution by natural selection could have given rise to subpopulations of social cheaters can inform accounts of psychopathy. It is certainly plausible that psychopathy evolved as a frequency-dependent life history strategy of defection, whereby psychopathic characteristics (manipulation, charm, dishonesty, callousness, aggression, irresponsibility, promiscuity, and a parasitic lifestyle) formed a suite of adaptive traits and behaviors that exploited a social environment mostly characterized by cooperation.

The Genetics of Psychopathy

There are two general approaches to studying the genetics of a trait. The first is quantitative genetics, the study of the relative contribution of genes and environment in explaining variance in the trait. The second is molecular genetics, the study of the role of particular genes in producing the phenotypic characteristic. These two approaches are often complementary (exceptions arise when a trait shows little variance—e.g., number of fingers—but has a clear genetic basis). Although the construct of psychopathy has a long history, its valid measurement is fairly recent, and therefore there are very few genetic studies of psychopathy proper. In addition, psychopaths are very socially mobile, so it might be difficult to include family members in genetic studies. In the following, we briefly review the few studies available, but first we discuss the relevance of such studies for testing the frequency-dependent selection account of psychopathy.

The frequency-dependent selection explanation discussed above makes the clear prediction that measures of psychopathy should show high heritability[2] in quantitative genetics studies and that gene variants unique to psychopathy would be identified in molecular genetics studies. Although these predictions are straightforward, there are a few complications to consider. First, almost all psychological traits show moderate to high heritability, but few evolutionary psychologists would suggest that these traits (e.g., major personality dimensions) are the result of frequency-dependent selection. High heritability can also result from weak ancestral selection pressure on the trait in question, high mutation rates, sexual recombination, or a history of host–parasite coevolution (see Tooby & Cosmides, 1990). At the very least, however, low heritability of psychopathy would seriously question the validity of the frequency-dependent selection account.

Second, gene variants might have low penetrance or require specific environmental triggers for expression and so would be difficult to detect with simple genetic linkage and association studies that do not examine contextual factors. For example, Caspi et al. (2002) found an interaction between allelic variation in a gene coding for a neurotransmitter enzyme and the experience of childhood maltreatment in predicting adult antisocial tendencies. Although frequency-dependent models imply genetic differences among individuals (or morphs), it is possible that gene expression for a particular trait still require some kind of environmental cue. Perhaps psychopathy remains "dormant" unless the relevant cues are present, increasing the challenge of genetic studies.

Third, how likely is it that just one or a few gene variants are contributing to the development of something as complex as psychopathy? One might think that a multitude of genes have to be involved, making the task of finding relevant genes almost impossible because molecular genetics typically has low statistical power to detect individual genes each with small effects. Recent studies in evolutionary developmental biology, however, suggest that the task might not be as hopeless as it looks. These studies show that some master genes (e.g., hox genes) control the activity of many other genes and thereby the development of complex phenotypic features. Perhaps one or a few "psychopathy" master genes affect the expression of other genes, leading to all characteristics of psychopathy. Psychopaths, after all, look very much like exaggerated young males (except that they display risk-taking, high mating effort, antisocial behavior, etc. throughout their lifetimes). That is, the human genome may already have the capacity to produce all or most of the characteristic phenotypic psychopathic traits. Perhaps all that evolution required was a master gene that controls the expression of such existing traits (for an accessible and fascinating introduction to the field of evolutionary developmental biology, see Carroll, 2005).

With these considerations in mind, we examine the few genetic studies of psychopathy. It should be noted that there have been dozens of studies of antisocial tendencies, conduct problems, delinquency, and criminality, but these studies have not distinguished between psychopathy and general antisociality. These studies have typically obtained fairly high heritability estimates (reviewed in Blonigen, Carlson, Krueger, & Patrick, 2003; Lykken, 1995; Quinsey et al., 2004) but it is unclear whether, and by how much, these estimates were influenced by psychopathy. The frequency-dependent selection account would suggest that heritability estimates in these studies would be positively affected by the number of psychopaths in the samples studied.

A study of children has revealed substantial heritability for callousness and unemotionality, traits that are strongly associated with psychopathy. Viding, Blair, Moffitt, and Plomin (2005) examined a large sample of 7-year-olds rated by teachers as extreme on a callous-unemotional scale. The monozygotic co-twins of these probands scored much more similarly to the probands on the same scale than dizygotic co-twins, with an estimated heritability value of 0.67 and no effect of the shared environment. The heritability of a measure of antisocial conduct was also found to be high, but only if the probands scored high on the measure of callous-unemotionality. In a subsequent analysis, Viding et al. (2007) reported a substantial genetic influence overlap for callous-unemotional traits and antisocial conduct.

In a twin study of older male children (ages 10–12) and adolescents (16–18), Taylor, Loney, Bobadilla, Iacono, and McGue (2003) examined the heritability of a self-reported psychopathy measure comprising two related factors: antisocial and impulsive behavior, and callousness and emotional detachment. The heritability estimates varied between 0.36 and 0.54 in the older age group and between 0.50 and 0.52 in the younger age group (our calculations). The univariate biometric analysis revealed a significant additive genetic effect and an unshared environment effect for both psychopathy factors.[3] The bivariate model suggested that the correlation between the two psychopathy factors could be attributed to additive genetic and unshared environmental effects.

In another large study of preadolescent twin boys and girls (9 to 10 years old), Baker et al. (2007) examined the heritability of a common factor underlying psychopathic traits, aggression, and conduct problems. Most of the variation was accounted for by additive genetic effects (0.96) and the remainder by unshared environment effects (0.04), in both sexes.

Blonigen et al. (2003) examined the heritability of a self-report measure of psychopathic personality in a cohort of young adult male twins. Twin correlations suggested perfect heritability, but the correlation for dizygotic twins was nonsignificantly different from zero. Biometric modeling suggested moderate nonadditive genetic effects due to epistasis (interactions between genes at different loci) and a moderate effect of unshared environment. Finally, in a large study of twins aged 16 to 17 using a self-report questionnaire assessing three correlated psychopathic characteristics, heritability estimates were 0.36 to 0.54 for boys and 0.52 to 0.70 for girls (our calculations). All remaining variance could be attributed to unshared environmental effects (Larsson et al., 2006). Additive genetic factors accounted for 63% of the variance in the latent psychopathy factor, with the remainder attributable to unshared environmental effects (see also Larsson et al., 2007).

In sum, these five studies of psychopathic traits revealed moderate to high heritability estimates and no effect of the shared environment (see also Waldman & Rhee, 2006). These results are consistent with the frequency-dependent selection account of psychopathy and not with facultative (conditional) explanations. If any aspect of the expression of psychopathy is conditional on environmental cues, those cues remain unidentified. More work remains to be done to elucidate the gene–environment interactions that influence psychopathy. Although these studies have used different measures specifically designed to assess psychopathy, three relied on self-report only, all used different measures, and none used samples likely to contain a high proportion of psychopaths (except perhaps for Viding et al., 2005). No study has yet examined the heritability of psychopathy using the PCL-R. We were unable to locate any research on the molecular genetics of psychopathy.

The Brains of Psychopaths

Although differential brain functioning in psychopaths is not surprising—after all, differences in behavior must be caused by some brain differences—studies that have investigated differences between "normal" brains and psychopathic brains are useful for understanding the mechanisms underlying psychopathy. It is a common mistake in studies of psychopathy to assume evidence of brain differences (especially between clinically identified subjects and unaffected controls) to be evidence of damage, dysfunction, defect, or pathology.

Kiehl (2006) reviewed several studies noting that damage to various components of the paralimbic system results in some symptoms and cognitive impairment associated with psychopathy. Changes in behavior associated with paralimbic damage, however, are also associated with impaired decision making and greater reactive (but not instrumental) aggression, both of which are strongly indicative of generalized criminal behavior but not psychopathy. There is little evidence to suggest that the very specific constellation of behaviors associated with psychopathy can be induced by any specific brain injury. The frequency-dependent selection explanation would suggest that the brains of psychopaths are necessarily different from the brains of nonpsychopaths but that this difference is not due to pathological causes. Although brain imaging studies cannot infer much about the pathological nature of brain differences, they can still shed light on patterns of brain functioning unique to psychopathy.

Imaging studies utilizing positron emission tomography (PET) and magnetic resonance imaging (MRI) test whether the unique pattern of behavior observed in psychopathy is due to differential anatomy or activation in the brain, as compared to "normal" populations. Several imaging studies have been conducted on violent offenders and those diagnosed with antisocial personality disorder (APD). The problem with these studies, however, is that these samples contained probable life-course-persistent offenders, only some of whom were psychopaths. As we mentioned already, an evolutionary view of psychopathy would expect important differences between psychopathic and non-psychopathic life-course-persistent offenders. Unless psychopathy is diagnosed using a validated measure, such as the PCL-R, it is difficult to know whether these imaging studies reveal brain structures or functions unique to psychopathy or structures or functions typical of violent offenders or those with APD more generally. In this section, we report on the few imaging studies conducted on psychopaths.

The paralimbic system has been identified as an important activating circuit possibly relevant to psychopathy. Damage to subcomponents of this system has been associated with an increase in some behaviors also symptomatic of psychopathy (e.g., extreme aggression, lack of empathy, general callousness), a phenomenon termed "pseudopsychopathy" (Kiehl, 2006). Behaviors similar to these have been observed in studies manipulating animal brains as well as case studies in humans where damage has occurred as a result of head injury (for a comprehensive review, see Kiehl, 2006). Although these studies provide evidence that some clinical features that resemble psychopathic traits can be due to brain damage, it is far from clear that the kind of damage studied so far can produce the full spectrum of psychopathic traits.

In the few studies that have investigated brain functioning in true psychopathic samples, little convergent evidence has emerged to indicate whether particular brain areas or systems are implicated in psychopathy. Two studies have found differences in amygdala functioning, and one found a difference in the frontal cortex. The amygdala plays a role in aversive conditioning, instrumental learning, and general processing of emotion and fear (Blair, 2003; LeDoux, 2003). Thus, differences in amygdala function could give rise to many of the characteristics of psychopathy, such as low empathy, minimal response to aversive stimuli, and general absence of emotional responding. Using volumetric MRI techniques, Tiihonen et al. (2000) found that high levels of psychopathy, as scored using the PCL-R, were associated with lower amygdala volume. In another study, Kiehl et al. (2001) used an emotional memory task in which participants processed words of neutral and negative valence. Participants who scored high on the PCL-R showed reduced MRI-measured amygdala response compared to lower-scoring individuals. These results are suggestive of potential differential amygdala function in psychopathy.

The frontal cortex, encompassing both the orbitofrontal and prefrontal cortices, is associated with conscious decision making and executive control. Thus, differences in the functioning of this region could also result in some behaviors typical of psychopaths, including social behavioral problems and high aggression (Blair, 2003). Damage to the frontal cortex, however, is inconsistent with other typical psychopathic behaviors, especially instrumental violence and, thus, planning ability. Raine et al. (2000) assessed individuals who scored high on the PCL-R using MRI and found that they showed reduced prefrontal gray matter volume but not white matter volume. Another MRI study by Laakso et al. (2002) found no difference between psychopathic and non-psychopathic populations in total prefrontal or prefrontal white and cortical volumes. Together, these findings provide little evidence for generalized frontal cortical dysfunction in psychopaths. Blair (2003) suggested, however, that differences in one particular area of the frontal cortex—the orbitofrontal cortex (OFC)—might be consistent with lower amygdala activity in psychopathy in that the OFC shares several neural projections to and from the amygdala. Blair also points out that parts of the OFC are associated with instrumental learning and response reversal, functions said to be different in psychopaths. Nevertheless, few empirical data exist to support the idea of *impaired* OFC functioning, and it remains unclear whether any differences in frontal cortical structure are associated with psychopathy.

Conclusion

Further understanding of psychopathy will benefit from studies aimed at refining its conceptualization and measurement. Much of the current debate focuses on the distinction between core personality features and more easily observable antisocial and externalizing traits, and on whether psychopathy is an aggregation of multiple and distinct factors or one general constellation of traits. It is also possible that some psychopathic features are missing or incorrectly conceptualized. One version of the frequency-dependent selection account of psychopathy suggests that early-onset and coercive mating effort might be a key feature of psychopathy, and this feature is not properly captured in the current version of the PCL-R, the gold standard assessment tool for offenders. Most of the theoretical work on psychopathy is traditionally bound to medical and pathological notions and has suffered from evolutionary neglect (the neglect of consideration of ultimate causes). So far, nonpathological (adaptationist) accounts have survived empirical disconfirmations, and research in the area of experimental games of cooperation, genetics, and brain imaging are likely to provide further insights.

Many people, scientists included, find the contemplation of psychopathy especially fascinating. The idea that a minority of male criminals is engaged in a life history strategy distinct from that of most people can be hard to accept at first—that is, most of us would like to believe that people are all generally alike and that the worst antisocial conduct would disappear if everyone had free and equal access to the best care, opportunities, and resources. Some selectionist accounts of psychopathy suggest, however, that these beliefs might not be completely correct—perhaps most people are alike and generally interested in mutual cooperation, and this has permitted a niche for a minority, alternative, nonpathological life history strategy characterized by social defection, emotional indifference to others, interpersonal exploitation, aggression, and coercive mating effort. If so, free and equal access to resources and opportunities (and providing psychotherapy) might have little effect on the prevalence of psychopathy, which might actually be altered only by the vigilance and contingencies non-psychopaths can bring to bear. It is somewhat curious in this context that few have noticed that phenotypes that include special skills (e.g., glibness and charm, manipulation, parasitic lifestyle) are rarely the result of pathology.

ACKNOWLEDGMENTS

The authors would like to thank Annabree Fairweather, Vern Quinsey, Marnie Rice, Michael Seto, Kelly Suschinsky, and, especially, Danny Krupp for commenting on a previous version of this chapter, and the Social Sciences and Humanities Research Council for its financial support in the form of a Standard Research Grant (M. L. L. and G. T. H.) and a Doctoral Fellowship (S. M.).

Notes

1. Readers might wonder how someone (with a maximal score on the PCL-R, for example) could simultaneously possess the traits of shallow affect and strong negative emotionality. In addition to the possibility of deliberate deception, the answer no doubt lies in the circumstances. Prototypical psychopaths are emotionally indifferent to the unhappiness and suffering of others (but not because they have any trouble perceiving it). They are, however, easily angered and upset by threats to their own interests. When institutionalized, for example, they worry about their fate (Cleckley, 1941), angrily guard their rights, and are prone to regard themselves as "victims of the system," their own misdeeds notwithstanding (Hare, 1998).

2. In quantitative genetics, *heritability* has a special technical meaning that is often misinterpreted. Heritability is the proportion of phenotypic variance that can be accounted for by genetic variance.

3. *Additive gene effects* refers to the simple combination of gene effects at different loci (as opposed to *nonadditive effects*, which refers to the interaction between different genes and gene dominance, among other things). *Unshared environmental effects* refers to environmental factors that operate to make siblings different from one another.

References

Axelrod, R. (1984). *The evolution of cooperation*. New York: Basic Books.
Axelrod, R., & Dion, D. (1988). The further evolution of cooperation. *Science, 242*, 1385–1390.
Axelrod, R., & Hamilton, W. (1981). The evolution of cooperation. *Science, 211*, 1390–1396.
Baker, L. A., Jacobson, K. C., Raine, A., Lozano, D. I., & Bezdjian, S. (2007). Genetic and environmental bases of childhood antisocial behavior: A multi-informant twin study. *Journal of Abnormal Psychology, 116*, 219–235.

Barr, K. N., & Quinsey, V. L. (2004). Is psychopathy a pathology or a life strategy? Implications for social policy. In C. Crawford & C. Salmon (Eds.), *Evolutionary psychology, public policy, and personal decisions* (pp. 293–317). Hillsdale, NJ: Erlbaum.

Benning, S. D., Patrick, C. J., Hicks, B. M., Blonigen, D. M., & Krueger, R. F. (2003). Factor structure of the psychopathic personality inventory: Validity and implications for clinical assessment. *Psychological Assessment, 15,* 340–350.

Blackburn, R. (2007). Personality disorder and psychopathy: Conceptual and empirical integration. *Psychology, Crime and Law, 13,* 7–18.

Blair, K. S., Richell, R. A., Mitchell, D. G. V., Leonard, A., Morton, J., & Blair, R. J. R. (2006). They know the words, but not the music: Affective and semantic priming in individuals with psychopathy. *Biological Psychology, 73,* 114–123.

Blair, R. J. R. (2003). Neurological basis of psychopathy. *British Journal of Psychiatry, 182,* 5–7.

Blonigen, D. M., Carlson, S. R., Krueger, R. F., & Patrick, C. J. (2003). A twin study of self-reported psychopathic traits. *Personality and Individual Differences, 35,* 179–197.

Book, A. S., Holden, R. R., Starzyk, K. B., Wasylkiw, L., & Edwards, M. J. (2006). Psychopathic traits and experimentally induced deception in self-report assessment. *Personality and Individual Differences, 41,* 601–608.

Book, A. S., Quinsey, V. L., & Langford, D. (2007). Psychopathy and the perception of affect and vulnerability. *Criminal Justice and Behavior, 34,* 531–544.

Budhani, S., Richell, R. A., & Blair, R. J. (2006). Impaired reversal but intact acquisition: Probabilistic response reversal deficits in adult individuals with psychopathy. *Journal of Abnormal Psychology, 115,* 552–558.

Burt, S. A., McGue, M., Carter, L. A., & Iacono, W. G. (2006). The different origins of stability and change in antisocial personality disorder symptoms. *Psychological Medicine, 37,* 27–38.

Carlson, S. R., McLarnon, M. E., & Iacono, W. G. (2007). P300 amplitude, externalizing psychopathology, and earlier- versus later-onset substance-use disorder. *Journal of Abnormal Psychology, 116,* 565–577.

Carroll, S. B. (2005). *Endless forms most beautiful: The new science of evo devo.* New York: W. W. Norton.

Caspi, A., McClay, J., Moffitt, T. E., Mill, J., Martin, J., Craig, I. W., et al. (2002). Role of genotype in the cycle of violence in maltreated children. *Science, 297,* 851–854.

Cleckley, H. (1941). *The mask of sanity.* St. Louis: Mosby.

Cooke, D. J., Michie, C., & Hart, S. D. (2006). Facets of clinical psychopathy: Toward clearer measurement. In C. J. Patrick (Ed.), *Handbook of psychopathy* (pp. 91–106). New York: Guilford Press.

Cooke, D. J., Michie, C., & Skeem, J. (2007). Understanding the structure of the Psychopathy Checklist-Revised. An exploration of methodological confusion. *British Journal of Psychiatry, 190,* 39–50.

Edens, J. F., Marcus, D. K., Lilienfeld, S. O., & Poythress, N. G. (2006). Psychopathic, not psychopath: Taxometric evidence for the dimensional structure of psychopathy. *Journal of Abnormal Psychology, 115,* 131–144.

Fu, P., Neff, B. D., & Gross, M. R. (2001). Tactic-specific success in sperm competition. *Proceedings of the Royal Society of London: Biological Sciences, 268,* 1105–1112.

Glass, S. J., & Newman, J. P. (2006). Recognition of facial affect in psychopathic offenders. *Journal of Abnormal Psychology, 115,* 815–820.

Glenn, A. L., Raine, A., Venables, P. H., & Mednick, S. A. (2007). Early temperamental and psychophysiological precursors of adult psychopathic personality. *Journal of Abnormal Psychology, 116*, 508–518.

Gross, M. R. (1996). Alternative reproductive strategies and tactics: Diversity within sexes. *Trends in Ecology and Evolution, 11*, 92–98.

Gross, M. R. (1991). Evolution of alternative reproductive strategies: Frequency-dependent sexual selection in male bluegill sunfish. *Philosophical Transactions of the Royal Society of London: Biological Sciences, 332*, 59–66.

Gross, M. R., & Charnov, E. L. (1980). Alternative life histories in bluegill sunfish. *Proceedings of the National Academy of Sciences USA, 77*, 6937–6940.

Hare, R. D. (1970). *Psychopathy: Theory and research.* New York: John Wiley.

Hare, R. D. (1998). *Without conscience: The disturbing world of the psychopaths among us.* New York: Guilford.

Hare, R. D. (2003). *Hare PCL-R: Technical Manual.* Toronto: MHS.

Hare, R. D., Clark, D., Grann, M., & Thornton, D. (2000). Psychopathy and the predictive validity of the PCL-R: An international perspective. *Behavioral Sciences and the Law, 18*, 623–645.

Hare, R. D., & Neumann, C. S. (2006). The PCL-R assessment of psychopathy: Development, structural properties, and new directions. In C. J. Patrick (Ed.), *Handbook of psychopathy* (pp. 58–90). New York: Guilford Press.

Harpending, H. C., & Sobus, J. (1987). Sociopathy as an adaptation. *Ethology and Sociobiology, 8*, 63S–72S.

Harpur, T. J., Hakstian, A. R., & Hare, R. D. (1988). Factor structure of the Psychopathy Checklist. *Journal of Consulting and Clinical Psychology, 56*, 741–747.

Harris, G. T., Rice, M. E., & Camilleri, J. A. (2004). Applying a forensic actuarial assessment (the Violence Risk Appraisal Guide) to nonforensic patients. *Journal of Interpersonal Violence, 19*, 1063–1074

Harris, G. T., Rice, M. E., & Cormier, C. A. (1994). Psychopaths: Is a therapeutic community therapeutic? *Therapeutic Communities, 15*, 283–300.

Harris, G. T., Rice, M. E., Hilton, N. Z., Lalumière, M. L., & Quinsey, V. L. (2007). Coercive and precocious sexuality as a fundamental aspect of psychopathy. *Journal of Personality Disorders, 21*, 1–27.

Harris, G. T., Rice, M. E., & Lalumière, M. L. (2001). Criminal violence: The roles of psychopathy, neurodevelopmental insults and antisocial parenting. *Criminal Justice and Behavior, 28*, 402–426.

Harris, G. T., Rice, M. E., & Quinsey, V. L. (1994). Psychopathy as a taxon: Evidence that psychopaths are a discrete class. *Journal of Consulting and Clinical Psychology, 62*, 387–397.

Harris, G. T., Skilling, T. A., & Rice, M. E. (2001). The construct of psychopathy. *Crime and Justice: A Review of Research, 28*, 197–264.

Hicks, B. M., & Patrick, C. J. (2006). Psychopathy and negative emotionality: Analyses of suppressor effects reveal distinct relations with emotional distress, fearfulness, and anger-hostility. *Journal of Abnormal Psychology, 115*, 276–287.

Hicks, B. M., Blonigen, D. M., Kramer, M. D., Krueger, R. F., Patrick, C. J., Iacono, W. G., et al. (2007). Gender differences and developmental change in externalizing disorders from late adolescence to early adulthood: A longitudinal twin study. *Journal of Abnormal Psychology, 116*, 433–447.

Hilton, N. Z., Harris, G. T., Rice, M. E., Houghton, R. E., & Eke, A. W. (2008). An indepth actuarial assessment for wife assault recidivism: The Domestic Violence Risk Appraisal Guide. *Law and Human Behavior, 31*, 150–163.

Kiehl, K. A. (2006). A cognitive neuroscience perspective on psychopathy: Evidence for paralimbic system dysfunction. *Psychiatry Research, 142,* 107–128.

Kiehl, K. A., Smith, A. M., Hare, R. D., Mendrek, A., Forster, B. B., et al. (2001). Limbic abnormalities in affective processing by criminal psychopaths as revealed by functional magnetic resonance imaging. *Biological Psychiatry, 50,* 677–684.

Kurzban, R., & Houser, D. (2005). Experiments investigating cooperative types in humans: A complement to evolutionary theory and simulations. *Proceedings of the National Academy of Sciences, USA, 102,* 1803–1807.

Laakso, M. P., Gunning-Dixon, F., Vaurio, O., Repo-Tiihonen, E., Soininen, H., et al. (2002). Prefrontal volumes in habitually violent subjects with antisocial personality disorder and type 2 alcoholism. *Psychiatry Research: Neuroimaging, 114,* 95–102.

Lalumière, M. L., Harris, G. T., Quinsey, V. L., & Rice, M. E. (2005). *The causes of rape: Understanding individual differences in male propensity of sexual aggression.* Washington, DC: American Psychological Association.

Lalumière, M. L., Harris, G. T., & Rice, M. E. (2001). Psychopathy and developmental instability. *Evolution and Human Behavior, 22,* 75–92.

Langton, C. M., Barbaree, H. E., Harkins, L., & Peacock, E. J. (2007). Sex offenders' response to treatment and its association with recidivism as a function of psychopathy. *Sexual Abuse: A Journal of Research and Treatment, 18,* 99–120.

Larsson, H., Andershed, H., & Lichtenstein, P. (2006). A genetic factor explains most of the variation in the psychopathic personality. *Journal of Abnormal Psychology, 115,* 221–230.

Larsson, H., Tuvblad, C., Rijsdijk, F. V., Andershed, H., Grann, M., & Lichtenstein, P. (2007). A common genetic factor explains the association between psychopathic personality and antisocial behavior. *Psychological Medicine, 37,* 15–26.

LeDoux, J. (2003). The emotional brain, fear, and the amygdala. *Cellular and Molecular Neurobiology, 23,* 727–738.

Leistico, A. R., Salekin, R. T., DeCoster, J., & Rogers, R. (2007). A large-scale meta-analysis relating the Hare measures of psychopathy to antisocial conduct. *Law and Human Behavior, 32,* 28–45.

Livesley, W. J. (1998). The phenotypic and genotypic structure of psychopathic traits. In D. J. Cooke, A. E. Forth, & R. D. Hare (Eds.), *Psychopathy: Theory, research and implications for society* (pp. 69–79). Dordrescht: Kluwer Academic.

Loney, B. R., Taylor, J., Butler, M. A., & Iacono, W. G. (2007). Adolescent psychopathy features: 6-year temporal stability and the prediction of externalizing symptoms during the transition to adulthood. *Aggressive Behavior, 33,* 242–252.

Looman, J., Abracen, J., Serin, R., & Marquis, P. (2005). Psychopathy, treatment change, and recidivism in high-risk, high-need sexual offenders. *Journal of Interpersonal Violence, 20,* 549–568.

Lykken, D. T. (1995). *The antisocial personalities.* Hillsdale, NJ: Erlbaum.

Lynam, D. R., Caspi, A., Moffitt, T. E., Loeber, R., & Stouthamer-Loeber, M. (2007). Longitudinal evidence that psychopathy scores in early adolescence predict adult psychopathy. *Journal of Abnormal Psychology, 116,* 155–165.

Maccoon, D. G., & Newman, J. P. (2006). Content meets process: Using attributions and standards to inform cognitive vulnerability in psychopathy, antisocial personality disorder, and depression. *Journal of Social and Clinical Psychology, 25,* 802–824.

Marinoff, L. (1990). The inapplicability of evolutionary stable strategy to the Prisoner's Dilemma. *British Journal for the Philosophy of Science, 41,* 461–472.

Mealey, L. (1995). The sociobiology of sociopathy: An integrated evolutionary model. *Behavioral and Brain Sciences, 18,* 523–599.

Moffitt, T. E., & Caspi, A. (2001). Childhood predictors differentiate life-course persistent and adolescence-limited antisocial pathways among males and females. *Development and Psychopathology, 13,* 355–375.

Moltó, J., Poy, R., Segarra, P., Pastor, M. C., & Montañés, S. (2007). Response preservation in psychopaths: Interpersonal/affective or social deviance traits? *Journal of Abnormal Psychology, 116,* 632–637.

Munro, G. E. S., Dywan, J., Harris, G. T., McKee, S., Unsal, A., & Segalowitz, S. J. (2007). Response inhibition in psychopathy: The frontal N2 and P3. *Neuroscience Letters, 418,* 149–153.

Neff, B. D. (2001). Genetic paternity analysis and breeding success in bluegill sunfish (*Lepomis macrochirus*). *Journal of Heredity, 92,* 111–119.

Neff, B. D., Fu, P., & Gross, M. R. (2003). Sperm investment and alternative mating tactics in bluegill sunfish (*Lepomis macrochirus*). *Behavioral Ecology, 14,* 634–641.

Oxford, M., Cavell, T. A., & Hugues, J. N. (2003). Callous/unemotional traits moderate the relation between ineffective parenting and child externalizing problems: A partial replication and extension. *Journal of Clinical Child and Adolescent Psychology, 32,* 577–585.

Patrick, C. J., Edens, J. F., Poythress, N. G., Lilienfeld, S. O., & Benning, S. D. (2006). Construct validity of the psychopathic personality inventory two-factor model with offenders. *Psychological Assessment, 18,* 204–208.

Porter, S., & Woodworth, M. (2006). Psychopathy and aggression. In C. J. Patrick (Ed.), *Handbook of psychopathy* (pp. 481–494). New York: Guilford Press.

Quinsey, V. L., Skilling, T. A., Lalumière, M. L., & Craig, W. M. (2004). *Juvenile delinquency: Understanding the origins of individual differences.* Washington: American Psychological Association.

Quinsey, V. L., Harris, G. T., Rice, M. E., & Cormier, C. A. (2006). *Violent offenders: Appraising and managing risk* (2nd ed.). Washington, DC: American Psychological Association.

Raine, A., Lencz, T., Bihrle, S., LaCasse, L., & Colletti, P. (2000). Reduced prefrontal gray matter volume and reduced autonomic activity in antisocial personality disorder. *Archives of General Psychiatry, 57,* 119–127.

Rice, M. E. & Harris, G. T. (1992). A comparison of criminal recidivism among schizophrenic and nonschizophrenic offenders. *International Journal of Law and Psychiatry, 15,* 397–408.

Rice, M. E. & Harris, G. T. (1995). Psychopathy, schizophrenia, alcohol abuse, and violent recidivism. *International Journal of Law and Psychiatry, 18,* 333–342.

Rice, M. E. & Harris, G. T. (1997). Cross validation and extension of the Violence Risk Appraisal Guide for child molesters and rapists. *Law and Human Behavior, 21,* 231–241.

Rice, M. E., Harris, G. T., & Cormier, C. A. (1992). Evaluation of a maximum security therapeutic community for psychopaths and other mentally disordered offenders. *Law and Human Behavior, 16,* 399–412.

Salekin, R. T., Rogers, R., & Sewell, K. W. (1996). A review and meta-analysis of the Psychopathy Checklist and Psychopathy Checklist-Revised. *Clinical Psychology, Science, and Practice, 3,* 203–215.

Seto, M. C., & Barbaree, H. E. (1999). Psychopathy, treatment behavior, and sex offender recidivism. *Journal of Interpersonal Violence, 14,* 1235–1248.

Seto, M. C., Harris, G. T., Rice, M. E., & Barbaree, H. E. (2004). The Screening Scale for Pedo-
    philic Interests and recidivism among adult sex offenders with child victims. *Archives of
    Sexual Behavior, 33*, 455–466.

Shaw, D. S., Bell, R. Q., & Gilliom, M. (2000). A truly early starter model of antisocial behavior
    revisited. *Clinical Child and Family Psychology Review, 3*, 155–172.

Shaw, D. S., Gilliom, M., Ingoldsby, E. M., & Nagin, D. S. (2003). Trajectories leading to school-
    age conduct problems. *Developmental Psychology, 39*, 189–200.

Skeem, J., Johansson, P., Andershed, H., Kerr, M., & Louden, J. E. (2007). Two subtypes of
    psychopathic violent offenders that parallel primary and secondary variants. *Journal of
    Abnormal Psychology, 116*, 395–409.

Skilling, T. A., Harris, G. T., Rice, M. E., & Quinsey, V. L. (2002). Identifying persistently anti-
    social offenders using the Hare Psychopathy Checklist and DSM antisocial personality
    disorder criteria. *Psychological Assessment, 14*, 27–38.

Skilling, T. A., Quinsey, V. L., & Craig, W. A. (2001). Evidence of a taxon underlying serious
    antisocial behavior in boys. *Criminal Justice and Behavior, 28*, 450–470.

Swogger, M. T., & Kosson, D. S. (2007). Identifying subtypes of criminal psychopaths: A repli-
    cation and extension. *Criminal Justice and Behavior, 34*, 953–970.

Taylor, J., Loney, B. R., Bobadilla, L., Iacono, W. G., & McGue, M. (2003). Genetic and envi-
    ronmental influences on psychopathy trait dimensions in a community sample of male
    twins. *Journal of Abnormal Child Psychology, 31*, 633–645.

Tiihonen, J., Hodgins, S., Vaurio, O., Laakso, M., Repo, E., Soininen, H., et al. (2000). Amygda-
    loid volume loss in psychopathy. *Society for Neuroscience Abstracts, 2017*.

Tooby, J., & Cosmides, L. (1990). On the universality of human nature and the uniqueness of
    the individual: The role of genetics and adaptation. *Journal of Personality, 58*, 17–67.

Vasey, M. W., Kotov, R., Frick, P. J., & Loney, B. R. (2005). The latent structure of psychopathy in
    youth: A taxometric investigation. *Journal of Abnormal Child Psychology, 33*, 411–429.

Viding, E., Blair, J. R., Moffitt, T. E., & Plomin, R. (2005). Evidence for substantial genetic risk
    for psychopathy in 7-year olds. *Journal of Child Psychology and Psychiatry, 46*, 592–597.

Viding, E., Frick, P. J., & Plomin, R. (2007). Aetiology of the relationship between callous-
    unemotional traits and conduct problems in childhood. *British Journal of Psychiatry, 190*,
    33–38.

Vizard, E., Hickey, N., & McCrory, E. (2007). Developmental trajectories associated with juve-
    nile sexually abusive behaviour and emerging severe personality disorder in childhood:
    3-year study. *British Journal of Psychiatry, 190*, 27–32.

Waldman, I. D., & Rhee, S. H. (2006). Genetic and environmental influences on psychopathy
    and antisocial behavior. In C. J. Patrick (Ed.), *Handbook of psychopathy* (pp. 205–228).
    New York: Guilford Press.

Widiger, T. A. (2006). Psychopathy and DSM-IV psychopathology. In C. J. Patrick (Ed.), *Hand-
    book of psychopathy* (pp. 156–171). New York: Guilford Press.

Wootton, J. M., Frick, P. J., Shelton, K. K., & Silverthorne, P. (1997). Ineffective parenting and
    childhood conduct problems: The moderating role of callous-unemotional traits. *Journal
    of Consulting and Clinical Psychology, 65*, 301–308.

PART FIVE

VICTIMS OF CRIME

11

Victim Adaptations

JOSHUA D. DUNTLEY AND TODD K. SHACKELFORD

What Is a Victim?

There are victims of disease, victims of natural disasters, and victims of circumstance. People may even be victims of their own actions, hoisted by their own petards. For forensic psychologists who work within the legal system, victims represent a more restricted class of individuals–people who have costs defined by legislators as criminal inflicted on them by others.

An evolutionary exploration of victimization demands a more inclusive definition of victimization. Specifically, we argue that the genetic relatives, romantic partners, and close allies of the primary victims of exploitative or violent strategies also incur costs and can be considered secondary victims. Primary victims of crime share genes with all of their living genetic relatives. Because natural selection operates through the differential replication of genes (Hamilton, 1963), costs to genetic fitness resulting from the victimization of a family member are shared across all of the person's genetic relatives. Because a victim's closer genetic relatives share more copies of the victim's genes, the costs that they incur are greater than those endured by more distant genetic relatives. Spouses and close social allies can also be secondary victims, incurring costs as a result of loss of investment or protection, and perhaps by gaining a reputation of being vulnerable to exploitation (Buss & Duntley, 2008; Duntley, 2005). We hypothesize that selection fashioned adaptations in both primary and secondary victims to prevent or stanch the costs of victimization.

Why Are Some Behaviors Considered Crimes?

Of all the human behaviors that inflict costs on others, only a subset are considered to be criminal. Derogating competitors, for example, is not criminal but is a competitive strategy that people use to inflict costs on intrasexual rivals (Buss & Dedden, 1990). How do individuals and societies decide whether a behavior should be legally vilified? Evolutionary psychologists propose that societal groups criminalize those behaviors that have the greatest negative consequences on reproductive fitness (Buss, 2007; Jones, 1997). Laws prohibiting cost-inflicting behaviors and the enforcement of those laws are argued to be outcomes of evolved psychological mechanisms. Individuals with psychological predispositions to prevent being victimized and to punish those who inflict costs would have had an evolutionary advantage over competitors who lack such predispositions. As a result, the genetic foundation for the development of mechanisms to punish exploitative behaviors would have been passed on with greater frequency to subsequent generations than other strategies that were less effective at stanching fitness losses from being victimized. Because all individuals in a group would benefit from preventing others from victimizing them, it is likely that selection favored cooperation among individuals in the same group, and especially the same family who have shared genetic interests, for the prevention and punishment of cost-inflicting behaviors against mutual allies.

Criminal Cost-inflicting Behaviors

The criminal cost-inflicting strategies that humans employ manifest in many different guises, including robbery, assault, rape, and murder. Many hostile human activities have been proposed to be the result of psychological adaptations. Researchers have found evidence for adaptations that contribute to the production of spousal violence (Buss & Shackelford, 1997a), aggression (Buss & Shackelford, 1997b; Campbell, 1993; Daly & Wilson, 1988), and rape (Thornhill & Palmer, 2000). At the core of the selection pressures that shaped these adaptations is conflict between individuals for limited resources. In this chapter, we will (a) discuss how natural selection shaped strategies to inflict costs on other humans and (b) explain how the recurrence of cost-inflicting strategies in predictable contexts of competition selected for specific patterns of victim defenses. Because of the high fitness consequences of homicide, we will focus on defenses against being murdered.

Contexts Selecting for the Infliction of Costs

To identify which individuals are in the greatest conflict over a limited resource, it is necessary to explore the adaptive problems leading to conflict between individuals. The conflict that exists between two individuals is tempered by genetic relatedness (Hamilton, 1963). Because selection operates by differential replication of genes, individuals should have evolved predispositions to favor genetic relatives who share copies of their genes over nonrelatives. Thus, closer genetic relatives should experience less conflict over resources than more distant relatives or unrelated individuals.

There can be dangers associated with adopting a strategy of cost-infliction against competitors. Individuals who inflict costs on others may gain unfavorable reputations, become injured, or die as a result of carrying out their attacks. Because of the potential dangers, the use of cost-inflicting strategies to best competitors should be most likely when the contested resources are uncommon and the fitness payoffs are great. For example, men who hold high positions in status hierarchies have greater success in attracting mates than do lower-status men (Buss et al., 1990). High-status positions in social hierarchies are rare and are valuable for the reproductive success of men, and would have created selection pressure for strategies capable of increasing status, including tactics of cost-infliction on rivals. In contrast, there would not have been ancestral selection pressures to compete against others for plentiful, easily obtainable resources or struggle to control items or entities that contributed little or nothing to human reproductive success.

Conflict over Status

One broad context of conflict is over position in status hierarchies. All available evidence indicates that high-status men have sexual access to a larger number of women (Perusse, 1993). Men who are high in status also seek younger and more fertile women (Grammer, 1992) and marry women who are more attractive (Taylor & Glenn, 1976; Udry & Eckland, 1984) than their low-status rivals. Although no comprehensive evolutionary theory of the importance of status over our evolutionary history has yet been proposed (Buss, 2007), the potential for large fitness gains associated with increases in status would have created selection pressure for cognitive adaptations that produce desires and behaviors that lead to hierarchy ascension and prevent large status falls.

Conflict over Material Resources

A second context of ancestrally recurrent conflict was conflict over *material resources* that helped to solve recurrent adaptive problems. Such resources include territory, food, weapons, and tools. There was also conflict over individuals who were the suppliers of material resources, such as conflict between siblings for investment from their parents and elder kin (Parker, Royle, & Hartley, 2002) and conflict between women for men with resources (Buss, Larsen, & Westen, 1996; Buss, Larsen, Westen, & Semmelroth, 1992). The scarcer and more valuable the resource in terms of its contribution to an individual's reproductive success, the greater the conflict is between individuals over access to the resource.

Conflict over Mating Resources

Whereas the minimum obligatory parental investment for women is nine months, the minimum investment for men can be as little as a few minutes. Because women's minimum investment in reproduction is greater, the costs of a poor mate choice are higher (Trivers, 1972). As a result, there is conflict between the sexes about the timing of sexual activity. Because sex is less costly for men, they desire sexual activity much earlier in a relationship than do women (Werner-Wilson, 1998). Men also desire a greater number of sexual partners than women (Schmitt, Shackelford, Duntley, Tooke, & Buss, 2002) and are more amenable to short-term, uncommitted sex (Buss, 1996).

In sum, each context of conflict results from individuals pursuing evolved strategies. Selection sculpted the adaptations that produce these strategies, including those that exploit others, because of their benefits to the reproductive success of the individuals who use them. It is important not to lose sight of the fact that, over human evolutionary history, there were at least two sides to every conflict.

The Coevolution of Cost-infliction and Victim Defenses

Coevolutionary arms races are part of the evolutionary history of all species. They can occur between species, as with the fox and the hare, or within species between different individuals' competing adaptations in contexts of social conflict. Coevolutionary arms races can create massive selection pressures capable of producing rapid evolutionary change (Phillips, Brown, & Shine, 2004). Any recurrent context of conflict between individuals has the potential to be a hotbed for the coevolution of competing strategies to best a competitor or to defend against being exploited.

The evolution of adaptations to inflict costs created selection pressures for the coevolution of counter-adaptations in victims to decrease or prevent incurring the costs. The strength of the selection pressure for victim adaptations is a function of the magnitude of costs inflicted, the frequency of such costs over evolutionary time, and the certainty that the costs would be inflicted. Once adaptations to prevent or minimize the costs of exploitation evolve in victims, they create new selection pressures on those who inflict costs for refinements in their adaptations capable of stanching the effectiveness of the victim adaptations. These refined adaptations for cost-infliction in turn create new selection pressures for refined victim adaptations capable of defending against the new cost-inflicting strategies. This antagonistic, coevolutionary arms race between adaptations to inflict costs and victim adaptations to defend against costs is hypothesized to have recurred over human evolutionary history.

Victim adaptations to competitors' cost-inflicting strategies can evolve only when the strategies have been recurrent in predictable contexts over evolutionary time. Many evolved victim adaptations function by making a competitor's cost-inflicting behavior too costly to perform. This would create selection pressure against the cost-inflicting strategy. If a cost-inflicting strategy persists over evolutionary time despite its costs, then the cost-inflicting strategy may be functional in producing a net benefit in a particular context. We propose that evidence of such functionality is evidence of adaptation.

The Three Temporal Contexts of Victim Defenses

There are important differences between the form and function of victim defenses depending on when they are enacted. Victims can defend themselves from the cost-inflicting strategies of others (1) before the victimization occurs, (2) while the cost-inflicting event is occurring, or (3) after being victimized. Each of these temporal contexts of victim defenses was selected to minimize the impact of the outcomes of victimization. We hypothesize that the strength of selection pressures operating to design adaptations to address each temporal context varies as a function of the nature of the costs inflicted. For example, there would be selection pressures on victim adaptations against rape in all three temporal contexts. Women should have adaptations to avoid victimization, to minimize costs during victimization, and to take steps to prevent reputational damage and future victimization in the aftermath of rape. However, there would not be selection pressures on all three temporal contexts of primary victims' adaptations against being murdered. The primary victims of homicide are incapable of directly influencing events after their deaths.

Adaptations to Prevent or Avoid Victimization

The best defense against being victimized is to never become a victim. To the extent that strategies of cost-infliction were perpetrated by predictable conspecifics in predictable contexts, there would have been selection pressures for the evolution of defensive adaptations to avoid them. Individuals with adaptations that led them to recognize situational cues and individual characteristics associated with a higher likelihood of incurring costs and to then avoid them would have had a large fitness advantage over competitors without these abilities. Fear while walking through dark alleys at night or of people who seem "shifty" and stranger anxiety in infants are examples of the hypothesized outcomes of adaptations to avoid falling victim to the cost-inflicting strategies of others.

Adaptations to Minimize Costs During Victimization

Selection also shaped adaptations to minimize the costs of victimization while it is occurring. Defensive postures, verbal attempts at manipulation, and seeking or creating opportunities to flee an attacker are defensive strategies hypothesized to have been selected because they decreased the costs of victimization. Curling into a fetal position may help to deflect blows from an attacker away from a victim's head and internal organs. The use of language to activate sympathy or empathy in an attacker or to frighten an attacker away may be effective in decreasing the duration or severity of the cost-infliction. Creating or waiting for an event that distracts an attacker or temporarily incapacitating the attacker might give victims an opportunity to escape or to hide and seek protection, decreasing the magnitude of costs they might otherwise have incurred. Finally, Bracha (2004) has hypothesized that fainting may be an evolved strategy to minimize the costs of being attacked or prevent victimization by sending an honest signal to attackers that one is not a threat.

Post-victimization Adaptations

Finally, we hypothesize that selection shaped victim adaptations activated after the occurrence of the cost-inflicting event that function to minimize the impact of the victimization and to prevent it from being repeated. For example, acting as though the injuries sustained during a fight are not as debilitating as they actually are or using verbal assaults on an attacker that impugn the effectiveness of a person's attack, such as "You fight like my grandmother," may decrease the status loss that can be associated with losing a fight.

There are numerous avenues for the prevention of future occurrences of victimization. One is learning cues to danger. By recognizing and subsequently avoiding dangerous contexts and individuals, victims make themselves less likely to incur costs in similar contexts in the future. A person victimized in a certain part of a city, for example, may be motivated to avoid that part of the city. Similarly, a victim may avoid future interactions with an attacker. Victims also may be proactive in avoiding future conflicts by developing or acquiring defenses against future attacks by conspecifics. For example, carrying a weapon for self-defense may decrease the likelihood of incurring serious costs in future confrontations.

Another avenue for the prevention of future victimization is retaliation against an attacker. Demonstrating an effective ability to retaliate may decrease the likelihood of future victimization by sending a message to the perpetrator and others that attacks or exploitation will be punished. Revenge has been suggested to be wired into our psychology by natural selection (Buss & Duntley, 2006). Functional magnetic resonance imaging (fMRI) research has demonstrated that pleasure centers of men's brains become activated when they are successful in obtaining revenge against someone they perceive to have crossed them (Singer et al., 2006). This suggests that the motivation for men to seek revenge may have evolutionary underpinnings and supports the contention that maintaining status in social competition was important for the reproductive success of ancestral men.

Selection pressures for each temporal category of victim adaptations are unlikely to have been equal. Since avoiding victimization entirely was ancestrally associated with the lowest costs, we hypothesize that there was proportionally more selection pressure for the evolution of previctimization adaptations than for victim adaptations that function during or after victims have incurred costs. As a result, previctimization adaptations are hypothesized to be larger in number and perhaps more elaborate in design than the other temporal categories of victim adaptations.

In sum, it is useful to consider three temporal categories of victim adaptations: those aimed at avoiding victimization, those that minimize the costs of victimization while it is occurring, and those that function after victimization to minimize its costs and prevent its recurrence. The nature of the victimization will determine the degree of selection pressure for adaptations in each of these contexts.

Adaptations to Damage Status

One strategy for inflicting costs on rivals in order to deprive them of reproductively relevant resources is to damage their reputations. An individual in a group cannot ascend in a status hierarchy without displacing someone above, bumping that person to a lower position than he or she occupied previously and inflicting costs associated with status loss. Higher-status men have greater access to resources and more mating opportunities than lower-status men (Betzig, 1993; Buss, 1996; Hill & Hurtado, 1996; Perusse, 1993). Because additional mating opportunities enhances the reproductive success of men more than it does that of women, it has been hypothesized that there should be greater status striving among men (Buss, 2003a). Research across the life span has found this to be the case, with men placing greater importance on coming out ahead and women tending to be more focused on maintaining social harmony (Maccoby, 1990; Pratto, 1996; Whiting & Edwards, 1988).

Defenses against Status Damage

A number of victim defenses may have evolved to combat the danger of status loss caused by the cost-inflicting tactics of competitors. First, individuals should be armed with the ability to constantly track their own position in a status hierarchy while also keeping track of their closest competitors (Buss, 2004; 2007). Individuals should be motivated to gather information about the strengths and weaknesses of their closest status rivals to inform strategies of status defense that may be required in the future. The strategic formation of alliances that will strengthen one's hold on a position in a status hierarchy can help defend against status assaults from others. Offensive tactics such as competitor derogation (Buss & Dedden, 1990) can assault the status of those most likely to challenge one's position in the future, forestalling a status conflict. Competitor derogation may also be an effective strategy after a status loss has occurred. Recouping status that has been lost, however, can be a more formidable task than maintaining one's position in a status hierarchy and may require more drastic measures. Social status was so important to the reproductive success of ancestral men that people may now resort to violence and even murder in response to public humiliation or challenges to status and social reputation. This made sense in the context of small-group living in which we evolved (Tooby & Devore, 1987), where a loss of status could have had devastating effects on survival and reproduction (Buss, 2007). The outcome of selection for victim adaptations to defend status in the small-group living conditions of our ancestors is evidenced today in research conducted on homicidal ideation that finds the most frequent triggers of homicidal fantasies are status related (Buss & Duntley, 1999) and in research on actual murders, which suggests that experiencing reputational damage contributes to the activation of the motivational mechanisms behind a substantial number of homicides (Daly & Wilson, 1988).

Adaptations for Theft and Cheating

A second strategy of cost-infliction that may be used to gain an advantage in competition for resources is to steal those resources (Cohen & Machalek, 1988; see also Chapter 9 of this volume) or or to cheat rivals out of their resources. A valuable weapon can be stolen and used against its owner. Valuable territory can be encroached upon and its vegetation, water, shelter, and wildlife exploited (Chagnon, 1996). Mates can be poached from rivals (Buss, 2000, 2003a; Schmitt & Buss, 2001). Public knowledge that an individual has been cheated or had valuables stolen also can affect the person's reputation. The person may gain a reputation as one who is easy to exploit, perhaps increasing the likelihood that others will attempt to cheat or steal from the person (Buss & Duntley, 2008). An easily exploitable person will likely be less attractive to members of the opposite sex. Cheating and the theft of resources, in short, can be effective strategies of cost-infliction for individual gain.

Defenses against Theft and Cheating

To prevent the threat of material resource theft, individuals are hypothesized to have evolved adaptations to defend against theft and being cheated. These mechanisms are hypothesized to motivate people to keep valuable items under protection, to conceal them, or to make valuable commodities seem less desirable to rivals. Humans may have also evolved adaptations to detect those who would cheat them. Deceiving rivals about the location of a valuable resource, such as food, has been shown to occur in other primates, like tufted capuchin monkeys (*Cebus apella*) (Fujita, Kuroshima, & Masuda, 2002), as well as in pigs (Held, Mendl, Devereux, & Byrne, 2002) and in ravens (*Corvus corax*) (Bugnyar & Kotrschal, 2004). The ability to detect cheaters in contexts of social exchange is another strategy for preventing the loss of resources to rivals. Sugiyama, Tooby, and Cosmides (2002) found evidence that the ability to detect violations of conditional rules in contexts of social exchange ("cheater detection") is likely a cross-cultural universal. In their research, the Shiwiar hunter-horticulturalists of the Ecuadorian Amazon performed similarly to Harvard under-graduates in their ability to detect rule violations in contexts of social exchange. Both groups, however, performed poorly when asked to detect violations of conditional rules in contexts other than social exchange.

When the resource that is threatened is a mate rather than a material commodity, Buss and Shackelford (1997a) found that men and women engage in tactics that range from vigilance to violence to defend their relationships. Fueled by jealousy, an emotion absent from contexts of material resource theft, men's tactics of defending against mate poachers were found to be different from women's. Men are more likely to conceal their partners, to display resources, and to resort to threats and violence, especially against rivals. Women are more likely to enhance their appearance and to induce jealousy in their partners, demonstrating their desirability by showing that they have other mating options.

Adaptations for Violence

A third strategy for inflicting costs on rivals is to injure them physically. Individuals should disengage from competition for a contested resource when the inclusive fitness costs of competing become greater than the benefits of controlling the resource. The direct infliction of costs on competitors in the form of violence can help tip the outcome of competition in favor of the cost-inflicting individuals, increasing the likelihood that they will gain control of contested resources. Healthy individuals can compete more effectively than their injured rivals. Rivals may be more likely to avoid or to drop out of competitions with individuals who have injured them in the past. Individuals capable of inflicting greater injuries on competitors than are inflicted on them may gain a reputation as being difficult to exploit. This reputation is hypothesized to help protect those successful in the use of violence against future violent confrontations and grant them easier access to resources with less resistance from competitors. Some strategies employed to win competitions for reproductively relevant resources offer a potential solution to a wider variety of problems than others. For example, violence can be used to help solve a broader range of problems than theft. In a single instance, violence can be used as a strategy to aid in theft, to demonstrate one's ability to acquire resources to potential mates, to intimidate rivals, making them less likely to seek retribution, and to make future threats of violence more credible.

Victim Defenses against Violence

The most effective strategy for dealing with violence capable of producing injuries is to avoid it altogether. Adaptations for alliance formation may provide one form of deterrence, as it is easier to attack an individual than a group. Adaptations that lead to the avoidance of contexts likely to make one the target of violence may provide another kind of protection against being injured in a violent confrontation. Humans may also possess adaptations designed for attempting to reason with an attacker, emphasizing the costs of their violent behavior or suggesting other resolutions to the conflict. Finally, if an attack cannot be avoided, individuals may resort to violence or even murder to defend themselves (Daly & Wilson, 1988).

Adaptations that Produce Rape

A fourth cost-inflicting strategy aimed directly at obtaining reproductive re-sources is rape. A rapist may benefit from the behavior by siring offspring that he may not have otherwise produced. Not only does rape inflict terrible emotional (Block, 1990; Burgess & Holmstrom, 1974) and physical (Geist, 1988) costs on women but it also inflicts fitness costs by bypassing female mechanisms of mate choice (Buss, 2007). Although some scholars have concluded that there is not enough evidence to determine whether men have adaptations for rape (Buss, 2003a, 2007; Symons, 1979), historical records and ethnographies suggest that rape occurs cross-culturally and has been recurrent over deep time (Buss, 2003a).

Victim Defenses against Rape

A number of researchers have proposed the existence of anti-rape adaptations. The formation of alliances with groups of other women and with men for protection has been argued to be an evolved counterstrategy to rape (Smuts, 1992). The "body-guard hypothesis" proposes that women's preference for mates who are physically formidable and high in social dominance is, in part, an adaptation to prevent rape (Wilson & Mesnick, 1997). Specialized fears that motivate women to avoid situations ancestrally predictive of an increased likelihood of being raped have been proposed to help preemptively defend against rape. To prevent conception resulting from rape, women may have evolved to avoid risky activities during ovulation (Chavanne & Gallup, 1998). The psychological pain of rape has been argued to motivate women to avoid being raped in the future (Thornhill & Palmer, 2000). In addition, women may possess adaptations to minimize the costs of rape after it has occurred. To avoid the reputational damage that can be associated with rape or to avoid losing their roman-tic partner, women may feel motivated to keep their ordeal a secret. We hypothesize that female rape victims' common urge to bathe themselves after their victimization functions to wash physical evidence of the forced encounter away so it cannot be de-tected, especially by their romantic partners who may be more likely to abandon a sex-ually exploited partner (Thornhill & Palmer, 2000). Finally, women may seek revenge against their attacker by marshaling male relatives and allies to attack him, especially if the rapist represents a persistent threat to the woman or her female relatives.

Adaptations that Produce Homicide

Buss and Duntley (1998, 1999, 2003, 2004) have proposed that humans possess adaptations for murder. According to their homicide adaptation theory, over the long expanse of human history there were recurrent sources of conflict between individuals, such as conflict over reputation and social status, conflict over resources, and conflict over romantic partners. Homicidal strategies are argued to be distinct from nonlethal solutions to conflict in that they lead to an absolute end to the competition between two individuals. Once dead, a person can no longer damage your reputation, steal your resources, prevent you from attracting a romantic partner, or have sex with your spouse.

Homicide is hypothesized to be the designed output of evolved psychological mechanisms. Killing conspecifics is argued to solve a variety of adaptive problems. Specifically, the killing of a conspecific could have contributed to (1) preventing the exploitation, injury, rape, or killing of self, kin, mates, and coalitional allies by conspecifics in the present and future; (2) reputation management against being perceived as easily exploited, injured, raped, or killed by conspecifics; (3) protecting resources, territory, shelter, and food from competitors; (4) eliminating resource-absorbing or costly individuals who are not genetically related (e.g., stepchildren); and (5) eliminating genetic relatives who interfere with investment in other vehicles better able to translate resource investment into genetic fitness (e.g., deformed infants, the chronically ill or infirm). Chapter 3 of this volume provides a more thorough exploration of homicide adaptation theory.

Homicide as a By-product of Other Evolved Mechanisms

Adaptations for homicide need not be involved in the production of all homicidal behavior. Another evolutionary explanation of conspecific killing was proposed by Daly and Wilson in their book *Homicide* (1988). According to Daly and Wilson, homicide may be considered an overreactive mistake, the by-product of adaptations designed for nonlethal outcomes. They argue that homicide can be used "as a sort of 'assay' of the evolved psychology of interpersonal conflict" (Wilson, Daly, & Daniele, 1995). For example, if cognitive adaptations for parenting fail to engage, it may lead a woman to abandon her infant in a dumpster. The resulting death, according to Daly and Wilson, is not the result of maternal adaptations to kill; rather, it is a byproduct of the activation failure of the woman's parenting mechanisms. Similarly, male adaptations for the experience of sexual jealousy and those that motivate men to coerce and control their female partners may overreact, leading some men to mistakenly use too much force when confronting an unfaithful partner, causing her death. In this case, again, the homicide is a byproduct of the function of other mechanisms that were designed by selection for their nonlethal consequences. In the case of a husband who kills his wife for being sexually unfaithful, Daly and Wilson have argued that male mechanisms for sexual jealousy and the coercion and control of their mates may mistakenly overreact, leading a man to kill his wife. Despite their contention that conspecific killing in humans is a maladaptive by-product of psychological adaptations, Although Daly and Wilson (1988) think that adaptations for homicide are very unlikely, they do emphasize that an evolutionary account of homicide is important: "[W]hat is needed is a Darwinian psychology that uses evolutionary ideas as a metatheory for the postulation of cognitive/emotional/motivational mechanisms and strategies" (pp. 108–109).

The Fitness Costs of Being Killed

Whether there are adaptations specifically for homicide or homicide is a byproduct of adaptations that were designed to have nonlethal consequences, conspecific killing was a recurrent feature of human evolutionary history (Chagnon, 1988; Trinkhaus & Shipman, 1993). Examining the costs of homicide through an evolutionary lens elucidates the nature and magnitude of the costs incurred by victims of homicide and gives us a better understanding of how other humans were a significant danger over our evolutionary history. A victim's death has a much larger impact on his or her inclusive fitness than just the loss of the genes housed in the person's body. The inclusive fitness costs of dying at the hands of another human can cascade to the victim's children, spouse, kin, and coalitional allies. The specific costs include the following.

Loss of future reproduction. A victim of homicide cannot reproduce in the future with a current mate or with other possible mates. On average, this cost would have been greater for younger individuals than for older individuals.

Damage to existing children. The child of a murdered parent receives fewer resources, is more susceptible to being exploited by others, and may have more difficulty in ascending status hierarchies or negotiating mating relationships, which will likely lead to poorer fitness outcomes. Children of a murdered parent may see their surviving parent's investment diverted away from them to a new mating relationship and to the children who are the product of that relationship. A single parent can invest less than two and might abandon his or her children in favor of better mating prospects in the future. Finally, the children of a murdered parent risk becoming stepchildren, a condition that brings with it physical abuse and homicide rates 40 to 100 times greater than those found among children who reside with two genetic parents (Daly & Wilson, 1988).

Damage to extended kin group. A homicide victim cannot protect or invest in kin. A victim's entire kin network can gain the reputation of being vulnerable to exploitation as a result of the person's death. A dead victim cannot influence the status trajectories or mating relationships of family members. And the open position left by the victim in a kin network's status hierarchy could create a struggle for power among the surviving family members.

A homicide victim's fitness losses can be a rival's fitness gains. Killers can benefit from the residual reproductive value and parenting value of the surviving mate of their victim, sometimes at the expense of the victim's children with that mate. Killers can ascend into the vacancies in status hierarchies left by their victims. The children of killers would thrive relative to the children of homicide victims, who would be deprived of the investment, protection, and influence of two genetic parents. Many family members who would have survived if the person were not killed will die before they can reproduce, and many children who would have been born to members of the family will never be born.

Defenses against Homicide

Of all the dangers created by other humans, homicide can be the most devastating in terms of its effect on the inclusive fitness of its victims. If homicide recurred in predictable contexts over our evolutionary history, it would have created selection pressures to avoid being killed in precisely those contexts. We propose that the selection pressures created by the costs of being killed were powerful enough to shape distinct adaptations to defend against homicide (Duntley & Buss, 1998, 2000, 2001, 2002; Buss & Duntley, 2006, under review).

The strength of selection for any adaptation, including defenses against being killed, is a function of the *frequency* of the event and the *fitness costs* of the event. Low base-rate events that impose heavy fitness costs, such as homicide, can create intense selection pressures for adaptations to prevent or avoid them. Ancestral homicides, however, may not have been as infrequent as they are in many modern societies. Homicide rates in hunter-gatherer societies, which more closely resemble the conditions in which humans evolved, are far higher than those in modern nation-states with organized judicial systems (Ghiglieri, 1999; Marshall & Block, 2004).

The Nature of Selection Pressures for Homicide
Defense Adaptations

Homicide defense adaptations would have been selected for only one function: to avoid the massive fitness costs of being killed. This could have been accomplished by (1) avoiding contexts that present a high risk of homicide, (2) manipulating contexts that have a high probability of prompting homicidal behavior in a conspecific so they were less or no longer dangerous, (3) defending oneself against homicidal conspecifics, and (4) stanching the costs of homicide among the genetic relatives of the victim after it occurred. Because homicide has unique fitness consequences, we hypothesize that the fear of being killed is a distinct emotional state. We propose that it is accompanied by specific decision rules that function to help individuals defend against being killed by a conspecific. Specifically, we propose that selection fashioned homicide defense adaptations that lead to the avoidance of unfamiliar surroundings, particularly those controlled by rivals; traveling through locations where one could be ambushed; traveling at night; interacting with individuals who are more likely to kill; and inflicting costs likely to motivate a conspecific to kill.

Avoiding Contexts Where Homicide Is Likely

One of the design features of homicide avoidance mechanisms is sensitivity to cues of high-risk contexts. Cues to the presence of such contexts are hypothesized to include the following.

Who controls the territory one occupies. Who controls the territory an individual is occupying at a given moment is an important cue that is hypothesized to have been reliably correlated with the ancestral likelihood of being killed by hostile conspecifics. Individuals are more vulnerable to attack when away from their home territory. Being in a rival's territory or even a neutral territory would be a cue to an increased risk of attack. Chagnon (1996) reports that the Yanomamo sometimes lure members of a rival group to their territory under the auspices of having a celebratory feast. Away from their home territory, the rival group is at a strategic disadvantage. The Yanomamo attempt to lull their rivals into a false sense of security only to ambush them. We hypothesize that individuals will experience more fear of being killed in the presence of cues indicative of being in hostile territory.

Characteristics of the physical surroundings. We propose that characteristics of the physical surroundings are another source of ancestrally relevant cues to the likelihood of being killed. It is easier for a competitor to hide in the shadows than in the light. Individuals are more likely to be ambushed in areas where there are visual obstacles than in areas affording unobstructed scanning of the surroundings. An individual is more vulnerable to attack when his back is to an open room than against a wall. Individuals should experience more fear of homicide and more ideation that their life may be in danger in the presence of such cues to their vulnerability. Evidence supporting this hypothesis comes from investigations of the Savanna hypothesis. Kaplan (1992) argued that the process of evaluating landscape involves information-gathering about places for surveillance, places for hiding, refuges from predators, and possible routes of escape.

Characteristics of the rival. Certain personality and life history characteristics of rivals are hypothesized to have been recurrently correlated over our evolutionary history with the likelihood that a rival will kill: high levels of narcissism, an antisocial personality, high impulsivity, low conscientiousness, high levels of hostility, and a history of committing acts of violence or homicide against others. A history of violent behavior is one of the strongest predictors of future violence (Douglas & Webster, 1999). Ethnographic evidence indicates that some men develop reputations as killers or thugs. The people who live in the same communities as these men give them a wide berth, trying to avoid doing anything that might antagonize them (Chagnon, 1996; Ghiglieri, 1999). We hypothesize that a design feature of defenses against homicide is the ability to recognize and track dangerous conspecifics, attributing to them states of mind that would assist in predicting and avoiding their violent tendencies.

Features of the situation. Specific adaptations are hypothesized to have evolved that lead people to be sensitive to circumstances ancestrally indicative of an increased probability of being killed. Individuals who recognized and avoided such situations would have had a survival advantage over those who did not. Examples of these situations include the following:

1. injuring, raping, killing, or inflicting other serious costs on a rival, his kin, his mates, or his coalitional allies;
2. damaging a rival's reputation, leading others to perceive him or his genetic relatives as easily exploited, injured, raped, or killed;
3. poaching the resources, mates, territory, shelter, or food that belongs to a rival;
4. absorbing the resources of a nongenetic relative (e.g., stepchildren); and
5. interfering with parents' or kin's investment in vehicles who are less able to translate resource investment into genetic fitness (e.g., deformed infants, the chronically ill).

The experience of fear may be one adaptive mechanism that helps us to avoid circumstances in which others may be threats to our lives. In his book *The Gift of Fear* (1997), De Becker argues that fear, when applied appropriately, is a signal that exists to aid in our survival, protecting us from violent situations. It is adaptive to experience fear, he argues, when the fear is enabling—allowing people to effectively address the danger they face. Real fear, according to De Becker, "occurs in the presence of danger and will always easily link to pain or death" (p. 285).

Marks (1987) has argued that fear and anxiety can be protective in four primary ways. First, they can immobilize a person. This could help to conceal people from a predator, allow them time to assess the situation, and perhaps decrease their likelihood of being attacked. This is a valuable strategy when there is uncertainty about whether one has been spotted by a predator or cannot determine a predator's exact location. Second, fear can motivate people to escape or avoid danger in the environment.

This can help to move out of harm's way and find a location that provides protection from future interactions with the source of the danger. Third, fear may lead people to adopt a strategy of aggression in self-defense. A dangerous conspecific or predator can be frightened away or killed through the successful employment of an aggressive strategy. Finally, fear and anxiety can lead people to adopt a strategy of submission as a way to appease a source of the hostility, usually another person.

Sometimes people do not detect or are unable (or unwilling) to avoid contexts in which someone may try to kill them. We hypothesize that humans have evolved defensive strategies to protect themselves from impending and actively occurring homicidal attacks. Such strategies are hypothesized to take three primary forms:

1. **Fleeing the potentially homicidal confrontation with the person.** An individual who is successful in fleeing from someone who tried to kill him may then attempt to change the situation in ways that will decrease the likelihood of being killed. One such strategy may be to leave the area he shares with the intended killer. An explanation that has been proposed for human migration out of Africa, across Europe and Asia, and into the Americas is that migrating groups were attempting to avoid hostile confrontations with conspecifics (Diamond, 1997; Richerson & Boyd, 1998). Fleeing homicidal rivals can be an effective strategy if the intended victims can move out of the attackers' reach. But fleeing often represents only a temporary solution: if nothing about the context of conflict between the killer and intended victim changes, it is likely that a homicidal person will attempt to kill their intended victim again.

2. **Manipulating the situation to make killing less beneficial and more costly.** A person who believes he might be killed may be able to alter aspects of the situation to increase the costs or decrease the benefits of a homicidal strategy, making homicide less attractive to the killer than nonlethal alternatives. Examples include forging alliances with powerful conspecifics; staying in the vicinity of coalitional allies who may serve as bodyguards; turning members of a group against the person who may intend to kill you; resolving the conflict with the conspecific by offering some form of benefit; helping the rival to salvage or restore a reputation that the victim had a part in impugning; bargaining or begging for one's life; threatening retaliation by one's kin and coalitional allies; and performing preemptive, perhaps homicidal, attacks against the would-be killer, his kin, or his coalitional allies.

Many of these strategies may be implemented up to the moment of the victim's death. The implementation of these defensive strategies may not always be enough to derail a homicidal strategy in favor of a nonlethal alternative. If not, the person targeted by a killer would have no recourse but to defend against the attack.

3. **Defending against homicidal attacks.** At the point at which a rival is engaging in behaviors capable of killing, it may be too late to flee or derail the homicidal strategy. In such face-to-face confrontations with a killer, the options are to defend oneself or to die. There are two strategies of self-defense: call for help by an individual under violent attack or physically incapacitate the would-be killer so the intended victim can flee. Screams for help by an individual under violent attack may be

uniquely identifiable from other calls for assistance. Selection could have fashioned this kind of honest signal if fitness gains flowed to rescuers, such as kin or coalitional allies who might benefit from reciprocal exchange with the intended victim. "Death screams" (Buss, personal communication, 2004) may represent another category of alarm: they do not function as a call for help but instead warn kin and mates of the presence of a killer as the victim dies. References to "blood-curdling screams" and "screaming bloody murder" may refer to such uniquely identifiable screams made by people who are battling off an attacker's attempts to kill them.

Physically incapacitating a would-be killer is another strategy a victim can use in self-defense. Invariably, this strategy involves physically attacking the killer in some way. At a minimum, the victim of a homicidal strategy must incapacitate the attacker enough so that the victim can flee or buy enough time for help to arrive. In some confrontations, the most practical strategy of physically incapacitating the killer may be to kill the person in self-defense. Contexts leading victims to kill in self-defense are hypothesized to include features such as a lack of kin or allies in close enough proximity to help, the failure of nonlethal strategies to incapacitate the attacker, and a lack of other possible options.

One of the key differences between a would-be killer and a victim in confrontations is that the killer is more often prepared to carry out his homicidal strategy than the victim is to defend against being killed. The killer can select the time and place best suited to carrying out homicidal plans. Selection would have favored psychological adaptations that led killers to favor contexts in which they could catch victims alone and by surprise, reducing the possible costs of killing (e.g., being injured or killed by the victim or the victim's kin). As a result, it is hypothesized that the majority of face-to-face confrontations between a would-be killer and the intended victim result in the death of the victim. Because the genetic relatives of a homicide victim suffer fitness costs, we propose that adaptations to defend against being killed are also found in victims' kin.

4. **Stanching the costs of homicide by genetic relatives after it has occurred.** At least two forces may have selected for adaptations in kin that function to minimize the negative consequences of the killing of a family member by a conspecific. First, damage to a homicide victim's family reputation may be at least partially repaired by inflicting roughly equivalent costs on the killer. A family that is capable of striking back against the killer may be able to demonstrate that it is not or is no longer exploitable. Second, the killer may be a persistent threat if he continues to live. Avenging the death of a family member by killing the person's killer may eliminate a source of recurrent fitness costs.

All of the proposed adaptations for defending against homicide function by derailing or thwarting homicidal strategies or by inflicting heavy costs on killers. Homicide defense adaptations are costly for killers. The evolution of adaptations to defend against being killed is hypothesized to have created selection pressure for the evolution of refined adaptations for homicide that were capable of circumventing the evolved homicide defenses. The presence of refined homicide adaptations, in turn, would have selected for refined homicide defenses, and so on, setting up an antagonistic coevolutionary arms race between adaptations to kill and adaptations to defend against being killed.

Evidence of Adaptations for Homicide and Homicide Defenses

Evidence for anti-homicide defenses has been documented across the lifespan (Duntley, 2005). In this section, we focus on early lifespan evidence for these defenses.

Homicide has the potential to occur wherever there are humans interacting with other humans. This is as true of interactions between mother and child as it is of those between enemy nations. It is even true of the relationship between a pregnant mother and her developing fetus. For a woman, the fetus she carries probably does not represent her last opportunity to reproduce. Women were selected to invest more in those offspring who are likely to yield the greatest reproductive benefit, even in utero. If a fetus is not viable, for example, it would make more sense in terms of inclusive fitness for a pregnant woman to forgo her investment in its development in favor of investing in a subsequent pregnancy. Most fertilized eggs do not result in a full-term pregnancy. Up to 78% fail to implant or are spontaneously aborted (Nesse & Williams, 1994). Most often, these outcomes occur because the mother's body detects chromosomal abnormalities in the fetus. The body's ability to detect such abnormalities is the result of adaptations that function to prevent the mother from investing in offspring that will likely die young. Most miscarriages occur during the first twelve weeks of pregnancy (Haig, 1993), when the mother has not yet invested heavily in a costly pregnancy and when the spontaneously aborted fetus is less likely to lead to infection (Saraiya et al., 1999). The fetus, however, is not a passive pawn in its mother's evolved reproductive strategy. The fetus has only one chance to live. Selection would have favored fetal genes that resist a mother's attempt to abort the pregnancy. The production and release of human chorionic gonadotropin (hCG) by the fetus into the mother's bloodstream, which is normally an honest signal of fetal viability, has been hypothesized to be an adaptation fetuses have evolved to defend against being spontaneously aborted. This hormone prevents the mother from menstruating, allowing the fetus to remain implanted in its mother's uterus. Maternal physiology reacts to the production of hCG as a sign that the developing fetus is viable (Haig, 1993). Children continue to face threats to their lives after they are born. Infancy is a time in every person's life when he or she is particularly vulnerable to the homicidal strategies of others, especially when the attackers are those responsible for the infant's care.

There is conflict between parents and their offspring about the best allocation of parental resources. Offspring have evolved to desire more investment than is optimal for their parents to provide. Rather than investing the majority of resources in their offspring, parents' fitness benefits from also investing in other relationships, such as mateships and friendships, and investing in their own survival. The optimal amount of investment a parent can make in his or her offspring also varies as a function of the parent's likely reproductive success in the future, known as reproductive value. (Trivers, 1974). The reproductive value of children is lowest at birth and increases as they age, a function of the likelihood that they will survive to reproductive age.

A newborn infant has few options for defending itself from homicidal attacks perpetrated by adults. To defend against maternal infanticide, a newborn's best strategy may be to display cues that it is a vehicle worthy of investment. Immediately after birth, an infant should display cues to its health and vigor, cues capable of satisfying maternal adaptations that evolved to judge the probability of fitness payoffs for investing in the infant (Soltis, 2004). Newborns who nurse in the first hour after birth stimulate a surge in maternal oxytocin levels, strengthening the bond between mother and newborn. Nursing mothers' priorities become shifted. They become less motivated to self-groom for the purposes of attracting a mate and more motivated to groom their infants (Insel, 1992). By contrast, new mothers who do not nurse are more likely to suffer from postpartum depression (Papinczak & Turner, 2000; Taveras et al., 2003), a condition associated with higher rates of maternal infanticide (Hagen, 1999; Knopps, 1993; Spinelli, 2004) and maternal thoughts of harming their newborns (Jennings, Ross, Popper, & Elmore, 1999; Kendall-Tackett, 1994). More active newborns, as evaluated by APGAR scores, are less likely to die (Chong & Karlberg, 2004; Morales & Vazquez, 1994), and, in terms of fitness, would be wiser objects of maternal investment than newborns that are not active. Selection is hypothesized to have favored early nursing, the production of loud cries, and robust movements in newborns as defenses against maternal infanticide.

As they develop, infants are increasingly aware of their environment and able to move about on their own. As a result, they are increasingly likely to encounter dangers while outside the range of their parents' and other genetic relatives' protection. Infants who possess some ability to recognize potential dangers in the environment would have a significant advantage over infants with no such ability. Selection is proposed to have favored knowledge in advance, in the form of specific fears, to steer infants away from threats to their survival. The developmental timing of the emergence of fears provides evidence that selection played a part in shaping them. Many fears do not emerge in development until individuals first encounter adaptive problems. For example, a fear of heights, if it emerges, does so when children begin to crawl. The emergence of this fear corresponds with infants' greater risk of falling. Fear of strangers emerges at about the same time (Scarr & Salapatek, 1970), corresponding with a greater risk of encountering hostile, unrelated conspecifics. Stranger anxiety provides powerful protection against dangerous conspecifics. It prevents children from approaching individuals they do not know and motivates them to seek parental protection. Stranger anxiety has been documented in many different countries and cultures, from Guatemala and Zambia, to the !Kung and the Hopi Indians (Smith, 1979). Infant deaths at the hands of unrelated conspecifics have been documented in humans (Daly & Wilson, 1988; Hrdy, 2000) and among nonhuman primates (Ghiglieri, 1999; Hrdy, 1977, 2000; Wrangham & Peterson, 1996). Human children are more fearful of male strangers than female strangers, corresponding to the greater danger posed by unrelated males than unrelated females over human evolutionary history (Heerwagen & Orians, 2002). Even though the majority of strangers may not intend to inflict harm on children, if a fear of strangers prevented even a tiny fraction of children from being killed over our evolutionary history, stranger anxiety would have been favored by natural selection.

Strangers are not the only threat to the lives of children. Children raised with a stepparent in the home are between 40 and 100 times more likely to be killed by their stepparent or parent than children raised by two genetic parents (Daly & Wilson, 1988). Stepfamilies were likely a recurrent feature of ancestral environments. Without modern medical treatments, disease killed many ancestral adults. Fathers sometimes died in battles or on hunts. Mothers sometimes died during childbirth. After their partner's death, it was probably not uncommon for a surviving parent to find a new mate. Along with the benefits that come from a new long-term relationship is the potential for significant costs to existing children. Because the risk of being killed is so much greater for children with a stepparent in the home, one risk that may have affected single parents' mate choice was the risk their new mate posed to their existing children. There would have been selection pressure for the evolution of adaptations in single parents to prefer partners who presented little risk to their existing children. Single parents' evolved preferences for new partners are hypothesized to be, at least in part, evolved defenses against homicide of their existing children (Buss, 2005).

Stepchildren may also possess adaptations to help defend against potentially homicidal stepparents. These adaptations are hypothesized to have been shaped to recognize characteristics of potential stepparents that may be predictive of their likelihood of inflicting costs on the children, including killing them. Children's evolved intuitions about potential stepparents are proposed to lead them to influence their surviving parent's mate choice, providing some measure of defense against the possibility of being killed by a stepparent.

Selection also is hypothesized to have favored adaptations to guide the behavior of children living with a stepparent. Stepchildren should take steps to minimize their costliness to their stepparent, such as keeping a low profile and demanding few resources. Stepchildren should also recognize opportunities to make themselves valuable to their stepparent, such as contributing to the care of children that result from the relationship between their genetic parent and stepparent. The best strategy of stepchildren who feel their life is in danger, however, may be to sabotage the relationship between their genetic parent and stepparent. This may involve stepchildren inflicting costs on their stepparents in an attempt to get the stepparents to abandon the romantic relationship. It may also involve stepchildren inflicting costs on themselves to compel their genetic parent to curb investment away from a new mateship and toward their children. Engaging in delinquent and self-injurious behaviors may be strategies that stepchildren use to inflict costs on themselves. Living in a stepfamily, as compared to living with two genetic parents, more than doubles a child's risk of engaging in juvenile delinquent behavior (Coughlin & Vuchinich, 1996).

The presence of a stepparent is a good example of a recurrent context of increased risk of homicide that may have selected for anti-homicide defenses in stepchildren and their kin. These adaptations are hypothesized to become activated in stepchildren but remain dormant in children who reside with both of their genetic parents. We propose that specialized adaptations to defend against homicide exist for all contextual domains where there was a recurrent risk of being killed. Many situations, however, do not provide complete information about the probability that a person may fall victim to homicide. Because being killed is so costly, it is likely that selection fashioned adaptively patterned biases that lead people to systematically overestimate the likelihood that they will be killed in conditions of uncertainty.

Managing Errors to Avoid Being Killed

Goleman (1995) argued that most of what people worry about has a low probability of happening, suggesting that people are wasting their time by ruminating on such issues. However, a cognitive system that "irrationally" overestimated the likelihood of violence, increasing the probability of avoiding attackers, would be favored by selection over an unbiased, "rational" cognitive system that led an individual to be more likely to incur the heavy costs of being victimized. Because many inferences about whether one will be targeted by a killer are clouded by uncertainty, contexts of homicide can be considered compatible with the logic of error management theory (Haselton, 2003; Haselton & Buss, 2000). In situations involving uncertainty, making an erroneous inference about the intentions of others can carry high fitness costs. There are two types of errors one can make when inferring the intentions of others: inferring an intention that is not present or inferring the absence of an intention that is present. In the case of avoiding homicide, selection pressure would have shaped cognitive biases that lead people to overinfer homicidal intent in others. It would be better, on average, to infer that someone might want to kill you when he really does not rather than to infer that someone does not want to kill you when he actually does. In this way, people would avoid making the more costly of the two errors. In sum, a design feature of the psychology of evolved homicide defenses is a cognitive bias that leads people to systematically overinfer homicidal intent in others who occupy adaptive problem contexts historically solvable by homicide.

The *amount* of uncertainty surrounding a potentially high-cost situation is also likely to have an effect. Imagine a man walking home from a bar late on a rainy night. He decides to take a shortcut through a dark alley to shorten the distance he must walk in the rain. As he is walking, he notices another man in the alley and immediately identifies the man as his brother. Assuming the two had a good relationship, there would be little reason for the man to infer that his brother might want to kill him. Indeed, no fears of being killed should be triggered in this situation. Now imagine that the same man takes a shortcut through an alley and sees another man whom he does not know. Greater uncertainty about the intentions of the unknown man, in addition to the other features of the context, may lead to an overinference of the likelihood that this man might intend to harm or kill. In conditions of uncertainty about the identity of another person, in vague situations, and in the absence of information to the contrary, the safer error would be to overinfer a conspecific's hostile intentions. In fact, the safest error would be to assume that the other person intended to kill you. Selection is hypothesized to have shaped adaptations to defend against the most costly possibility first. When the chaos of environmental cues creates uncertainty, selection should mold psychological design to assume that the worst possible fitness event is going to occur, facilitating the avoidance of fitness costs. The strategies that people employ to defend against homicide (e.g., avoiding contexts solvable by killing, fleeing from attackers, or killing one's attacker) would also be effective in defending against a number of nonlethal, cost-inflicting strategies, such as assault, robbery, and rape, possibly providing additional selection pressure for the evolution of victim defenses against the cost-inflicting strategies of others.

In sum, we propose that adaptations to minimize costly errors evolved in the form of cognitive biases that overestimate the likelihood that another individual intends to inflict costs proportional to the uncertainty surrounding the individual's intentions and the context. The bias toward inferring that another individual plans to inflict costs should increase as uncertainty about the individual's intentions and the context increases. This is not to say that such an error management bias will be applied equally to all, different individuals. The bias should be proportional to the ancestral threat that different individuals posed. It should be especially strong for those who posed the greatest threat, such as members of out-groups and young adult males, and less strong or absent for others (e.g., infants, young children, the elderly).

There is evidence that people's perceptions are biased in the direction predicted by error management theory (Haselton & Buss, 2000). Experiments using schematic facial stimuli demonstrate that different facial expressions are not processed the same way (Öhman, Lundqvist, & Esteves, 2001). Participants in this research viewed stimuli of threatening and friendly faces that were constructed from identical physical features. The threatening face was identified more quickly than the happy face from among neutral distracters. Additionally, faces with V-shaped eyebrows of a schematic angry facial display were more quickly and accurately identified than were faces with inverted V-shaped eyebrows (friendly faces) among both neutral and emotional distracters. These results are consistent with a perceptual bias as predicted by error management theory that leads individuals to be especially sensitive to the presence of potentially hostile conspecifics. Natural selection would have favored a greater sensitivity to angry faces over friendly faces, as those with hostile intentions would have posed an adaptive problem often requiring immediate action to avoid incurring the potentially heavy costs resulting from being a victim of exploitation or murder.

Despite the proposed evolved defenses against being killed discussed previously, many people still willingly enter into situations that could get them killed. People have extramarital affairs. People derogate others to ascend status hierarchies. People poach the material and mating resources of others. Why would people risk engaging in such high risk strategies?

Secrecy

The answer may lie in the use of secrecy as a defense against being killed. People become homicidal only if they are aware that someone else is inflicting heavy costs on them or great benefits will flow to them as a result of the kill. Ignorance can provide them bliss and provide those who sneak behind their backs some measure of protection from being killed. A sexual relationship carried on behind the back of one's partner, for example, has the potential to confer fitness benefits to men in the form of more offspring. It can confer benefits to women as well, such as access to superior or different genes and access to additional resources from an affair partner (Greiling & Buss, 2000). Selection is hypothesized to have favored the use of secrecy to defend against the costs of discovered infidelity, which includes being killed by a jealous partner. This logic also applies to other behaviors that benefit one individual at a cost to another. In the case of sexual infidelity, there is a clear pattern in the risks of being killed. Men are more likely than women to kill their partner for a sexual infidelity. As a result, selection pressures are proposed to have been stronger on women to adopt clandestine tactics to conduct their affairs than it was on men. Women may have evolved to be more motivated to hide, and better at hiding, their infidelities from their partners than men. This may help to explain why men indicate a greater amount of uncertainty about whether their romantic partner is having an affair than women do (Buss, 2000): men encounter fewer cues to their partner's infidelity. Clandestine strategies, however, are not always successful. Sometimes men discover their partner's infidelity. As homicide statistics demonstrate (Buss, 2005; Daly & Wilson, 1988; Ghiglieri, 1999), perhaps the most dangerous human a woman will encounter in her lifetime is her romantic partner.

Killing in Self-defense: Preemptive Homicide to Prevent Being Killed

In a review of 223 appellate opinions of the homicide cases of battered women in Pennsylvania, 75% of the homicides occurred while the woman was being assaulted by her romantic partner (Maguigan, 1991). In a study of mate homicides in North Carolina between 1991 and 1993, violence perpetrated by men preceded 75% of cases in which women killed their romantic partners. In contrast, there is no evidence that violence perpetrated by women preceded any of the homicides committed by men (Smith, Moracco, & Butts, 1998). It can be argued that the majority of women who kill their romantic partners do so in self-defense. The example provided by these female-perpetrated mate homicides is illustrative of the ultimate anti-homicide defense: killing an attacker before the attacker kills you.

We propose that the costs of being murdered were substantial enough to select for adaptations designed to eliminate the threat of homicidal conspecifics by killing them. Selection for homicide defenses was unlike selection for the psychology of homicide. Whereas adaptations for homicide are argued to have been selected to favor killing only when available nonlethal alternatives delivering equivalent benefits were exhausted, selection likely favored psychological design to prefer homicide as a strategy of self-defense in some face-to-face confrontations with a would-be killer. Killing someone to prevent him or her from killing you would have had distinct evolutionary advantages over strategies of nonlethal violence. By killing a homicidal conspecific, you eliminate any future threat the person may pose. Whereas an injured rival can recuperate and attempt to kill you again, a dead rival cannot. By killing your would-be killer, you also demonstrate a willingness and ability to kill, sending a powerful signal to others that attempts on your life will be met with the ultimate cost.

Most legal systems do not treat homicides committed in self-defense the same as other homicides. The law considers killing in self-defense to be a form of justifiable homicide if the person who kills "reasonably believes that killing is a necessary response to a physical attack that is likely to cause serious injury or death" (Costanzo, 2004, p. 83). In the evolutionary history of adaptations to produce preemptive homicides, however, the management of errors in conditions of uncertainty would have played a pivotal role in determining what a person reasonably believes. Individuals in the past who erred on the side of preemptively killing those whom they perceived to be a credible threat to their life or the lives of their genetic kin would have had an advantage over individuals who erred in the opposite direction. The likely consequence is the overestimation of the threat that some conspecifics pose and the preemptive killing of some people who were not pursuing a strategy of lethal aggression. In the calculus of natural selection, however, it is better to be in error and alive than risk being killed.

Conclusion

The evolution of adaptations to inflict costs created selection pressures for the coevolution of victim adaptations to avoid or prevent incurring the costs. These coevolved victim adaptations in turn created selection pressure for the evolution of refined adaptations and new adaptations for cost-infliction, setting up antagonistic, coevolutionary arms races between strategies to inflict costs and victim strategies to defend against them. Coevolutionary arms races can be extremely powerful. They can exert selection pressure on numerous physiological and psychological systems simultaneously, leading to rapid evolutionary change and great complexity of adaptive design. Adaptations for homicide and adaptations to defend against being killed are hypothesized to be the results of such an antagonistic coevolutionary arms race. The costs to genetic fitness of being killed are among the greatest an individual can endure at the hands of a conspecific. These tremendous costs are proposed to have created unique and powerful selection pressures for the evolution of victim adaptations to defend against being killed. The available evidence is consistent with the theory that coevolved adaptations for homicide and victim defenses against homicide guide human behavior when we face contexts ancestrally solvable through the use of lethal aggression. We are likely the only species that possess psychological adaptations that function specifically to kill humans.

ACKNOWLEDGMENT

Portions of this chapter are based, in part, on the following works: Duntley, J. D. (2005). Adaptations to dangers from humans. In D. Buss (Ed.), *The handbook of evolutionary psychology* (pp. 224–249). New York: Wiley; and Duntley, J. D., & Shackelford, T. K. (2008). Adaptations to avoid victimization. Manuscript under editorial review.

References

Betzig, L. L. (1993). Sex, succession, and stratification in the first six civilizations. In L. Ellis (Ed.), *Social stratification and socioeconomic inequality* (pp. 37–74). Westport, CT: Praeger.

Block, A. P. (1990). Rape trauma syndrome as scientific expert testimony. *Archives of Sexual Behavior, 19*, 309–323.

Bracha, H. S. (2004). Freeze, flight, fight, fright, faint: Adaptationist perspectives on the acute stress response spectrum. *CNS Spectrums, 9*, 679–685.

Bugnyar, T., & Kotrschal, K. (2004). Leading a conspecific away from food in ravens (*Corvus corax*)? *Animal Cognition, 7*, 69–76.

Burgess, A. W., & Holmstrom, L. L. (1974). Rape Trauma Syndrome. *American Journal of Psychiatry, 131*, 981–986.

Buss, D. M. (1996). Sexual conflict: Evolutionary insights into feminism and the "battle of the sexes." In D. M. Buss & N. M. Malamuth (Eds.), *Sex, power, conflict* (pp. 296–318). New York: Oxford University Press.

Buss, D. M. (2000). *The dangerous passion*. New York: Free Press.

Buss, D. M. (2003a). *The evolution of desire* (rev. ed.). New York: Free Press.

Buss, D. M. (2003b, June). *Sexual conflict*. Paper presented at the Annual Meeting of the Human Behavior and Evolution Society, University of Nebraska.

Buss, D. M. (2005). *The murderer next door*. New York: Penguin.

Buss, D. M. (2007). *Evolutionary psychology* (3rd ed.). New York: Allyn & Bacon.

Buss, D. M., Abbott, M., Angleitner, A., Asherian, A., Biaggio, A., Blanco-Villasenor, A., et al. (1990). International preferences in selecting mates: A study of 37 cultures. *Journal of Cross-Cultural Psychology, 21*, 5–47.

Buss, D. M., & Dedden, L. A. (1990). Derogation of competitors. *Journal of Social and Personal Relationships, 7*, 395–422.

Buss, D. M., & Duntley, J. D. (1998, July). *Evolved homicide modules*. Paper presented at the Annual Meeting of the Human Behavior and Evolution Society, Davis, CA.

Buss, D. M., & Duntley, J. D. (1999, June). *Killer psychology: The evolution of intrasexual homicide*. Paper presented at the Annual Meeting of the Human Behavior and Evolution Society, Salt Lake City, UT.

Buss, D. M., & Duntley, J. D. (2003). Homicide: An evolutionary perspective and implications for public policy. In N. Dess (Ed.), *Violence and public policy* (pp. 115–128). Westport, CT: Greenwood.

Buss, D. M., & Duntley, J. D. (2008). Adaptations for exploitation. *Group Dynamics: Theory, Research, and Practice.*

Buss, D. M., & Duntley, J. D. (2006). The evolution of aggression. In M. Schaller, J. A. Simpson, & D. T. Kenrick (Eds.), *Evolution and Social Psychology* (pp. 263–286). New York: Psychology Press.

Buss, D. M., & Duntley, J. D. (under review). *Homicide Adaptation Theory.*

Buss, D. M., Larsen, R. R., & Westen, D. (1996). Sex differences in jealousy: Not gone, not forgotten, and not explained by alternative hypotheses. *Psychological Science, 7,* 373–375.

Buss, D. M., Larsen, R. R., Westen, D., & Semmelroth, J. (1992). Sex differences in jealousy: Evolution, physiology, and psychology. *Psychological Science, 3,* 251–255.

Buss, D. M., & Shackelford, T. K. (1997a). From vigilance to violence: Mate retention tactics in married couples. *Journal of Personality and Social Psychology, 72,* 346–361.

Buss, D. M., & Shackelford, T. K. (1997b). Human aggression in evolutionary psychological perspective. *Clinical Psychology Review, 17,* 605–619.

Campbell, A. (1993). *Men, women, and aggression.* New York: Basic Books.

Chagnon, N. (1996). *Yanomamo* (5th ed.). New York: Holt, Rinehart, & Winston.

Chagnon, N. (1988). Life histories, blood revenge, and warfare in a tribal population. *Science, 239,* 985–992.

Chavanne, T. J., & Gallup, G. G. Jr. (1998). Variation in risk taking behavior among female college students as a function of the menstrual cycle. *Evolution and Human Behavior, 19,* 27–32.

Chong, D. S., & Karlberg, J. (2004). Refining the Apgar score cut-off point for newborns at risk. *Acta Paediatrica, 93,* 53–59.

Cohen, L. E., & Machalek, R. (1988). A general theory of expropriative crime: An evolutionary ecological approach. *American Journal of Sociology, 94,* 465–501.

Costanzo, M. (2004). *Psychology applied to law.* New York: Thomson Wadsworth.

Coughlin, C., & Vuchinich, S. (1996). Family experience in preadolescence and the development of male delinquency. *Journal of Marriage and the Family, 58,* 491–501.

Daly, M., & Wilson, M. (1988). *Homicide.* Hawthorne, NY: Aldine.

Daly, M., & Wilson, M. (1990). Killing the competition. *Human Nature, 1,* 83–109.

De Becker, G. (1997). *The gift of fear.* New York: Little, Brown.

Diamond, J. (1997). *Guns, germs, and steel.* New York: W. W. Norton.

Douglas, K. S., & Webster, C. D. (1999). Predicting violence in mentally and personality disordered individuals. In R. Roesch, S. D. Hart, & J. R. P. Oglof (Eds.), *Psychology and law: The state of the discipline* (pp. 175–239). New York: Kluwer/Plenum.

Duntley, J. D. (2005). Adaptations to dangers from other humans. In D. Buss (Ed.), *The handbook of evolutionary psychology* (pp. 224–249). New York: Wiley.

Duntley, J. D., & Buss, D. M. (1998, July). *Evolved anti-homicide modules.* Paper presented at the Annual Meeting of the Human Behavior and Evolution Society, Davis, CA.

Duntley, J. D., & Buss, D. M. (1999, June). *Killer psychology: The evolution of mate homicide.* Paper presented at the Annual Meeting of the Human Behavior and Evolution Society, Salt Lake City, UT.

Duntley, J. D., & Buss, D. M. (2000, June). *The killers among us: A co-evolutionary theory of homicide.* Invited paper presented at a special symposium organized by the Society for Evolution and the Law at the Annual Meeting of the Human Behavior and Evolution Society, Amherst, MA.

Duntley, J. D., & Buss, D. M. (2001, June). *Anti-homicide design: Adaptations to prevent homicide victimization.* Paper presented at the Annual Meeting of the Human Behavior and Evolution Society, London.

Duntley, J. D., & Buss, D. M. (2002, July). *Homicide by design: On the plausibility of psychological adaptations for homicide.* Invited presentation for the First Annual AHRB Conference on Innateness and the Structure of the Mind, University of Sheffield, England.

Fujita, K., Kuroshima, H., & Masuda, T. (2002). Do tufted capuchin monkeys (*Cebus apella*) spontaneously deceive opponents? A preliminary analysis of an experimental food-competition contest between monkeys. *Animal Cognition, 5,* 19–25.

Geist, R. F. (1988). Sexually related trauma. *Emergency Medicine Clinics of North America, 6,* 439–466.

Ghiglieri, M. P. (1999). *The dark side of man.* Reading, MA: Perseus Books.

Goleman, D. (1995). *Emotional intelligence.* New York: Bantam.

Grammer, K. (1992). Variations on a theme: Age dependent mate selection in humans. *Behavioral and Brain Sciences, 15,* 100–102.

Greiling, H., & Buss, D. M. (2000). Women's sexual strategies: The hidden dimension of extra pair mating. *Personality and Individual Differences, 28,* 929–963.

Hagen, E. H. (1999). The functions of postpartum depression. *Evolution and Human Behavior, 20,* 325–359.

Haig, D. (1993). Genetic conflicts in human pregnancy. *Quarterly Review of Biology, 4,* 495–532.

Hamilton, W. D. (1963). The evolution of altruistic behavior. *American Naturalist, 97,* 354–356.

Hassell, M. P. (1975). Density-dependence in single-species populations. *Journal of Animal Ecology, 44,* 283–295.

Haselton, M. G. (2003). The sexual overperception bias: Evidence of systematic bias in men from a survey of naturally occurring events. *Journal of Research on Personality, 37,* 34–47.

Haselton, M. G., & Buss, D. M. (2000). Error Management Theory: A new perspective on biases in cross-sex mind reading. *Journal of Personality and Social Psychology, 78,* 81–91.

Heerwagen, J. H., & Orians, G. H. (2002). The ecological world of children. In P. H. Kahn Jr. & S. R. Kellert (Eds.), *Children and nature* (pp. 29–64). Cambridge, MA: MIT Press.

Held, S., Mendl, M., Devereux, C., & Byrne, R. W. (2002). Foraging pigs alter their behavior in response to exploitation. *Animal Behavior, 64,* 157–166.

Hill, K., & Hurtado, A. M. (1996). *Ache life history.* New York: Aldine De Gruyter.

Hrdy, S. B. (1977). Infanticide as a primate reproductive strategy. *American Scientist, 65,* 40–49.

Hrdy, S. B. (2000). *Mother nature.* London: Vintage.

Insel, T. R. (1992). Oxytocin—A neuropeptide for affiliation: Evidence from behavioral, receptor autoradiographic, and comparative studies. *Psychoneuroendocrinology, 17,* 3–35.

Jennings, K. D., Ross, S., Popper, S., & Elmore, M. (1999). Thoughts of harming infants in depressed and nondepressed mothers. *Journal of Affective Disorders, 54,* 21–28.

Jones, O. (1997). Law and biology: Toward an integrated model of human behavior. *Journal of Contemporary Legal Issues, 8,* 167–208.

Kaplan, S. (1992) Environmental preference in a knowledge-seeking, knowledge-using organism. In J. H. Barkow, L. Cosmides, and J. Tooby (Eds.), *The adaptive mind* (pp. 535–552). New York: Oxford University Press.

Kendall-Tackett, K. A. (1994). Postpartum depression. *Illness, Crisis, and Loss, 4,* 80–86.

Knopps, G. (1993). Postpartum mood disorders: A startling contrast to the joy of birth. *Postgraduate Medicine, 103,* 103–116.

Maccoby, E. E. (1990). Gender and relationships: A developmental account. *American Psychologist, 45,* 513–520.

Maguigan, H. (1991). Myths and misconceptions in current reform proposals. *University of Pennsylvania Law Review, 140,* 379–486.

Marks, I. M. (1987). *Fears, phobias, and rituals.* New York: Oxford University Press.

Marshall, I. H., & Block, C. R. (2004). Maximizing the availability of cross-national data on homicide. *Homicide Studies, 8,* 267–310.

Morales, V. Z., & Vazquez, C. (1994). Apgar score and infant mortality in Puerto Rico. *Puerto Rico Health Science Journal, 13,* 175–181.

Nesse, R. M., & Williams, G. C. (1994). *Why we get sick.* New York: Times Books/Random House.

Öhman, A., Lundqvist, D., & Esteves, F. (2001). The face in the crowd revisited: A threat advantage with schematic stimuli. *Journal of Personality and Social Psychology, 80,* 381–396.

Papinczak, T. A., & Turner, C. T. (2000). An analysis of personal and social factors influencing initiation and duration of breastfeeding in a large Queensland maternity hospital. *Breastfeeding Review, 8,* 25–33.

Parker, G. A., Royle, M. J., & Hartley, I. R. (2002). Intrafamilial conflict and parental investment: A synthesis. *Philosophical Transactions of the Royal Society of London B, 357,* 295–307.

Perusse, D. (1993). Cultural and reproductive success in industrial societies: Testing the relationship at proximate and ultimate levels. *Behavioral and Brain Sciences, 16,* 267–322.

Phillips, B., Brown, G. P., & Shine, R. (2004). Assessing the potential for an evolutionary response to rapid environmental change: Invasive toads and an Australian snake. *Evolutionary Ecology Research, 6,* 799–811.

Pratto, F. (1996). Sexual politics: The gender gap in the bedroom, the cupboard, and the cabinet. In D. M. Buss & N. M. Malamuth (Eds.), *Sex, power, conflict* (pp. 179–230). New York: Oxford University Press.

Richerson, P. J., & Boyd, R. (1998). The evolution of human ultra-sociality. In I. Eibl-Eibesfeldt & F. K. Salter (Eds.), *Indoctrinability, warfare, and ideology* (pp. 71–95). New York: Berghahn Books.

Saraiya, M., Green, C. A., Berg, C. J., Hopkins, F. W., Koonin, L. M., & Atrash, H. K. (1999). Spontaneous abortion-related deaths among women in the United States—1981–1991. *Obstetrics & Gynecology, 94,* 172–176.

Scarr, S., & Salapatek, P. (1970). Patterns of fear development during infancy. *Merrill Palmer Quarterly, 16,* 53–90.

Schmitt, D. P., & Buss, D. M. (2001). Human mate poaching: Tactics and temptations for infiltrating existing mateships. *Journal of Personality and Social Psychology, 80,* 894–917.

Schmitt, D. P., Shackelford, T. K., Duntley, J. D., Tooke, W., & Buss, D. M. (2001). The desire for sexual variety as a tool for understanding basic human mating strategies. *Personal Relationships, 8,* 425–455.

Singer, T., Seymour, B., O'Dojerty, J., Stephan, K. E., Dolan, R, J., & Frith, C. D. (2006). Empathic neural responses are modulated by the perceived fairness of others. *Nature, 439,* 466–469.

Smith, P. H., Moracco, K. E., & Butts, J. D. (1998). Partner homicide in context: A population-based perspective. *Homicide Studies, 2,* 400–421.

Smith, P. K. (1979). The ontogeny of fear in children. In W. Sluckin (Ed.), *Fear in animals and man* (pp. 164–168). London: Van Nostrand.

Smuts, B. B. (1992). Men's aggression against women. *Human Nature, 6,* 1–32.

Soltis, J. (2004). The signal functions of early infant crying. *Behavioral and Brain Sciences, 27,* 443–490.

Spinelli, M. G. (2004). Maternal infanticide associated with mental illness: Prevention and the promise of saved lives. *American Journal of Psychiatry, 161,* 1548–1557.

Sugiyama, L. S., Tooby, J., & Cosmides, L. (2002). Cross-cultural evidence of cognitive adaptations for social exchange among the Shiwiar of Ecuadorian Amazonia. *Proceedings of the National Academy of Sciences of the United States of America, 99,* 11537–11542.

Symons, D. (1979). *The evolution of human sexuality.* New York: Oxford University Press.

Taveras, E. M., Capra, A. M., Braveman, P. A., Jensvold, N. G., Escobar, G. J., & Lieu, T. A. (2003). Clinician support and psychosocial risk factors associated with breastfeeding discontinuation. *Pediatrics, 112,* 108–115.

Taylor, P. A., & Glenn, N. D. (1976). The utility of education and attractiveness for females' status attainment through marriage. *American Sociological Review, 41,* 484–498.

Thornhill, R., & Palmer, C. (2000). *A natural history of rape.* Cambridge, MA: MIT Press.

Tooby, J., & DeVore, I. (1987). The reconstruction of hominid behavioral evolution through strategic modeling. In W. G. Kinzey (Ed.), *The evolution of human behavior* (pp. 183–237). New York: State University of New York Press.

Trinkaus, E., & Shipman, P. (1993). *The Neandertals: Changing the image of mankind.* New York: Alfred A. Knopf.

Trivers, R. L. (1972). Parental investment and sexual selection. In B. Campbell (Ed.), *Sexual selection and the descent of man: 1871–1971* (pp. 136–179). Chicago: Aldine.

Trivers, R. L. (1974). Parent–offspring conflict. *American Zoologist, 14,* 249–264.

Udry, R. R., & Eckland, B. K. (1984). Benefits of being attractive: Differential payoffs for men and women. *Psychological Reports, 54,* 47–56.

Werner-Wilson, R. J. (1998). Gender differences in adolescent sexual attitudes: The influence of individual and family factors. *Adolescence, 33,* 519–531.

Whiting, B., & Edwards, C. P. (1988). *Children of different worlds.* Cambridge, MA: Harvard University Press.

Wilson M. I., Daly, M., & Daniele, A. (1995) Familicide: The killing of spouse and children. *Aggressive Behavior, 2,* 275–291.

Wilson, M., & Mesnick, S. L. (1997). An empirical test of the bodyguard hypothesis. In P. A. Gowaty (Ed.), *Feminism and evolutionary biology: Hormones, brain, and behavior* (pp. 505–511). New York: Chapman & Hall.

Wrangham, R. W., & Peterson, D. (1996). *Demonic males.* Boston: Houghton Mifflin.

12

The Evolution of a Sense of Justice

DENNIS L. KREBS

Everyone possesses a sense of justice, however misguided it may be. How do people acquire this sense? Where does it come from? In this chapter, I argue that to account for the acquisition of a sense of justice, we must identify the mental mechanisms that produce it and explain how they originated and became refined in the course of human evolution. Explaining how a sense of justice originated in the human species helps us understand what it is, what it is for, how it is designed, what activates it, and why it sometimes fails to give rise to fair judgments and behaviors.

A Working Definition of a "Sense of Justice"

A sense of justice consists of thoughts and feelings about what is fair and unfair and what people deserve from and owe others (rights and duties). When we think of justice, we think of balanced scales. In *Nicomachean Ethics*, Aristotle distinguished three forms of justice. The first pertains to how resources should be distributed (*distributive justice*)—for example, in terms of principles of equality, equity, desert, and merit. The second pertains to agreements between people—promises, commitments, and other kinds of social contracts (*commutative justice*). The final type pertains to the righting of wrongs (*corrective justice*). It includes ideas such as forgiveness and a bunch of "r" words—revenge, reparation, restitution, and retribution ("getting even"). Overriding all of these forms of justice is *procedural justice*. To make fair decisions, people must use fair and impartial procedures such as the Golden Rule, balanced discussion, or democratic decision making.

Psychological Accounts of the Origin of a Sense of Justice

If you ask people how they acquired their sense of justice, most people, from the Western world at least, would advance a social learning account. They would say that they acquired a sense of justice from their parents and other mentors, who taught them to behave fairly, to share, to take turns, to keep their promises, and so on. Although it would be foolish to deny that social learning plays a role in the acquisition of a sense of justice, more is involved. If children internalized their parents' ideas about fairness, then children would possess the same ideas their parents do, but they do not. Children argue with their parents. They have minds of their own. They are able to think for themselves. And the ways in which they think about fairness changes as they develop. Cognitive-developmental theorists such as Kohlberg (1984) and Piaget (1932) have argued that children derive their conceptions of justice from structures of moral reasoning.

Like social learning, reasoning plays a role in determining people's sense of justice. However, like social learning, it does not account for all aspects of this sense. As demonstrated by Haidt (2001), people sometimes simply feel that a behavior is fair or unfair, right or wrong, without thinking about it or engaging in moral reasoning. If someone cheats you or breaks a promise to you, you may experience an immediate sense of righteous indignation without engaging in rational deliberation.

The goal of virtually all psychological research on a sense of justice is to decipher the design of the proximate mechanisms that produce it. Theoretical differences arise with respect to the types of mechanisms responsible for producing it (e.g., social learning versus reasoning versus affective mechanisms), the ways in which they are designed (e.g., whether people possess one overriding structure of moral reasoning or a bunch of different, domain-specific structures designed to deal with different aspects of justice), and the ways in which they interact (e.g., whether reason structures affective reactions, or whether affective reactions structure reason). Although adherents of different psychological approaches each tend to assume that their approach offers a full account of the acquisition of a sense of justice, it is clear that each approach accounts for only part of the process. A sense of justice stems from a system of mechanisms. Sometimes people derive conceptions of justice from one mechanism, sometimes from another. Sometimes more than one mechanism is activated, and when this occurs, the activated mechanisms may work in concert to support the same decision, or they may engender internal conflict. What is needed is an overarching framework that accounts for the origin of this system and integrates its components in meaningful ways. The thesis of this chapter is that evolutionary theory fills this bill.

An Overview

The mechanisms that produce a sense of justice did not emerge in the human species one sunny morning in full-blown glory. They emerged slowly over eons, through the modification of more primitive mechanisms. Although this was a continuous process, it is helpful heuristically to break it down into overlapping phases. I will suggest that the first phase in the evolution of a sense of justice involved the evolution of cooperative behavioral dispositions and the affective reactions that support them. Precursors of this sense can be seen in chimpanzees and other primates. In the second phase, this primitive sense became refined and elaborated in the context of strategic interactions among members of groups motivated to induce one another to behave in cooperative ways. The acquisition of the capacity for symbolic language, perspective-taking, and sophisticated forms of intelligence played important roles in this process, which gave rise to moral judgments and moral norms. In the final phase, humans acquired the capacity to imagine ideal social systems; to reflect on moral issues; to figure out how, in principle, to solve complex moral problems; and to develop ideal conceptions of justice.

The Evolution of Cooperation

From an evolutionary perspective, the key to understanding the origin of a sense of justice lies in identifying the adaptive functions it evolved to serve. I will argue that the overarching function of a sense of justice is to induce members of groups to uphold fitness-enhancing forms of cooperation. To understand the emergence of the mechanisms that produce a sense of justice, we must first understand the emergence of the mechanisms that induce animals to cooperate.

There is tremendous adaptive potential in cooperation. In conducive contexts, two or more animals that work together and exchange goods and services can enhance their fitness much more effectively than they could by going it on their own. This does not, however, guarantee the evolution of cooperative dispositions. All kinds of traits and behaviors could enhance animals' fitness better than those they already possess. For cooperative dispositions to evolve, individuals must inherit genes that guide the creation of mechanisms that dispose them to behave in cooperative ways, and these mechanisms must pay off better genetically than competing mechanisms such as those that dispose them to behave in selfish ways.

The Fundamental Social Dilemma

Assume that, originally, animals were disposed to help only themselves. It is relatively easy to account for the evolution of mutualistic behaviors such as group hunting and group defense, because the animals that engage in such behaviors could be coordinating their efforts to maximize their own biological gains, helping others only incidentally. In contrast, it is considerably more difficult to account for the selection of mechanisms that dispose animals to engage in equitable exchanges. As expressed by the philosopher Rawls (1999) in the opening pages of *A Theory of Justice*,

> Although a society is a cooperative venture for mutual advantage, it is typically marked
> by a conflict as well as by an identity of interests. There is an identity of interests since

social cooperation makes possible a better life for all than any would have if each were to live solely by his own efforts. There is a conflict of interests since persons are not indifferent as to how the greater benefits produced by their collaboration are distributed, for in order to pursue their ends they each prefer a larger to a lesser share. (Rawls, 1999, p. 4)

Modeled in evolutionary terms, assume that members of a group inherit genes that dispose them to adopt one of two strategies—either to behave fairly (i.e., to cooperate) or to behave selfishly (i.e., to cheat). If all members of a group inherited genes that disposed them to cooperate, everyone could obtain more for himself or herself though gains in trade than he or she could by failing to cooperate, and the group could prevail in competitions against less cooperative groups. Cooperation could produce a utopia for all. The problem is, if other members of one's group behave cooperatively, each individual can come out ahead by doing less than his or her share and taking more. If those who are disposed to behave selfishly contribute more replicas of their genes to future generations than those who are disposed to behave fairly, selfish dispositions will be selected and evolve. Ironically, however, as the number of selfish members of a group increases, there are fewer and fewer cooperative individuals to exploit, jeopardizing the system of cooperation and forcing selfish individuals to interact with one another, to their mutual detriment.

Theoretical Resolutions of the Fundamental Social Dilemma:
The Selection of Cooperative Strategies

Game theorists have created computerized simulations of evolution in which they have pitted cooperative strategies against selfish strategies. These theorists have found that certain conditionally cooperative strategies, such as various forms of tit-for-tat (that is to say, strategies based on the decision rule, "make an initial cooperative overture, then copy the response of your partner,") and variations such as tit-for-two-tats, are equipped to defeat unconditionally selfish strategies and evolve in favorable conditions. The cooperative strategies gain their power either by reducing the costs and increasing the benefits of behaving fairly or by increasing the costs and reducing the benefits of behaving unfairly. The genetic costs of contributing one's share can be reduced by engaging in cooperative exchanges with those who share one's genes, by selectively engaging in exchanges with other cooperators, and by reaping indirect benefits from acquiring a reputation as a cooperator. The net genetic costs of failing to contribute one's share can be increased by diminishing the probability that recipients or others will interact with those who behave selfishly and by increasing the probability that selfish individuals will be punished—either by their interaction partners or by other members of their group. Accounting for the evolution of dispositions to punish third parties is tricky, because if we assume that it is costly to inflict punishments, those who refused to accept responsibility for administering punishments would fare better than those who accepted responsibility.

Reciprocity in Nonhuman Animals

The most appropriate place to look for precursors of the forms of cooperation practiced by humans is in other primates. Studies by de Waal and others (see Kappeler & Schaik, 2006, for a review) have established that chimpanzees engage in calculated forms of delayed reciprocity in which they remember who has helped them, track credits and debts to particular partners, and repay them either in kind or in some other currency. For example, chimpanzees are more likely to assist those who have assisted them in agonistic exchanges with others ("one good turn deserves another") and to aggress against those who have sided with others against them ("an eye for an eye") (De Waal & Luttrell, 1988). In addition, chimpanzees are more likely to share food with those who have groomed them earlier in the day. If we accept the idea that chimpanzees inherit mechanisms that dispose them to reciprocate and engage in other forms of cooperation, we can conclude that they possess mental mechanisms that enable them to solve fundamental social dilemmas and induce them to engage in primitive forms of fairness.

Games that Primates Play

The social lives of chimpanzees and members of other social species are dynamic. Members of primate groups engage in ongoing contests in which they attempt to induce one another to behave in ways that benefit them by invoking tactics such as begging, offering, enticing, screaming, threatening, attacking, and shunning. De Waal (1991) has suggested that the "active reinforcement of others" (p. 338) is responsible for the emergence of prescriptive rules in groups of chimpanzees.

In their essence, the games that humans play when they are in small groups are the same as the games that other primates play. Like other primates, humans engage in strategic interactions and attempt to press one another's prosocial buttons. They use physical, material, and social rewards and punishments to induce others to treat them right. In Darwin's (1874) words, "man [is] influenced in the highest degree by the wishes, approbation, and blame of his fellow-men, as expressed by their gestures and language" (p. 106).

The Origin of a Sense of Justice

Trivers (1985) suggested that "a sense of fairness has evolved in the human species as the standard against which to measure the behavior of other people, so as to guard against cheating in reciprocal relationships" (p. 388). According to Trivers (2006), "such cheating is expected to generate strong emotional reactions, because unfair arrangements, repeated often, may exact a very strong cost in inclusive fitness" (p. 77). In a similar vein, de Waal and Brosnan (2006) have suggested that "the squaring of accounts in the negative domain . . . may represent a precursor to

human justice, since justice can be viewed as a transformation of the urge for revenge, euphemized as retribution, in order to control and regulate behavior" (p. 88).
On the positive side, "the memory of a received service, such as grooming, induces a
positive attitude toward the same individual, a psychological mechanism described
as 'gratitude' by Trivers (1971)" (p. 93).

The affective precursors to a sense of justice discussed by Trivers and de Waal
stem primarily from the reactions of animals to the ways in which *they* are *treated* by
members of their groups. There is, however, more to humans' sense of justice than
these reactions. Humans also experience emotional reactions to the ways in which
they and others treat third parties.

Affective Reactions to Third-Party Injustice

Although other primates display negative reactions to members of their troupes who
violate prosocial norms and take measures to punish them (Boehm, 2000), humans
may be the only species that is disposed to punish free riders and those who behave
unfairly toward third parties. Summarizing the findings from several studies, Gachter
and Herrmann (2006) conclude:

> Overall, the results suggest that free riding causes negative emotions . . . [that are] con-
> sistent with the hypothesis that emotions trigger punishment. . . . [T]he majority of pun-
> ishments are executed by above-average contributors and imposed on below-average
> contributors. . . . [P]unishment increases with the deviation of the free rider from other
> members' average contribution. . . . [E]vidence from neuroscientific experiments supports
> the interpretation that emotions trigger punishment. (p. 297)

Although evolutionary theorists agree that humans are disposed to punish third-
party cheaters, they do not agree about how the mechanisms that give rise to these
dispositions evolved. On one side, mainstream evolutionary theorists argue that the
disposition to punish free riders evolved through standard forms of selection (kin selection, reciprocal altruism, indirect reciprocity, and costly signaling). For example,
Trivers (2006) has suggested that because the groups formed by early humans consisted mainly of kin, we would expect the mechanisms that dispose contemporary
humans to punish third parties to "misfire" by being activated by members of groups
who are not kin. Trivers's account implies that "the human brain applies ancient
cooperative heuristics even in modern environments" (Gachter & Herrmann, 2005).
Other mainstream evolutionary theorists such as Alexander (1987) and Nowak and
Sigmund (1998) have argued that the disposition to punish third parties could have
been reinforced by the fitness-enhancing gains of an enhanced social image or a reputation for cooperation. On the other side, theorists such as Fehr and Gächter (2002)
and Gintis, Bowles, Boyd, and Fehr (2003) have argued that biological evolution is
not, by itself, equipped to account for the disposition to punish free riders in one-shot
games among anonymous players and that this disposition could have evolved only
through gene-culture coevolution. The theoretical differences between theorists who

have advanced exclusively individual-level selection models and theorists who have advanced coevolutionary models are significant psychologically mainly with respect to their potential to produce hypotheses about how the mechanisms in question are designed.

Affective Reactions to Treating Others Fairly and Unfairly

When we attribute a sense of justice to people, we imply that they possess standards of fairness that they apply to themselves as well as to others. If the function of negative reactions to unfair behaviors committed by others is to motivate people to uphold systems of cooperation by punishing cheaters, we might also expect people to feel bad when they cheat and to be inclined to punish themselves. In fact, people often do feel bad when they cheat others, but it is unclear whether such negative reactions stem from the same mechanisms as their reactions to the transgressions of others.

There is an important difference between inducing oneself to cooperate and inducing others to cooperate. As discussed, in most contexts people are able to maximize their benefits by inducing others to do their share, or more than their share, while doing less than their share themselves. From an adaptive perspective, we would not expect people to be unconditionally motivated to behave fairly or to be naturally inclined to pass judgment on themselves in an impartial way. Rather, we would expect the mechanisms that guide decisions about fairness to be calibrated in ways that maximized the genetic benefits to early humans, inducing individuals to feel inclined to behave only as fairly as they needed to maximize their benefits from social exchanges. In support of these expectations, there is a great deal of evidence that people are inclined to react more strongly to being treated unfairly by others than to treating others unfairly, to hold others to higher standard of fairness than they hold themselves, and to reckon costs and benefits for themselves and others in different ways (Greenberg & Cohen, 1982). As expressed by Trivers (2006), "[A]n attachment to fairness or justice is self-interested and we repeatedly see in life . . . that victims of injustice feel the pain more strongly than do disinterested bystanders and far more than do the perpetrators" (p. 77).

People's negative reactions to others' injustices usually involve anger, which seems to emerge automatically. In contrast, people's negative reactions to their own injustices may be acquired more indirectly, through social learning. As emphasized by Darwin (1874), humans are highly motivated to seek the approval and avoid the disapproval of members of their groups. Contemporary learning theorists such as Aronfreed (1968) have adduced evidence that children acquire negative reactions to their own transgressions through classical and instrumental conditioning. Children come to feel good about behaving fairly and bad about cheating because they are rewarded when they behave fairly and punished when they behave unfairly. Although such inputs structure children's early conceptions of right and wrong, they do not account for a fully developed sense of justice, as I will explain.

The Expansion and Refinement of Cooperative Systems in the Human Species

Humans engage in concrete forms of reciprocity and feel angry when others cheat them in much the same way as chimpanzees do. However, *in addition*, humans engage in more complex forms of social exchange. They give to others over long periods of time before receiving any returns; they invest in long-term relationships; they trade across widely diverse domains (often using money as a common medium); they reckon equity in highly refined ways; they engage in indirect forms of reciprocity; they create rules and formalize systems of sanctions that uphold cooperative systems; they coordinate their efforts on a massive scale to accomplish such tasks such as constructing skyscrapers and building bridges.

The unique forms of cooperation practiced by modern humans became possible when early humans acquired the intellectual and linguistic abilities necessary to create them and uphold them. As expressed by Williams (1989), "the unparalleled human capability for symbolic communication has an incidental consequence of special importance for ethics. In biological usage, communication is nearly synonymous with attempted manipulation. It is a low-cost way of getting someone else to behave in a way favorable to oneself" (p. 211). Coupled with intelligence, symbolic language would have enabled early humans to translate their affective reactions to the behavior of members of their groups into words and communicate such reactions to those who performed the behaviors and to third parties. Not only would it have enabled them to express their immediate approval and disapproval with words such as "good" and "bad," but it would also have enabled them to pass judgment on events that occurred in the past and to make judgments about events that could occur in the future. It would have enabled them to transform primitive threats and promises into long-term social contracts and commitments (Nesse, 2001) and to verbalize disapproval when others violated implicit social contracts such as those that govern monogamous marriages. It would have enabled them to enhance or diminish others' reputations through gossip (Alexander, 1987; Dunbar, 1996) and to buttress their judgments with reasons, explanations, and justifications designed to increase their persuasive power.

The Expansion and Refinement of a Sense of Justice

Intelligence and language are two-edged swords. On the one hand, they enable humans to create and uphold significantly more complex forms of cooperation than those practiced by any other species. On the other hand, they enable humans to engage in significantly more complex forms of cheating. Although we would expect people to be naturally inclined to make self-serving moral judgments, the process of strategic interaction is equipped to counteract such biases. Because recipients are unreceptive to judgments that exhort them to behave in ways that do not advance their interests, blatantly self-serving judgments do not work, and because they do not work, people are disinclined to make them.

Moral Argumentation

Language and intelligence endow humans with the capacity to resolve their conflicts of interest through negotiation and discussion. Many theorists have focused on the significance of moral argumentation in the production of standards of justice (e.g., Damon & Hart, 1992; Habermas, 1993; Piaget, 1932). When people engage in moral argumentation, they may attempt to push one another's emotional buttons (Haidt, 2001), or they may appeal to one another's rational faculties (Saltzstein & Kasachkoff, 2004). As explained by the philosopher Singer (1981), publicly expressed rational arguments tend to generate universal and impartial standards: "[I]f I claim that what I do is right, while what you do is wrong, I must give some reason other than the fact that my action benefits me (or my kin, or my village) while your action benefits you (or your kin or your village)" (p. 118). When people use reason and logical consistency as weapons in moral arguments, they often end up hoist on their own petards.

The Evolution of Rules and Justice Norms

The process of strategic interaction and the adaptive value of resolving conflicts of interest through moral argumentation have implications for the evolution of rules of conduct and universal norms of justice. Members of groups make rules to formalize their agreements about how they should be treated by others, and they invoke sanctions to induce others to uphold the rules. What goes around comes around (Alexander, 1987), such that the rules that members of groups invent to control the behavior of others end up controlling their behavior. Inasmuch as recipients are more receptive to some moral prescriptions than to others, recipients serve as agents of selection, determining which prescriptions succeed, get repeated, and develop into rules and moral norms. We would expect people to be particularly receptive to moral judgments and rules that prescribe fitness-enhancing forms of cooperation and to judgments that enable them to resolve conflicts of interest in mutually beneficial ways. Consistent with these expectations, there is evidence that judgments and rules that uphold fair, balanced, and reversible solutions to social conflicts—such as those prescribed by the norm of reciprocity and the Golden Rule—constitute universal moral norms (Brown, 1991; Gouldner, 1960; Sober & Wilson, 1998; Wright, 1994).

Clearly, however, not all moral rules and norms are fair or rational. Following Aristotle, Darwin (1874) distinguished between two types of rules, akin to culturally universal and culturally relative moral norms. He suggested the following:

> The higher [moral rules] are founded on the social instincts, and relate to the welfare of others. They are supported by the approbation of our fellowman and by reason. The

lower rules . . . arise from public opinion, matured by experience and cultivation . . . [and may lead to] the strangest customs and superstitions, in complete opposition to the true welfare and happiness of mankind. (p. 118)

Earlier I discussed differences between negative affective reactions to injustices committed by others and negative reactions to injustices committed by oneself. In the same vein, there is a significant difference between believing that others should uphold standards of justice and believing that one is obliged to uphold them. People could espouse norms of justice in order to manipulate others into behaving in cooperative ways without believing in the norms or incorporating them into their own conceptions of justice. We would, however, expect the process of strategic interaction to reduce the gap between conceptions of one's own and others' rights and duties.

To begin with, as emphasized by socialization theorists, people may be persuaded to accept as valid the standards preached by others. Evolutionary theory offers a basis for predicting which, of the many ideas to which people are exposed, they will be disposed to accept. It leads us to expect people to be most receptive to norms and standards that have enhanced their fitness in the past and that they believe will enhance their fitness in the future. Thus, for example, we would expect people to be receptive to standards preached by those with a vested interest in their welfare and to standards that are widely accepted by other members of their groups (see Richerson & Boyd, 2005, for a more extended discussion of this issue).

In addition, preaching standards of justice to others may induce those who preach them to accept them as their own. Believing in the validity of the prescriptive judgments one makes may reap adaptive benefits by increasing their persuasive power (Trivers, 1985). People may persuade themselves in the process of persuading others (Festinger, 1964). People may be inclined to believe moral judgments and standards generated during moral negotiations because they actively participated in generating them, because they are supported by others, because they are backed up by reasons, and because they enable them to advance their own interests in optimal ways.

The Origin of Conscience

Most people locate their sense of justice in a mental mechanism they call their conscience. The conditioned reactions to one's transgressions discussed earlier may form the core of conscience. Animals such as dogs appear to display affective reactions akin to guilt when they anticipate punishment for their transgressions (Aronfreed, 1968). Humans differ from other animals, however, in their ability to construct portable cognitive representations of others and store them in their minds, to view events from others' perspectives, and to imagine how others will respond to their behavior (Selman, 1980). In their imagination, people experience others as observing them when they are in private and passing judgment on their behavior (Aronfreed, 1968; Higgins, 1987).

Ironically, perhaps, the mechanisms that enable people to take the perspective of others may have evolved as tools designed to improve early humans' ability to manipulate others in the context of strategic interactions. There is tremendous adaptive potential in the ability to anticipate the moves of others in social games—what they are thinking; what they intend to do; whether they will cooperate, pay one back, detect one's deception; and so on. To accomplish this, people internalize mental representations of others and view events, including those which they themselves are directly involved in, from their perspectives. After people internalize mental images of others, they may experience these images as approving and disapproving of the things they do in private, and this may be experienced as a "voice of conscience."

As children's perspective-taking abilities develop, their cognitive representations of others become increasingly abstract, integrated, and general (Selman, 1980). As expressed by Wilson (1993), "At first we judge others; we then begin to judge ourselves as we think others judge us; finally we judge ourselves as an impartial, disinterested third party might" (p. 33). We would expect highly developed perspective-taking processes to give rise to fairer decisions than more primitive perspective-taking processes.

To summarize, an evolutionary analysis suggests that conscience is a mental mechanism that originated as a tool in strategic interaction. Conscience consists of internalized images of others that enable people to predict how others will react to their behaviors. In imagining the negative reactions of others, people experience an anticipatory fear or embarrassment, which they experience as a sense of guilt or shame. As people internalize an increasingly large number of cognitive representations and as they integrate them in their minds, the perspective from which they judge themselves becomes increasingly abstract and impartial.

Reframing Traditional Psychological Accounts of the Acquisition of a Sense of Justice

An evolutionary framework supplies a basis for reconceptualizing psychological models of the acquisition of a sense of justice in ways that integrate their insights and redress their limitations. The family contexts in which parents teach children to behave fairly are microcosms of larger social groups. Members of families face fundamental social dilemmas. Because parents and children need each other to propagate their genes, it is in their genetic interest to help one another and uphold familial systems of cooperation. However, it may be in each member's interest to favor himself or herself and those with whom he or she shares the largest complement of genes (Trivers, 1974). Conflicts of interest precipitate strategic interactions in which members of families attempt to induce one another to behave in ways that maximize their genetic benefits. The ways in which members of families resolve their conflicts of interest affect the ways in which their conceptions of justice are structured and calibrated.

Evolutionary theory leads us to expect the mechanisms that regulate strategic interactions between parents and children to be designed in fitness-enhancing ways. It follows that we would not expect children to conform to their parents' injunctions indiscriminately or docilely. We would expect children to resist injunctions that run contrary to their interests and actively attempt to manipulate and control other members of their families. Contemporary accounts of conscience that view the child "as an agent in moral socialization who actively processes parental moral messages" and engages in "discourse" with his or her parents (Kochanska & Aksan, 2004, p. 303) fit comfortably in an evolutionary framework that emphasizes the role of strategic interaction in the development of a sense of justice. From this perspective, the key to instilling a balanced sense of justice in children lies in structuring their early interactions in fair ways and inducing them to discover by their experience that it pays to cooperate and treat others fairly.

An evolutionary analysis implies a different interpretation from that offered by cognitive-developmental theorists of evidence that children acquire increasingly sophisticated structures of justice reasoning as they develop. The anthropologist Fiske (1992) has amassed evidence that people from all cultures are innately disposed to develop cognitive "schemata" that organize information about four types of social relations—(1) affectionate relations among people who share social bonds, (2) hierarchical relations among people who differ in social rank, (3) egalitarian exchanges among equals, and (4) economic relations aimed at maximizing cost/benefit ratios across different commodities. Chimpanzees possess the first three schemata; the fourth appears to be unique to the human species (de Waal, 1996; Haslam, 1997).

Life history theory implies that the reason people are prone to invoke increasingly sophisticated schemata and structures of moral reasoning as they develop is that they need increasingly sophisticated schemata and standards of justice to solve the increasingly complex and embedded social problems they encounter as they progress through the life span. The reason young children view justice primarily in terms of obedience to authority (Kohlberg, 1984) is that it is adaptive for young children to subordinate themselves to older, wiser, and more powerful members of their groups. The reason older children view justice primarily in terms of concrete reciprocity is that reciprocity is a more adaptive strategy than obedience in egalitarian relations among peers (Piaget, 1932). The reason young adults view justice primarily in terms of principles that uphold long-term commitments, harmonious in-group relations, and systems of indirect reciprocity is that these forms of cooperation are best equipped to foster their interests (see Krebs, 2005a, 2005b, for elaborations of these ideas). The sophisticated forms of justice reasoning that define Kohlberg's highest stages of moral development constitute creative ideas about how to resolve conflicts of interest and reap the benefits of cooperation in optimal ways. From an evolutionary perspective, cardinal moral principles such as "foster the greatest good for the greatest number" equate to injunctions to foster one's ultimate adaptive interests by upholding the standards, forms of conduct, and systems of cooperation that, if adopted by everyone, would produce the greatest gains.

From a life history perspective, we would not expect new structures of justice reasoning to "transform and displace" older structures, as Colby and Kohlberg (1987) have hypothesized. We would expect people to acquire structures of justice reasoning in an "additive-inclusive" way (Eisenberg, 1982; Levine, 1979), because adults continue to experience the kinds of adaptive problems that early structures evolved to solve. Adults may, for example, find themselves in subordinate positions in which it would be adaptive for them to believe that they should show deference to authority (Milgram, 1974). Viewed in this manner, the acquisition of a sense of justice consists more in the acquisition of the flexibility necessary to solve social problems in the most efficient, effective, and adaptive ways than in the ability to make highly sophisticated moral judgments in every context (Krebs & Denton, 2005). Although the justifications that adults advance for obeying authority and engaging in tit-for-tat exchanges may be more sophisticated than those advanced by children—for example, because adults embed their justifications in principles that uphold more broadly based systems of cooperation—their decisions may stem from essentially the same affective and cognitive processes.

The Activation of Mechanisms that Produce a Sense of Justice

Given a suite of evolved mechanisms equipped to contribute to people's sense of justice, the main task for those who seek to account for this phenomenon is to explain how these mechanisms are activated and, if more than one is activated, how they interact. Because complex forms of moral cognition are more costly than simpler forms, we would expect people to be inclined to use simple, automatic forms as their default (Gigerenzer, 2000; Gilovich, Griffin, & Kahneman, 2002). We would expect affective reactions such as gratitude and righteous indignation to exert an immediate effect on people's sense of justice (Haidt, 2001; Sunstein, 2005), and we would not be surprised that people have difficulty justifying decisions derived in these ways or, if called upon to justify them, that they offer plausible but invalid post hoc rationalizations (Haidt, 2001).

We also would expect people to invoke simple forms of justice reasoning to solve simple, recurring social problems (Fiske, 1992), to make quick decisions in contexts in which the costs of deliberation are high, and to generate simple judgments when such judgments constitute the most effective forms of persuasion and impression management (such as, for example, when they are directed toward children) (Krebs & Janicki, 2004). We would expect people to adopt and to preach the moral norms of their cultures without thinking much about them, as long as they worked reasonably well, and to use mental shortcuts in contexts in which heuristics generate acceptable moral decisions (Chaiken, 1987; Gigerenzer, 2000; Sunstein, 2005).

We would expect conceptions of justice to be customized to solve different kinds of social problems and, therefore, for people to invoke different conceptions of justice in different domains, contexts, and conditions (Damon, 1980; Eisenberg, 1982;

Krebs & Denton, 2005; Krebs, Vermeulen, Carpendale, & Denton, 1991). We would expect the cognitive apparatus that gives rise to conceptions of justice to be susceptible to framing, directional, motivational, self-serving, nepotistic, and group-serving biases (Chaiken, Giner-Sorolla, & Chen, 1996; Krebs & Laird, 1998; Kunda, 2000; Pyszczynski & Greenberg, 1987; Richerson & Boyd, 2005). And we would not be surprised to find that people sometimes use justice reasoning for immoral purposes, such as avoiding responsibility and justifying immoral acts (Bandura, 1991; Haidt, 2001).

There is nothing in this evolutionary analysis of the acquisition of a sense of justice that is inconsistent with the idea that people have the capacity to derive conceptions of justice from sophisticated forms of moral reasoning. As demonstrated by cognitive-developmental theorists, most people do possess this capacity. However, an evolutionary framework induces us to ask how often, and in what contexts, people invoke this tool rather than other tools in their moral-decision-making tool boxes. We would expect people to invoke sophisticated forms of moral reasoning to derive decisions about justice when they work better than alternative methods and when the biological benefits from invoking them outweigh the costs. For example, we would expect people to invoke sophisticated forms of moral reasoning to resolve conflicts among moral intuitions and moral norms (Haidt, 2001) and the rights and duties of people participating in embedded systems of cooperation (Kohlberg, 1984). We would expect people to engage in reflective moral reasoning when they possess ample processing capacity, when they are challenged (e.g., in moral argumentation), when they have time to deliberate, when the costs of deliberation are low, when the benefits of deliberation are high, when they are motivated to be accurate, when audiences are impressed by sophisticated moral judgments, and so on. Note that these conditions are characteristic of those in which cognitive-developmental theorists assess moral reasoning.

Conclusion

To understand how people acquire a sense of justice, we must understand why people need one and what goals it helps them to achieve. The mechanisms that give rise to a sense of justice evolved to help early humans maximize their gains from cooperative social interactions. A sense of justice induces members of groups to distribute resources in fair ways (distributive justice), to honor the commitments they make to others (commutative justice), to punish cheaters (corrective justice), and to develop effective ways of resolving conflicts of interest and making fair decisions (procedural justice).

Contemporary humans inherit primitive predispositions to react positively to being treated fairly and negatively to being treated unfairly, to pass judgment on those who treat others fairly or unfairly, and to feel obliged to pay others back. This core is refined and expanded during the process of strategic interaction in every generation as people reward and punish one another for behaving in cooperative and uncooperative ways, preach norms of fairness, negotiate mutually beneficial solutions to their conflicts of interest, and attempt to create ever more effective systems of cooperation. To achieve these goals, people use the tools with which they have been endowed by natural selection, especially language, perspective-taking abilities, and social intelligence. Although it is naïve to expect people to possess a universal sense of justice that consistently disposes them to make fair and impartial decisions that jeopardize their adaptive interests, it is realistic to expect people to be able to counteract one another's biases in ways that enable them to make fair decisions in contexts in which such decisions advance everyone's interests in optimal ways.

References

Alexander, R. D. (1987). *The biology of moral systems*. New York: Aldine de Gruyter.

Aronfreed, J. (1968). *Conduct and conscience*. New York: Academic Press.

Bandura, A. (1991). Social cognitive theory of moral thought and action. In W. M. Kurtines & J. L. Gewirtz (Eds.), *Handbook of moral behavior and development* (Vol. 1, pp. 54–104). Hillsdale, NJ: Erlbaum.

Boehm, C. (2000). Conflict and the evolution of social control. *Journal of Consciousness Studies, 7*, 79–101.

Brown, D. E. (1991). *Human universals*. New York: McGraw-Hill.

Chaiken, S. (1987). The heuristic model of persuasion. In M. P. Zanna, J. M. Olson, & C. P. Herman (Eds.), *Social influence: The Ontario Symposium* (pp. 3–39). Hillsdale, NJ: Erlbaum.

Chaiken, S., Giner-Sorolla, R., & Chen, S. (1996). Beyond accuracy: Defense and impression motives in heuristic and systematic information processing. In P. M. Gollwitzer & J. A. Bargh (Eds.), *The psychology of action: Linking cognition and motivation to behavior* (pp. 553–578). New York: Guilford Press.

Colby, A., & Kohlberg, L. (Eds.). (1987). *The measurement of moral judgment* (Vols. 1–2). Cambridge: Cambridge University Press.

Gachter, S., & Herrmann, B. (2006). Human cooperation from an economic standpoint. In P. M. Kappeler & C. P. van Schaik (Eds.), *Cooperation in primates and humans: Mechanisms and evolution* (pp. 275–302). Berlin: Springer-Verlag.

Damon, W. (1980). Patterns of change in children's social reasoning: A two-year longitudinal study. *Child Development, 46*, 1010–1017.

Damon, W., & Hart, D. (1992). Self-understanding and its role in social and moral development. In M. H. Bornstein & E. M. Lamb (Eds.), *Developmental psychology: An advanced textbook* (2nd ed., pp. 421–465). Hillsdale, NJ: Erlbaum.

Darwin, C. (1874). *The descent of man and selection in relation to sex*. New York: Rand McNally.

de Waal, F. B. M. (1991). The chimpanzee's sense of social regularity and its relation to the human sense of justice. *American Behavioral Scientist, 34*, 335–349.

de Waal, F. B. M. (1996). *Good natured: The origins of right and wrong in humans and other animals*. Cambridge, MA: Harvard University Press.

de Waal, F. B. M., & Brosnan, S. F. (2006). Simple and complex reciprocity in primates. In P. M. Kappeler & C. P. van Schaik (Eds.), *Cooperation in primates and humans: Mechanisms and evolution* (pp. 85–106). Berlin: Springer-Verlag.

De Waal, F. B. M., & Luttrell, L. M. (1988). Mechanisms of reciprocity in three primate species: Symmetrical relationship characteristics or reciprocity? *Ethology and Sociobiology, 9*, 101–118.

Dunbar, R. I. M. (1996). Determinants of group size in primates: A general model. In G. Runciman, J. Maynard Smith, & R. I. M. Dunbar (Eds.), *Evolution of social behavior patterns in primates and man* (pp. 33–58). Oxford: Oxford University Press.

Eisenberg, N. (1982). *The development of prosocial behavior*. New York: Academic Press.

Fehr, E., & Gächter, S. (2002). Altruistic punishment in humans. *Nature, 415*, 137–140.

Festinger, L. (1964). *Conflict, decision, and dissonance*. Stanford, CA: Stanford University Press.

Fiske, A. P. (1992). Four elementary forms of sociality: Framework for a unified theory of social relations. *Psychological Review, 99*, 689–723.

Gachter, S., & Herrmann, B. (2006). Human cooperation from an economic perspective. In P. M. Kappeler & C. P. van Schaik (Eds.), *Cooperation in primates and humans: Mechanisms and evolution* (pp. 275–301). Berlin: Springer-Verlag.

Gigerenzer, G. (2000). *Adaptive thinking: Rationality in the real world*. New York: Oxford University Press.

Gilovich, T., Griffen, D., & Kahneman, D. (2002). *Heuristics and biases: The psychology of intuitive judgment*. New York: Cambridge University Press.

Gintis, H., Bowles, S., Boyd, R., & Fehr, E. (2003). Explaining altruistic behavior in humans. *Evolution and Human Behavior, 24*, 153–172.

Gouldner, A. W. (1960). The norm of reciprocity: A preliminary statement. *American Sociological Review, 25*, 161–78.

Greenberg, J., & Cohen, R. L. (1982). *Equity and justice in social behavior*. New York: Academic Press.

Habermas, J. (1993). *Justification and application*. Cambridge, MA: MIT Press.

Haidt, J. (2001). The emotional dog and its rational tail: A social intuitionist approach to moral judgment. *Psychological Review, 108*, 814–834.

Haslam, N. (1997). Four grammars for primate social relations. In J. A. Simpson & D. T. Kenrick (Eds.), *Evolutionary social psychology* (pp. 297–316). Mahwah, NJ: Erlbaum.

Higgins, E. T. (1987). Self-discrepancy: A theory relating self and affect. *Psychological Review, 94*, 319–340.

Kappeler, P. M., & van Schaik, C. P. (2006). *Cooperation in primates and humans: Mechanisms and evolution*. Berlin: Springer-Verlag.

Kohlberg, L. (1984). *Essays in moral development: The psychology of moral development* (Vol 2.). New York: Harper & Row.

Kochanska, G., & Aksan, N. (2004). Conscience in childhood: Past, present, and future. *Merrill-Palmer Quarterly, 50*, 299–310.

Krebs, D. L. (2005a). An evolutionary reconceptualization of Kohlberg's model of moral development. In R. Burgess & K. MacDonald (Eds.), *Evolutionary perspectives on human development* (pp. 243–274). Thousand Oaks, CA: Sage.

Krebs, D. L. (2005b). The evolution of morality. In D. Buss (Ed.), *The handbook of evolutionary psychology* (pp. 747–771). Hoboken, NJ: John Wiley.

Krebs, D. L., & Denton, K. (2005). Toward a more pragmatic approach to morality: A critical evaluation of Kohlberg's model. *Psychological Review, 112*, 629–649.

Krebs, D. L., & Janicki, M. (2004) The biological foundations of moral norms. In M. Schaller & C. Crandall (Eds.), *Psychological foundations of culture* (pp. 25–148). Hillsdale, NJ: Erlbaum.

Krebs, D. L., & Laird, P. (1998). Judging yourself as you judge others: Perspective-taking, moral development, and exculpation. *Journal of Adult Development, 5*, 1–12.

Krebs, D. L., Vermeulen, S. C., Carpendale, J. I., & Denton, K. (1991). Structural and situational influences on moral judgment: The interaction between stage and dilemma. In W. Kurtines and J. Gewirtz (Eds.), *Handbook of moral behavior and development: Theory, research, and application (pp. 139–169)*. Hillsdale, NJ: Erlbaum.

Kunda, Z. (2000). *Social cognition: Making sense of people*. Cambridge MA: MIT Press.

Levine, C. G. (1979). Stage acquisition and stage use: An appraisal of stage displacement explanations of variation in moral reasoning. *Human Development, 22*, 145–164.

Milgram, S. (1974). *Obedience to authority*. New York: Harper.

Nesse, R. M. (Ed.). (2001). *Evolution and the capacity for commitment*. New York: Russell Sage Foundation.

Nowak, M. A., & Sigmund, K. (1998). Evolution of indirect reciprocity by image scoring. *Nature, 393*, 573–577.

Piaget, J. (1932). *The moral judgment of the child*. London: Routledge & Kegan Paul.

Pyszczynski, T., & Greenberg, J. (1987). Toward an integration of cognitive and motivational perspectives on social inference: A biased hypothesis-testing model. *Advances in Experimental Social Psychology, 20*, 297–340.

Rawls, J. (1999). *A theory of justice* (rev. ed.). Cambridge, MA: Harvard University Press.

Richerson, P. J., & Boyd, R. (2005). *Not by genes alone: How culture transformed human evolution*. Chicago: University of Chicago Press.

Saltzstein, H. D., & Kasachkoff, T. (2004). Haidt's moral intuitionist theory: A psychological and philosophical critique. *Review of General Psychology, 8*, 273–282.

Selman, R. L. (1980). *The growth of interpersonal understanding*. New York: Academic Press.

Singer, P. (1981). *The expanding circle: Ethics and sociobiology*. New York: Farrar, Straus and Giroux.

Sober, E., & Wilson, D. S. (1998). *Unto others: The evolution and psychology of unselfish behavior*. Cambridge, MA: Harvard University Press.

Sunstein, C. R. (2005). Moral heuristics. *Behavioral and Brain Sciences, 28*, 531–573.

Trivers, R. (1974). Parent-offspring conflict. *American Zoologist, 14*, 249–264.

Trivers, R. (1985). *Social evolution*. Menlo Park, CA: Benjamin Cummings.

Trivers, R. (2000). The elements of a scientific theory of self-deception. In D. LeCroy & P. Moller (Eds.), *Evolutionary perspectives on human reproductive behavior* (pp. 114–131). New York: New York Academy of Sciences.

Trivers, R. (2006). Reciprocal altruism: 30 years later. In P. M. Kappeler & C. P. van Schaik (Eds.), *Cooperation in primates and humans: Mechanisms and evolution* (pp. 67–84). Berlin: Springer-Verlag.

Williams, G. C. (1989). A sociobiological expansion of *Evolution and Ethics*. In J. Paradis & G. Williams (Eds.), *Evolution and Ethics* (pp. 179–214). Princeton, NJ: Princeton University Press.

Wilson, J. Q. (1993). *The moral sense*. New York: Free Press.

Wright, R. (1994). *The moral animal*. New York: Pantheon Books.

PART SIX

APPLICATIONS AND FUTURE DIRECTIONS

13

Reducing Crime Evolutionarily

LEE ELLIS

The evidence for genetic influences on criminality is no longer scientifically questionable (reviewed by Anderson, 2007, pp. 95–124; Rose, 2000). This is not all that surprising if one simply realizes that the brain—obviously a genetically influenced biological organ—guides all behavior, including that which is socially defined as criminal.

Even today, most criminologists only study social influences on criminal behavior. That narrow-minded tradition should be in our past; the era of neurologically specific theories has arrived (Rafter, 2006). These are theories that identify how the brains of offenders differ on average from the brains of nonoffenders, whether the causes are genetic or environmental. I have devised such a theory that I will briefly present. Then, I will discuss a variety of ways in which it suggests criminal and delinquent behavior can be prevented and treated.

The Evolutionary Neuroandrogenic Theory

The theory is called the *evolutionary neuroandrogenic (ENA) theory* of criminal behavior (for more details, see Ellis 2003, 2004, 2005). In a nutshell, ENA theory asserts that genes have evolved ways of altering human brain functioning—particularly among males—to exhibit increased criminality during their early reproductive years. Theoretically, males as a whole have evolved greater tendencies than females to victimize others. These male victimizing tendencies have been naturally selected for because females have been favored for choosing mates who are reliable and capable provisioners of resources. Some details surrounding these basic arguments appear below.

The Evolutionary Proposition

ENA theory asserts that both evolution and genetics are central to understanding criminal/antisocial behavior, a view that is foreign to most criminologists. In particular, the theory asserts that natural selection has favored the evolution of a broad class of behavioral tendencies known as competitive/victimizing behavior, one form of which is behavior socially recognized as criminal.

The most fundamental premise of ENA theory derives from noting that among mammals, only the females can gestate offspring. This simple fact drives the theory. As the amount of time and energy required by females to produce an offspring increased—which was certainly the case in our species—females came to exhibit a phenomenon known as female choice, meaning that they exercise primary discretion in terms of mating decisions—becoming the mating gatekeepers, so to speak (Geary, 2000, p. 59).

According to ENA theory, female choice has had considerable influence on the evolution of male behavior. In particular, it has led to the formation of social hierarchies within which males compete for dominance (or status) throughout their reproductive careers (Ellis, 2001). Males who exhibit at least modest success in status attainment will pass more copies of their genes onto subsequent generations than males who have little or no status attainment. The main reason for this is that females use status (and status potential) as a criterion for choosing mates.

Females have been favored by natural selection for biasing their mate choice toward males with status because doing so allows females to focus greater time and energy on bearing and rearing offspring. Otherwise, a female will need to divert time and energy toward provisioning resources on her own.

ENA theory asserts that female choice has imposed continuous natural selection pressure on males to focus their time and energy on provisioning, and in most societies this has entailed functioning within social hierarchies for status. Due to this natural selection pressure, males throughout the world are found to be much more prone toward overtly competitive activities than are females (Ellis et al., 2008, Table 6.2.3.13).

According to ENA theory, competitive/victimizing behavior exists along a continuum of crude to sophisticated expressions, and victimizing criminality is a crude expression. Close to the sophisticated end of the same continuum are the sorts of business and commercial activities that make life in complex societies possible. Near the middle of the continuum are deceptive and shady business practices that may or may not be considered criminal (Ellis, 2004, p. 147).

For natural selection to impinge upon a trait, the trait must be at least partially influenced by genes (Pinker, 2002, p. 50). Thus, at the heart of ENA theory is the assumption that genetic factors are contributing to people's varying tendencies to engage in crime (as well as other forms of competitive/victimizing behavior).

The Neuroandrogenic Proposition

As to how genes have made males more criminal than females, ENA theory asserts that testosterone and other so-called male hormones (collectively known as androgens) operate on the brain to facilitate the learning of competitive/victimizing behavior, including its criminal forms. Theoretically, androgen-motivated inclinations to learn competitive/victimizing behavior are partially wired into the brains of males even before birth but begin to be much more fully expressed at the onset of puberty. The most widespread manifestation of competitive/victimizing behavior with the onset of puberty is juvenile delinquency, although general aggressiveness and reduced compliance with authority are also common.

Eventually, these early postpubertal expressions of competitive/victimizing behavior will be tempered with tendencies to compete within a hierarchical social system. Rapid transition to the latter (sophisticated) forms of competitive/victimizing behavior is facilitated by agile reasoning and learning abilities. Consequently, individuals who have low intelligence or learning disabilities will be relatively slow to transition from crude to sophisticated forms of competitive/victimizing behavior. These slow learners are most likely to become what Moffitt (1997) has termed "life-course-persistent offenders," whereas males with average or above average learning ability are most likely to be what she has termed "adolescence-limited offenders."

It is important to mention that more detailed descriptions of the theory (e.g., Ellis, 2005) specify aspects of brain functioning that affect the probability of criminal behavior, all of which are androgen influenced. They involve (a) the arousal control process, mainly in the brain stem; (b) emotion control mechanisms, primarily in the limbic system; (c) executive functioning processes, mainly in the prefrontal portion of the neocortex; and (d) the relative strength of the left and right hemispheres. I briefly allude to these brain functions as they pertain to specific crime prevention and treatment approaches in the following section.

Using ENA Theory for Crime Prevention and Treatment

Numerous applications of ENA theory are possible regarding both the prevention and treatment of criminality. These applications can be conceptualized within the following three categories: social learning approaches, pharmacological/neurological approaches, and eugenic approaches.

Social Learning Approaches

ENA theory suggests that several social learning approaches to crime prevention and recidivism reduction should have their intended crime-reducing effects. These approaches involve recognizing that while the motivation for criminal behavior is largely unlearned, the behavior itself is learned. For example, largely unlearned desires for creature comforts may lead to thefts, those for sexual satisfaction may cause rape, and those for envy and revenge may induce many assaults and murders. Accordingly, any treatment programs that help offenders (or prospective offenders) to identify and utilize alternatives to illegal means to satisfy innate desires should help to reduce crime. Following are some of those programs and a review of the main evidence pertaining to their effectiveness.

Mentoring Programs

Begun in the 1930s, the first mentoring type of crime prevention program came to be known as Big Brother/Big Sister (Reymert, 1940). In such a program, a same-sex adult is teamed with a delinquent or "at-risk" youth. The adult befriends, counsels, and participates in recreational activities with the youth in order to guide him or her toward becoming a responsible citizen. Do such programs have their intended effects? The empirical evidence is limited but suggests that they have significant tendencies to prevent delinquency, at least in terms of illegal drug use and truancy (Grossman & Tierney, 1998).

Parenting Management Training

Anyone who has ever witnessed a mother yelling obscenities at her child in a grocery store knows that some parents are atrocious when it comes to helping their children learn to behave within acceptable social limits. Studies have shown that a lack of parental competence is a significant predictor of offspring delinquency (Farrington, 1987, p. 32; Simons, Wu, Conger, & Lorenz, 1994). According to most research, the most effective parenting for preventing delinquency involves firm but minimally punitive discipline (Kandel, 1982; Patterson & Stouthamer-Loeber, 1984).

Assessments of programs designed to help parents acquire these types of child management skills have suggested that most of them have modest success at reducing delinquency (Klein et al., 1977; Woolfenden, Williams, & Peat, 2002; but for no significant long-term effect see Bank, Marlowe, Reid, Patterson, & Weinrott, 1991). Theoretically, these programs are only modestly successful because the personalities of children vary considerably independent of parental treatment. Most children have personalities that allow them to rather quickly learn acceptable behavior even with relatively poor parental guidance. On the other hand, children who are most likely to become delinquent and criminal later in life demand much more skilled and patient parenting to prevent antisocial behavior. ENA theory predicts that considerably greater parental skills will be required to keep males from engaging in delinquency than females.

Language-Focused Programs

Research has repeatedly shown that persons with serious criminal histories exhibit unusually high rates of deficits in language skills (e.g., Moffitt, Silva, Lynam, & Henry, 1994; Rodriguez, 1993). Reflecting these language-related deficits are studies showing that offenders score distinctly lower on verbal aspects of standardized IQ tests relative to their scores on nonverbal (performance) aspects of these tests, a phenomenon known as "intellectual imbalance" (e.g., Henry, Moffitt, & Silva, 1992; Lynam, Moffitt, & Stouthamer-Loeber, 1993).

To explain such language deficiencies, ENA theory contends that testosterone causes the brain to shift away from its normal left-dominated hemispheric brain-functioning pattern toward a greater involvement of the right hemisphere (Ellis, 2005). Theoretically, this shift makes it difficult for individuals to maintain attention on and to intelligibly process linguistic stimuli. Not only do they perform poorly in school as a result but they are also more likely to ignore laws and most other language-based rules of socially acceptable conduct.

If ENA theory is correct regarding the left hemisphere being less dominant among offenders than among nonoffenders, it may be possible to prevent offending by immersing crime-prone individuals into language-oriented learning throughout childhood. No specific programs directly bearing on this theoretical prediction were located.

Self-Control and Moral Reasoning Training

According to ENA theory, the frontal lobes perform important "master control" functions that help humans organize their daily activities into coherent themes (life's plans) and do so without routinely harming others (Ellis, 2005). Collectively known as *executive functioning*, these higher thought processes make moral reasoning and so-called self-control possible.

Can the frontal lobes be taught to improve in moral reasoning and self-control? Without delving into the details of what "improve" means, one can think of the brain in ways that might pertain to muscle tissue. Even though some people are naturally much stronger than others, everyone can still enhance his or her muscularity through exercise. Likewise, neurological processes can be substantially enhanced through "exercise" by socially practicing moral reasoning and self-regulation.

Most moral issues boil down to weighing short-term versus long-term consequences of one's actions. The more individuals can be taught to focus on the long-term consequences of their actions, the better their moral reasoning will be. Similarly, self-control is usually achieved by being able to foresee the long-term advantages of postponing immediate gratification.

Crime prevention programs having to do with promoting self-control are currently conceptualized mainly in terms of Gottfredson and Hirschi's (1990) self-control theory. Thinking about self-control in terms of ENA theory, on the other hand, has at least two advantages. First, unlike control theory, ENA theory recognizes that people do not simply vary in self-control due to upbringing. Instead, genetically regulated brain processes are seen as having much to do with how quickly people mature in their self-control. Second, ENA theory forces one to think of self-control, moral reasoning, and long-term planning as interconnected phenomena. This communality largely resides in executive functioning of the prefrontal lobes. Morgan and Lilienfeld (2000) reviewed considerable evidence that deficient executive functioning of the prefrontal lobes is a significant contributor to delinquent and criminal behavior. Beaver, Wright, and Delisi (2007) went on to argue that the well-established link between poor self-control and antisocial behavior is the result of deficiencies in prefrontal executive functioning.

Even though much of the variation in executive functioning appears to be under genetic control, there are ways it can be enhanced through social training and reinforcement (Baumeister, Heatherton, & Tice, 1994; Strayhorn, 2002a). Accordingly, at least one program for promoting self-control has shown promise for crime prevention (Strayhorn, 2002a, 2002b).

Additional research supports the idea that even though executive functioning of the prefrontal lobes has a major role to play in maintaining self-control, such control can still be modified through social training. For example, clinical psychologists were able to teach mothers how to instill more effective self-control strategies for resisting temptation and being less impulsive in troublesome preschoolers (Mauro & Harris, 2000). Likewise, a set of reinforcement techniques have been developed that appears to promote the learning of socially responsible behavior among conduct-disordered children (reviewed by McMahon & Wells, 1998). The hope is that these children will thereby avoid antisocial behavior later in life.

Pharmacological/Neurological Approaches

If ENA theory is true, there should be numerous ways to reduce crime through our growing understanding of the brain. As discussed in the following sections, these approaches would include the use of drugs for alleviating neurological symptoms that are often precursors for criminal and antisocial behavior. Before exploring these approaches, it should be emphasized that no neurochemical treatment program should be employed as a first-line strategy but rather as a possible secondary or tertiary approach when learning-based approaches prove to be unsatisfactory. Even then, pharmacological therapies should only be used in conjunction with learning-based approaches, not simply on their own (Harrington & Bailey, 2003, p. 27).

Stimulant Arousal Control Medication

Methylphenidate (Ritalin) has been used to treat symptoms of Attention-Deficit/ Hyperactivity Disorder (ADHD) for the past couple of decades (Swanson, McBurnett, Christian, & Wigal, 1995). This and other stimulant drugs appear to have their main effect by allowing the brains of ADHD sufferers to focus greater proportions of their attention on ordinary incoming stimuli (as most people do) rather than attending only to unusually intense and often socially disruptive stimuli (Polanczyk et al., 2007).

According to ENA theory, fairly high proportions of delinquents exhibit neurological underarousal, as do ADHD children (Ellis, 2005), a view supported by empirical evidence (Sullivan & Rudnik-Levin, 2001). If so, stimulant medications may help to suppress delinquent activities. One study did report that methylphenidate reduced aggressive behavior among conduct-disordered children (Kaplan, Busner, Kupietz, Wassermann, & Segal, 1990). However, too little research pertaining to its postpubertal therapeutic effects is currently available to make a judgment with confidence (see Garland, 1998). Nevertheless, one experimental study suggested that methylphenidate helped reduce aggressive behavior among young adolescents (Hinshaw & Erhardt, 1991), and another concluded that antisocial behavior generally was diminished with this medication (Klein, Alexander, & Parsons, 1997).

A stimulant drug that produces a more extended therapeutic response per dose than methylphenidate is an amphetamine marketed under the brand name Adderall (Pelham et al., 1999; Swanson et al., 1998). For this reason, it should be explored as more appropriate for treating severe delinquency symptoms.

Anti-androgens

At the heart of ENA theory is the premise that testosterone and other androgens operate on the brain in ways that promote criminal behavior. This leads one to expect drugs that reduce testosterone levels to help reduce the probability of offending. Consequently, a class of drugs called anti-androgens—primarily cyproterone acetate and medroxyprogesterone acetate (trade name Depo-Provera)—should reduce the incidence of crime and delinquency.

So far, the best-documented effects of anti-androgens in treating criminality have involved sex offenders. Provided that these offenders maintain their treatment regimen, studies suggest that the commission of new sex offenses is substantially diminished (reviewed by Grossman, Martis, & Fichtner, 1999; Maletzky, Tolan, & McFarland, 2006; Rosler & Witztum, 2000).

According to ENA theory, anti-androgens should also help to reduce nearly all types of offenses, not just those of a sexual nature. For example, administering anti-androgens to young postpubertal males at high risk of offending, especially regarding violent offenses, should help to suppress the dramatic surge in testosterone in the years immediately following puberty. Males with the greatest difficulty learning may need to be maintained on anti-androgen treatment for as much as a decade. No specific evidence was located to assess the merits of this hypothesis.

Anti-androgens (the administration of which is also called *chemical castration*) are often discussed in tandem with actual (surgical) castration. The main difference between the two is that chemical castration is reversible and thereby less punitive than surgical castration. Nevertheless, studies of the effects of surgical castration have indicated that rapists, pedophiles, and exhibitionists who have undergone the procedure have much lower sex offense recidivism rates than do comparable sex offenders who are not surgically castrated (Hansen, 1991; Wille & Beier, 1989).

Antipsychotic Medication

Research indicates that criminality, especially of a violent nature, is more common among schizophrenics (Tengstrom, Hodgins, Grann, Langstrom, & Kullgren, 2004; Walsh, Buchanan, & Fahy, 2002) and manic depressives (Feldmann, 2001; Harrer & Kofler-Westergren, 1986) than among persons in general. Various drugs known as antipsychotics are often used in treating persons with these ailments. This has raised the possibility that antipsychotics might also be helpful in preventing at least some types of criminal behavior. The research bearing on this possibility is limited but worth briefly exploring.

One study indicated that two drugs often used in treating schizophrenia—chlorpromazine and thioridazine—were helpful in reducing assaultive behavior among mentally retarded children (Campbell, Rapoport, & Simpson, 1999). Another drug also used mainly to treat schizophrenia—risperidone—was deemed fairly effective in temporarily reducing aggression and other symptoms of childhood conduct disorders (Findling et al., 2000).

A medication with a long history in treating symptoms of manic depression is lithium carbonate (Baldessarini, Tondo, & Hennen, 1999). Actually the lightest known metal, lithium in granulated form has helped for decades to manage ungovernable tempers and acts of impulsive aggression among persons diagnosed with manic depression (Shader, Jackson, & Dodes, 1974; Sheard, Marini, Bridges, & Wagner, 1976). It has also been found to alleviate explosive outbursts of aggression among children and young adolescents with conduct disorders (Campbell et al., 1984; Malone, Delaney, Luebbert, Cater, & Campbell, 2000).

ENA theory would attribute the success of these antipsychotic medications to evidence that they all tend to temper the emotion control centers in the brain's limbic system (Ellis, 2005). From an evolutionary standpoint, the limbic system houses many key survival instincts that help humans and other mammals to make judgments about social relationships.

Atypical Antipsychotic Medication

In recent years, several antipsychotic medications have been developed that differ substantially from more established antipsychotic medications in how they affect the brain; thus they have been dubbed atypical. The main distinguishing feature of atypical antipsychotics is that they target the type 2 neurotransmitter receptors for both dopamine and serotonin in the limbic system much more directly than is true for earlier developed antipsychotic drugs (Worrell & Marken, 2000).

One atypical antipsychotic medication, known as quetiapine, has been used in treating conditions as diverse as schizophrenia (Kasper & Muller-Spahn, 2000) and Parkinson's disease (Targum & Abbott, 2000) with at least modest promise. However, in a limited clinical trial, it seemed to be very helpful in reducing impulsivity, hostility, and aggression among four maximum-security inmates diagnosed with antisocial personality disorder (Walker, Thomas, & Allen, 2003).

The Walker et al. study obviously needs to be extended before its findings can be considered established. Nonetheless, it offers a ray of hope in terms of alleviating behavior traits that are very common among persons with extremely high offending rates—that is, psychopaths (Hare, 1993). ENA theory envisions the limbic system as one of the key areas of the brain in which emotions conducive to criminality reside.

Anticonvulsant Medication

Anticonvulsant medications are primarily prescribed to persons with a history of epileptic seizures. Numerous studies have found a statistical link between epilepsy and episodic bursts of aggression (e.g., Devinsky et al., 1994; Marsh & Krauss, 2000).

ENA theory can explain links between epilepsy and aggression in various neurologically specific ways. One is to note that many types of epilepsy involved disturbances primarily in the limbic system and its connections with the prefrontal areas of the frontal lobes (Dougherty et al., 2004; Raine & Yang, 2006; Trimble & Tebartz van Elst, 2003). Since these are areas crucial to social emotions, long-term planning, and moral reasoning, epilepsy may disturb the functioning of brain regions critical to the control of emotionally charged aggression (Woermann et al., 2000). If this line of reasoning is correct, it should be possible to treat impulsive types of criminal behavior with anticonvulsant drugs.

Researchers have sought to determine whether anticonvulsant drugs can reduce the incidence of episodic aggression. Results have been positive, especially for carbamazepine, which has been found to reduce the incidence of such aggression in patients generally (reviewed by Young & Hillbrand, 1994), among conduct disordered children (Kafantaris et al., 1992), and for epileptic and manic depressive adults (Post, Rubinow, & Uhde, 1984). Other anticonvulsants that have shown promise in suppressing violent outbursts among convicted offenders with and without a history of seizures are Propranolol (Mattes, 1990; Sheard, 1984) and Valproate (Wilcox, 1995; Donovan, Susser, & Nunes, 1997).

Serotonin-altering Medications

Serotonin is an important neurotransmitter associated with feelings of calm and contentment (Kalus, Asnis, & Van Praag, 1989; Plaznik, Kostowski, & Archer, 1989). Typically, low or unstable serotonin activity in the brain is linked to irritability and impulsive violence (Matykiewicz, La Grange, Vance, Wang, & Reyes, 1997; Virkkunen, Eggert, Rawlings, & Linnoila, 1996).

While the research is still limited and preliminary, a few studies suggest that serotonin-altering drugs can be used to prevent recidivism among violent psychopaths (reviewed by Dolan, Deakin, Roberts, & Anderson, 2002) as well as deviant sex offenders (Fedoroff, 2004). Serotonergic drugs may also help to reduce violence among conduct-disordered children (Staller, 2007), marijuana use by ADHD adolescents (Solhkhah et al., 2005), and cocaine addiction (Liu & Cunningham, 2005).

ENA theory predicts that serotonergic therapy would provide effective treatment for criminal and antisocial behavior partly because serotonin pathways connect the brain's prefrontal areas with the emotion control centers in the limbic system (Davidson, Purtnam, & Larson, 2000, p. 592). Theoretically, serotonin facilitates executive cognitive functioning that is required to restrain impulses that often originate in the limbic system, especially those of rage and social frustration (Ellis, 2005). Another noteworthy point is that testosterone seems to fundamentally alter serotonergic pathways in the brain (Birger et al., 2003; Fink, Sumner, & Rosie, 1999). Understanding the impact that testosterone has on serotonin could have a major impact on pharmacologically regulating impulsive types of human aggression.

Reducing Lead Exposure

Lead was widely used in paint until the 1940s and is still peeling from the walls of some old homes. It was also an additive in gasoline until the 1970s, thereby contaminating the atmosphere of many large cities. Exposing the brain to lead lowers intelligence-test scores (Bellinger et al., 2003; Canfield, Kreher, Cornwell, & Henderson, 2003) and probably learning ability in general (Yuan et al., 2006).

ENA theory states that any suppression of learning ability or executive functioning will increase the likelihood of a sustained criminal career. Over the years, numerous studies have indicated that bodily exposure to lead, even prenatally, is associated with later delinquency and criminality, especially of a violent nature (e.g., Dietrich, Ris, Succop, Berger, & Bornschein, 2001; Needleman, McFarland, Ness, Fienberg, & Tobin, 2002; Nevin, 2000). Even when the detrimental effects of lead exposure on IQ are controlled, links between this exposure and so-called externalizing behavior problems remain (Chen, Cai, Detrich, Radcliffe, & Rogan, 2007). If ENA theory is correct, this latter finding suggests that executive functioning is also compromised by brain exposure to lead.

Criminologists should collaborate with other scientists to help reduce lead exposure for persons of all ages. They should also seek to identify other neurotoxins that may adversely affect learning ability and related aspects of human temperament. In this regard, prenatal exposure to manganese appears to enhance the symptoms of conduct-disordered behavior and ADHD (Ericson et al., 2007).

EEG Biofeedback

The brain is the most direct controller of behavior. Therefore, the brains of chronic offenders must be functioning in ways that significantly differ from the brains of nonoffenders. Some have proposed that it may be possible to use EEG biofeedback techniques to divert the brains of chronic offenders away from functioning patterns that are most conducive to offending (Raine, 1996, p. 56). So far, clinical research suggests that ADHD symptoms can be at least partially suppressed with biofeedback (reviewed by Monastra et al., 2005). Whether this can be extended into preventing delinquent and criminal behavior remains to be determined.

Eugenic Approaches

The biggest concern that many have surrounding biosocial criminology is that it could resurrect the twentieth-century eugenics movement and even Nazism. Despite the controversy, this section will explore how two social/governmental policies may in fact be having eugenic effects on criminality even though they were not specifically instituted for this purpose. The two policies to be explored are the U.S. legalization of abortion in the early 1970s and the dramatic increase in the rate of incarceration beginning in the 1980s.

The context within which this exploration takes place involves noting that the rate of crime, especially for violent crimes, began to decline in the United States in the early to mid-1990s, and this decline can only be partially explained in terms of shifts in population-age-related factors (Fox, 2000; Zimring, 2006). Similarly, the rates of child abuse have also declined substantially in this same time period (Finkelhor & Jones, 2006).

Because ENA theory is firmly embedded in evolutionary thinking, it inescapably assumes that genetic factors contribute to criminality. Therefore, curtailing the reproduction rates of persons with "crime-prone genes" relative to persons with few such genes should reduce a country's crime rates. Is there any evidence that political/governmental policies in the United States could have so altered people's reproduction rates as to have significantly impacted crime rates?

Abortion Legalization

In 1972, a Supreme Court decision known as *Roe v. Wade* legalized abortions in the United States. Since then, approximately one in six U.S. pregnancies have been terminated, roughly 1.2 million per year (Spitz et al., 1996), with the greatest proportion of terminations occurring in teenage pregnancies (Darroch, Singh, & Frost, 2001).

Beginning in the twenty-first century, research began to implicate the decriminalization of abortion as a possible contributor to the U.S. declining crime rate that became evident in the 1990s (Berk, Sorenson, Wiebe, & Upchurch, 2003; Donohue & Levitt, 2001; Joyce, 2004; Sorenson, Wiebe, & Berk, 2002; for an exception see Zimring, 2006). To explain how such a connection might occur, the main argument has been that women who were unprepared for motherhood (at least at the time they became pregnant) were most likely to obtain an abortion (Donohue & Levitt, 2001). This could cause a decrease in criminality in the next generation of children, as unwanted pregnancies and out-of-wedlock births are predictive of offspring criminality (Jonsson, 1967, p. 209; Kubicka et al., 1995; Walsh, 1990).

Eugenically speaking, an additional factor may be involved. Among both sexes, out-of-wedlock pregnancies may be most common among persons who have genetic propensities toward providing poor parental care to their offspring (Burt, Krueger, McGue, & Iacono, 2003; Perusse, Neale, Heath, & Eaves, 1994). Diminished parental care may increase the likelihood of criminal and antisocial behavior in offspring (Reiss et al., 1995). Another possibility is that many of the same genes that contribute to antisocial behavior also contribute to substandard parenting. In either case, offending-prone parents may have been considerably more likely to have terminated a pregnancy than parents in general, thereby lowering the proportion of children being born with antisocial tendencies.

Incarceration Rates

Prior to 1970, the United States incarceration rate was "only" about twice as high as other Western countries (Freeman, 1996), but in the late 1970s, imprisonment rates began climbing so that by the 1990s they were over five times higher (Tonry, 1999; Uggen & Manza, 2002).

Many factors may have contributed to the high and growing rate of U.S. incarceration. These include racism, poverty, out-of-wedlock parenthood, and increases in the availability of hard street drugs such as heroin and crack cocaine, all of which are arguably more prevalent in the United States than elsewhere in the Western world (Blumstein & Rosenfeld, 1998; Bridges & Crutchfield, 1988; Levitt, 1996). Setting aside the causes of high incarceration rates, the issue at hand is whether these rates may be so high as to actually impact the reproduction rates of offenders relative to the general population, thereby diminishing crime rates in subsequent generations.

Obviously, high incarceration rates may have deterrent and incapacitation effects (Levitt, 1996), but these would occur fairly soon (i.e., within two or three years) after an incarceration rate increase. The sort of effects at issue here would not be apparent until a new generation began to enter its crime-prone years (i.e., approximately fifteen years following birth). This line of reasoning is obviously not "politically correct," but it is worth considering in the context of evolutionary approaches to crime prevention.

So far, the evidence is difficult to assess, partly because crime statistics are influenced by numerous factors, not the least of which are changes in the proportions of offenses being reported to police (O'Brien, 1996). Also, if there are effects due to legalized abortion (as discussed above), these may be interacting with the effects of increased incarceration. Nevertheless, the decline in the U.S. crime rates throughout the 1990s (although irregularly), especially for violent offenses (Blumstein & Rosenfeld, 1998), is consistent with the view that it is at least partly the result of removing increasing proportions of offenders from contributing to the nation's gene pool beginning in the late 1970s.

Conclusion

This chapter describes the evolutionary neuroandrogenic (ENA) theory of criminal behavior, a theory that can be characterized in terms of two propositions, one evolutionary and the other neurohormonal. The evolutionary proposition states that criminality is part of a spectrum of largely male responses to female preferences for mates who are capable provisioners of resources. This spectrum is in the form of a neurologically programmed continuum of competitive/victimizing behavior patterns that vary from very crude (usually criminal) to very sophisticated (rarely criminal) behavior. Theoretically, at puberty, all males start near the crude end of the continuum, and as they mature they move toward more and more sophisticated expressions. Males who learn quickly will transition rapidly from crude to at least moderately sophisticated expressions. Those with low intelligence, learning disabilities, or few opportunities to practice competitive/victimizing behavior will transition more slowly.

According to the theory's second proposition, male brains on average are inclined more than female brains toward competitive/victimizing behavior as they are exposed to higher levels of testosterone and other androgens. Theoretically, the most permanent effects of androgens on brain functioning occur prior to birth, but the most dramatic behavioral activation of these perinatal effects awaits the surge in testosterone at puberty.

If the theory is true, three categories of treatment approaches to crime prevention or treatment should all have some beneficial effects. These categories are (1) social learning approaches, (2) pharmacological/neurological approaches, and (3) eugenic approaches. Examples of each of these three approaches are discussed. Overall, the theme of this chapter is that Darwinian evolutionary thinking is relevant not only to understanding criminal behavior but also to preventing and treating such behavior. Especially promising in recent years have been a number of pharmacological approaches to the prevention and treatment of antisocial precursors of criminality.

ACKNOWLEDGMENTS

I thank Dr. Kevin Beaver and Dr. Anthony Walsh for providing helpful comments on drafts of this chapter.

References

Anderson, G. S. (2007). *Biological influences on criminal behavior.* New York: CRC Press.

Baldessarini, R. J., Tondo, L., & Hennen, J. (1999). Effects of lithium treatment and its discontinuation on suicidal behavior in bipolar manic-depressive disorders. *Journal of Clinical Psychiatry, 60,* 77–84.

Bank, L., Marlowe, J. H., Reid, J. B., Patterson, G. R., & Weinrott, M. R. (1991). A comparative evaluation of parent-training interventions for families of chronic delinquents. *Journal of Abnormal Child Psychology, 19,* 15–33.

Baumeister, R. F., Heatherton, T. F., & Tice, D. M. (1994). *Losing control: How and why people fail at self-regulation.* San Diego, CA: Academic Press.

Beaver, K. M., Wright, J. P., & Delisi, M. (2007). Self-control as an executive function: Reformulating Gottfredson & Hirschi's parental socialization thesis. *Criminal Justice and Behavior, 34,* 1345–1361.

Bellinger, D. C., Needleman, H. L., Eden, A. N., Donohoe, M. T., Canfield, R. L., Henderson, C. R., et al. (2003). Intellectual impairment and blood lead levels. *New England Journal of Medicine, 349,* 500–502.

Berk, R., Sorenson, S., Wiebe, D., & Upchurch, D. (2003). The legalization of abortion and subsequent youth homicide: A time series analysis. *Analyses of Social Issues and Public Policy, 3,* 45–64.

Birger, M., Swartz, M., Cohen, D., Alesh, Y., Grishpan, C., & Kotelr, M. (2003). Aggression: The testosterone-serotonin link. *Israeli Medical Association Journal, 5*, 653–657.

Blumstein, A., & Rosenfeld, R. (1998). Explaining recent trends in U.S. homicide rates. *Journal of Criminal Law and Criminology, 88*, 1175–1216.

Bridges, G. S., & Crutchfield, R. D. (1988). Law, social standing, and racial disparities in imprisonment. *Social Forces, 66*, 699–724.

Burt, S. A., Krueger, R. F., McGue, M., & Iacono, W. (2003). Parent-child conflict and the comorbidity among childhood externalizing disorders. *Archives of General Psychiatry, 60*, 505–513.

Campbell, M., Rapoport, J. L., & Simpson, G. M. (1999). Antipsychotics in children and adolescents. *Journal of the American Academy of Child and Adolescent Psychiatry, 38*, 537–545.

Campbell, M., Small, A. M., Green, W. H., Jennings, S. J., Perry, R., & Bennett, W. G. (1984). Behavioral efficacy of haloperidol and lithium carbonate. A comparison in hospitalized aggressive children with conduct disorder children. *Archives of General Psychiatry, 41*, 650–656.

Canfield, R. L., Kreher, D. A., Cornwell, C., & Henderson, C. R. (2003). Low-level lead exposure, executive functioning, and learning in early childhood. *Child Neuropsychology, 9*, 35–53.

Chen, A., Cai, B., Detrich, K. N., Radcliffe, J., & Rogan, W. J. (2007). Lead exposure, IQ, and behavior in urban 5- to 7-year olds: Does lead affect behavior only by lowering IQ? *Pediatrics, 119*, 650–658.

Darroch, J. E., Singh, S., & Frost, J. J. (2001). Differences in teenage pregnancy rates among five developed countries: The roles of sexual activity and contraceptive use. *Family Planning Perspectives, 33*, 244–250, 281.

Davidson, R. J., Purtnam, K. M., & Larson, C. L. (2000). Dysfunction in the neural circuitry of emotion regulation: A possible prelude to violence. *Science, 289*, 591–594.

Devinsky, O., Ronsaville, D., Cox, C., Witt, E., Fedio, P., & Theodore, W. H. (1994). Interictal aggression in epilepsy: The Buss-Durkee hostility inventory. *Epilepsia, 35*, 585–590.

Dietrich, K. N., Ris, M. D., Succop, P. A., Berger, R. L., & Bornschein, R. L. (2001). Early exposure to lead and juvenile delinquency. *Neurotoxicology and Teratology, 23*, 511–518.

Dolan, M., Deakin, W. J. F., Roberts, N., & Anderson, I. (2002). Serotonergic and cognitive impairment in impulsive aggressive personality disordered offenders: Are there implications for treatment? *Psychological Medicine, 32*, 105–117.

Donohue, J., & Levitt, S. (2001). The impact of legalized abortion on crime. *Quarterly Journal of Economics, 116*, 379–420.

Donovan, S. J., Susser, E. S., & Nunes, E. V. (1997). Divalproex treatment of disruptive adolescents: A report of 10 cases. *Journal of Clinical Psychiatry, 58*, 12–15.

Dougherty, D. D., Rauch, S. L., Deckersbach, T., Marci, C., Loh, R., Shin, L. M., et al. (2004). Ventromedial prefrontal cortex and amygdala dysfunction during an anger induction positron emission tomography study in patients with major depressive disorder with anger attacks. *Archives of General Psychiatry, 61*, 795–804.

Ellis, L. (2001). The biosocial female choice theory of social stratification. *Social Biology, 48*, 297–319.

Ellis, L. (2003). Biosocial theorizing and criminal justice policy. In A. Somit & S. Peterson (Eds.), *Human nature and public policy: An evolutionary approach* (pp. 97–120). New York: Palgrave.

Ellis, L. (2004). Sex, status, and criminality: A theoretical nexus. *Social Biology, 51*, 144–160.

Ellis, L. (2005). Theoretically explaining biological correlates of criminal behavior. *European Journal of Criminology, 2*, 287–315.

Ellis, L., Hershberger, S., Field, E., Wersinger, S., Pellis, S., Geary, D., et al. (2008). *Sex differences: Findings from more than a century of scientific research.* New York: Psychology Press (Taylor and Francis).

Ericson, J., Crinella, K., Clarke-Stewart, A., Allhusen, V., Chan, T., & Robertson, R. (2007). Prenatal manganese levels linked to childhood behavioral disinhibition. *Neurotoxicology Teratology, 29*, 181–187.

Farrington, D. P. (1987). Early precursors of frequent offending. In J. Q. Wilson & G. C. Loury (Eds.), *From children to citizens. Vol. 3: Families, schools, and delinquency prevention* (pp. 27–50). London: Springer-Verlag.

Fedoroff, J. P. (2004). Serotonergic drug treatment of deviant sex interests. *Sexual Abuse: A Journal of Research and Treatment, 6*, 105–121.

Feldmann, T. B. (2001). Bipolar disorder and violence. *Psychiatric Quarterly, 72*, 119–129.

Findling, R. L., McNamara, N. K., Branicky, L. A., Schluchter, M. D., Lemon, E., & Blumer, J. L. (2000). A double-blind pilot study of risperidone in the treatment of conduct disorder. *Journal of the American Academy of Child and Adolescent Psychiatry, 39*(4), 509–516.

Fink, G., Sumner, B., & Rosie, R. (1999). Androgen actions on central serotonin neurotransmission: Relevance for mood, mental state and memory. *Behavioral Brain Research, 105*, 53–68.

Finkelhor, D., & Jones, L. (2006). Why have child maltreatment and child victimization declined? *Journal of Social Issues, 62*, 685–716.

Fox, J. A. (2000). Demographics and U.S. homicide. In A. Blumstein & J. Wallman (Eds.), *The crime drop in America* (pp. 288–318). Cambridge: Cambridge University Press.

Freeman, R. B. (1996). Why do so many young American men commit crimes and what might we do about it? *Journal of Economic Perspectives, 10*, 25–42.

Garland, E. J. (1998). Reviews: Pharmacotherapy of adolescent attention deficit hyperactivity disorder: Challenges, choices and caveats. *Journal of Psychopharmacology, 12*(4), 385–395.

Geary, D. C. (2000). Evolution and proximate expression of human paternal investment. *Psychological Bulletin, 126*, 55–77.

Gottfredson, M. R., & Hirschi, T. (1990). *A general theory of crime.* Stanford, CA: Stanford University Press.

Grossman, J. B., & Tierney, J. P. (1998). Does mentoring work? An impact study of the Big BrothersBig Sisters program. *Evaluation Review, 22*, 403–426.

Grossman, L. S., Martis, B., & Fichtner, C. G. (1999). Are sex offenders treatable? A research overview. *Psychiatric Service, 50*, 349–361.

Hansen, H. (1991). *Treatment of dangerous sex offenders.* Helsinki, Finland: Ministry of Justice, Government Printing Centre.

Hare, R. D. (1993). *Without conscience: The disturbing world of psychopaths among us.* New York: Pocket Books.

Harrer, G., & Kofler-Westergren, B. (1986). Depression and criminality. *Psychopathology, 19* supplement 2, 215–219.

Harrington, R. C., & Bailey, S. (2003). *The scope for preventing antisocial personality disorder by intervening in adolescence.* Manchester, England: National Programme on Forensic Mental Health R&D Seminar.

Henry, B., Moffitt, T. E., & Silva, P. A. (1992). Disentangling delinquency and learning disability: Neuropsychological function and social support. *International Journal of Clinical Neuropsychology, 13*, 1–6.

Hinshaw, S. P., & Erhardt, D. (1991). Attention-deficit hyperactivity disorder. In P. C. Kendall (Ed.), *Child and adolescent therapy: Cognitive-behavioral procedures* (pp. 98–128). New York: Guilford Press.

Jonsson, G. (1967). Delinquent boys: Their parents and grandparents. *Acta Psychiatrica Scandinavia*, Supplement 43, 1–264.

Joyce, T. (2004). Did legalized abortion lower crime? *Journal of Human Resources, 39*, 1–28.

Kafantaris, V., Campbell, M., Padron-Gayol, M. V., Small, A., Locascio, J., & Rosenberg, C. R. (1992). Carbamazepine in hospitalized aggressive conduct-disordered children: An open pilot study. *Psychopharmacology Bulletin, 28*, 193–199.

Kalus, O., Asnis, G. M., & Van Praag, H. M. (1989). The role of serotonin in depression. *Psychiatric Annals, 19*, 348–353.

Kandel, D. B. (1982). Epidemiological and psychosocial perspectives on adolescent drug use. *Journal of Child Psychiatry, 21*, 328–347.

Kaplan, S. L., Busner, J., Kupietz, S., Wassermann, E., & Segal, B. (1990). Effects of methylphenidate on adolescents with aggressive conduct disorder and ADHD: A preliminary report. *Journal of the American Academy of Child and Adolescent Psychiatry, 29*, 719–723.

Kasper, S., & Muller-Spahn, F. (2000). Review of quetiapine and its clinical applications in schizophrenia. *Expert Opinion on Pharmacotherapy, 1*, 783–801.

Klein, N. C., Alexander, J. F., & Parsons, B. V. (1977). Impact of family systems intervention on recidivism and sibling delinquency: A model of primary prevention and program evaluation. *Journal of Consulting and Clinical Psychology, 3*, 469–474.

Klein, R. G., Abikoff, H., Klass, E., Ganeles, D., Seese, L. M., & Pollack, S. (1997). Clinical efficacy of methylphenidate in conduct disorder with and without attention deficit hyperactivity disorder. *Archives of General Psychiatry, 54*, 469–474.

Kubicka, L., Matejcek, Z., David, H. P., Dytrych, Z., Miller, W. B., & Roth, Z. (1995). Children from unwanted pregnancies in Prague, Czech Republic, revisited at age thirty. *Acta Psychiatrica Scandinavica, 91*, 361–369.

Levitt, S. D. (1996). The effect of prison population size on crime rates: Evidence from prison overcrowding litigation. *Quarterly Journal of Economics, 111*, 319–351.

Liu, S., & Cunningham, K. A. (2005). Serotonin2c receptors (5-ht2c r) control expression of cocaine-induced conditioned hyperactivity. *Drug and Alcohol Dependence, 81*, 275–282.

Lynam, D., Moffitt, T. E., & Stouthamer-Loeber, M. (1993). Explaining the relation between IQ and delinquency: Class, race, test motivation, school failure, or self control? *Journal of Abnormal Psychology, 102*, 187–196.

Maletzky, B. M., Tolan, A., & McFarland, B. (2006). The Oregon depo-Provera program: A five-year follow-up. *Sexual Abuse: A Journal of Research and Treatment, 18*, 303–316.

Malone, R. P., Delaney, M. A., Luebbert, J. F., Cater, J., & Campbell, M. (2000). A double-blind placebo-controlled study of lithium in hospitalized aggressive children and adolescents with conduct disorder. *Archives of General Psychiatry, 57*(7), 649–654.

Marsh, L., & Krauss, G. L. (2000). Aggression and violence in patients with epilepsy. *Epilepsy & Behavior, 1*, 160–168.

Mattes, J. A. (1990). Comparative effectiveness of carbamazepine and propranolol for rage outbursts. *Journal of Neuropsychiatry and Clinical Neuroscience, 2*, 159–164.

Matykiewicz, L., La Grange, L., Vance, P., Wang, M., & Reyes, E. (1997). Adjudicated adolescent males: Measures of urinary 5-hydroxyindoleacetic acid and reactive hypoglycemia. *Personality and Individual Differences, 22,* 327–332.

Mauro, C. F., & Harris, Y. R. (2000). The influence of maternal child-rearing attitudes and teaching behaviors on preschoolers' delay of gratification. *Journal of General Psychology, 161,* 292–306.

McMahon, R. J., & Wells, K. C. (1998). Conduct problems. In E. J. Mash & R. A. Barkley (Eds.), *Treatment of childhood disorders* (pp. 111–207). New York: Guilford.

Moffitt, T. E. (1997). Adolescence-limited and life-course-persistent offending: A complementary pair of developmental theories. In T. P. Thornberry (Ed.), *Developmental theories of crime and delinquency* (pp. 11–54). New Brunswick, NJ: Transaction.

Moffitt, T. E., Silva, P. A., Lynam, D. R., & Henry, B. (1994). Self-reported delinquency at age 18: New Zealand's Dunedin multidisciplinary health and development study. In J. Junger-Tas, G.-J. Terlouw, & M. W. Klein (Eds.), *Delinquent behavior among young people in the western world: First results of the international self-report delinquency study* (pp. 354–369). Amsterdam: Kugler.

Monastra, V. J., Lynn, S., Linden, M., Lubar, J. F., Gruzelier, J., & LaVaque, T. J. (2005). Electroencephalographic biofeedback in the treatment of attention-deficit/hyperactivity disorder. *Applied Psychophysiology and Biofeedback, 30*(2), 95–114.

Morgan, A. P., & Lilienfeld, S. O. (2000). A meta-analytic review of the relation between antisocial behavior and neuropsychological measures of executive function. *Clinical Psychology Review, 20,* 113–156.

Needleman, H. L., McFarland, C., Ness, R. B., Fienberg, S. E., & Tobin, M. J. (2002). Bond lead levels in adjudicated delinquents: A case control study. *Neurotoxicology and Teratology, 24,* 711–717.

Nevin, R. (2000). How lead exposure relates to temporal changes in IQ, violent crime, and unwed pregnancy. *Environmental Research, 83*(1), 1–22.

O'Brien, R. M. (1996). Police productivity and crime rates 1973–1992. *Criminology, 34,* 183–207.

Patterson, G. R., & Stouthamer-Loeber, M. (1984). The correlation of family management practices and delinquency. *Child Development, 55,* 1299–1307.

Pelham, W. E., Aronoff, H. R., Midlam, J. K., Shapiro, C. J., Gnagy, E. M., Chronis, A. M., et al. (1999). A comparison of Ritalin and Adderall: Efficacy and time-course in children with attention-deficit/hyperactivity disorder. *Pediatrics, 103*(4), 43–57.

Perusse, D., Neale, M. C., Heath, A. C., & Eaves, L. J. (1994). Human parental behavior: Evidence for genetic influence and potential implications for gene-culture transmission. *Behavior Genetics, 24,* 327–335.

Pinker, S. (2002). *The blank slate: The modern denial of human nature.* New York: Viking.

Plaznik, A., Kostowski, W., & Archer, T. (1989). Serotonin and depression: Old problems and new data. *Progress in Neuro-Psychopharmacology and Biochemical Psychiatry, 13,* 623–633.

Polanczyk, G., Zeni, C., Genro, J. P., Guimaraes, A. P., Roman, T., Hutz, M. H., et al. (2007). Association of the adrenergic alpha 2a receptor gene with methylphenidate improvement of inattentive symptoms in children and adolescents with attention-deficit/hyperactivity disorder. *Archives of General Psychiatry, 64*(2), 218–224.

Post, R. M., Rubinow, D. R., & Uhde, T. W. (1984). Biochemical mechanisms of action of carbamazepine in affective illness and epilepsy. *Psychopharmacology Bulletin, 20,* 585–590.

Rafter, N. H. (2006). H. J. Eysenck in Fagin's kitchen: The return to biological theory in the 20th-century criminology. *History of the Human Sciences, 19,* 37–56.

Raine, A. (1996). Autonomic nervous system factors underlying disinhibited, antisocial, and violent behavior: Biosocial perspectives and treatment implications. *Annals of the New York Academy of Sciences, 794,* 46–59.

Raine, A., & Yang, Y. (2006). Neural foundations to moral reasoning and antisocial behavior. *Social Cognitive and Affective Neuroscience, 1,* 203–213.

Reiss, D., Hetherington, E. M., Plomin, R., Howe, G. W., Simmens, S. J., Henderson, S. H., et al. (1995). Genetic questions for environmental studies. Differential parenting and psychopathology in adolescence. *Archives of General Psychiatry, 52,* 925–936.

Reymert, M. L. (1940). Prevention of juvenile delinquency. *Journal of Exceptional Children, 6,* 300–303.

Rodriguez, M. (1993). Cognitive functioning, family history of alcoholism, and antisocial behavior in female polydrug abusers. *Psychological Reports, 73,* 19–26.

Rose, N. (2000). The biology of culpability: Pathological identity and crime control in a biological culture. *Theoretical Criminology, 4*(1), 5–34.

Rosler, A., & Witztum, E. (2000). Pharmacotherapy of paraphilias in the next millennium. *Behavioral Sciences & the Law, 18,* 43–56.

Shader, R. I., Jackson, A. H., & Dodes, L. M. (1974). The antiaggressive effects of lithium in man. *Psychopharmacology, 40,* 17–24.

Sheard, M. H. (1984). Clinical pharmacology of aggressive behavior. *Clinical Neuropharmacology, 7,* 173–183.

Sheard, M. H., Marini, J. L., Bridges, C. I., & Wagner, E. (1976). The effect of lithium on impulsive aggressive behavior in man. *American Journal of Psychiatry, 133,* 1409–1413.

Simons, R. L., Wu, C. I., Conger, R. D., & Lorenz, F. O. (1994). Two routes to delinquency: Differences between early and late starters in the impact of parenting and deviant peers. *Criminology, 32,* 247–276.

Solhkhah, R., Wilens, T., Daly, J., Prince, J., Van Patten, S., & Biederman, J. (2005). Bupropion SR for the treatment of substance-abusing outpatient adolescents with attention-deficit/hyperactivity disorder and mood disorders. *Journal of Child and Adolescent Psychopharmacology, 15,* 777–786.

Sorenson, S., Wiebe, D., & Berk, R. (2002). Legalized abortion and the homicide of young children: An empirical investigation. *Analyses of Social Issues and Public Policy, 2,* 239–256.

Spitz, A. M., Velebil, P., Koonin, L., Strauss, L. T., Goodman, K. A., Wingo, P., et al. (1996). Pregnancy, abortion, and birth rates among U.S. adolescents—1980, 1985, and 1990. *Obstetrical & Gynecological Survey, 51,* 659–660.

Staller, J. A. (2007). Psychopharmacologic treatment of aggressive preschoolers: A chart review. *Progress in Neuropsychopharmacology and Biological Psychiatry, 31*(1), 131–135.

Strayhorn, J. M. (2002a). Self-control: Theory and research. *Journal of the American Academy of Child and Adolescent Psychiatry, 41,* 7–16.

Strayhorn, J. M. (2002b). Self-control: Toward systematic training programs. *Journal of the American Academy of Child and Adolescent Psychiatry, 41,* 17–27.

Sullivan, M. A., & Rudnik-Levin, F. (2001). Attention deficit/hyperactivity disorder and substance abuse: Diagnostic and therapeutic considerations. *Annals of the New York Academy of Sciences, 931*(1), 251–270.

Swanson, J. M., McBurnett, K., Christian, D. L., & Wigal, T. (1995). Stimulant medication and treatment of children with ADHD. In T. H. Ollendick & R. J. Prinz (Eds.), *Advances in clinical child psychology* (Vol. 17, pp. 265–322). New York: Plenum.

Swanson, J. M., Wigal, S., Greenhill, L., Browne, R., Waslick, B., Lerner, M., et al. (1998). Objective and subjective measures of the pharmacodynamic effects of Adderall in the treatment of children with ADHD in a controlled laboratory classroom setting. *Psychopharmacology Bulletin, 34,* 55–60.

Targum, S. D., & Abbott, J. L. (2000). Efficacy of quetiapine in Parkinson's patients with psychosis. *Journal of Clinical Psychopharmacology, 20,* 54–60.

Tengstrom, A., Hodgins, S., Grann, M., Langstrom, N., & Kullgren, G. (2004). Schizophrenia and criminal offending. *Criminal Justice and Behavior, 31,* 367–391.

Tonry, M. (1999). Why are U.S. incarceration rates so high? *Crime and Delinquency, 45,* 419–437.

Trimble, M. R., & van Elst, L. T. (2003). The amygdala and psychopathology studies in epilepsy. *Annals of the New York Academy of Sciences, 985,* 461–468.

Uggen, C., & Manza, J. (2002). Democratic contraction? Political consequences of felon disenfranchisement in the United States. *American Sociological Review, 67,* 777–803.

Virkkunen, M., Eggert, M., Rawlings, R., & Linnoila, M. (1996). A prospective follow-up study of alcoholic violent offenders and fire setters. *Archives of General Psychiatry, 53,* 523–529.

Walker, C., Thomas, J., & Allen, T. (2003). Treating impulsivity, irritability, and aggression of antisocial personality disorder with quetiapine. *International Journal of Offender Therapy and Comparative Criminology, 47,* 556–567.

Walsh, A. (1990). Illegitimacy, abuse and neglect, and cognitive development. *Journal of Genetic Psychology, 151,* 279–285.

Walsh, E., Buchanan, A., & Fahy, T. (2002). Violence and schizophrenia: Examining the evidence. *British Journal of Psychiatry, 180,* 490–495.

Wilcox, J. A. (1995). Divalproex sodium as a treatment for borderline personality disorder. *Annals of Clinical Psychiatry, 20,* 33–37.

Wille, R., & Beier, K. M. (1989). Castration in Germany. *Annals of Sex Research, 2,* 103–133.

Woermann, F. G., van Elst, L. T., Koepp, M. J., Free, S. L., Thompson, P. J., Trimble, M. R., et al. (2000). Reduction of frontal neocortical grey matter associated with affective aggression in patients with temporal lobe epilepsy: An objective voxel by voxel analysis of automatically segmented MRI. *Journal of Neurology, Neurosurgery, and Psychiatry, 68*(2), 162–169.

Woolfenden, S. R., Williams, K., & Peat, J. (2002). Family and parenting interventions for conduct disorder and delinquency: A meta-analysis of randomized controlled trials. *Archives of Diseases in Childhood, 86,* 251–256.

Worrell, J. A., & Marken, P. A. (2000). Atypical antipsychotic agents: A critical review. *American Journal of Health-System Pharmacy, 57,* 238–255.

Young, J. L., & Hillbrand, M. (1994). Carbamazepine lowers aggression: A review. *Bulletin of the American Academy of Psychiatry and the Law, 22,* 53–61.

Yuan, W., Holland, S. K., Cecil, K. M., Dietrich, K. N., Wessel, S. D., Altaye, M., et al. (2006). The impact of early childhood lead exposure on brain organization: A functional magnetic resonance imaging study of language function. *Pediatrics, 118,* 971–977.

Zimring, F. (2006). *The great American crime decline.* New York: Oxford University Press.

14

Did the Victim Deserve to Die?

Darwin Goes to Court

J. ANDERSON THOMSON JR.

The real voyage of discovery consists not in seeking new landscapes but in having new eyes.
—Marcel Proust

Not long ago, at an annual meeting of trial attorneys, a famous criminal defense lawyer who made his reputation by defending accused murderers spoke about defendants' rights. During the questioning phase, he was asked how he approached a capital murder case. He paused and then said, "I approach a murder case by asking myself two questions. Did the victim deserve to die? And, was the defendant the right man for the job?"

The audience burst out laughing. But laughter quickly changed to nervous chuckling when the group realized he was serious. He approached each murder case with those questions firmly in mind. This attorney is not the originator of those questions, nor is he the only person to think that way. The Texas Constitution once had an amendment nicknamed the "He needed killin'" clause. That someone "needed killin'" was—and some say still is—a valid defense in a Texas courtroom.

The lawyer's answer to the question of how he approached a capital murder case reflects what we all now know: murder can be natural and understandable. Through the lenses of evolutionary psychology, we can see how homicide may be produced by design features of human minds, particularly men's minds (Buss, 2005; also see Chapter 3 of this volume). But I didn't know that when I heard the famous lawyer speak. I trained as a psychiatrist in the 1970s. My background is in psychodynamics, psychoanalysis, general psychiatry, and traditional forensic psychiatry. In the early days of my career, when someone committed murder, my colleagues and I believed that psychopathology caused the violence. Murder meant madness. Who in his "right mind" would kill? Now we know that there are parts of the mind that originated much further back in deep time that can make killing quite natural, given our species' evolutionary history.

Shortly after hearing the attorney's speech, I was asked to evaluate Willie, a 19-year-old single man who, with his 17-year-old half-brother Steve, killed his father. The father arrived home one afternoon with his fourth wife, the defendants' stepmother, to be met by a hail of bullets from Willie and Steve. Willie fired the first shots, which killed his father. Steve shot seconds later and struck the stepmother, who survived but was made paraplegic, wheelchair bound for life by Steve's bullets.

The young men gathered up their father's gun collection and fled. Their father was a relatively poor man, an auto mechanic, but he had built a gun collection of considerable value relative to his lot in life. State police soon caught Willie and Steve in North Carolina. They were charged with multiple firearm offenses and with capital murder. They faced the death penalty.

Willie's capital-murder-certified attorneys asked my partner and me to evaluate their client. I told them about the famous trial lawyer's approach to murder cases, and they decided to use it. Willie and Steve's father truly was a monster. His modus operandi remained consistent throughout his adult life. He raped a 13- or 14-year-old girl and then married his victim. After having one or more children with his victim-turned-wife, he discarded her and moved on to more fertile fields. Several of his former wives came forth at the trial to testify about his monstrous nature. Auto mechanics who worked with him testified that during work hours, even in the sweltering summers, he kept whoever was his current wife and their youngest children in his car in the parking lot of whichever auto dealer then employed him. He physically and sexually abused all of his children, male and female alike, including both of the defendants. Emergency room records surfaced on my defendant and confirmed one early episode of sexual abuse, even though Willie did not remember that particular incident.

A psychiatric examination of Willie indicated that he suffered chronic depression and post-traumatic stress disorder (PTSD). All of that was presented at trial. Willie's attorneys portrayed him as a victim who was protecting the family and ridding them of a dangerous and potentially deadly man. They implied that Willie shot the father to protect Steve. The father had sexually abused Steve several months before the killing. Willie knew this, and indeed, Steve still may have been in the father's cross hairs. Abuse caused the murders. Protection of the family was paramount. Revenge was implied. Parent–offspring conflict and theft were ignored.

A Transitional Species

Before we continue to Willie's fate, I offer thanks to the editors of this volume, Joshua Duntley and Todd Shackelford, for inviting a practicing forensic psychiatrist to contribute. Unbeknown to them, they asked a transitional species to weigh in as this new field of evolutionary forensic psychology emerges. Thanks to a good friend and gifted lawyer, Willis Spaulding, who gave me Robert Wright's *The Moral Animal* ten years ago, the lens of evolutionary psychology now influences my clinical and forensic practices. Wright's book ushered in a sea change in my understanding of human behavior, psychology, psychiatry, psychopathology, and, in this instance, how I approach forensic cases. This opportunity gives me, as just one forensic practitioner, the opportunity to share my views of the current impact and future directions of evolutionary forensic psychology. In this chapter I illustrate my points with my own cases, such as Willie's capital murder case.

As Owen Jones notes, the law is about human behavior. To the degree that we have an accurate understanding of human nature, the law will be more effective. There is almost no area of the law where psychology, clinical psychology, and psychiatry fail to have impact. Clinicians are asked to determine competence to stand trial (CST) and mental state at the time of the offense (MSO). Within our justice system, every criminal defendant now has a constitutional right to a psychiatric evaluation (*Ake v. Oklahoma*). Sex offenders are mandated by law to have psychiatric or psychological evaluations and treatment. In domestic relations courts, partner violence, child abuse, divorce, and child custody and visitation require clinicians' reports and testimony. Parent–offspring conflict always surfaces in trust and estates litigation and in the frequent challenges to wills.

There are few judges, civil litigators, criminal defense lawyers, prosecutors, and clinicians familiar with evolutionary psychology. That will change as evolutionary psychology becomes part of mainstream psychology. Future college graduates who choose legal professions will know more about the discipline of evolutionary psychology. As clinical programs incorporate more of an evolutionary perspective, future forensic clinicians will both need and utilize it in ways we are beginning to see, and which are discussed in the preceding chapters.

Willie's Fate

Willie and Steve were convicted of second-degree murder, a victory for the defendants and their attorneys. All of us involved in the case came away with the impression that had the stepmother not been permanently paralyzed, the young men would have received an even lesser sentence.

At the time of the trial, I certainly believed, "to a reasonable degree of medical certainty," that Willie's depression, PTSD, and the horrendous abuse suffered at the hands of his father *caused* the father's murder and the stepmother's malicious wounding. Since learning evolutionary psychology, I have reason to reevaluate that conclusion. The murder was premeditated. The defendants' behavior and the history of the case suggest that these impoverished boys, consciously or not, were concerned about the distribution of sparse paternal assets. Their motives are better understood through parent–offspring conflict, a concept unknown to me at the time. Willie had lost his job shortly before the murder and needed money; this is a more immediate motive, and one in keeping with what we now know. Willie had years of ample opportunity and provocation to exact revenge or protect his siblings from the father's predation. Why did he kill when he did?

What evolutionary psychology helps one see in Willie's case may be character-ized as intentionality, which, for Willie, involved the pursuit of fundamental adaptive goals. "Intent" in criminal law comprises concepts of *mens rea*, a mental state inferred from conduct, and *actus reus*, a voluntary act. When there is a claim of "automatism" (in cases of involuntary intoxication, temporal lobe epilepsy, dissociative reactions to medication, etc.), the forensic evaluation usually focuses on the *actus reus*. Whether *mens rea* was impaired is not an issue.

Many crimes, most notably homicide, are graded in terms of "intent," with first-degree murder requiring proof of the highest level of intent, "malice aforethought." Capital murder requires proof of other aggravating circumstances not directly involving intent beyond malice aforethought. Capital murder defendants, however, may offer by way of defense *any* evidence of impaired intent. By contrast, most non-capital criminal defendants may not use expert testimony to mitigate or negate crim-inal intent unless it is done in the form of an insanity defense.

An insanity defense in most states concedes that the requisite criminal intent existed but that intent, in ways defined by the applicable law, was affected by mental disorder to such an extent that the defendant is nonetheless not guilty "by reason of insanity." The insanity defense is thus called the NGRI (not guilty by reason of insan-ity) or MSO (mental state at the time of the offense).

There is a long, rich history of insanity standards:

Wild beast test (Rex, B. Arnold, 1724). A man must be totally deprived of his understanding and memory so as not to know what he is doing any more than an infant, a brute, or a wild beast.

Irresistible impulse test (*Regina v. Oxford*, 1940). If some controlling disease was, in truth, the acting power within him, which he could not resist, then the defendant will not be held responsible.

McNaghten rule (*McNaghten's Case*, 1743). A mental disease or defect at the time of the act that caused the defendant not to know the nature and quality or the wrongfulness of the act.

Durham rule (*Durham v. United States*, 1954). The accused is not criminally responsible if his unlawful act is the product of a mental disease or defect.

Model Penal Code (American Law Institute, 1955). A person is not responsible for criminal conduct if at the time of such conduct, as a result of mental disease or defect, he lacked substantial capacity to appreciate the wrongfulness of his conduct (cognitive arm) or to conform his conduct to the requirements of the law (volitional arm). (Adapted from Simon & Gold, 2004.)

In my state, and in many others, the traditional McNaghten rule together with some version of the irresistible impulse defense guides assessment. In conducting an evaluation, a clinician has to assess the evidence of mental illness at the time of the evaluation, at the time of the offense, and in the time prior to the offense. Simple presence of a mental illness is not necessarily sufficient. A clinician then has to determine evidence for impaired functioning within a few days of the offense and at the time of the offense. The motive for the offense must be determined to the extent possible. The clinician attempts to gain a detailed understanding of the criminal defendant's thinking and behavior before, during, and after the offense. Also taken into consideration is the prior legal history of the defendant.

The particular legal rules of the jurisdiction in which the evaluation is conducted have two principal effects, one of which is more speculative than the other. The first effect is to act as a guide to and sometimes a restraint on the testimony of a forensic expert. Can the expert witness testify as to intent apart from an insanity defense? Can the witness express an opinion on the "ultimate" issue of whether the defendant is "insane"? Must the witness express the opinion in terms of "reasonable medical certainty"? The answer to these questions will differ from jurisdiction to jurisdiction and from court to court within those jurisdictions. Knowing the answers to these questions—and the referring attorney may not always know the answers—is of course important in conducting and reporting the results of an evaluation, but not as important as the second effect, or lack of effect, of the legal rules.

The second effect of the rules comes in the form of jury instructions, which state the law to the jury at the conclusion of the trial and by which they are supposed to reach a decision. The jury, particularly on questions of credibility, on which point expert testimony is almost always prohibited, does what nature, not the law, dictates.

An understanding of evolutionary psychology better enables the forensic evaluator to speak to the real concerns of the jury (or, in the absence of a jury, the judge). Legal rules are institutionalized versions of our rules of thumb or heuristics, products of human evolution no less than an upright gait or speech.

Litigation is an elaborate system of "cheater detection," a basic condition of human sociality, which enables us to determine, for example, whether to punish or reward another who appears not to reciprocate our generosity.

One of the rules of thumb that we use in cheater detection, and indeed in responding to other threats of harm, is that "intentional" acts can be deterred by punishment more than nonintentional acts. Another basic rule of thumb is to help rather than punish someone whose lack of reciprocity is somehow related to his or her sickness. Regardless of the legal rules, evolutionary psychology suggests that these are the rules that juries struggle with.

But sickness and intent can overlap, putting these two rules of thumb in conflict. It is the job of the evaluator to reconcile them. When I was working with Willie, it was difficult for me to see anything other than the mental disorder. The adaptive, albeit primitive, goals achieved by the murder are easier to spot from the long view of evolution, and indeed some real mental disorders, such as depression or dissociation, may themselves be ways of achieving adaptive goals. Of course, the mental disorder may be feigned, but it's not that simple to reconcile the two rules of thumb regarding intentionality and sickness. Both can be present.

It is not simple because a very ill defendant can know both "nature and consequence" and the difference between right and wrong. Todd, a young man with untreated paranoid schizophrenia, believed that two tourists who sat eating ice cream by a university were sent by the Central Intelligence Agency to spy on him. He assaulted both of them and fled. He knew the nature of what he was doing—that is, striking them with his fists. He also knew the consequences: the police would be called. He knew it was wrong to hit someone, but he believed he had no alternative and acted in perceived self-defense. He was found not guilty by reason of insanity.

The crucial areas, once a severe mental illness is identified, are the defendant's ability not only to know the difference between right and wrong but also to refrain from the action. The tangled web of mental disease or defect and impairment of the knowledge of wrongfulness will certainly benefit from an evolutionary perspective. Krebs's (Chapter 12 in this volume) and others' ideas on the evolution of morality need to be applied to this prong of the insanity defense. A basic, ancient, evolved sense of right and wrong is not easily overridden even by the severest of mental illnesses. Individuals who most of us agree should fall under the protection of an insanity defense can fail to secure its protection because of the way laws are written and interpreted. Andrea Yates, the Texas mother who killed her children, was undoubtedly psychotic at the time of the offense. All the experts on both sides of the case agreed on the severity of her mental illness, but by law the focus needed to be on her ability to tell right from wrong. The testifying forensic psychiatrists' disagreements centered on her ability to know the wrongfulness of her acts. Her insanity defense initially failed in 2002, and she was convicted of capital murder. Due to the false testimony of Park Dietz, one of the prosecution's forensic psychiatrists, her conviction was overturned, and in 2006 she was finally acquitted by reason of insanity.[1] Even in Texas, even when psychosis was obvious, the jury struggled with the idea that young children "needed killin'." The teachings of evolutionary psychology about the adaptive nature of infanticide might have made this act easier to understand.

Rape and Sexual Coercion

Evolutionary psychology, through the work of legal scholars such as Owen Jones (1999) and investigators such as Randy Thornhill and Craig Palmer (2000), the Gottschalls (2003), McKibbin et al. (Chapter 6 in this volume), and others, has advanced our understanding of rape. We can now discern the adaptive logic of rape more than that of many other crimes.

One of my duties is to conduct the forensic evaluations at a local community mental health center. Within the space of several months, two defendants were charged with rape, and evaluations were ordered for both. Each case was unusual, the likes of which I had never seen, and that there were two of them simultaneously was especially surprising.

The facts of the cases were almost identical. Both defendants had followed a lone young woman unknown to them to her apartment, broken in, and raped her. Because the rapes occurred at night, neither woman was able to give a clear description of her assailant, identify him from pictures, or provide enough details to generate an artist's approximation. However, that turned out to be unnecessary: within several weeks of each attack, the perpetrators returned to the apartment of their particular victim, knocked on the door, and politely asked the victim for a date. That led to positive identification, confessions, and two convictions. Neither young man had identifiable major psychopathology. They genuinely had no conception of the harm caused by their attack. They truly believed their victims might have found the experience pleasurable and might be interested in a relationship. Their self-deception was breathtaking in its cruelty and stupidity.

At the time of those evaluations, my earlier training held sway. With both cases, I concluded that the defendant did not suffer from any major psychopathology, and neither case yielded a plausible explanation.

The traditional view—that rape has a contributing or causative psychopathology—is so ingrained in the system that the following case was sent to me. A young man, John, came to Charlottesville, Virginia, with no unusual developmental history. He was born to an intact family and was educated. He dropped out of college after two years. A long-term girlfriend broke up with him shortly before he settled in Charlottesville, which is dominated by the University of Virginia. John worked below his intellectual capacity at a pizza restaurant, where the workers partied hard. John frequently drank to excess after closing the restaurant.

On one such work night, John planned to meet friends for late-night drinks. He began to drink before he drove to rendezvous with them. When his friends failed to show at the chosen bar, he set out to look for them. He first went to one friend's apartment, but the friend was not there. However, the friend's girlfriend was there with their infant child. She told the defendant that her partner, his drinking buddy, had gone out to party. John was already intoxicated. He forced her upstairs and, while she was bent over on the bed, lying over her child to protect the little boy, raped her; he then fled. Later he told me that he had immediately realized what he had done and felt intense shame and guilt. He fled in his car toward Richmond, sixty miles east. Acute remorse made him drive onto the shoulder of the interstate and stop. He decided to turn himself in, and he called the police.

At the preliminary hearing, the judge was stunned and insisted there must be something terribly wrong with John. Only a very ill young man, he emphasized, could rape a friend's girlfriend, whom he barely knew and toward whom he allegedly held no animosity, and do so in the presence of her child. The judge ordered the psychiatric evaluation before the defense attorney moved to request it.

John suffered no major mental illness or personality disorder, and could be given no Axis I or Axis II diagnosis. John remembered meeting the victim only once before the rape and had only the vaguest recollection of that occasion. When he met her, he remembered thinking she was attractive, but he maintained that she made no large or lasting impression. The evaluation brought forth some evidence to suggest that John might have been depressed at the time of the rape, feeling like his life was on a downward trajectory. But by the time of the evaluation, he was depressed by his charges and his life in jail. Determining his level of depression before the rape was problematic. He knew he was drinking excessively, but that was all. There were no long-standing psychiatric symptoms, personality disorder, hatred of women, or any of the usual explanations for rape. Even though John pled guilty, the presence of the child at the time of the offense contributed to his receiving a long prison sentence.

One of my roles is staff psychiatrist at the university's student health center. Date rape occurs often. When the perpetrator is known to the mental health staff, a consistent finding is no major psychopathology or even a consistent type of personality disorder. How does one understand such behavior?

In the AEP years of my life (after evolutionary psychology), my reading of the literature and such rape cases convince me that rape is an adaptation, not a by-product of male sexual aggressiveness. Owen Jones's (1999) superlative law review article, although neutral on the "adaptation versus by-product" debate, lays out the evidence for rape as an adaptation. Randy Thornhill and Craig Palmer's (2000) book convinced me of Thornhill's position that rape is produced by psychological adaptation. The Gottschalls' (2003) evidence that there are increased pregnancy rates with rape relative to consensual sex adds additional evidence. Women's evolved mechanisms for avoiding rape suggest that rape lurked as an ever-present threat in ancestral environments. If we look at the large disparity between the sexes in parental investment, would we not be surprised if *Homo sapiens* males contained no rape adaptation? The disparity in parental investment in our species provides fertile soil for the evolution of a mechanism to override female choice.

What are the implications for the evaluation of a defendant charged with murder or rape? The forensic clinician should now look at psychopathology as just one of a multitude of factors that influence a defendant to deploy the adaptations for killing or rape. Stupidity, personality disorders, depression, substance abuse, and even psychosis may impair cost/benefit decision making, causing a young man like John to deploy what was once adaptive behavior: ensuring survival of his DNA through a forced coupling with a woman already shown to be fertile.

In short, and in any case involving both mental illness and adaptive behavior, it would behoove those of us who practice forensic psychiatry to look at the illness as something that triggers the behavior that is in our civilized society criminal but which was once adaptive. We can consider it as a sort of mental "oncogene"—many people have the genetic potential for various cancers, but most researchers now realize that there may be some trigger that turns a normal gene into an oncogene and begins the abnormal cell division. The relationship between psychopathology and adaptive behavior may be the same.

Domestic Violence

> Papa loved Mamma.
> Mamma loved men.
> Mamma's in the graveyard.
> Papa's in the pen.

Male sexual jealousy, arguably another aspect of cheater detection, is the most combustible element in domestic violence. Yet it is remarkable that such a relatively simple concept has been ignored in teaching professionals how to conduct forensic evaluations, although daytime talk shows that offer public revelations of DNA paternity tests are oddly popular and can clearly show the doubt and anger that can arise from a man's concern that he has been deceived—or, in the sense of adaptation, that the DNA carried in a child is not his.

No defendant has ever volunteered to me that he was unsure his children were his own or that he believed his mate to be unfaithful. The most obvious and common shift in my forensic assessments since learning of evolutionary psychology has been to begin asking the relevant in-depth questions on fidelity and paternity. Does the defendant think his partner has been unfaithful in the past, is unfaithful in the present, and/or might be unfaithful in the future? Has he ever harbored doubts about the paternity of his children? Such questions never fail to reveal information that would remain hidden had the questions not been asked—information that invariably influences the psychiatric conclusions.

Bill, a 30-year-old manual laborer, was charged with burning down his home. He did have a psychotic illness, probably a bipolar illness, though we debated that. Most clinicians on the staff emphasized his bipolar illness as the explanation for his crime. But on close questioning he revealed doubts about his wife's faithfulness and the paternity of one of their children. In my opinion, that was the real spark for his arson.

Larry, a man who had no prior criminal history but did have a history of depression and suicidal threats in earlier years, incurred within the space of six months numerous domestic charges centered around a turbulent second marriage. The charges included assault, threatening to burn down a house, and intimidating a witness. His first marriage had not been marked with violence, and he had a son with his first wife. He claimed that the marriage ended because of his ex-wife's "controlling nature." He could never go fishing, he said. He claimed that fidelity was not an issue—he had never been unfaithful to his first wife, nor, in his opinion, had she to him.

Within a year of the first marriage's end, Larry met and married his second wife, who also had been previously married. Larry was aware that her first husband had strayed and that she had retaliated with an affair. When Larry and his second wife came into conflict, he accused her of infidelity, frequently drove by her workplace, and became criminally hostile. In my opinion, it was the infidelity in his second wife's past that cued his hostile behavior, and his suspicions, unreported to prior examiners, led to the assaults, threats, and intimidation. A remarkable impression I took away from his evaluation was of his otherwise mild and quiet nature.

Lee Harvey Oswald's murder of President Kennedy drew fuel from male sexual jealousy. The evidence is considerable and includes Oswald's wife Marina's testimony to the Warren Commission that she was "in love" with JFK and that the President reminded her of a medical student she regretted not marrying. Oswald's marriage to Marina was characterized by domestic abuse. Several months before the assassination, Oswald discovered that Marina had been unfaithful while they were still in Russia, where they met and married. These may be crucial pieces of Oswald's motive for murder (Thomson, Boissevain, & Aukofer, 1997).

Slip-up versus Homicide Adaptation

One of the current debates in the field is noted in Chapter 4 of this volume. It is the slipup explanation for homicide (Daly & Wilson, 1988) versus dedicated mechanisms for murder (Buss, 2005; see also Chapter 3 of this volume). Chagnon's (1997) work with the Yanomamo provides an unambiguous view of the adaptive logic of murder. Helene Valero's memoir of her years with the Yanomamo counters the idea of murder as a "slipup." The Yanomamo men she described knew when they intended to wound versus when they were attempting to murder (Biocca, 1996). Daly and Wilson (1988) put to rest the idea that a face-off between two men is ever "trivial." My reports no longer mention such incidents with puzzlement or veiled condescension. Although I disagree with their "slipup" hypothesis, their focus on the dynamics of male–male competition and its centrality to homicide should guide forensic clinicians' formulation of murder cases.

Charles, a 50-year-old man, was charged with the capital murder of his 33-year-old wife. Her body was discovered in a motel; she was on her back, in bed, nude, with her legs pulled up and knees splayed open. She died of a single gunshot wound that had entered her right chest and pierced major blood vessels. The husband was apprehended in another state several weeks later. He had visited his extended family and appeared normal.

Charles claimed he had been in a car with his estranged wife when he pulled out a gun and threatened to kill himself. She had grabbed the gun barrel, he said, and the gun discharged and fatally wounded her. Charles checked into a motel, carried her into the room, and tried to tend to her wound. She died, and he fled. That was his story.

There were holes in his story and major inconsistencies in the forensic evidence. She was his third wife and he was her first husband. He was seventeen years older than she was. She had been morbidly obese but had undergone bariatric surgery, and had shed over one hundred pounds. Photographs indicated that at the time of her death she was attractive. Several weeks before the murder, she moved out of the home she shared with the defendant and into an apartment. Unbeknownst to the defendant, but confirmed through others, she started to date two new men.

However, she maintained contact with her husband, and on the morning of the murder she went to the home she formerly shared with him. He claimed they had sex that morning, and that subsequently he drove her around town in the car, begging her to return to their marriage. Charles had a well-documented history of depression and substance abuse. In a prior marriage, he had been tried and acquitted of marital rape. Those problems became the focus of the efforts to have psychiatric evidence of mitigation introduced at trial or sentencing in the current case. But the evidence suggested a deliberate murder. The way the body was left suggested a warning. His behavior fits Buss and Duntley's (1998, 1999) model of mate homicide (see also Buss, 2005; Duntley, 2005). The latent intent was the literal death of a mate, a desire to send a warning to other men, and the need to deprive rivals of the wife's attentions.

Substance Use

For the practicing forensic clinician, one of the most important developments will be an evolutionary understanding of substance use. Most criminal defendants suffer from substance abuse and are intoxicated at the time of their offense. An article in *Science* by Nesse and Berridge (1997) and a special issue of *Addiction* (2002) devoted to evolutionary psychology views of substance abuse light the way forward.

Our brains are not designed for supernormal substances like drugs. Our drugs of abuse invariably act directly on limbic areas of the brain and activate old instincts that suggest a fitness benefit is right around the corner. Drugs dissolve a sober assessment of a situation, leading to an inaccurate analysis of the cost of deploying an ancestrally adaptive, but currently criminal, behavioral solution such as rape or murder. Abused substances override negative emotions, particularly the emotions that might inhibit these dangerous actions.

A Savanna IQ Goes to Court

Kanazawa's ideas on a Savanna-IQ interaction (Chapter 9 in this volume) reorient any assessment for competence, particularly competence to stand trial (CST). A courtroom is a novel situation. Any forensic clinician will tell you that evaluations have been conducted in which the evidence suggests the defendant is incompetent, even though in other areas of his life he functions relatively well. In the following case, the defendant also demonstrated the ability to deceive. Findings of incompetence like these are often challenged. The Savanna-IQ Interaction Hypothesis provides a testable way of understanding these cases.

In 1960, the U.S. Supreme Court detailed the current standard for competency to stand trial (*Dusky v. United States*, 1960). The standard is whether a criminal defendant "has sufficient ability to consult with his lawyer with a reasonable degree of rational understanding, and whether he has a rational as well as factual understanding of the proceedings against him." All states have a similar test for competence. A defendant is found incompetent if, because of a mental disorder, either of the following is true:

1. The defendant is unable to understand the nature and objectives of the court proceedings.
2. The defendant is unable to assist in the defense.

A problem in either part of this test can lead to a finding of incompetence. The standard for proving incompetence is a preponderance of the evidence (*Cooper v. Oklahoma*, 1996) by the defense. The standard in federal courts is similar to state standards. Incompetence is proven when the defendant "is presently suffering from a mental disease or defect rendering him mentally incompetent to the extent that he is unable to understand the nature and consequences of the proceedings against him or to assist properly in his defense" (19 U.S.C. §4241).

This is translated into assessing a defendant in the following areas:

1. *Charges.* Does the criminal defendant understand the nature of the charges? Is he or she knowledgeable of the official name of the charge? But it is more important that the person understand the nature of the act that he or she is accused of committing.
2. *Severity of the charge.* A criminal defendant should understand the severity, whether it is a misdemeanor or a felony, and the possible range of sentence if he or she is convicted.
3. *Pleas.* A criminal defendant is assessed to see whether he or she understands various pleas that are available, including guilty, not guilty, no contest, or not guilty by reason of insanity.
4. *Courtroom personnel roles.* A criminal defendant is assessed regarding his or her understanding of the roles of the defendant, the defense attorney, the judge, the commonwealth's attorney/prosecutor, the jury, witnesses, and the victim.
5. *The adversarial nature of the courtroom.* A criminal defendant has to understand which court personnel oppose his or her interest. The person must demonstrate some self-protective awareness.

With regard to ability to assist their attorney, defendants are assessed in the following areas: ability to work with their attorney; understanding of their current legal situation; comprehension of plea bargaining; ability to enter, if applicable, a mental illness defense; capacity to appraise evidence and outcome; memory and concentration for trial decision making; awareness of appropriate courtroom behavior; consistent and organized narrative of the offense; and the presence of self-defeating behavior (Simon & Gold, 2004).

David, a 29-year-old single man who lived with his father and stepmother, allegedly approached a woman at a bus stop, poked her face with his finger, and, when she walked away, pushed her from behind. He was charged with assault. A competency evaluation was ordered upon the motion of his defense attorney.

He was given the Wechsler Adult Intelligence test (WAIS-III). His verbal IQ was 71, which falls in the range of borderline intellectual functioning and indicated verbal performance in the lowest 3% of the population his age. His performance IQ of 60 and his full-scale IQ of 64 were in the markedly impaired range of intelligence classification and indicated nonverbal and overall intellectual test performance in the lowest 1% of the population his age. His current WAIS subtest performances were deemed valid estimates of his current and recent levels of intellectual abilities. Five of six verbal subtest performances fell in the impaired range. His elevated performance on the digit span subtest indicated ability for passive attention and accounted for his verbal IQ score being above the markedly impaired range.

The psychologist who tested David thought his level of skills was more consistent with a diagnosis of mental retardation than with a diagnosis of borderline intellectual functioning.

David's Competency Exam

The defendant was brought to the community mental health center by his stepmother and was left in the waiting room. He responded to his name being called and accompanied the evaluator to the interview room without problem. He presented as a young male dressed in blue jeans, shirt, and winter coat. He wore running shoes, and the clothes appeared clean. His hygiene seemed without problem.

He could maintain eye contact with the examiner. His speech was generally coherent. His thought processes tended to be linear and logical, though, as will be noted, he made some nonsensical responses. There was no evidence of psychosis. He denied psychotic symptoms.

He was asked first if he knew why he was at the interview. He said that he didn't know. When asked if he currently had legal charges against him, he said he didn't know. He then spontaneously said that, "C [stepmother] told me I have to go to court on March 30." When asked about what matters involving him are before the court, he said he did not know. He then said it was "something about a girl." He was asked if he remembered anything about it. He said, "It has to do with speaking to somebody."

He was asked if he had been to court before. He said, "Plenty of times, but I wouldn't know what it is about." This struck the examiner as a spontaneous claim that he was not competent.

When asked what the judge's job in a court is, he said, "He speaks to you." When asked what other jobs the judge had, he said, "That's all I know." When he was pressed about other roles for the judge, he said, "He places your bail, he gives you counseling and help or he'll suspend your license." When asked what bail meant, he said, "Money." When asked what the money was for, he said, "Anything. For going to a store."

He was asked if he knew his attorney's name. He said he had forgotten. When pressed, he said, "Susan." When told that his attorney was Valerie [last name], he mimicked the last name with a word approximate to it.

When asked what his attorney's job is, he said, "She gives you counsel." When asked what that meant, he said, "Help. She asks me questions. She tells me if I am right or if I am wrong." When pressed about other functions of his attorney, he said, "Those were all." He was again asked the name of his attorney, and he said, "Valerie [correct last name]."

When asked the commonwealth attorney or prosecutor's job, he said, "They arrest you. They talk to you for a long time. They ask you how you like things around the community. They tell you about different jobs that are going on. They talk to the judge. They answer the questions for the judge." When asked who presented the evidence against him, he said, "Anybody."

When asked if he knew the term plea bargain, he said he did not know what it meant. Interestingly, he spelled plea, "p-l-e-a." When asked what "plea" meant, he said, "It's when someone talks to you about money. It means not having authority over me. It means talking to you about committing a crime." When asked if he knew what "to plead guilty" meant, he said, "Arrested."

When asked if he had ever heard of the terms *confidentiality* or *lawyer/client privilege*, he said, "I've heard of privacy." When asked what that meant, he said, "Getting along with the next human being."

When asked if anyone could order his attorney to reveal what they have talked about, he said, "I don't think so, unless it is coming from a judge or an attorney. It is confidential. It is secret."

When asked what he would do if someone on the witness stand said something that was not true, he said, "I'd ignore it." When asked if he would say something or stand up or yell at the witness or to the judge, he said, "Only if it is the right thing to do."

David's Mental Status Examination

David knew the name of the month, that the day was the eighth, and that the year was 2007. When asked who the president was, he said, "Clinton?" When told it was not Clinton and again asked who it was, he said, "George Bush." When asked who the vice president was, he said he did not know. Similarly, he did not know the name of the governor.

He said he lived on [street address in Charlottesville] and in [a neighboring rural county]. When asked whom he lived with, he said, "A bunch of brothers, Chris and R. J." He said they lived in [the rural county] and were "out and about."

The examiner said that he understood he lived with his stepmother, C, and her sons. He said he did live with them and "her husband." When asked who lived in the home, he said, "People that are close kin to a lot of people." When it was pointed out that the man he referred to as C's husband was his father, he said, "Well, that just ran off my mind."

When asked again about whom he lived with, he said that he lived in Charlottesville with his mother, his stepfather, and his stepmother's two sons, Junior and Germaine.

When asked if he watched television, he said yes. When asked what was in the news, he said, "The weather, I watch the weather report."

The above is just a brief part of a several-hours-long interview, but I hope it gives the reader a sense of David. In my report to the court, I concluded that David was not competent to stand trial. Aspects of his competency exam suggested that he attempted to deceive me, wanting me to see him as incompetent. He responded to several questions with answers he knew were false and would portray him as less intelligent. For example, he referred to his father as his stepmother's husband. His attempt to deceive me was detailed in the report. However, even if he was aware enough to feign greater deficits than he suffered, his history and baseline intellectual function indicated to me that David was incompetent and not restorable to competence.

This conclusion was challenged in court by the prosecutor. "If he could fake it, being worse than he is, he could make it," captures the prosecutor's argument. A second exam has been ordered. My contention is that the ability to deceive is ancient and can be present even in individuals with demonstrable IQ problems that render them incompetent.

Daubert and Darwin

The U.S. Supreme Court's 1993 decision in *Daubert v. Merrell Dow Pharmaceuticals, Inc.* substituted a test grounded in Karl Popper's conceptualization of falsifiability as a hallmark of science. That test requires the trial judge to consider whether the technique or theory has been tested and whether it has been subjected to professional scrutiny through peer review and publication, whether it yielded an acceptable rate of error, and whether it has been accepted by the relevant scientific community. This will only help evolutionary psychology, which is committed to empirical validation. All too frequently in the psychiatric profession, theories have been promulgated and used in courts of law when they have little or no empirical support.

Teaching Forensic Evolutionary Psychology

How does one teach forensic evolutionary psychology to clinicians and court personnel? Walsh and Beaver (Chapter 2 of this volume) captured my attention with their succinct explanation of the well-known sex differences in criminal behavior. Why is the greatest risk factor for crime maleness? With crime, we must confront the naturalistic fallacy. Crime is an abridgment of/challenge to the rules of cooperation and reciprocity. If life is mating effort and parenting effort, and mating effort dominates men's lives far more than it does women's, crime covers the behaviors that promote mating effort: deceitfulness, impulsiveness, sensation seeking, and aggression.

The crucial corrective idea to teach is the Darwinian bedrock of criminal behavior. Psychopathology, personality disorders, substance abuse, and the other diagnosable problems identified by clinicians are incapable of generating organized behavior by themselves. Organized behavior requires a foundation of functional mechanisms capable of producing the behavior in appropriate circumstances. The cognitive structures for the production of criminal behaviors were shaped by Darwinian natural selection and the selection pressure created by recurrent exposure to contexts affecting reproductive success.

Policy Implications

How many judges know that theft is a mammalian trait (see Chapter 9 of this volume)? If they knew its origin and presence in the other animals, might they view the crime differently when certain individuals appeared before them? How would they view it when committed by an individual who suffers from chronic schizophrenia? One of my tasks is to evaluate the criminal defendant who is one of the chronically mentally ill and who has incurred enough misdemeanor charges to qualify as a felon, a "habitual offender." Designed to identify repeat offenders who are antisocial, habitual offender laws routinely ensnare the chronically mentally ill who shoplift cigarettes or food. Their clumsiness secures their easy arrest, and then their attorneys often ask whether they qualify for the insanity defense. Even though they are ill, they know the nature and consequences of their actions. They know they are breaking the law and risking arrest and prosecution. Their illnesses leave them poor and relatively helpless.

In my state, since 1978, the life-or-death decision in capital murder cases rests in part on whether the Commonwealth can prove, beyond a reasonable doubt, that there is a probability that in the future the defendant "would commit criminal acts of violence that would constitute a continuing serious threat to society" (Va. Code Ann. 19.2–264[C]). Since Virginia abolished parole, the only society to which a life-sentenced capital defendant can pose a "continuing serious threat" is prison society. But juries are not allowed to hear evidence of security and actual rates of violence in Virginia's prisons. None of this information can enter through mental health experts, and they must assess the defendant's future dangerousness with no regard to the environment in which he or she will live.

Mental health experts must base their capital mitigation prediction on past history and other indices of risk. Often they approach the assessment as if they are measuring the heat level of a continuously boiling cauldron of homicidal fury. There remains little comprehension that violence is context dependent, the probable deployment of adaptations. The prison that any capital murderers inhabit defangs their violence. In 2005, there were 26,581 inmates in Virginia's prisons, including 385 convicted of capital murders and 2,000 convicted of first-degree murder. There was one homicide, nineteen aggravated assaults on other prisoners (0.61 per 1,000), and two aggravated assaults on prison guards (0.06 per 1,000).

Society now sees life imprisonment without hope of release as both retributive and protective. Cruelty has been replaced with long-term imprisonment. Death sentences might decrease if court personnel, mental health experts, and juries were to understand that violence is context dependent, with the deployment of homicidal adaptations occurring only in certain situations. Those contexts have been effectively removed by the prison system (Bruck, 2007).

Conclusion

My daughter's attribution for someone of considerable intelligence is *MOFO*, her acronym for "Master of the F—— Obvious." That captures my inevitable reaction as I delve into evolutionary psychology and learn its explanations for human nature and criminal behavior. I was trained in a psychodynamic model that often led to tortured and incomprehensible formulations. They utilized little or no empirical support, showed wide subjectivity, and offered no avenue for empirical verification.

As this chapter was being written, Seung-Hui Cho slaughtered thirty-two people at Virginia Tech. Mental health experts and forensic clinicians have weighed in with diagnostic assessments of him, which include psychotic illnesses such as paranoid schizophrenia. An evolutionary psychology–informed view is that he was extremely socially isolated and inept as a result of Asperger's, pervasive developmental disorder, or another nonpsychotic impairment of social functioning. This fits with Lee Kirkpatrick's research that found people low in social inclusion and high in feelings of superiority are most likely to be aggressive (Kirkpatrick, Waugh, Valencia, & Webster, 2002). The descriptions of Cho's father's isolation are eerily similar to the younger Cho's, but without the violent edge. There are no reports to date of psychotic episodes or symptoms in Cho. Marginalized, rebuffed in his clumsy attempts to approach women, and defeated socially, he would be more clearly motivated by a desire to get revenge against those who represented the people who had excluded him than by psychopathology. Revenge is an evolved aspect of the mind that functioned as deterrence (Daly & Wilson, 1988). Men's pleasure from revenge and absence of empathy for those they dislike are now verified and supported by fMRI studies (Singer et al., 2006). Cho took his revenge on those who he felt were responsible for his marginalized status. Unlike our ancestors, he had access to far deadlier weapons and could slaughter many before being stopped. As much as we hate to entertain the idea, Seung-Hui Cho may have been less distant from all men than we might at first believe.

As Duntley and Shackelford argue in their introduction to this volume, if knowledge is like a river, new knowledge can raise the level of the water until it overflows its banks. The new streams it creates, the landscape it submerges, and the hills that are carved away cannot be predicted. Evolutionary psychology will be like an overflow of knowledge, cutting new rivers through once familiar lands. We can only guess how it will change the shape of the legal landscape. What will happen when judges, prosecutors, and defense attorneys have familiarity with an evolutionary psychology perspective? What will happen when expert witnesses who are called to provide testimony are familiar with forensic evolutionary psychology? What happens when we have new and different understandings of the various behaviors that bring people into court?

The MOFO reaction doubtlessly occurs among those who have discovered the evolutionary paradigm and its application to human nature. Darwin, more than Freud, gave us the tools to understand defendants and the juries who pass judgment on them. My hope and hypothesis are that as more forensic clinicians learn evolutionary psychology, the more its discoveries will be applied to the forensic setting. That will lead us closer to assisting courts and juries in answering the questions about the defendants that have been with us for all of human history.

ACKNOWLEDGMENTS

Clare Aukofer worked her magic on my prose. Willis Spaulding sharpened the discussion of intent and contributed insights about expert testimony and legal rules as institutionalized rules of thumb. Owen Jones made helpful comments on a late draft. Joshua Duntley and Todd Shackelford gave me this opportunity, editorial assistance, and several superb new ideas. Over many years I have learned from Marilyn Minrath, my partner in private forensic practice, and Richard Bonnie, Bruce Cohen, Dewey Cornell, John Monahan, Daniel Murrie, Eileen Ryan, William Stejskal, and Janet Warren, my colleagues at University of Virginia's Institute of Law, Psychiatry and Public Policy, who provide unparalleled opportunities for case consultation.

Notes

1. Fortunately, in my opinion, the case was retried. At the first trial in 2002, Dr. Park Dietz, one of the prosecution psychiatrists, testified about an episode of *Law & Order* in which a woman got away with drowning her children in a bathtub by pleading insanity. During the first trial, prosecutors suggested that Ms. Yates watched the show and saw it as "a way out." But it was soon discovered that no such episode existed. The conviction was successfully overturned, and a retrial led to the 2006 finding of not guilty by reason of insanity.

References

Addiction. (2002, April). Special issue: Evolutionary psychobiological approaches to addiction, *97*.

Biocca, E. (1996). *Yanomamo: The story of Helena Valero, a girl kidnapped by Amazonian Indians*. New York: Kodansha International.

Bruck, David I. (2007, April 13). *The "dangerousness" scam: How Virginia substitutes fear and fiction for fact in jury sentencing*. Virginia Trial Lawyers annual meeting, White Sulphur Springs, WV.

Buss, D. (2005). *The murderer next door: Why the mind is designed to kill*. New York: Penguin Press.

Buss, D. M., & Duntley, J. D. (1998, July). *Evolved homicide mechanisms*. Paper presented at the annual meeting of the Human Behavior and Evolution Society, Davis, CA.

Buss, D. M., & Duntley, J. D. (1999). *Killer psychology*. Paper presented at the annual meeting of the Human Behavior and Evolution Society, Salt Lake City, UT.

Chagnon, N. (1997). *Yanomamo* (5th ed.). Fort Worth: Harcourt Brace College.

Daly, M., & Wilson, M. (1988). *Homicide*. New York: Aldine de Gruyter.

Duntley, J. D. (2005). Adaptations to dangers from humans. In D. M. Buss (Ed.), *The handbook of evolutionary psychology* (pp. 224–249). Hoboken, NJ: John Wiley.

Gottschall, J. A., & Gottschall, T. A. (2003). Are per-incident rape-pregnancy rates higher than per-incident consensual pregnancy rates? *Human Nature, 14*, 1–20.

Jones, O. (1999) Sex, culture, and the biology of rape: Toward explanation and prevention. *California Law Review, 87*, 827–941.

Kirkpatrick, L. A., Waugh, C. E., Valencia, A., & Webster, G. D. (2002). The functional domain specificity of self-esteem and the differential prediction of aggression. *Journal of Personality and Social Psychology, 82*, 756–767.

Nesse, R. M., & Berridge, K. (1997). Psychoactive drug use in evolutionary perspective. *Science, 277*, 63–65.

Simon, R. I., & Gold, L. H. (2004). *Textbook of forensic psychiatry*. Washington, DC: American Psychiatric.

Singer, T., Seymour, B., O'Doherty, J. P., Stephan, K. E., Dolan, R. J., & Frith, C. D. (2006). Empathic neural responses are modulated by the perceived fairness of others. *Nature, 439*, 466–469.

Thomson, J. A., Boissevain, J., & Aukofer, C. (1997). Lee Harvey Oswald: Another look. *Mind and Human Interaction, 8*, 119–138.

Thornhill, R., & Palmer, C. (2000). *A natural history of rape: Biological bases of sexual coercion*. Cambridge, MA: MIT Press.

Author Index

Subject Index